382

Rigged Rules and Double Standards:
trade, globalisation, and
the fight against poverty

Contents

Acknowledgements

This report was written by Kevin Watkins, with the exception of Chapter 4, which was written by Penny Fowler. Its preparation has been a co-operative effort, involving Oxfam staff and partner organisations. It draws upon the findings of a research programme which was managed by Kevin Watkins, Penny Fowler, Celine Charveriat, and Gonzalo Fanjul.

Special mention should be made of the contributions of the following people to specific chapters: Jeff Atkinson, Oli Brown, Celine Charveriat, Sumi Dhanarajan, Gonzalo Fanjul, Penny Fowler, Charis Gresser, Antonio Hill, Ruth Mayne, Robin Palmer and Sophia Tickell. Sally Baden and Thalia Kidder made significant contributions to the gender analysis in the report as a whole.

Many background studies, papers, and notes were prepared on thematic issues. These were written by Allison Aldred, Francisco Amador, Carlos Ancona, Jeff Atkinson, Néstor Avendaño, Rosanna Barbero, Michelle Beveridge, Frans Bieckmann, Mike Bird, Fiona Black, John de Boer, Chris van der Borgh, David Boyer, Megan Bradley, Oli Brown, Tony Burdon, John Burstein, CEDLA, Edith Cervantes, Celine Charveriat, Jean Marie Robert Chery, Hadi Cordera, John Crabtree, Anand Kishore Das, Siddharth Deva, Sumi Dhanarajan, Peter Drahos, Dominic Eagleton, Gonzalo Fanjul, Tricia Feeney, Mark Fried, Carlos Galián, Beatriz González-Manchón, Paul Goodison, Emma Gough, Charis Gresser, Yohannes Habtu Atsbeha, Barend Hazeleger, Jon Hellin, Sophie Higman, Hoang Xuan Thanh, IIEP, INESA, Thalia Kidder, Margarita Maffii, Marika McCauley, Ruth Mayne, the Oxfam team in Hanoi, Francis Perez, Victor Pérez-Grovas, Jacquelyn M. Pinat, Jonathan Pitts, J. Mario Ponce, Mario Posas, Anjali Raj, José Juan Romero, Allen Rosenfeld, Natalie Rowe, Jan Ruyssenaars, Robert Scott, Jung-ui Sul, Widyono Sutjipto, Cesar Allan Vera, Malou Vera, Bayu Wicaksono, and Dini Widiastuti. Caterina-Ruggeri Laderchi provided technical support and Jung-ui Sul research assistance on Chapter 5. A full list of background studies is appended to the report; some of them can be accessed from the Oxfam Trade Campaign website at **http://www.maketradefair.com**

Colleagues from Oxfam offices across the world provided useful comments and suggestions during the drafting process. They included Sally Baden, Bert Beekman, Kelly Brooks, Celine Charveriat, Peggy Connolly, Sumi Dhanarajan, Ashvin Dayal, Gonzalo Fanjul, Marlies Filbri, Rian Fokker, Justin Forsyth, Mark Fried, Heather Grady, Allert van den Ham, Gina Hocking, Thalia Kidder, Joyce Kortlandt, Greetje Lubbi, Francis Perez, Alex Renton, Chris Roche, Ken Smith, Severina Rivera, and Jasmine Whitbread.

The editorial and advisory group for the overall report consisted of Peggy Connolly, Gonzalo Fanjul, Justin Forsyth, Penny Fowler, and Phil Twyford.

The production and consultation process for the report was managed by Izzy Birch. The text was edited by Catherine Robinson and designed by Paul Gallagher.

Foreword

Global interaction, rather than insulated isolation, has been the basis of economic progress in the world. Trade, along with migration, communication, and dissemination of scientific and technical knowledge, has helped to break the dominance of rampant poverty and the pervasiveness of 'nasty, brutish, and short' lives that characterised the world. And yet, despite all the progress, life is still severely nasty, brutish, and short for a large part of the world population. The great rewards of globalised trade have come to some, but not to others.

What is needed is to create conditions for a fuller and fairer sharing of the enormous benefits from trade. Can this be done without destroying the global market economy? The answer is very firmly yes. The use of the market economy is consistent with many different resource distributions, rules of operation (such as patent laws and anti-trust regulations), and enabling conditions for participating in the market economy (such as basic education and health care). Depending on these conditions, the market economy itself would generate different prices, dissimilar terms of trades, distinct income distributions, and more generally diverse overall outcomes. Institutional change and policy reform can radically alter the prevailing levels of inequality and poverty, without wrecking the global economy.

This report is concerned precisely with that task. The work involves the diagnosis of institutional features that impede a more equitable sharing of the fruits of trade and exchange. The organisational arrangements that require reform include, for example, the prevailing patent laws that effectively exclude the use of the most needed drugs by the most needy people (while giving little incentive for the development of particularly appropriate drugs, such as preventive vaccines, which are less attractive to pharmaceutical companies).

I will not try to summarise the report. There is a very useful executive summary – the excellence of which would not, I hope, deter the reading of the entire report. The authors of the report have proposed specific institutional changes which deserve serious attention. In addition, the broader object of the report is to promote discussion of the kind of institutional architecture that may best serve the interests of the poor and the deprived. The basic objective is to combine the great benefits of trade to which many defenders of globalisation point, with the overarching need for fairness and equity which motivates a major part of the anti-globalisation protests. The constructive agenda of the report draws on both concerns.

Amartya Sen
Honorary President of Oxfam
March 2002

Executive summary

There is a paradox at the heart of international trade. In the globalised world of the early twenty-first century, trade is one of the most powerful forces linking our lives. It is also a source of unprecedented wealth. Yet millions of the world's poorest people are being left behind. Increased prosperity has gone hand in hand with mass poverty and the widening of already obscene inequalities between rich and poor. World trade has the potential to act as a powerful motor for the reduction of poverty, as well as for economic growth, but that potential is being lost. The problem is not that international trade is inherently opposed to the needs and interests of the poor, but that the rules that govern it are rigged in favour of the rich.

The human costs of unfair trade are immense. If Africa, East Asia, South Asia, and Latin America were each to increase their share of world exports by one per cent, the resulting gains in income could lift 128 million people out of poverty. Reduced poverty would contribute to improvements in other areas, such as child health and education.

In their rhetoric, governments of rich countries constantly stress their commitment to poverty reduction. Yet the same governments use their trade policy to conduct what amounts to robbery against the world's poor. When developing countries export to rich-country markets, they face tariff barriers that are four times higher than those encountered by rich countries. Those barriers cost them $100bn a year – twice as much as they receive in aid.

Various polite formulations can be found to describe the behaviour of rich-country governments. But the harsh reality is that their policies are inflicting enormous suffering on the world's poor. When rich countries lock poor people out of their markets, they close the door to an escape route from poverty.

If Africa, East Asia, South Asia, and Latin America were each to increase their share of world exports by one per cent, the resulting gains in income could lift 128 million people out of poverty.

Lack of market access is not an isolated example of unfair trade rules, or of the double standards of Northern governments. While rich countries keep their markets closed, poor countries have been pressurised by the International Monetary Fund and World Bank to open their markets at breakneck speed, often with damaging consequences for poor communities. The problem of low and unstable commodity prices, which consigns millions of people to poverty, has not been seriously addressed by the international community. Meanwhile, powerful transnational companies (TNCs) have been left free to engage in investment and employment practices which contribute to poverty and insecurity, unencumbered by anything other than weak voluntary guidelines. The World Trade Organisation (WTO) is another part of the problem. Many of its rules on intellectual property, investment, and services protect the interests of rich countries and powerful TNCs, while imposing huge costs on developing countries. The WTO's bias in favour of the self-interest of rich countries and big corporations raises fundamental questions about its legitimacy.

Reform of world trade is only one of the requirements for ending the deep social injustices that pervade globalisation. Action is also needed to extend opportunity, and reduce inequalities in health, education, and income distribution. However, world trade rules are a key part of the poverty problem. Fundamental reforms are needed to make them part of the solution.

The Oxfam Trade Campaign

This report sets out Oxfam's analysis of the rules that govern world trade. The campaign that it launches aims to change those rules in order to unleash the potential of trade to reduce poverty. It is motivated by a conviction that it is time to end double standards and to make trade fair. The following are among Oxfam's main policy goals:

- Improving market access for poor countries and ending the cycle of subsidised agricultural over-production and export dumping by rich countries.

- Ending the use of conditions attached to IMF-World Bank programmes which force poor countries to open their markets regardless of the impact on poor people.

- Creating a new international commodities institution to promote diversification and end over-supply, in order to raise prices to levels consistent with a reasonable standard of living for producers, and changing corporate practices so that companies pay fair prices.

- Establishing new intellectual-property rules to ensure that poor countries are able to afford new technologies and basic medicines, and that farmers are able to save, exchange, and sell seeds.

- Prohibiting rules that force governments to liberalise or privatise basic services that are vital for poverty reduction.

- Enhancing the quality of private-sector investment and employment standards.

- Democratising the WTO to give poor countries a stronger voice.

- Changing national policies on health, education, and governance so that poor people can develop their capabilities, realise their potential, and participate in markets on more equitable terms.

Why campaign on trade, and why now? There are three answers to this question. The first is that the existing trade system is indefensible. No civilised community should be willing to tolerate the extremes of prosperity and poverty that are generated by current trade practices. And none of us should be willing to accept the abuse of power, injustice, and indifference to suffering that sustains those practices.

The second reason for action can be summarised in a simple phrase: 'enlightened self-interest'. What is happening today is not just indefensible, it is also unsustainable. Large parts of the developing world are becoming enclaves of despair, increasingly marginalised and cut off from the rising wealth generated through trade. Ultimately, shared prosperity cannot be built on such foundations. Like the economic forces that drive globalisation, the anger, despair, and social tensions that accompany vast inequalities in wealth and opportunity will not respect national borders. The instability that they will generate threatens us all. In today's globalised world, our lives are more inextricably linked than ever before, and so is our prosperity. As a global community, we sink or swim together. No country, however strong or wealthy, is an island.

As a global community, we sink or swim together.

The third motivation for Oxfam's trade campaign is the conviction that change is possible. The international trading system is not a force of nature. It is a system of exchange, managed by rules and institutions that reflect political choices. Those choices can prioritise the interests of the weak and vulnerable, or they can prioritise the interests of the wealthy and powerful. Trade is reinforcing global poverty and inequality because the international trading system is managed to produce these outcomes. The rules of the game reflect the power of vested interests. Concerted public campaigning can change this. As demonstrated by the international campaign to cancel the debts of poor countries, public action can force the interests of the poor on to the international agenda. And it can achieve real gains for human development.

Ultimately, there is a clear choice to be made. We can choose to allow unfair trade rules to continue causing poverty and distress, and face the consequences. Or we can change the rules. We can allow globalisation to continue working for the few, rather than the many. Or we can forge a new model of inclusive globalisation, based on shared values and principles of social justice. The choice is ours. And the time to choose is now.

1. Trade and globalisation in the twenty-first century

Well-managed trade has the potential to lift millions of people out of poverty. However, increased trade is not an automatic guarantee of poverty reduction. The experience of developing countries exposes the gap between the great potential benefits of trade on the one side, and the disappointing outcomes associated with growing integration through trade on the other.

'We are told that the American computer market is failing. They say that means there will be less production here. Without this job, my life will be very hard.'

JOSEPHINE LARANJA, EMPLOYED IN AN ELECTRONICS FACTORY SOUTH OF MANILA, THE PHILIPPINES

Current debates about trade are dominated by ritualistic exchanges between two camps: the 'globaphiles' and the 'globaphobes'. 'Globaphiles' argue that trade is already making globalisation work for the poor. Their prescription for the future is 'more of the same'. 'Globaphobes' turn this world-view on its head. They argue that trade is inherently bad for the poor. Participation in trade, so the argument runs, inevitably leads to more poverty and inequality. The corollary of this view is 'the less trade the better'.

The anti-globalisation movement deserves credit. It has raised profoundly important questions about social justice – and it has forced the failures of globalisation on to the political agenda. However, the war of words between trade optimists and trade pessimists that accompanies virtually every international meeting is counter-productive. Both world views fly in the face of the evidence – and neither offers any hope for the future. The false debate raging on trade is an unfortunate diversion, not least because of the revolutionary changes that are transforming the global trading system. Those changes have profound implications for all countries – and their future direction will determine the prospects for success in eradicating poverty.

Part of the change is quantitative. Exports have been growing much faster than global gross domestic product (GDP), so that trade now accounts for a greater share of world income than ever before. As a result, changes in trade patterns will have an increasing influence on patterns of income distribution – and on the prospects for poverty reduction. Developing countries have registered particularly rapid increases in their ratios of exports to GDP. Exports now account for more than one-quarter of their combined GDP, a proportion which is higher than for rich countries.

The composition of exports from developing countries has also been changing. While many remain dependent on primary commodities, the share of manufactured goods has been growing. Over the past decade, there has been a boom in high-technology exports, with countries such as China, India, and Mexico emerging as major suppliers of cutting-edge technologies, as well as labour-intensive goods.

The changing role of developing countries in the international division of labour reflects powerful technological forces that are driving globalisation. The marriage of computer technology and telecommunications – or digitalisation – is revolutionising international economic relations. Under the auspices of TNCs, it has facilitated the development of global production systems. Increased trade within companies has been one of the most powerful forces behind the expansion of world trade. The foreign sales of the largest 100 TNCs are equivalent in value to one-quarter of world trade; approximately two-thirds of all trade takes place within companies.

Through their production, investment, and marketing activities, TNCs are linking producers in developing countries ever more closely with consumers in rich countries. From women workers in Bangladesh's garment factories, to workers in China's special economic zones and workers in the free-trade zones of Central America, to small farmers and agricultural labourers across the developing world, globalisation is generating forces which create major opportunities, along with huge threats.

2. Trade as a force for poverty reduction

'If you ask me how our lives compare with our parents' lives, I will tell you that things are better. We are still vulnerable. But there is less poverty today.'

LAM VAN, RICE FARMER, MEKONG DELTA, VIETNAM

History makes a mockery of the claim that trade cannot work for the poor. Participation in world trade has figured prominently in many of the most successful cases of poverty reduction – and, compared with aid, it has far more potential to benefit the poor.

If developing countries increased their share of world exports by just five per cent, this would generate $350bn – seven times as much as they receive in aid. The $70bn that Africa would generate through a one per cent increase in its share of world exports is approximately five times the amount provided to the region through aid and debt relief.

Apart from the financial benefits, export growth can be a more efficient engine of poverty reduction than aid. Export production can concentrate income directly in the hands of the poor, creating new opportunities for employment and investment in the process. However, the 'aid versus trade' dichotomy can be overstated: aid can play a critical role in enabling poor people to benefit from trade, notably by supporting investments in health and education services and economic infrastructure.

Export success can play a key role in poverty reduction. Simulations conducted for this report have attempted to capture the potential impact on poverty of an increased share of world exports for developing countries. At one level, these simulations are artificial. Gains from trade are dynamic and cumulative: they cannot be captured by a static snapshot. Even so, the figures are striking. They suggest that a one per cent increase in world-export share for each developing region could reduce world poverty by 12 per cent. The decline would be greatest in sub-Saharan Africa and South Asia, the two regions with the highest concentrations of poverty.

This shift in distribution of world export activity implied by our simulation is very modest, especially when measured against the current imbalance between population and world-export shares. Low-income developing countries account for more than 40 per cent of world population, but less than 3 per cent of world trade. Whereas rich countries export goods and services worth approximately $6000 per capita, the equivalent figure for developing countries is $330, and less than $100 for low-income countries.

Experience from East Asia illustrates what is possible when export growth is broad-based. Since the mid-1970s, rapid growth in exports has contributed to a wider process of economic growth which has lifted more than 400 million people out of poverty. In countries such as Vietnam and Uganda, production for export markets has helped to generate unprecedented declines in the levels of rural poverty. Where export growth is based on labour-intensive manufactured goods, as in Bangladesh, it can generate large income gains for women.

There are caveats to be attached to all of these success stories. Rising inequality has slowed the rate of poverty reduction in East Asia, and export growth has been accompanied by extreme forms of exploitation, especially among female workers. Yet these outcomes are not inevitable. They are the result of governments failing to protect the interests of the poor.

The benefits of trade are not automatic – and rapid export growth is no guarantee of accelerated poverty reduction. Yet when the potential of trade is harnessed to effective strategies for achieving equitable growth, it can provide a powerful impetus to the achievement of human-development targets. Access to larger markets and new technologies creates incentives for investment, which in turn generates economic growth and employment. If countries are able to engage in higher-value-added trade, as in East Asia, export growth can contribute to rapid increases in living standards.

3. Left behind: poor countries and poor people in the global trading system

Despite some notable successes, the expansion of world trade under globalisation has produced disappointing outcomes for poverty reduction. Rising tides are supposed to lift all boats; but the rising tide of wealth generated by trade has lifted some boats higher than others, and some are sinking fast.

Persistent poverty and increasing inequality are standing features of globalisation. In the midst of the rising wealth generated by trade, there are 1.1bn people struggling to survive on less than $1 a day – the same number as in the mid-1980s. Inequalities between rich and poor are widening, both between and within countries. With only 14 per cent of the world's population, high-income countries account for 75 per cent of global GDP, which is approximately the same share as in 1990.

Inequalities in trade are reinforcing these wider inequalities. For every $1 generated through exports in the international trading system, low-income countries account for

Some countries that appear to be successfully integrating through trade are trapped in low-value-added ghettoes, and the growth in their exports has little impact on their levels of poverty.

only three cents. Even though developing countries have been increasing their exports more rapidly than rich countries, large initial inequalities mean that the absolute gap between them is widening. In the 1990s, rich countries increased the per capita value of their exports by $1938, compared with $51 for low-income countries and $98 for middle-income countries.

Export success in developing countries has been highly concentrated. East Asia accounts for more than three-quarters of manufactured exports, and an even larger share of high-technology products. South Asia and sub-Saharan Africa together account for less than two per cent, and (with the exception of Mexico) Latin America's share is shrinking.

Some countries that appear to be successfully integrating through trade are trapped in low-value-added ghettoes, and the growth in their exports has little impact on their levels of poverty. International trade data identify Mexico as a major exporter of high-technology goods and services. However, less than two per cent of the value of its exports derives from local inputs. The same is true of a number of countries with high rates of export growth in the garments sector, such as Bangladesh and Honduras. In each case, export production is dominated by the simple assembly and re-export of imported components under TNC auspices, with limited transfer of technology.

Other countries have failed to escape long-standing problems. Exporters of primary commodities have seen their shares of world trade shrink, with sub-Saharan Africa bearing the brunt of problems associated with low prices. Deteriorating terms of trade since the late 1970s have cost the region the equivalent of 50 cents for every $1 that it receives in aid.

Trade theory predicts that poor people in developing countries will benefit from integration through trade, but the theory has been confounded by reality. In Latin America, rapid growth in exports has been associated with rising unemployment and stagnating incomes. Real minimum wages in the region were lower at the end of the 1990s than at the start of the decade. Evidence presented in this report shows that the rural poor in particular are losing out.

Not all of the problems associated with trade can be assessed through their effects on incomes. In many countries, export growth has been built on highly exploitative employment practices. Women employed in China's economic zones are often forced to work twelve-hour days in appalling conditions. Garment workers in Bangladesh are denied the right to join unions. Long working days for poverty-level wages make heavy demands on the time and energy of women. Meanwhile, many governments have imposed 'flexible' labour practices – a euphemism, in this context, for violating basic employment rights.

4. Market access and agricultural trade: the double standards of rich countries

Northern governments reserve their most restrictive trade barriers for the world's poorest people…Trade restrictions in rich countries cost developing countries around $100bn a year – twice as much as they receive in aid.

The full potential of trade to reduce poverty cannot be realised unless poor countries have access to markets in rich countries. Unfortunately, Northern governments reserve their most restrictive trade barriers for the world's poorest people.

Competition in the international trading system can be likened to a hurdle race with a difference: the weakest athletes face the highest hurdles. When desperately poor smallholder farmers or women garment workers enter world markets, they face import barriers four times as high as those faced by producers in rich countries. Trade restrictions in rich countries cost developing countries around $100bn a year – twice as much as they receive in aid. Sub-Saharan Africa, the world's poorest region, loses some $2bn a year, India and China in excess of $3bn. These are only the immediate costs. The longer-term costs associated with lost opportunities for investment and the loss of economic dynamism are much greater.

Trade barriers in rich countries are especially damaging to the poor, because they are targeted at the goods that they produce, such as labour-intensive agricultural and manufactured products. Because women account for a large share of employment in labour-intensive export industries, they bear a disproportionate share of the burden associated with the lower wages and restricted employment opportunities imposed by protectionism.

Who are the worst offenders in damaging the interests of developing countries through trade barriers? Oxfam has attempted to answer this question through its Double Standards Index (DSI). This measures ten important dimensions of rich-country trade policies, including average tariffs, the sizes of tariffs in textiles and agriculture, and restrictions on imports from the Least Developed Countries. We call it the Double Standards Index, because it measures the gap between the free-trade principles espoused by rich countries and their actual protectionist practices. No industrialised country emerges with credit, but the European Union (EU) emerges as the worst offender, beating the United States by a short head.

Nowhere are the double standards of industrialised-country governments more apparent than in agriculture. Total subsidies to domestic farmers in these countries amount to more than $1bn a day. These subsidies, the benefits of which accrue almost entirely to the wealthiest farmers, cause massive environmental damage. They also generate over-production. The resulting surpluses are dumped on world markets with the help of yet more subsidies, financed by taxpayers and consumers.

Oxfam has developed a new measure of the scale of export dumping by the EU and the United States. It suggests that both these agricultural superpowers are exporting at prices more than one-third lower than the costs of production. These subsidised exports from rich countries are driving down prices for exports from developing countries, and devastating the prospects for smallholder agriculture. In countries such as Haiti, Mexico, and Jamaica, heavily subsidised imports of cheap food are destroying local markets. Some of the world's poorest farmers are competing against its richest treasuries.

Rich countries have systematically reneged on their commitments to improve market access for poor countries. Instead of reducing their own farm subsidies, they have increased them. Having pledged to phase out the Multi-Fibre Arrangement, which restricts imports of textiles and garments, they have liberalised fewer than one-quarter of the products for which they had agreed to open their markets.

Improved market access could provide a powerful impetus to poverty-reduction efforts, especially if linked to domestic strategies for extending opportunities to the poor and overcoming gender-based barriers to market access. Among the priorities are the following.

- Duty-free and quota-free access for all low-income countries.

- A general reduction in tariff peaks, so that no tariffs applied against developing-country exports exceed five per cent.

- Accelerated phase-out of the Multi-Fibre Arrangement, to allow market access for textiles and garments, which are the main labour-intensive exports of the developing world.

- A comprehensive ban on export subsidies, and a restructuring of farm subsidies to achieve social and environmental objectives, rather than increased output.

- Recognition of the right of developing countries to protect their agricultural systems for food-security purposes.

Reforms such as these would create an enabling environment for poverty reduction. They would offer new opportunities for poor countries and poor people. However, improved market access is only one of the requirements for strengthening the links between trade and poverty reduction. Many of the poorest countries lack the infrastructure to take advantage of market openings. Within countries, poor people similarly lack access to productive assets – such as land and credit – and to health care, education, and infrastructure provision.

5. Trade liberalisation and the poor

'Imports are killing our markets and our communities.'

HECTOR CHAVEZ,
SMALLHOLDER FARMER, CHIAPAS, MEXICO

The removal of trade barriers in rich countries would produce clear benefits for poor countries. Carefully designed and properly sequenced import liberalisation in developing countries can also benefit the poor, especially when the lowering of trade barriers is part of a coherent poverty-reduction strategy. However, rapid import liberalisation in developing countries has often intensified poverty and inequality. Loan conditions attached to IMF and World Bank programmes are a major part of the problem.

The IMF, the World Bank, and most Northern governments are strong advocates of trade liberalisation. In the case of the IMF and the World Bank, advocacy has been backed by loan conditions which require countries to reduce their trade barriers. Partly as a result of these loan conditions, poor countries have been opening up their economies much more rapidly than rich countries. Average import tariffs have been halved in sub-Saharan Africa and South Asia, and cut by two-thirds in Latin America and East Asia.

International financial institutions and governments have sought to justify their support for rapid import liberalisation by reference to World Bank research which seeks to establish that trade liberalisation is good for growth, and that the poor share in the benefits of growth on an equitable basis. In this report we challenge the evidence presented by the World Bank. We show that the research on which it is based is deeply flawed, and that it is producing bad policy advice.

One of the problems stems from confusion over the meaning of 'openness'. The World Bank uses an economic outcome (ratio of trade-to-GDP) as an indirect measure of the impact of policy changes in favour of liberalisation. Using a different indicator of openness, based on the speed and scale of import liberalisation, we show that many of the countries that are integrating most successfully into world markets – such as China, Thailand, and Vietnam – are not rapid import liberalisers. Conversely, many rapid import liberalisers have a weak record on poverty reduction, despite following the spirit and the letter of World Bank–IMF policy advice.

In many countries, rapid liberalisation has been associated with rising inequality. Case studies from Peru show smallholder farmers in highland areas operating at a disadvantage, compared with commercial farms. In Mexico, the 'poverty belt' states in the south are becoming poorer, in comparison with states in the north. In India, import liberalisation is intensifying inequalities within rural areas, and between urban and rural areas. These inequalities matter, because they slow the rate at which economic growth is converted into poverty reduction.

Poverty Reduction Strategy Papers (PRSPs) provide the IMF and the World Bank with an opportunity to place trade at the centre of their dialogue with governments on poverty. That opportunity is being lost. In a review of twelve PRSPs we found that only four mentioned the possible impact of trade reform on poor people, of which two considered measures to protect the losers. In Cambodia, the IMF and the World Bank are supporting a strategy which will sharply reduce import tariffs on agricultural goods, exposing millions of rice farmers to competition from Thailand. Yet no poverty assessment has been carried out.

Among the recommendations set out in this report are the following.

- IMF–World Bank programmes should not impose further loan conditions requiring trade liberalisation.

- Rich countries should reciprocate past liberalisation undertaken by developing countries under IMF–World Bank conditions by making equivalent reductions in their own import barriers.

- All PRSPs should include a detailed analysis of the potential impact of trade liberalisation on income distribution and poverty reduction.

6. Primary commodities: trading into decline

'Proper economic prices should be fixed not at the lowest possible level, but at a level sufficient to provide producers with proper nutritional and other standards.' (John Maynard Keynes, 1944)

Coffee...prices have fallen by 70 per cent since 1997, costing developing-country exporters some $8bn in lost foreign-exchange earnings.

More than half a century has passed since Keynes argued for a new international institution to address the problems facing exporters of primary commodities. Today, low and unstable prices for commodities are among the most powerful influences that prevent trade from working for the poor.

Many of the world's poorest countries remain heavily dependent on primary commodities. More than fifty developing countries depend on three or fewer such commodities for more than half of their export earnings. The national economies of these countries and the household economies of millions of poor people have been devastated by a protracted decline in prices.

Coffee has been one of the commodities worst affected. Prices have fallen by 70 per cent since 1997, costing developing-country exporters some $8bn in lost foreign-exchange earnings. For some countries, these losses have outweighed the benefits of aid and debt relief. Poor households have suffered particular hardship. Our research among coffee farmers in Tanzania, southern Mexico, and Haiti found families reducing their general consumption, taking children out of school, and facing extreme difficulties in meeting health costs. Family and community structures were coming under strain, as women were forced to increase their off-farm labour, and men to migrate in search of work.

The underlying causes of the crisis in commodity markets vary from product to product. However, the general problem is one of structural over-supply. Output across a wide range of products is consistently exceeding demand, which leads to excessive stocks and periodic price collapse.

'The price of coffee is destroying this community.'

TATU MUSEYNI, COFFEE FARMER, KILIMANJARO REGION, TANZANIA

Any change in world market prices generates winners and losers, and commodity markets are no exception. The losers include in their ranks millions of the world's most vulnerable households. The winners, in this case, include the large TNCs that dominate global markets. These TNCs – such as the Nestlé corporation – have been able to take advantage of ruinously low producer prices to enjoy high profit margins.

Resolving the protracted crisis in commodity markets is a fundamental requirement for more inclusive globalisation. The issues raised are complex, but the current piecemeal approach to reform is not working. This report sets out an agenda for reform, including the following recommendations:

- **A new institution to oversee global commodity markets, and a new system of commodity agreements.** This would seek to reduce price volatility. In contrast to the failed agreements of the past, the new institution would include financing mechanisms designed to bring supply back into balance with demand, at reasonable price levels. It would also work to support diversification, and to increase the value of exports through strategies for adding value to the products of low-income countries.

- **The adoption by TNCs of socially responsible purchasing operations.** This would include an increase in the proportion of commodities purchased under long-term contract arrangements, and a fair price when world market prices fall below levels consistent with reasonable living standards in exporting countries.

7. Transnational companies: investment, employment, and marketing

Technological change has made globalisation possible. Transnational companies have made it happen. Through their investment, production, and marketing activities, TNCs bring the world's economies and people more closely together. They have the potential to spread the benefits of globalisation more widely, but they are failing to do so.

Many developing-country governments have introduced an 'open door' policy for foreign investment. Encouraged by Northern governments and financial institutions, they have sought to generate rapid export growth by attracting TNCs. But this strategy is flawed.

Foreign direct investment (FDI) has many potential benefits. It can provide access to new financial resources, technologies, and markets. However, the current financial benefits have been exaggerated. High levels of profit repatriation, high-cost incentives to attract investors, and tax avoidance combine to reduce real financial transfers. For every $1 of foreign investment, around 30 cents are repatriated through profit transfers.

Not all investment is good investment. In development terms, good-quality investment transfers skills and technology, and creates dynamic linkages with local firms. Much FDI does not fit into this category. In Latin America, increased FDI has been associated with reduced capacity for research and development, and a growing dependence on technology imports. Free-trade zones appear to attract the worst-quality FDI. In many cases – as in Bangladesh and Mexico – these zones operate as enclaves, almost totally isolated from the domestic economy. FDI in the extraction of mineral resources has a particularly bad development record. It has often intensified conflicts, caused extreme environmental damage, and led to the displacement of local communities.

TNCs have a major influence on employment standards in developing countries, partly as direct employers, but mainly through their sub-contracting activities. While most TNCs have adopted codes of conduct on employment, the benefits have been limited. With their emphasis on voluntarism, these codes have failed to address the erosion of workers' rights, or to prevent the emergence of extreme inequalities based on gender.

Weak auditing of corporate codes is a serious problem, but even the best auditing practices would not resolve the deeper tensions. In many major exporting economies, governments have dismantled employment protection in order to attract FDI, often with the encouragement of TNCs. This report documents cases in which Northern-based companies, many of which have exemplary codes of conduct, are being supplied by sub-contractors which violate basic employment rights on a systematic basis. Moreover, the market conditions created by TNCs, including intense price pressures on suppliers and stringent delivery deadlines, make it difficult to raise standards.

As the most vulnerable members of the workforce in export industries, women face special challenges. Inadequate social-insurance rights, obligatory over-time work, hazardous work conditions, and poverty-level wages are common. In many countries, export-led success is built on the exploitation of women and girls.

> '**Work in the factory is hard. We are not well treated. Do people in your country think about our condition when they buy the shirts we make?**'
>
> NAWAZ HAZARI, SEWING-MACHINE OPERATOR, GANAKBARI EXPORT-PROCESSING ZONE, DHAKA, BANGLADESH

Through their marketing activities, some TNCs are posing grave threats to public health. Efforts to create markets for tobacco and infant-formula milk are two activities which inflict especially serious damage.

The recommendations presented in this report include the following:

- Governments should enact and enforce national employment laws consistent with the core standards of the International Labour Organisation (ILO).

- The WTO's Trade Policy Reviews should report on trade-related labour standards.

- Employment rights in export-processing zones should be strengthened, with an emphasis on improving the employment status of women.

- The ILO's capacity to monitor and enforce core labour standards should be strengthened.

- Northern governments should establish (under their Guidelines for Multinational Enterprises) better mechanisms for investigation, monitoring and reporting, in order to hold TNCs accountable for their actions in developing countries.

- Governments should establish a legally binding international protocol, based on the (currently draft) UN Fundamental Human Rights Principles for Business Enterprises, to govern the production, trade, and consumption of natural resources from conflict areas.

8. International trade rules as an obstacle to development

Good international trade rules can create an enabling environment for poverty reduction. Bad rules have the opposite effect. They can prevent governments from initiating the strategies that are needed to make trade work for the poor. Many of the provisions of the World Trade Organisation are bad rules.

The agreement on the Trade-Related Aspects of Intellectual-Property Rights (TRIPs) is

The TRIPs agreement is an act of institutionalised fraud, sanctioned by WTO rules…Developing countries will lose approximately $40bn a year in the form of increased licence payments to Northern-based TNCs.

a prime example. Adam Smith once warned governments to guard against the instincts of private traders: 'People of the same trade seldom meet together, even for merriment and diversion, but the conversation ends in a conspiracy against the public, or in some diversion to raise prices.' He could have been writing about the TRIPs agreement. More stringent protection for patents will increase the costs of technology transfer. Developing countries will lose approximately $40bn a year in the form of increased licence payments to Northern-based TNCs, with the USA capturing around one-half of the total. Behind the complex arguments about intellectual-property rights, the TRIPs agreement is an act of institutionalised fraud, sanctioned by WTO rules.

The application of the TRIPs agreement to medicines will have grave consequences for public health. Evidence from developing countries suggests that reinforced patent protection could double the costs of medicines. Given that poor households already spend more on drugs than on any other item of health care, this will significantly raise the cost of treating illness. Premature death and unnecessary sickness are inevitable corollaries. Because of their higher levels of vulnerability to illness and their role as primary carers, women will suffer the gravest consequences.

Current approaches to patenting directly threaten the interests of small farmers. Northern governments have effectively authorised corporate investors to undertake acts of bio-piracy, by permitting them to patent genetic materials taken from developing countries. If a royalty of two per cent were to be levied on these materials, it would generate some $5bn. To add to their problems, smallholder farmers could lose the right to save, sell, and exchange seeds.

Under the General Agreement on Trade in Services (GATS), industrialised countries are seeking to open new markets for TNC investors. These include markets for financial services and basic utilities, such as water. Service-sector activities in which developing countries stand to benefit – such as labour supply – have not been prioritised. Meanwhile, by applying free-market principles to the provision of essential utilities, the GATS agreement threatens to promote forms of privatisation which will damage the interests of the poor.

Many of the industrial policies that facilitated successful integration into world markets in East Asia are now either restricted or prohibited by WTO rules. These include policies that would require TNCs to source products locally, along with restrictions on foreign investment. By requiring countries at very different levels of economic development to apply the same rules, the WTO system is out of touch with the challenges that confront poor countries.

Among the reforms advocated in this report are the following:

- An end to the universal application of the WTO intellectual-property blueprint: developing countries should retain the right to maintain shorter and more flexible systems of intellectual-property protection.

- A clear commitment to put public-health priorities before the claims of patent holders, building on the commitments made at the Doha Ministerial Conference in 2001.

- A prohibition on patent protection for genetic resources for food and agriculture, and stronger rights for poor countries to develop more appropriate forms of plant-variety protection, and to protect farmers' rights to save, sell, and exchange seeds.

- A rebalancing of the services agreement in order to prioritise development objectives, to exclude essential public services from liberalisation negotiations, and to strengthen national sovereignty.

- Strengthening of the WTO's provisions for the 'special and differential treatment' of developing countries; and the removal of restrictions on the rights of governsments to regulate foreign investment and protect their countries' infant industries.

9. Making trade work for the poor

Trade can realise its full potential only if rich and poor countries alike take action to redistribute opportunities in favour of the poor. This requires action at the national level, new forms of international co-operation, and a new architecture of global governance at the WTO.

The challenge of extending opportunity at the national level goes beyond the narrow confines of trade policy. Inequalities in health and education services, and in the ownership of assets, are a formidable barrier to making markets work for poor people. Lacking access to land, marketing infrastructure, and financial resources, the poor are often least equipped to take advantage of market opportunities, and the most vulnerable to competition from imports. In many countries, extensive corruption and excessive bureaucracy act as a tax on trade – and the tax falls most heavily on the poor.

International co-operation must be strengthened in a range of areas. Developing countries need development assistance if they are to integrate into world markets on more favourable terms and to extend opportunities to the poor. Yet rich countries reduced their aid budgets by $13bn between 1992 and 2000. Some of the heaviest cuts fell on the poorest countries and in areas – such as agriculture – where well-targeted aid can make a difference to levels of poverty. Failure to resolve the long-standing debt problems of low-income countries, and to respond effectively to new problems in private capital markets, poses further threats. There is a growing danger that many developing countries will be forced by unsustainable debt to transfer the wealth that is generated by exports to creditors in rich countries.

> **Trade can realise its full potential only if rich and poor countries alike take action to redistribute opportunities in favour of the poor.**

The WTO is one of the youngest international institutions, but it is old before its time. Behind the façade of a 'membership-driven' organisation is a governance system based on a dictatorship of wealth. Rich countries have a disproportionate influence. This is partly because of a failure of representational democracy. Each WTO country may have one vote, but eleven of its members among the least-developed countries are not even represented at the WTO base in Geneva. Informal power-relations reinforce inequalities in negotiating capacity at the WTO. Meanwhile, beyond the WTO, powerful TNCs exercise a disproportionate influence over the direction of trade policy.

Reforms to trade governance are needed in order to make trade work for the poor at all levels. They include the following:

- Redistributive reforms linked to national poverty-reduction strategies. These reforms include land redistribution, changes in public-spending priorities, infrastructural development, and measures to overcome gender-based barriers to equity in local markets.

- Action to tackle the problems of corruption. At the national level, this implies stronger auditing through bodies answerable to the legislature, along with adherence to the OECD anti-bribery convention and guidelines on corruption.

- Increased technical support for poor countries through a Financing Facility for Trade-Related Capacity Building. This would include an annual budget of approximately $250m to enhance the negotiating capacity of developing countries at the WTO.

- Improved transparency and accountability in developing countries. All governments should submit to their respective legislative bodies an annual report on their activities at the WTO. Trade-policy reviews at the WTO should include an assessment of the quality of dialogue between governments and civil society on trade-policy reform.

- Greater transparency on informal influence. All national governments should be required to disclose contacts and submissions made by organisations that seek to influence trade-negotiating policies.

- The development of a Global Anti-Trust Mechanism. In view of the massive concentration of corporate power in the global economy, the principles of anti-monopoly legislation should be extended beyond national borders to the international economy.

Just as in any national economy, economic integration in the global economy can be a source of shared prosperity and poverty reduction, or a source of increasing inequality and exclusion. Managed well, the international trading system can lift millions out of poverty. Managed badly, it will leave whole economies even more marginalised. The same is true at a national level. Good governance can make trade work in the interests of the poor. Bad governance can make it work against them.

At present, trade is badly managed, both at the global level and, in many countries, at the national level. Continuing on the current path is not an option. But a retreat into isolationism would deprive the poor of the opportunities offered by trade. It would counteract a powerful force for poverty reduction. That is why we need a new world trade order, grounded in new approaches to rights and responsibilities, and in a commitment to make globalisation work for the poor.

'In my village we were very poor. I came here to find a better life. Today, I have more money. My job here means that I can give my children an education, and we are not hungry. They will have the chance of a better future. But work in the factory is hard. We are not well treated. And if we become sick, we have no protection. Do people in your country think about our condition when they buy the shirts we make?'

NAWAZ HAZARI,
SEWING-MACHINE OPERATOR, GANAKBARI EXPORT-PROCESSING ZONE, DHAKA, BANGLADESH

'The price of coffee is destroying this community. When the price was better a few years ago, I could afford to send my children to school, and to feed them well. Now I can't afford to buy enough food. How can I send them to school when I cannot even feed them well? The price of coffee is destroying us.'

TATU MUSEYNI,
COFFEE FARMER, KILIMANJARO REGION, TANZANIA

INTRODUCTION

These five people, from five different countries, quoted above, have two things in common: poverty, and a dependence on international trade. Each is connected through international markets to consumers or producers in the industrialised world. And the life of each is profoundly affected by what happens in the international trading system.

The term 'international trade' conjures up images of big companies, rivalries between economic superpowers, and impenetrable negotiations at the World Trade Organisation (WTO). But global trade also has a human face. In South Asia it is the face of a young woman producing shirts for chain-stores in Europe and the USA. In Africa it is the face of a coffee farmer. In East Asia it is the face of a woman assembling circuit boards for state-of-the art computer systems. And in Latin America it is the face of a small farmer trying to compete against imports from the USA. Ultimately, trade links the lives of ordinary people like these to businesses and consumers in the world's richest countries.

For many of the communities with whom Oxfam works, international trade raises issues that are fundamental to their poverty and vulnerability. The terms on which poor people participate in world markets can determine whether or not their families have enough to eat, whether their children can attend school, whether their basic employment rights are respected, and – in the last analysis – whether they can work their way out of poverty. All too often the human face of trade is forgotten. It is conspicuous by its absence from the negotiating tables of the WTO, and from the trade ministries of Northern governments. Trade is at the centre of current debates about globalisation, yet poor people figure in those debates only as marginal spectators.

In the globalised world of the early twenty-first century, the lives of people in rich and poor countries are inextricably linked – and trade is one of the strongest ties that bind 'if you ask me how our lives compare with our parents' lives, I will tell you that everything has changed. Things are better. We have opportunities that they never had. Life is hard. We are still vulnerable. But there is less poverty today.'

LAM VAN,
RICE FARMER, MEKONG DELTA, VIETNAM

'Of course I am fearful of losing my job. Some factories have already closed. Now we are told that the American computer market is failing. They say that means there will be less production here. Without this job, my life will be very hard. My parents and children also depend on me, so it will be hard on them.'

JOSEPHINE LARANJA,
EMPLOYED IN AN ELECTRONICS FACTORY SOUTH OF MANILA, THE PHILIPPINES

'I don't know how American farmers can sell corn to this country at such low prices. I have heard that their government gives them money. What I know is that we cannot compete with their prices. Imports are killing our markets and our communities.'

HECTOR CHAVEZ,
SMALLHOLDER FARMER, CHIAPAS, MEXICO

us. Whenever a European or North American buys a cup of tea or coffee, puts on a shirt or a pair of shoes, logs on to a computer, or picks up a mobile phone, he or she is using things produced by people in developing countries. At its simplest, the international trading system is a marketplace where consumers enter into exchanges with people who may be invisible to them, but whose lives are affected by the rules that govern behaviour in that marketplace. Those rules can change the lives of poor people for better, or for worse. They can create an environment in which the benefits of trade are shared, or they can marginalise the vulnerable and bias advantage towards the wealthy. Ultimately, the rules matter, because trade is about human relations, and the shared destinies and responsibilities that those relations create.

Increased interdependence has implications for the rich world as well as for the poor world. For much of history, trade has been an exercise in exploitation. The world's richest countries have used it as a means of transferring wealth from the world's poorest countries, whether through outright plunder or unequal exchange. Mass poverty in developing countries inevitably accompanied the growth of their exports. But in the interdependent world of today, mass poverty in the midst of plenty is not a sustainable option. The prosperity of any one country is linked to the prosperity of all. We sink or swim together.

This report is about people. Drawing on Oxfam's work with communities and partners in more than 80 developing countries, it examines how the rapid growth of world trade is affecting the lives of the poor. One of its central findings is that the huge increase in wealth generated by trade under globalisation has not been matched by parallel progress in poverty reduction, or in broader progress towards human development. The economist and Nobel laureate, Amartya Sen, powerfully expressed the great paradox at the heart of globalisation when he wrote: 'We live in a world of unprecedented opulence ... And yet we also live in a world with remarkable deprivation, destitution and oppression. There are many new problems as well as old ones, including persistence of poverty and unfulfilled elementary needs' (Sen 1999).

Part of the problem with international trade is that the unprecedented opulence associated with it is not being shared on an equitable basis. Wealth is trickling down to many developing countries far too slowly; income differences between rich and poor countries, already obscene, are widening, and undermining the potential for poverty reduction. That is not the only problem. Development is not solely concerned with economic growth and rising incomes. It is also about expanding choice and enhancing the quality of life – what Sen calls 'a process of expanding the real freedoms that people enjoy' (op. cit.). All too often the price of expanding international trade is oppression and injustice. Old divisions based on wealth and gender are being reinforced by new patterns of inequality. Exploitative employment practices are denying millions of women who work in export industries their most basic rights, increasing their vulnerability as they generate wealth for their employers. In many poor countries, trade is undermining the livelihoods of the poor, while concentrating advantage in the hands of the wealthy. Environmental problems that threaten the welfare of future generations are being ignored.

Not all of the problems can be traced to international rules and the behaviour of Northern governments. Developing countries have much to answer for. Southern governments rightly condemn rich countries for denying them the opportunities that trade can provide. They call for policies to redistribute wealth and opportunity. Yet the vast majority are loathe to apply the same principles at home. Trade policies reinforce other policies that perpetuate inequality and injustice.

None of this is inevitable. The international trading system is not a force of nature beyond human control. The way in which it operates, the way in which it distributes costs and benefits, and the opportunities that it provides or destroys are the consequences of political choices – choices that are reflected in the rules, policies, and institutions that dictate the direction of global economic integration. The vast potential of trade to act as a force for economic growth, human development, and shared prosperity is being lost, not because trade is inherently opposed to the interests of the poor, but because it is being managed in a way that concentrates wealth and undermines freedom.

'Globaphobes' and 'globaphiles'

Current debates on trade are dominated by clashes between two great fundamentalist camps: the 'globaphobes' and the 'globaphiles'. In recent years, every major international event in the world economic calendar has been marked by confrontations between these camps, with the mass media selecting and magnifying the most extreme views. The endless arguments over whether globalisation is inherently good or bad for poor people are not helpful terms on which to conduct dialogue about an issue of such profound importance.

There is a difference between 'globaphobia' and the mainstream anti-globalisation movement. That movement has sought to focus public debate on the policies and institutions that deny poor countries an opportunity to participate in world trade on reasonable terms (Khor 2001; World Development Movement 2001a; Porto Alegre 2002). It represents a challenge to the existing trading system and the rules that govern it, but not a rejection of trade *per se*. 'Globaphobes', by contrast, are acutely pessimistic about trade. They believe that it leads inevitably to more poverty, deeper social divisions, the exploitation of poor countries and poor people by rich countries and transnational companies (TNCs), and environmental destruction (Goldsmith 2001).

Evidence that trade can produce such outcomes is not hard to find. Yet 'globaphobia' is refuted by the evidence of history. In East Asia, trade contributed to a dynamic process of economic growth that from the mid-1970s to the mid-1990s lifted more than 300 million people out of poverty. In other developing countries, participation in trade has given people opportunities that would otherwise have been denied to them. Whatever problems may be associated with the expansion of exports, their contraction would destroy the livelihoods of millions of women workers and small farmers. Nor is trade necessarily damaging to the environment, as some critics allege. There is no doubt that badly managed trade can contribute to environmental damage, both locally and globally. But the same applies to any form of production, whether for local or global markets, which fails to take into account the need for environmental sustainability.

If 'globaphobes' are prone to terminal pessimism, 'globaphiles' tend towards fundamentalist optimism. Strongly represented in the World Bank, the International Monetary Fund (IMF), the WTO, and Northern-government circles, they see no problems in export growth, import liberalisation, and rapid integration into the world economy. In their eyes, all trade is good trade – and every trade barrier is a bad barrier (Legrain 2000). The dominant view among 'globaphiles' is that 'globalisation has been a force for poverty reduction' (World Bank 2001a). Some have gone so far as to describe globalisation as 'the most effective force for reducing poverty known to mankind' (*The Economist* 2001a). Increased trade, so the argument runs, is generating the employment and economic growth needed to reduce poverty, and reducing income inequalities between rich and poor countries. While it is recognised that trade creates losers as well as winners, standard economic theory dictates that in the long run everybody wins.

Unfortunately, international trade is an area in which economic theory becomes divorced from observed reality. As globalisation has gathered pace, the world has become more polarised. Already divisive inequalities between rich and poor are widening by the day, both between and within countries. Meanwhile, deep and absolute poverty persists. Today, after two decades of rapid export growth, more than one billion people – one-fifth of the population of the developing world – are struggling to survive on less than $1 a day. That number has barely changed since the mid-1980s. From the viewpoint of the developing world, the argument of the globaphile camp – that in the long run the poor will benefit from unregulated trade – is unconvincing. It recalls the words of the British economist, John Maynard Keynes: 'In the long run we are all dead.'

International trade is not the primary force that drives global poverty and inequality, but it is failing the poor. Rich countries continue to capture the lion's share of world export markets, while whole swathes of the developing world fall further behind. Within developing countries too, integration into international markets often intensifies inequality. The rising prosperity associated with the rapid increase in high-technology exports from India's 'Silicon Valley' contrasts starkly with that country's lack of progress in reducing rural poverty. Export growth is widening economic divisions: between coastal and inland China, between northern Mexico and the 'poverty-belt' states of the south, and between rural and urban areas of Thailand. Male/female disparities are also widening, as power relations within the household and beyond ensure that men benefit at the expense of women.

Advocates for globalisation on the current model claim that it creates high levels of employment-creation; but they ignore the high levels of exploitation associated with that employment. In Bangladesh and Cambodia, Oxfam's partners are supporting women who work 14-hour days for a poverty-level wage. Women working in export-processing zones, from China to Honduras, are denied the most basic employment rights, including maternity provision, social insurance, and the right to join a trade union. Such practices deny millions of people a fair share in the export wealth that they create, reinforcing their poverty and vulnerability in the process.

None of this is inevitable. In itself, trade is not inherently opposed to the interests of poor people. International trade can act as a force for good, or for bad. Trade rules can be designed to disadvantage the poor and concentrate benefits in the hands of the rich, or they can be designed to create an enabling environment in which poor countries can catch up with the rest of the world. Trade can create jobs – or destroy them. It can close the gaps in national societies, or it can exacerbate inequalities based on class, gender, and region. It can enhance the livelihoods of poor people, or it can devastate their environments. It can provide the foreign exchange that countries need in order to import new technologies, or it can furnish the means to import military hardware and enrich corrupt political leaders. The outcomes are not pre-determined. They are shaped by the way in which international trade relations are managed, and by national policies.

The real challenge is to make trade contribute to poverty reduction by changing the institutions, rules, and policies that marginalise the poor. 'Globaphiles' have failed to address that challenge. They offer only more of the same: more liberalisation and more rapid integration into global markets. Given the failure of this model to date, the case for its continued application is indefensible.

'Globaphobes' offer something radically different. Behind the banner of 'national sovereignty' they propose a retreat from trade in favour of increased 'self-reliance'. Perhaps unsurprisingly, such thinking is more attractive to political constituencies in the rich world, where globalisation is increasing insecurity, than in developing countries. Hostility to immigration, scepticism about international co-operation, and suspicion about trade are starting to unite extreme nationalists, ultra right-wing parties, and other 'globaphobes' in potentially dangerous political coalitions. The ethos was well expressed by the Russian politician Vladimir Zhirinovsky, who asked: 'Why should we create suffering for ourselves? We should create suffering for others' (Freeland 1993).

This opposition to trade poses serious threats to developing countries. There are good grounds for challenging many aspects of globalisation, including the liberalisation of capital markets. As in the 1920s, many countries have seen the benefits of trade jeopardised and, in some cases, destroyed by opening their economies to the global financial system. However, integration through trade is not the same as integration through capital markets. Withdrawal from the international trading system and exclusion from Northern markets would deny developing countries and their populations a chance to share in global prosperity. The world's poor would be left even further adrift and isolated. 'National sovereignty', without a systematic strategy for poverty reduction, is little more than a one-way street leading to self-sufficient misery.

None of this is to deny the legitimacy of the fears, or the anger, engendered by globalisation in developing countries. Many of Oxfam's partners in the developing world, and the communities with whom it works, see international trade as a game governed by rules which are constructed to ensure that they cannot win. And they are right. Unless these rules are changed, and participation in trade is seen to deliver something more than continued poverty and inequality, the international trading system will continue to lack legitimacy.

Double standards in high places

Anti-trade views did not arrive with the latest phase of globalisation. Throughout history, international trade has been a subject of extreme controversy. The Greek philosopher, Aristotle, reluctantly conceded that some trade was imperative, even though he thought that it was disruptive of community life (Aristotle 1967: 51). Until the nineteenth century, most European powers viewed trade as a form of undeclared warfare. Their objective was to maximise benefits to themselves, while minimising those to rival nations, and their prime weapons were import barriers. It was not until David Ricardo elaborated the theory of comparative advantage in 1817 that the idea of trade as a mutually beneficial activity gained political momentum. Today, the doctrine of free trade reigns supreme. So pervasive is the belief, so absolute the conviction of its adherents, that it has emerged as the economic religion of globalisation. But it is a curious religion. Throughout history its followers have applied the creed to their own behaviour on a selective basis.

The world's first free-trade evangelist was Great Britain. Having nurtured its own industries behind high import barriers, Britain partially converted to free trade in the first half of the nineteenth century. At home, the power of vested interests meant that many trade barriers were kept intact. Such constraints did not apply overseas. When it encountered trade barriers in other countries, Britain could display all the zeal of a late convert. The nation's 'civilising mission', in the eyes of its political leaders of the day, was to eliminate all import restrictions, by persuasion if possible and by force if necessary. When China banned the sale of opium by the British East India Company on public-health grounds, the Prime Minister of the day, Lord Palmerston, decided to assert the right to free trade. He despatched a naval squadron to bombard Canton and other ports. The result was the 1842 Treaty of Nanking, under which the Chinese emperor was forced to establish free-trade zones. It was one of the world's first free-trade treaties.

The gunboats have gone, but much else remains the same. Lord Palmerston himself would have been impressed by the capacity of rich-country governments to combine double standards in trade policy with recourse to power politics. Indeed, he would not have been out of place leading the European Union or United States delegations in talks at the WTO.

Nowhere are the Palmerston principles more evident today than in the area of market access. Rich countries are fierce advocates of liberalisation in developing countries, while retaining high trade barriers against exports from the same countries. Competition in international trade can be likened to a hurdle race with a difference: the weakest athletes face the highest hurdles. Moreover, the trade barriers imposed by industrialised countries are concentrated in areas such as agriculture and textiles, in which developing countries have the greatest competitive advantage. These barriers are among the main obstacles to the development of a trading system capable of reducing poverty and inequality.

As in the era of coercive trade diplomacy, rich countries combine protectionism at home with the aggressive pursuit of markets overseas, especially when powerful private interests are at stake. The European Union and the United States have used the WTO to extend the investment rights of transnational companies, to enforce their claims for stringent protection of intellectual property, and to prise open key markets. The great corporations of the early twenty-first century are every bit as effective in projecting their commercial interests through powerful governments as the East India Company was in the nineteenth century.

Some of the double standards evident in the rules that govern world trade suggest some interesting historical analogies. During their own industrial development, today's rich countries insisted on the right to nurture infant industries behind protective tariffs. Countries such as the USA and Germany categorically rejected free trade until they had established themselves as major economic powers. Unfortunately, the analogies are not just items of historical interest. While rich countries keep the door to their own markets firmly closed, they use their control over institutions such as the WTO, the World Bank, and the IMF to open up developing-country markets. The message from rich countries to poor countries can be simply summarised: 'Do as we say, not as we do'. Unbalanced liberalisation is one of the reasons why the benefits of world trade are biased in favour of rich countries (Khor 2001).

The crisis of legitimacy

Double standards and the hypocrisy of Northern governments help to explain one of the great paradoxes of the international trading system. Measured by the criterion of wealth creation, the strength of the international trading system has reached an unprecedented peak. Yet the legitimacy of the rules and institutions which govern that system has never been weaker. There is a pervasive – and justified – feeling that industrialised countries are managing the global economy in a manner designed to maintain the privileges of the wealthy, at the expense of the poorest nations and communities.

That feeling was powerfully captured in the course of Oxfam's research among communities in developing countries with whom it works. One young Thai student expressed a sentiment felt by many: *'International trade is like bigger fish eating smaller fish. The big countries set the standards, and they use them to suppress the smaller countries. The weaker nations should have more power. Whatever we try to do ... the bigger nations get in first and try to take it all.'*

Officials in the WTO and spokespersons for Northern governments like to regard public concern about existing trade rules and global institutions as limited to a few protestors in the industrialised world (Legrain 2000). But they are wrong. What emerges from Oxfam's survey is a pervasive sense of powerlessness, mixed with anger, among many people in the developing world. Like the Thai student quoted above, millions of people in the world's poorest countries perceive and experience the global trading system as a source of injustice and unfairness.

These themes emerged repeatedly in interviews with producers in developing countries. Small farmers in Mexico know that their livelihoods are being destroyed not by the 'free' market, but by subsidies and unfair trade practices in Europe and the USA. One of them told Oxfam staff: *'You want to know why I can't compete with American farmers? It is because the market is not fair. We are poor, and they are rich – but they get subsidies and we get nothing.'* Women working in the free-trade zones of Bangladesh, Mexico, and

Honduras expressed deep grievances over the employment practices that link them to Northern consumers. One Bangladeshi woman commented: *'Nobody should have to work without some dignity and some rights. Do people in your rich countries who wear the shirts [we make] know about our conditions – do they care?'* Smallholder farmers growing coffee in Tanzania and cocoa in Ghana know that they are not getting a fair price for their products. As one Tanzanian farmer put it: *'Somebody must make money from our coffee, but all we have here is poverty.'*

In various ways, all these comments point to the crisis of legitimacy in the multilateral trading system, which has failed to give poor countries and poor people a reasonable stake in global prosperity. As the weakest parties in international trade, developing countries need a rules-based system. In fact, they need it even more than rich countries do. Without the capacity to retaliate, rules offer them their only protection from the abuse of economic power. However, viewed from the developing world, existing rules and institutions are distinctly biased towards the interests of the rich world. Instead of countervailing economic power, these rules and institutions are strengthening the position of the strong and undermining that of the vulnerable.

It is not simply international trade rules that need to change. When countries such as India, Brazil, and Mexico send representatives to WTO meetings, they rightly stress the case for redistributing the benefits of trade to poorer countries. Along with the rest of the developing world, they argue that Northern governments should place the interests of poor countries at the top of the agenda. Yet many of the same governments have a lamentable record on poverty reduction. The principles that they advocate at the WTO, with their emphasis on international equity, are not applied at home.

Unequal systems of distribution and inequitable public spending deny poor people access to the assets that they need in order to take advantage of the opportunities provided by trade – assets such as land, marketing infrastructure, and education. Deep-rooted gender-based inequalities go unaddressed. Meanwhile, trade liberalisation is frequently managed in a way that imposes costs on the most vulnerable sections of society – such as small farmers and low-paid workers – while concentrating advantage in the hands of the wealthy. In short, most developing-country governments are only too happy to inflict on their own people the very inequities that they justifiably accuse rich countries of inflicting on the developing world.

Institutional failure

The central argument of this report is that there is no automatic guarantee that increased trade will reduce poverty, but that, managed wisely, trade can help to lift millions of people out of poverty, creating new opportunities for broad-based economic growth. Managed badly, as it is now, it will leave millions of the world's poorest people ever more marginalised. No country will be immune to the instability attendant on the poverty, inequality, and resentment that will follow.

Rich countries have a moral responsibility and reasons of collective self-interest to avert this outcome. The moral responsibility derives from the imperative that poverty, and the enormous waste of human potential that it causes, should not be tolerated in the midst of plenty. The collective self-interest derives in part from economic considerations: all countries stand to benefit from the prosperity that trade can create. But there is also a deeper concern: in a globalised world, social and economic problems do not respect national borders. If whole swathes of the developing world are denied an opportunity to escape poverty, they will not remain as self-contained ghettoes of misery. The conflict, the refugees, and the health problems that poverty creates will be exported to other countries.

History offers some important lessons. After the First World War, the last great episode of globalisation collapsed, creating the conditions for the Great Depression of the 1920s and the nationalist tensions that led to the Second World War. Having gathered pace over the previous 75 years, the integrated global economy of the 1920s fell like a pack of cards. Financial instability, the collapse of international trade, and declining commodity prices created a self-reinforcing cycle (James 2001). The institutions created to manage international co-operation were too weak either to contain the destructive power of markets, or to spread the benefits of globalisation sufficiently widely to avert catastrophe.

Parallels with the 1920s can be overstated, but they should not be ignored. Then, as now, the world lacked the institutions needed to prevent financial crises, or to stop their transmission through the trading system. Then, as now, international trade was felt by many to be a threat to national prosperity. Then, as now, there were no institutions or mechanisms to address a protracted crisis in global commodity markets. Above all, the widespread resentment felt today in developing and developed countries alike at the failures of global institutions to defend the public good poses a challenge to multilateralism which recalls the mood of the 1920s.

Learning from the past

For the generation of post-1945 leaders, the lessons of the inter-war period were clear. Seeing that global prosperity and peace were mutually dependent, they sought a world order and global institutions which would expand opportunity – not just for some, but for all. As President Franklin Roosevelt said in his fourth inaugural address: 'We have learned that we cannot live alone, at peace; that our own well-being is dependent on the well-being of other nations, far away ... We have learned to be citizens of the world, members of the human community' (Roosevelt 1945).

The human community of the first decade in the new millennium is in urgent need of institutions which will govern markets in the common good. The financier and philanthropist George Soros has observed that global markets operate on the basis of fewer and fewer shared values, and that markets dictate politics, rather than vice versa. He describes the greatest threat to stability as being a general political failure at both the national and international levels (Soros 1998). Writing on the same theme, Paul Volcker, the Chair of the US Federal Reserve System, has drawn attention to the failure of global institutions to manage relations between countries in a manner that meets the basic criteria for fairness: 'When the IMF consults with a poor and weak country, the country gets in line. When it consults with a big and strong country, the IMF gets in line. When big countries are in conflict, the IMF gets out of the line of fire' (Volcker and Gyohten 1992).

These twin themes of political failure and institutional failure are fundamental to the crisis of legitimacy that faces multilateralism in international trade. In some areas, the WTO has been used as a blunt instrument to force open developing-country markets and advance the interests of Northern-based TNCs. In others, it adopts rules which seek to legitimise double standards, allowing levels of subsidies for agriculture or tariffs on textiles to accommodate US and European demands. Such practices are hardly consistent with the principles of fairness and balance that are vital requirements for a functioning rules-based system.

The clock is ticking at the WTO. At the end of 1999, the WTO ministerial meeting in Seattle broke down in the face of the developing world's collective refusal to participate in a round of talks which failed to reflect their interests. Media attention may have focused on the protestors, but the meeting collapsed because the major trading powers lacked the political will to accommodate the interests of developing countries. Calls to honour commitments made in the past, such as accelerating the phased removal of textile and agricultural trade barriers, were ignored.

Two years later, a follow-up meeting held in Doha, following the terrorist attacks in the USA on 11 September 2001, illustrated the collective inability of governments in rich countries to learn from their own mistakes. Having initially pledged their commitment to a new round of trade negotiations, focused on development (a so-called 'development round'), they proceeded to conduct business as usual. Vague commitments to improve market access have not been translated into a considered strategy for delivering real change. The already strained credibility of the multilateral system is being stretched to breaking point. Failure to develop new rules and end old injustices will jeopardise the survival of the WTO, and with it the stability of the global trading system.

After the terrorist attacks in New York and Washington in September 2001, many industrialised-country governments acknowledged the threat to collective security posed by poverty and inequality. One finance minister, the UK Chancellor Gordon Brown, set out a bold vision for reform. Recalling the spirit of the Bretton Woods conference at the end of the Second World War, he called for a commitment to 'inclusive globalisation' (Brown 2001). That goal is achievable. What is needed are the vision, the policies, and the institutions to make it happen.

CHAPTER 1
Trade and globalisation in the twenty-first century

The idea that globalisation is something new is a conceit of the late twentieth century. Developing countries have been progressively integrated into a global economy ever since the discovery of the New World more than five centuries ago. There are some powerful elements of continuity between past and present, including the role of rich countries in managing global markets to advance their own interests. Yet globalisation in the early twenty-first century is revolutionising economic relations between countries, and the future direction of change will have profound implications for poverty reduction.

The depth of interdependence in the new global economy means that the welfare of all countries is now more closely linked than ever before. Prosperity in any one country is increasingly dependent on prosperity elsewhere. The saying 'we sink or swim together' has taken on a new meaning in international economic relations. But globalisation is not just about abstract economic relations between countries. Behind the powerful global economic forces are processes that are transforming the lives of ordinary people in developing countries.

Globalisation manifests itself in strange ways. Five years ago, Shawaz Begum left her rural village in south-east Bangladesh to find work in the capital city of Dhaka. Today, she lives in Ashulia, a sprawling slum on the city's northern outskirts, a place of relentless poverty. Water supply and sanitation are major problems, especially in the rainy season. Shawaz rents a one-room home that is little more than a shack, made of a mud wall, wooden slats, and a plastic roof. But six days a week she enters a different world. Like most young women in Ashulia, Shawaz works as a machinist in a garments factory. Located in an export-processing zone and owned by a South Korean company, the factory produces designer-label shirts for a supply chain which leads to clients ranging from Pierre Cardin to Adidas. The labels on the shirts read 'Made in Bangladesh'; but the factory imports yarn from India, cloth from Taiwan and Korea, lining and packaging materials from China, and buttons from Indonesia. For her part in the operation, Shawaz is paid $1.50 for a ten-hour day.

Contacts between developing-country poverty and industrialised-country prosperity are not new, but globalisation is making those contacts more frequent and more intensive.

The contrasts that emerge are striking. Some of the world's most expensive shirts are produced by some of its poorest women, like Shawaz Begum. Blue-chip companies, such as Microsoft, IBM, and Intel, operate software-development facilities in the midst of India's mass poverty and illiteracy (Nicholson and Taylor 1997). Top-of-the-range computer systems are assembled by women workers from poor rural districts in China, the Philippines, and Mexico (Bank 1996). Some of the world's most advanced automobile factories, supplying markets in Europe and North America, are now located in developing countries.

In the most general terms, 'globalisation' describes the growing interdependence of the countries of the world. International trade, allied to huge increases in capital movements, the rapid expansion of transnational companies (TNCs), and technological change, is one of the most powerful motors driving that interdependence. But behind the abstract economic factors, globalisation is also transforming the lives of ordinary people, and re-configuring economic relations between countries.

This chapter analyses the role of international trade in shaping trade relations between countries. The first part considers international trade as a motor of globalisation, and shows how it is changing world trade patterns. The second part describes some of the technological forces that are shaping globalisation and highlights the role of TNCs. The third part briefly reviews some of the elements of continuity and some of the differences between globalisation at the start of the twenty-first century and that of earlier periods.

International trade and globalisation

In the last decade of the sixteenth century, Elizabethan England was at war with Spain and Portugal. It was the first real war of the globalisation era, and the stakes were high. Spain and Portugal, having opened up the East Indies and the New World, were reaping the benefits of access to precious metals and commodities prized in European markets. Plunder was generating lucrative trade. Anxious to redistribute some of the benefits, Queen Elizabeth I gave her blessing to acts of piracy. English naval squadrons lined up off the Azores to intercept and capture Spanish ships, sailing from the New World laden with treasure plundered from Mexico and Peru. In 1592, they struck lucky. The y intercepted the Portuguese ship *Madre de Deus* on its way back from the East Indies. It was filled with 425 tons of pepper, 45 tons of cloves, and 3 tons each of mace and nutmeg, along with large amounts of gold and silver coin, huge quantities of cloth, and chests full of jewels. The estimated value of the cargo was equivalent to half of all the money in the British Exchequer.

Robbery and plunder are recurrent themes in the history of trade, especially when viewed from the developing world. When economists write about globalisation today, they usually describe a process of world market integration that started at the end of the nineteenth century, suffered a reversal between the First and Second World Wars, and gathered force again in the 1980s (see, for example, O'Rourke and Williamson 2000, World Bank 2001b). The previous five centuries, during which today's industrialised countries extended their domination over the global economy, disappear from history. During that period, developing countries were integrated into the global trading system on terms designed to benefit the nations which constitute today's industrialised world. Trade was a vehicle for transferring wealth and power from poor to rich. Traffic in precious metals from the New World was an early example of globalisation. In the seventeenth century, the imposition of forced cultivation systems by Dutch colonists in the East Indies laid the foundations for a huge transfer of income through the spice trade. Slavery and colonialism were decisive stages in the creation of genuinely global markets, all of which were operated in order to concentrate wealth and advantage. Political power, as much as economic exchange, shaped the distribution of the benefits from trade. And in this, as in other respects, there are strong elements of continuity between past and present forms of globalisation.

Globalisation and trade in perspective

At the end of the nineteenth century, the world was highly integrated through the movement of goods, capital, and people. Steamships and railways connected countries and opened up national markets. The telegraph system facilitated the emergence of international capital markets. During the thirty years to 1914, the ratio of trade to world gross domestic product (GDP) doubled (Hirst and Thompson 1995). It was not until the 1970s that most industrial countries were exporting the same share of GDP as they had been exporting before 1914. When measured in relation to national wealth, imports and exports of capital were greater in the early twentieth century than they are today (James 2001:11-12). Above all, *people* crossed borders. More than 36 million people, most of them from poor rural backgrounds, left Europe between 1871 and 1915, the majority destined for the New World (Faini et al. 1999).

Early twentieth-century globalisation had major effects on global income distribution. Capital flows created the infrastructure for the export of labour-intensive agricultural goods, which were exchanged for manufactured goods. Average incomes grew and started to converge as inequalities narrowed. Wealth gaps diminished by about one-third in the last quarter of the nineteenth century (O'Rourke and Williamson 2000). Flows of capital and trade facilitated export growth and increased demand for labour in the New World, enabling migrant labour to be absorbed at higher income levels. Migration is estimated to have accounted for more than two-thirds of the income convergence that happened in the second half of the nineteenth century, with trade accounting for the rest (Lindert and Williamson 2001).

The inter-war period in the twentieth century saw a rapid retreat from global integration. A crisis in capital markets spread and internationalised the Great Depression. As banks called in loans, governments responded by cutting demand, attempting to pass the cost of adjustment on to each other. Every country responded to the balance-of-payments pressures created by the collapse of imports by restricting the imports of competitors, creating a downward spiral (James 2001). Ruthlessly competitive protectionism was the order of the day. The chosen weapon was tariff protection, with the USA leading the way through the imposition of high tariffs in 1929. Capital and trade flows collapsed, and world economic growth fell by one-third. Mass unemployment led to rising poverty within countries, while the degree of inequality between countries increased (Maddison 2001).

The experience of the 1930s holds important lessons for the rich world today. It graphically illustrates what happens when interconnected countries pursue policies that damage the interests of their trade partners. When the USA closed its markets, its exports promptly collapsed as a result of falling purchasing power overseas. When British banks called in their loans, they irrevocably damaged the interests of manufacturing exporters. Interdependence offers benefits; but when it goes wrong, it also has the potential to inflict social and economic costs.

Trade and interdependence: developing countries in the globalised economy

The integrated global economy at the start of the last century bears more than a passing resemblance to conditions that prevail today. Is there anything different about contemporary globalisation? And how is it shaping relations between developed and developing countries?

The answer to these questions is partly quantitative. Economic integration is proceeding at a dramatic pace, and one of its most powerful motors has been international trade. During the past 20 years, the volume of world trade has grown twice as fast as world GDP, or by six per cent versus three per cent. This means that the value of exports has tripled, while world GDP has doubled over the same period. Exports now represent almost one-fifth of global GDP. The result is that countries are more tightly integrated through trade than ever before, and increasingly depend on each other for their prosperity. (See Figure 1.1.)

Developing countries as a group have participated in this process. Exports have been growing faster than GDP in most developing regions, in some cases dramatically so. As a result, dependence on exports as a source of wealth has been growing far more rapidly in developing countries than in industrialised countries. Over the past decade, the share of trade in GDP increased by seven per cent for developing countries, and by ten per cent for low-income countries. Exports now account for more than one-quarter of GDP in developing countries. Rates of increase in export-dependence have been most rapid in East Asia and (albeit from a low base) in South Asia (Figure 1.2). Although the rate of increase in sub-Saharan Africa has been far slower, the ratio of regional trade to GDP is still more than twice as high as for the USA.

High levels of dependence on exports have important implications. Most obviously, they leave developing countries dangerously susceptible to changing conditions in global markets. At the same time, the rising share of national wealth accounted for by exports means that international trade exercises an increasingly important influence on average income levels.

It is not simply that the *volume and value* of trade have been growing under globalisation. *Patterns of trade* are also changing. International trade is becoming an increasingly knowledge-intensive activity. The share of manufacturing trade in general is rising relative to primary commodities, while the share of high-technology goods is rising fastest of all (Lall 2001a). Since the mid-1980s, world manufacturing trade has grown at three times the rate of trade in primary products, and now accounts for more than four-fifths of all world trade (Figure 1.3).

Technologies requiring heavy investments in research and development (R&D) and sophisticated technology infrastructures are now the most dynamic growth areas of international trade, led by electronics (see Figure 1.4). The share of this product group in the past 15 years has increased by a factor of three, to constitute more than one-quarter of world trade. Over the same period, medium-technology goods, such as auto parts, engineering, and other industrial products, have doubled their share. Meanwhile, the bottom is dropping out of world commodity markets. Their share of world trade has halved since the mid-1980s, and the overall trend is unmistakably downwards.

Developing countries have contributed to these structural changes in international trade under globalisation. Not only are they participating more extensively in the global

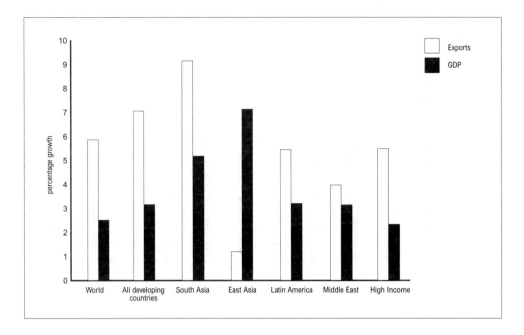

Figure 1.1
Average annual growth of exports and GDP (%) (1990-1999)

Source: World Bank 2001d, IMF 2001a

trading system, but they are also more prominent exporters of high-technology products. Because their exports have been growing faster than those of the industrialised world, developing countries' share in world trade has climbed from around one-fifth to one-quarter over the past decade. Export growth has been combined with a transformation in the structure of exports. Manufactured goods now account for more than four-fifths of total exports from developing countries, compared with only one-quarter at the start of the 1980s. These exports have been growing more rapidly than in developed countries, especially in the high-technology sectors. Over the 15 years from the mid-1980s, exports of manufactured goods rose at 12 per cent a year, and exports of high-technology goods at more than 20 per cent a year – double the rate of growth, in the latter case, achieved by industrialised countries. As a result, developing countries' share in global export markets for high-technology products has been increasing (Figure 1.5).

The expansion of international trade is intimately linked to flows of capital, just as it was during the last wave of globalisation a century ago. Foreign direct investment (FDI) has played a critical role in many developing countries in generating exports, with Northern TNCs locating production facilities overseas. The scale of FDI as a source of finance can be illustrated by comparing it with development assistance. At the start of the 1990s, aid flows to developing countries were roughly equivalent to flows of FDI. By 2000, FDI in developing countries amounted to $240bn, while official development assistance stood at $56bn. FDI has grown almost continuously for the past decade (World Bank 2001a). While it is true that foreign investment still accounts for a small share of GDP for developing countries, and that domestic savings will remain the main source of investment, FDI is growing in importance.

FDI is not the only source of financial integration. The biggest increase in private capital flows has been in portfolio investments, such as government and company bonds. The development of global capital markets has given institutional investors in the industrialised world access to assets (such as equity, government bonds, and company bonds) in the developing world. Pension funds, mutual funds, and hedge funds have been channelling equity flows to developing countries on a large scale, amounting to more than $100bn in 1997 (Schmukler and Lobaton 2001).

Figure 1.2
Exports as % of GDP
(1990 and 1999)

Source: World Bank 2001b

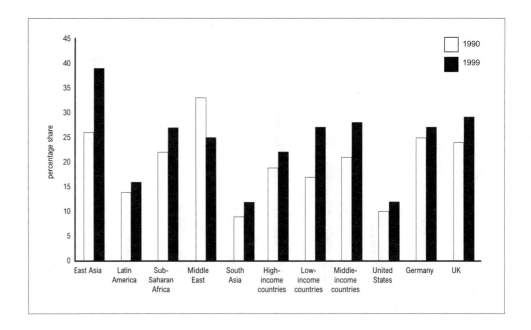

Developing countries have not been immune to another distinctive aspect of contemporary globalisation: the separation of currency and trade markets. New electronic technologies have made international currency an increasingly tradable commodity. The worldwide *daily* turnover in foreign-exchange markets in 1998 was approximately $1.5 trillion. That figure represents 78 times the daily volume of exports of goods and services, which is an increase of one-third in a decade (Bird and Rajan 2001).

New technologies and globalised production

Economic indicators of globalisation point to important changes in the way that countries interact in the international economy. Yet these quantitative indicators reflect far more profound qualitative changes, which are the result of three interactive forces: new technologies, the emergence of global production systems, and the operations of transnational companies.

The new technological revolution

Perhaps the decisive difference between globalisation today and a century ago is technological change. Advances in computing and telecommunications have brought unprecedented opportunities for the expansion of trade. New technologies are creating an ever-denser network of connections, both electronic and production-based, between the developed and the developing worlds.

The first industrial revolution in the eighteenth century was driven by steam power and textiles production. It was strengthened in the nineteenth century by the development of the railways, and given a powerful new impetus by electricity and the rise of science-based industries. Globalisation today has been made possible by another wave of technological change. The defining features of the revolution in information technology (IT) are, as in earlier periods, rapid advances in materials science and the diffusion of new technology. Arguably, however, the IT revolution is more far-reaching in its effects than anything seen before.

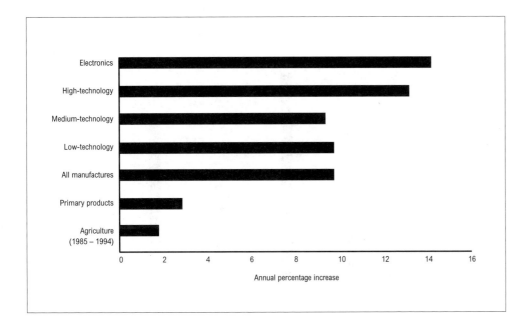

Figure 1.3
Average annual export growth rates
by selected product groups:
1985-98

Sources: UNCTAD 1999 and OECD 2001a

The semi-conductor is at the centre of this new revolution. Computing capacity is expanding at a staggering pace. Over the past decade, the capacity of semi-conductor chips has doubled every 18–24 months, and the processing power of computers has increased by a factor of 100 (IMF 2001a). The capacity of computers, communications networks, and information-storage and retrieval systems has probably grown faster than any technology in history (Castels 2000). Increased capacity has been accompanied by reduced costs. When Intel launched its Pentium 4 chip in mid-2001, the price was half that of the previous generation of chips, illustrating the inverse relationship between price and the development of processing speed (Abrams and Harney 2001).

The marriage of computer technology and telecommunications – or 'digitalisation' – is one of the defining features of contemporary globalisation (Schiller 2000). It has made possible the creation of new production systems, based on vast networks of information that can be shared at low cost by many users. The cost of transmitting information between and across these systems has fallen dramatically (Wristin 1997). Ten years ago, a 15 minute phone call from New York to Manila would have cost $40 at today's prices. It now costs less than 10 cents to e-mail a 50-page document over the same distance. Internet use has grown exponentially. The World Wide Web took just three years from its launch in 1989 to reach a global user network of 50 million people. Internet traffic is doubling every 100 days (Yusuf 2000); by 2005, an estimated one billion people will have access.

However, technology enthusiasts tend to make exaggerated claims about the power of computers to transform the world. They forget that half the world's population has never made a phone call, let alone logged on to the Internet (UNDP 2001a). There are limits to the reach of new technologies, but nevertheless they are revolutionising trade.

Transferability is one of the defining features of the IT revolution. In earlier industrial revolutions, new technologies such as railways and power-generation plants were dispersed across the world fairly slowly, especially in the developing world. Digital technologies are different. Their high price-to-weight ratio makes them far more easily transferable, with the result that goods embodying these new technologies are being more rapidly globalised (IMF 2001a:105).

Figure 1.4
Share of selected product groups
in world exports: 1985 and 1998

Source: Lall 2001a

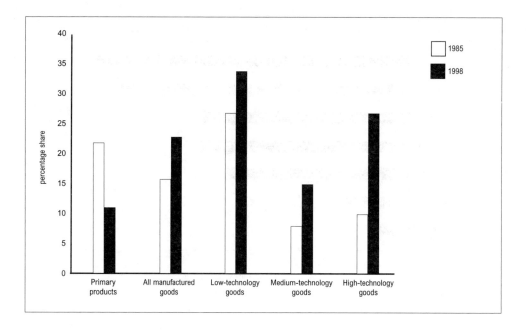

All this has had major implications for the nature of international trade. In the classic model based on comparative advantage, the location of industry is explained by two factors: natural-resource endowments, and the relative abundance of capital and labour. Britain led the first industrial revolution because it had the capital to build the factories, and the water and then coal to drive them. Pittsburgh became the iron and steel capital of the United States because the locations of the country's coal, iron ore, rivers, and lakes made it the most viable option. Developing countries, so the argument went, produced cheap textiles and agricultural exports because they had an abundance of cheap labour and land. Rich countries produced more sophisticated products because they had the education and skills needed to operate them, and because the technologies involved were not readily transferable.

Globalisation and the IT revolution have not completely invalidated simple models of comparative advantage. There are still limits to the transferability of technology, defined by factors such as levels of education and the quality of infrastructure. Even so, former theories of comparative advantage and the division of labour that they implied have been severely weakened, as witnessed by the rapid growth of high-technology exports from developing countries. In the new order, it is increasingly possible to leap over frontiers, linking high-productivity technologies to low-cost labour.

Global production systems

The combination of technological change and rapid liberalisation has pushed back the frontier of the production options available to transnational companies. Global production systems are consequently now increasingly complex, with firms able to produce and assemble components across a wide range of locations. A century ago, globalisation was driven by a simple transfer of goods and money between countries. Today, it is being driven by the development of production systems which span national borders, including the borders that separate rich and poor countries.

Through foreign investment or sub-contracting arrangements, firms can locate almost any value-added activity in any part of the world, subject to the availability of local skills and infrastructure. Much of the expansion of world trade over the past decade reflects the development of global production systems. One of the features of these systems is

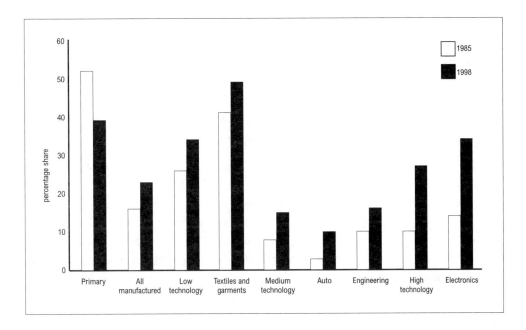

Figure 1.5
Share of developing countries in world exports: selected product groups (1985 and 1998)

Source: Lall 2001a

a high degree of specialisation. Products that might 20 years ago have been produced in one country are now made up of components that have crossed dozens of borders before final assembly.

In characteristically opaque terms, economists refer to this trend as the 'vertical disintegration of production', or 'intra-product' trade (Arndt 1998). In simple language, this means that products are increasingly being reduced to constituent components, sub-components, and processes that can be manufactured, assembled, or operated anywhere in the world. 'Intra-product' trade, involving the export and import of components used in creating a final product, now accounts for almost one-third of total world trade.

Intra-product trade has driven the rapid growth of high-technology exports from developing countries. Through their foreign-investment activities, TNCs have created vast networks and supply chains, whose importance can be obscured by international trade data. For example, the large increase in regional trade between East Asian countries represents a surge in trade *within* corporate production systems. In 1990, the Japanese company Fujitsu opened a new factory on an industrial estate just outside Bangkok. That factory, which now produces more than one million disk drives each month, is one part of a wider system, linked through import and export activity to other Fujitsu factories in China, Malaysia, the Philippines, and Vietnam, as well as to dozens of contractors and sub-contractors supplying electrical components (Arnold 2001).

Nowhere captures the spirit and meaning of globalisation quite like the Chinese city of Dongguan. Twenty years ago it was an insignificant town which few executives of the world's largest TNCs would have been able to find on a map. Today, it is a hub for one of the largest manufacturing export bases in the world. The city houses almost 3000 computer- and IT-related industrial enterprises, producing and assembling everything from disk drives and electronic circuit boards to scanners, keyboards, and magnetic heads. All the big players in the corporate IT world – IBM, Hewlett Packard, Fujitsu, and Dell, to name a few – have facilities in Dongguan. Turnover in the IT sector alone amounts to $10bn a year. Much of that turnover happens within the Hong Kong-Shenzhen-Guangzhou economic corridor, astride which Dongguan sits. Factories in the city take inputs from factories along the corridor, and supply outputs back to them; all are linked to larger networks of factories in the region and beyond. The pivotal role of Dongguan was well expressed by the Deputy Director of IBM for Asia, when he commented: 'If there is a traffic jam between Dongguan and Hong Kong, 70 per cent of the world's computer market will be affected' (Dongguan Information Centre 2001). The 'Dongguan factor' illustrates the transferability of new technologies. Of the 14 'super' semi-conductor plants under construction by US companies in 1997 and involving investments of more than $1.5bn, four were in East Asia.

Change is not restricted to the electronics industry. The large increases in trade connected with the automobile industry are also the product of global corporate restructuring. The new Volkswagen Beetle, a best-selling model in Europe, is produced in a state-of-the-art car factory using the most advanced robotic technologies. That factory is located not in Germany, but in Volkswagen's Puebla plant, 90 miles south-east of Mexico City. In 1995, Volkswagen decided to produce the new Beetle for worldwide distribution exclusively in Puebla, investing $1bn in a new factory. The 14,000 workers in the plant are linked to thousands of other workers across the world through Volkswagen's global network of suppliers (Harrison 1998).

Globalisation has rendered the 'national car' a thing of the past, dismantling borders between rich and poor countries in the process. When Henry Ford's 'Model T' car rolled off the assembly line in Detroit at the end of the last century, almost every component, apart from the rubber on the wheels, had been manufactured in the USA. It was, for practical purposes, 'made in America'. Today, new models are 'made worldwide'. In the mid-1990s the Fiat Palio entered the market, promoted by the company as the first 'world car'. The company was referring to its plans for producing the same model across the developing world, and has since started production in China, India, Egypt, Turkey, and Venezuela. But what is really international about the Palio is its composition. Each Fiat plant is linked through Fiat's 'World Information Flow' computer networks to other Fiat plants and to hundreds of suppliers in a global production system stretching across dozens of countries (Camuffo and Volpato 2000).

New technologies, trade liberalisation, and foreign investment are strengthening the links between developed and developing countries in the automobile industry. In 1990, General Motors (GM) had only one-fifth of its production capacity located outside the USA. By 2005 that figure will have risen to half (Hanson 2001). Brazil has been made the showcase for GM's new global production strategy, based on simple and flexible manufacturing plants, global sourcing, and regional marketing. Production has increased three-fold over the past decade. Component manufacturers are following in the wake of the car manufacturers. In the mid-1980s, the French auto-parts giant Valeo had only seven of its 33 plants located in developing countries. It now operates 43 plants in the developing world, including 21 in Latin America (Humphreys 1999).

While labour-intensive manufacturing sectors are falling behind in terms of world export growth, they have not escaped the revolutionary impact of new technologies and increased capital mobility. Two mutually reinforcing processes are underway. The first involves an acceleration of long-established trends. Trade liberalisation, new technologies, and capital mobility have made it increasingly easy to transfer factories to sites offering cheaper labour. Five years ago, Bloomington, Indiana was the self-proclaimed 'colour-TV capital of the world'. It was home to Thomson Consumer Electronics, which operated the world's largest television factory in the town. Today, the Thomson factory stands not in Bloomington, but in a free-trade zone near the northern Mexican town of Cuidad Juarez (Abrams and Harney 2001). It now exports its TV sets to the USA. The northern region of Mexico is now the largest exporter of colour televisions to the countries of the OECD, and accounts for almost two-thirds of US imports.

The second process is new. When the Singer corporation relocated its factories from Europe and the USA to East Asia in the 1960s, and then to South Asia, the factories were largely self-contained. That has changed. Today, even simple garment exports from developing countries frequently comprise products made in a large number of production sites. Cheap labour is still a magnet for foreign investors, but factories in developing countries are now part of far more complex global systems, linked to consumers through the purchasing activities of Northern retail chains.

Take the case of Fashun Wears, a thriving medium-sized factory located on the Okhla industrial estate on the northern outskirts of Delhi. In early 2001, the factory successfully tendered to produce 20,000 children's corduroy dresses for the chain-store group Gap at a going rate of $2.50 per item. It was competing against dozens of other factories in Gap's international supply network. And it will produce the dresses as one component in that network. Under the terms of the contract, Fashun Wears is required to import the synthetic lining and buttons from specified suppliers in China, the zip from South Korea, and the linen collar from another supplier in India. Workers in Fashun Wears are part of a global network, co-ordinated through Gap's international purchasing system.

New communication technologies make it easier to manage and control geographically dispersed supply chains. Flows of information within these chains can be maintained at virtually no cost, since digitalised information transfers are 'weightless'. This has led some commentators to predict the 'death of distance' in economic activity. That assessment may be premature, especially for landlocked countries and small island economies. Even so, the falling costs of containerisation and airfreight are reinforcing the effects of new communication technologies which are reducing the barriers of distance.

While the impact of globalisation on agricultural trade is superficially less marked than in manufacturing, it should not be under-estimated. Important shifts are taking place. These shifts are manifested in the rapid growth in industrialised-country demand for exotic fruits and off-season vegetables. New technologies and reduced transport costs have reduced the distance between the supermarket shelves of rich countries and farmers in poor countries. Mexico is now the single biggest source of avocados and tomatoes imported into the United States. In European supermarkets, *mange touts* and beans from Africa are now standard features, alongside a range of fruits that were rarities a decade ago. The rapid growth of fruit, vegetable, and other agricultural exports from developing countries is creating forms of employment for women – and new problems – across the developing world (Barrientos 2001).

The development of global retail chains provides further evidence of the new forces of globalisation at work. Once again, there is nothing new about TNCs investing in developing countries to get access to markets. High import barriers have given large retailing companies an incentive to locate in developing countries in order to gain access to protected markets. Unilever developed a major stake in the Indian detergents market, and General Motors a major stake in Brazil's car market, because these markets were very large. What has changed is the pattern of TNC operations.

No company embodies the values and activities of the new global retailer more than Wal-Mart, middle-America's most popular merchant. Today, it also dominates Mexico's retail sector. Wal-Mart de Mexico's 520 stores generate annual sales of $9bn, and account for about one-third of the $1.1bn in overseas profit generated by the parent company (Luhnow 2001). In the past, import duties forced foreign retailers in Mexico to source from local suppliers. Tariff and non-tariff restrictions gave home producers an advantage. Since the liberalisation of trade in 1994, this has changed. Mexico may be one of the world's largest producers of corn; it may be facing a social crisis in the corn sector, with the livelihoods of almost one million people under threat in the impoverished 'poverty-belt' states of the south; but Wal-Mart de Mexico does not source its corn from Mexican farmers. Its best-selling popcorn – Act II – is imported from the US company Con-Agra, with which Wal-Mart has negotiated a global supply contract. Act II is not an exception. Almost everything on the shelves of Wal-Mart de Mexico's stores is either imported, or produced in the plants of foreign companies in the country's free-trade zone. Products for the Mexican subsidiary are supplied through the same vast global purchasing system that links Wal-Mart stores across the world. With its emphasis on centralisation and standardisation, Wal-Mart embodies many of the values of the new global order (Zeller et al. 1997).

The role of TNCs

New technologies have made globalisation possible. Transnational companies make it happen. Through their purchasing, production, and investment decisions, they create a global market place and provide the impetus which drives increased interdependence.

TNCs are not new arrivals on the international stage. Since the days of the East India Company in the eighteenth and nineteenth centuries, private firms have been the main link between producers in the developing world and consumers in the industrialised world. During and after colonialism, TNCs brought these consumers the tea, coffee, sugar, and raw materials produced across the developing world. They still do. Small numbers of TNCs still dominate global commodity markets, often on a quasi-monopolistic basis. What has changed is the broader role and importance of TNCs in the international trading system. As with other aspects of globalisation, part of the change is qualitative, and part quantitative. Size may not be everything in economic life under globalisation, but it counts for a lot – and TNCs have it in gathering abundance.

Collectively, corporations operating in more than one country now account for about one-quarter of global output. International production carried out under the auspices of these companies is growing far more rapidly than other economic indicators. Global economic integration is, in large measure, the product of integrated corporate production systems. The annual foreign sales of the largest 100 TNCs amount to $2.1 trillion (United Nations 2000). To put that figure in context, it is equivalent to about seven per cent of global GDP and more than 25 per cent of world trade. It is also larger than the combined GDPs of South Asia and sub-Saharan Africa, home to one-third of the world's population.

At one level, such comparisons are of limited relevance. It is impossible to draw meaningful comparisons between the size of TNCs and the size of national economies. Company assets are not the same as national assets, and company sales or turnover are different from national income. National product is a measure of value-added in national economic activity, while company turnover represents value-added plus the costs of inputs. But while direct comparison may be of dubious relevance in technical or analytical terms, it does provide some indication of the sheer scale of corporate power. (The following data are derived from United Nations 2000.)

Comparing company turnover with GDP, half of the world's largest 100 economic entities are not countries, but corporations.

- Wal-Mart, General Motors, and Ford have a bigger turnover than Africa's entire combined GDP.

- Mitsubishi and Toyota have a turnover comparable to the GDP of countries such as Greece and Portugal.

- The combined sales of Wal-Mart, IBM, and Nestlé are equivalent to the GDP of Mexico or India.

In the past, Northern-based TNCs invested in developing countries for one of essentially three reasons: access to cheap labour, access to raw materials and commodities, and access to local markets. Most TNC activity was a simple bilateral operation, involving the transfer of goods between two countries, or the location of plants in countries to produce for a domestic market. Under globalisation, nothing has changed – and everything has changed.

Cheap labour, raw materials, and local markets are still magnets for investment. However, the role of TNCs as intermediaries between countries has changed out of all recognition. They are now gatekeepers to markets, investment, and technology: three of the key requirements for successful integration into the global economy.

- **Corporate markets.** The idea that world trade is about countries exchanging goods with each other has become an anachronism. Trade is an increasingly intra-corporate affair. Exchanges *within* TNCs now account for around two-thirds of world trade flows, reflecting the growth of 'intra-product' trade (Bird and Rajan 2001: 3). Access to 'world' markets is increasingly a function of participation in internal corporate markets, especially in high-technology sectors such as micro-electronics and automobiles. Much of the rapid growth in South–South trade that has accompanied globalisation is matched by the growth of intra-company trade. Through their control over market information and brand names, TNCs are also gatekeepers for access to consumer markets in products such as textiles and garments.

- **Corporate foreign investment.** The relentless rise of intra-company trade has been driven by FDI. Control over FDI is heavily concentrated. The largest 500 TNCs account for more than 80 per cent of foreign investment, and their share is growing over time (United Nations 1999: Ch 3). Export activity is intimately linked to investment for a growing number of developing countries. TNCs account for more than one-third of exports from rapidly globalising countries such as Mexico, China, and Malaysia, and more than 80 per cent of manufacturing exports from countries such as Bangladesh and Honduras (United Nations 1999: 245).

- **New technologies.** In a global marketplace dominated by new technologies, access to technology is a requirement for successful entry. Technologies which are used to produce the micro-electronic goods exported from the Philippines, the auto-parts from Mexico, and the garments from Bangladesh are all imported. Technology transfer is not a simple exchange. The new technologies needed to compete in global markets are the products of research and development (R&D) carried out under the auspices of TNCs. For instance, just 100 TNCs account for almost two-thirds of all R&D activity in the USA, which accounts in turn for 40 per cent of global R&D (United Nations 1999: 199). Cutting-edge technology is often patented – and the patent holder can dictate the terms of exchange. Control over technology, and the profits that technology offers in a knowledge-based economy, are at the heart of protracted disputes over intellectual-property rights at the WTO.

Old tensions and new developments

The idea that globalisation is something new is a conceit of the late twentieth century. Many of the themes that currently dominate debates on trade and finance would have been familiar to an audience in the 1930s. There are important elements of continuity with the past, but also wider differences.

One feature of globalisation that has a powerful resonance with the 1920s is the destabilising effects of capital markets. The catalyst for the collapse of the last great wave of integration in the 1920s was a financial implosion, which in turn destabilised world trade. Over the past decade, a succession of financial crises, in Mexico (the end of 1995), East Asia, Brazil, and Russia (1997), and Argentina (2001) has provided a timely reminder of the scope for systemic crisis. Each crisis has been accompanied by speculative attacks on national currencies and largely mismanaged rescue efforts. The fact that the international financial system has emerged intact after each episode should not detract from the scale of the disaster visited on some developing countries. Ordinary Indonesians and Argentinians have suffered major economic losses and political instability, just as people in inter-war Europe did.

Similar observations could be made in relation to trade. One of the reasons why so many countries turned inwards in the 1930s was because they shared a (mistaken) belief that participation in international trade offered limited benefits at high cost. Slumping commodity markets caused widespread poverty and instability. There was no confidence that the League of Nations, the institution set up partly to manage trade relations at the end of the First World War, could resolve the problem. Today, the benefits of trade may appear self-evident to the winners in rich countries, but developing countries are asking legitimate questions about the benefits of the current trade order – an order which imposes high adjustment costs on them as they liberalise, while denying them access to Northern markets. It also fails to address their commodity-trade problems (see Chapter 6). The WTO is widely – and rightly – perceived as part of the problem.

There are other striking parallels. During the 1930s, the crisis in international trade was accompanied by the rise of xenophobic nationalist movements. 'Anti-foreigner' sentiment was widespread, as was the feeling that poorer countries were trading unfairly, taking advantage of low wages, child labour, and weak employment standards. The International Labour Organisation (ILO), the body created to prevent 'unfair' trade, was widely seen as a failure. Similarly, there is a commonly held view in industrialised countries today that world trade rules and TNC practices are generating a 'race to the bottom', dragging all workers down to the level of the most exploited.

The world of today is different from that of the 1920s and 1930s. Yet a feature common to both worlds is a process of rapid economic integration which has not been complemented by the development of credible global institutions. The resulting risks are remarkably similar.

New developments in globalisation are transforming the lives of millions of people, and nowhere more so than in the sphere of employment. One of the most striking developments of the past two decades has been the 'feminisation' of workforces across much of the developing world (Fontana et al. 1998). At the start of the 1990s, one-fifth of Latin America's workforce was female. That figure has now risen to one-third (Mehra and Gammage 1999:536). Female employment creation has been especially strong in export industries. It is estimated that more than 90 per cent of the work force in export-processing zones (more than 20 million people) is made up of women (van Heerden 1999). China's phenomenal export growth has been driven increasingly by a workforce numerically dominated by women, with an estimated 24 million female assembly workers located in the special economic zones alone (Knox 1997). Female bias is especially strong in old labour-intensive industries such as garments, and dynamic growth sectors such as micro-electronics, which have hired young, literate, usually single women in large numbers. Employment has generated income and opportunity, along with practices which increase the insecurity of workers (see Chapter 3).

In the industrialised world too, labour markets are changing. The shift brought about by globalisation has resulted in more job insecurity, often allied to diminished social insurance. Unskilled workers are increasingly disadvantaged. The reasons are complex: increased trade, technological change, and political choice all interact. But there is a widespread, though largely mistaken, view that employment gains in developing countries are being won at the expense of industrialised countries (see Chapter 3).

For all the revolutionary changes associated with integration, we should bear in mind that globalisation has its limits. While capital markets may have become globalised, nothing remotely comparable has happened in labour markets. The number of people living outside the country of their birth is rising relatively slowly, at around two per cent a year. However, globalisation is creating new demands for labour mobility. There are now an estimated 20 million legal immigrants in the European Union, and three million illegal aliens. One recent study suggests that there are seven million Mexican-born immigrants in the USA, of whom only five million have legal status (Oxford Analytica 2000).

In contrast to the last wave of globalisation at the end of the nineteenth century, the movement of labour is strictly controlled – at least for the poor. Skilled workers already operate in a largely borderless world. More than one-third of the work force in the US Silicon Valley originates from the Indian sub-continent (*Financial Times* 2000). In the case of Africa, surveys have shown that one-third of the population who have completed a tertiary education live outside their country of birth. Despite remittances, which amounted to $52bn in 1998, the costs implied by the 'brain drain' in a knowledge-based global economy are very large. India alone loses the equivalent of $700m in revenue (Desai 2001).

Unlike their skilled counterparts, unskilled workers are subjected to stringent controls. Flows of human capital are today determined more by rich-country immigration policies than by differences in economic opportunity. Coupled with the grinding poverty and instability experienced by large sections of the world's population, these controls are stimulating a fast-growing area of trade: namely illegal trafficking of people. The return to an unskilled Mexican successfully entering the job market in the USA is a nine-fold salary increase. Such rewards encourage high levels of risk taking, sometimes with fatal consequences. Estimates suggest that more than $9bn is spent annually by people seeking to circumvent immigration controls (Bloom and Murshed 2001).

International trade is widely assumed to promote peace by linking the economic destinies of countries. That is one possible outcome: it was an objective that guided the founders of the European Union. However, the effects of globalisation are not always benign. In situations of State failure, international trade can generate destructive forces. The same technologies and transport infrastructures that facilitate legitimate economic transfers can be used to launder money and trade in arms. Illegal drugs-trafficking is an industry that generates some $500bn per annum, helping to sustain a civil war in Colombia (Bloom and Murshed 2001). More generally, trade in primary commodities can perpetuate cycles of conflict and poverty, as in West Africa and Angola. As in the case of capital markets, the world has yet to develop institutions and systems of co-operation capable of responding to the problems created by globalisation (see Chapter 7).

CHAPTER 2
Trade as a force for poverty reduction

International trade is often viewed as a threat to the poor. The opportunities that it creates for poverty reduction and human development are frequently overlooked. These opportunities are not an automatic corollary of increased trade; but, where good policies enable poor countries and poor people to participate in markets on equitable terms, trade can act as a powerful force for change. This chapter considers the potential inherent in trade as a force for poverty reduction.

The first part looks at the old adage that 'trade is more important than aid' in a new light. It shows that the potential benefits of trade massively outweigh those associated with aid, even though development assistance has an important role to play. The second part considers the role of trade in reducing poverty in developing countries, highlighting the experience of East Asia. The third section briefly examines some of the broader arguments in favour of trade.

Trade and aid

Northern governments often defend reductions in their overseas aid budgets with the claim that 'trade matters more than aid' (Stiglitz 2001: 8). That claim is accurate, but misleading. Aid can play a vital role in enabling poor countries and poor people to participate in trade on more favourable terms, for instance by improving transport infrastructure, or by raising standards of health and education. Reducing aid is not a good strategy for promoting developing-country trade interests. Yet, lamentable as the record of Northern governments may be, they are right about the relative importance of trade and aid.

The financial transfers from development assistance are dwarfed by the potential benefits that would result if developing countries increased their share of world exports. As a group, developing countries generate more than 30 times as much revenue per capita through exports ($322) as they receive in aid ($10). Low-income countries generate 12 times as much from exports ($113 per capita) as from aid ($9). These figures demonstrate a simple truth: even modest increases in developing countries' share of the world export market will massively outweigh any conceivable increase in aid. If they

Figure 2.1
Trade and aid: the impact on per capita income of a 1 per cent increase in world export market shares for selected regions

Source: Derived from World Bank 2001c

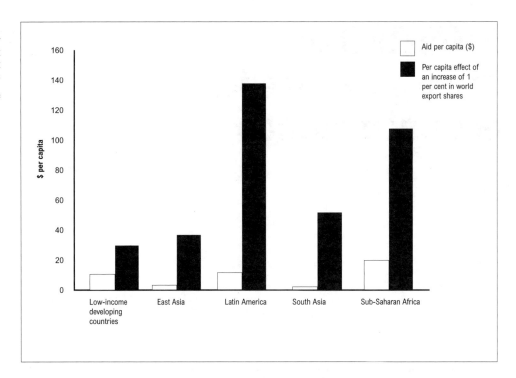

increased their share of world exports by five per cent, this would generate more than $350bn – seven times as much as they receive in aid. Such figures graphically illustrate the losses associated with policies that deprive developing countries of world-market shares. As Chapter 4 will demonstrate, the trade policies of rich countries are a major part of the problem.

Even modest increases in the share of world exports captured by developing countries would have the potential to generate large increases in income. Figure 2.1 compares aid levels with the foreign-exchange gains from a one per cent increase in exports. Expressed in income terms, those gains would be equivalent to the following:

- an increase of $30 per capita in low-income countries, representing an increase of seven per cent;

- an increase of one-fifth in average income for sub-Saharan Africa;

- an increase of $53 per capita, or 12 per cent, for South Asia;

- an increase of around four per cent of per capita income for Latin America and East Asia.

Once again, comparisons with aid transfers are telling. For low-income countries as a group, the one per cent increase in world export market share would generate almost four times as much income per capita as existing aid transfers. For sub-Saharan Africa, that figure would rise to five times more than per capita aid, and for South Asia to ten times more.

There are other reasons why trade is more important than aid as a force for poverty reduction. Broad-based economic growth provides an outlet for the productive potential of poor people, enabling them to produce their way out of poverty. Unlike aid, it directly generates income, employment, and investment resources for the household. Contrary to some widespread myths, trade can also help poor countries to achieve a greater level of self-reliance. By generating the foreign exchange needed to sustain imports, it can reduce dependence on aid, and with it exposure to the whims and fads of donors who govern access to aid budgets.

Implications for poverty

What impact would an increased share in world export markets have on poverty levels in developing countries? There is no simple answer to this question. The gains to be derived from exports are dynamic, and cannot readily be captured in static snapshots. In East Asia, large increases in export demand increased incentives for investment, generated employment, raised the overall rate of economic growth, and generated the savings on which future investment depended. As countries converted increased investment into rising productivity and more knowledge-intensive production, they were able to penetrate markets with higher-value-added goods, which in turn reinforced the links between export growth and rising living standards. The benefits were dynamic and cumulative, resulting from a mixture of efficiency gains and participation in an expanding market.

Notwithstanding the dynamic nature of advantages associated with international trade, static measurements can provide some insight into the potential order of magnitude of the income change that would be associated with an increased share of world exports. Converting the levels of per capita income growth presented in Figure 2.2 into poverty-reduction estimates is a hazardous exercise. Even so, it is an exercise that offers some important insights.

Changes in income poverty can be analysed in terms of the effects of changes in total GDP and changes in income distribution. Overall growth will determine the rate at which average incomes increase, while the proportion of any increment to growth accruing to the poor will determine the rate at which growth is converted into poverty reduction (we return to this issue in Chapter 5). It follows from this that the nature of the growth associated with increased exports has an important bearing on poverty outcomes. In countries with high concentrations of rural poverty, broad-based agricultural growth will have stronger effects on poverty. Similarly, labour-intensive manufactured exports that generate income and employment for the poor will have more impact on poverty than capital-intensive exports. More generally, the bigger the share of growth generated and captured by the poor, the bigger the impact on poverty.

Cross-country studies have found large variations in the rate at which income growth translates into poverty reduction. They have also generated divergent conclusions about the average relationship.[1] We have used one of the most conservative estimates of the ratio of per capita income growth to poverty reduction in order to quantify the potential impact on poverty levels of the average income gain that would accrue if each developing region captured 1 per cent more of world exports. This estimate suggests a ratio of income growth to poverty reduction of 1:0.9 in situations of low-income inequality, with the ratio falling to 1:0.3 in situations of high-income equality (Hanmer, Healey, and Naschold 2000).[2]

Converting the per capita income gain from a redistribution of world export shares in favour of developing countries produces some striking results (Figures 2.2a and 2.2b).[3] Under a low-level inequality scenario, an aggregate redistribution of 4 per cent (i.e. 1 per cent for each region) would reduce the number of people in poverty by 128 million. This is equivalent to around 12 per cent of the world total. The decline would be largest in sub-Saharan Africa, where 60 million people would be brought above the poverty line – a reduction of just over one-fifth. In South Asia, poverty would fall by around 56 million. Although the effects are far smaller in East Asia and Latin America, numbers in poverty would fall by over 9 million and around 3 million

Figures 2.2a and 2.2b
Effect on the incidence of poverty (2.2a) and headcount poverty (2.2b) of a 1 per cent increase in world export market share under high-inequality and low-inequality scenarios: major developing regions (2000)

Figure 2.2a

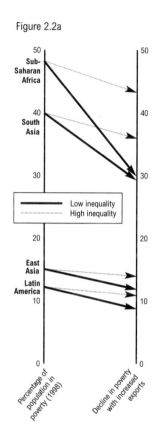

Figure 2.2b

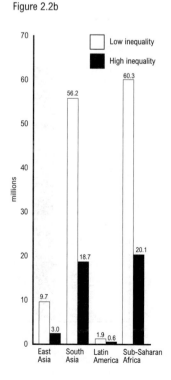

Figure 2.3
Africa's share of world trade,
1979 – 1999

Source: IMF

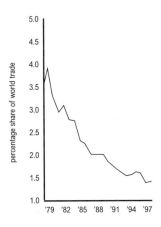

Figure 2.4
Sub-Saharan Africa: aid and debt
relief versus foreign-exchange
gains from a 1 per cent increase in
world market shares ($bn)

Source: World Bank 2001c, 2001a

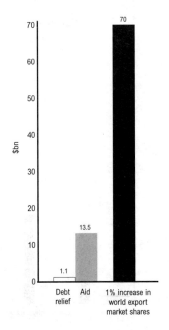

respectively. Higher levels of inequality would significantly reduce these effects, with poverty declining by only 43 million under an unequal income-distribution scenario.

The costs of marginalisation

Sub-Saharan Africa demonstrates the huge losses associated with a reduction in world-market share. Over the past two decades, the region has suffered a dramatic decline in its share of world exports (see Figure 2.3). It currently accounts for only 1.3 per cent of exports of goods and services – one-third of the level at the start of the 1980s (Subramanian 2001). The factors behind that decline are the subject of contentious debate. What is not in doubt is the enormous decline in living standards, and the associated increase in poverty, that it has produced. If sub-Saharan Africa had the same share of world exports today as it had in 1980, the foreign-exchange equivalent would be in the order of $278bn. Expressed in per capita terms, the income gain would be $432, which would almost double the current average income.

Northern governments congratulate themselves on what they perceive as their high levels of generosity in providing sub-Saharan Africa with aid and debt relief, but the extent of that generosity is open to question. Between 1994 and 1999, rich countries reduced their aid transfers from $34 to $20 per capita (World Bank 2001c). Moreover, many of the countries currently receiving debt relief under the Heavily Indebted Poor Countries (HIPC) Initiative are still spending more on debt servicing than on health and education services. The record looks even less impressive when assessed against what could be achieved through an improved trade performance. If Africa increased its share of world exports by just one per cent, it would generate $70bn – a sum that dwarfs the $14.6bn provided through debt relief and aid combined (see Figure 2.4). Even if rich countries' aid and debt-relief policies matched their rhetoric, sub-Saharan Africa would benefit far more from an enhanced trade performance than from development assistance.

It should be emphasised that a one per cent increase in world export market share is an exceptionally modest aspiration, in view of the discrepancy between the distribution of world population on the one side, and the distribution of export activity on the other. Low-income countries account for 40 per cent of the world's population, but only three per cent of exports. Sub-Saharan Africa, which accounts for ten per cent of the world's population, generates only one per cent of world exports. As such figures demonstrate, very small steps towards distributional equity in the global trading system could generate very large benefits for the world's poorest regions.

There is certainly more than enough room for distributional equity. At present, exports from rich countries amount to almost $6000 per person. The equivalent figure for developing countries is $330, and for low-income countries it is less than $100 (see Figure 2.5). If South Asia enjoyed the same share of world exports as Canada, the foreign-exchange gain would translate into an increase in income of $132, or just under one-third of average income. An enlarged share of world markets could also generate important benefits for middle-income countries. Were Latin America to capture a share of world trade commensurate with its share of world population, the equivalent gain would be $460 per capita, or more than ten per cent of average income.

Trade as an engine for poverty reduction

Increased trade does not automatically translate into poverty reduction. However, when trade is harnessed to effective economic policies and positive poverty-reduction strategies, it can act as a powerful force for change.

Evidence from East Asia

Over the past 40 years, the countries of East Asia have registered some of the most rapid rates of poverty reduction ever recorded. Whether measured by numbers below the poverty line, life expectancy, education, nutrition, or other human-development indicators, welfare has improved dramatically. To attribute these achievements to 'export-led growth' would require a rewriting of history, but to deny the role of exports in supporting national poverty reduction would do the same.

The facts of East Asia's achievements speak for themselves. In the mid-1970s, six out of every ten people in the region lived in extreme poverty. Today, fewer than two in ten are in this position. The number of people living on less than $1 a day has fallen from 720 million in the mid-1970s to 278 million (Ahuja et al. 1997, World Bank 2001c). Rapid and broad-based income growth has driven the decline in income poverty. Average incomes across much of the region grew at more than five per cent a year in per capita terms during the 1980s and 1990s. By virtue of compound interest, this translates into a doubling of average per capita income every 14 years. Between 1978 and 1997, average incomes in China doubled. To put this achievement in context, it took Britain half a century to double average incomes after the first industrial revolution (Levine 1997). In China, the rise in living standards lifted more than 200 million people out of poverty and reduced child-mortality rates by half (World Bank 1997).

Some economists claim that rapid integration into the world economy through trade and import liberalisation has been the main impetus for rapid growth and poverty reduction; but they are wrong. Most economies in East Asia did not start to liberalise imports until export growth was already well established (Rodrik 2001a). In China, domestic marketing reforms generated the initial wave of economic growth, which exports then helped to accelerate. Earlier, Taiwan and Korea developed behind protective import barriers, once again generating a dynamic export sector before liberalising imports (Wade 1990: Ch 4). 'Free trade' was not a major feature of East Asia's success, but exports did play a critical role in sustaining economic growth and poverty reduction.

Exports have consistently grown faster than GDP in East Asia – more than twice as fast in Korea, Taiwan, and China. In the case of China, exports have been increasing at more than 13 per cent a year, and now account for just under 25 per cent of GDP. They account for more than half of GDP in Korea, Indonesia, Malaysia, and Thailand. For the region as a whole, the export/GDP ratio has increased from around 25 to 39 per cent, higher than for any other developing region.

How did export growth contribute to poverty reduction in East Asia? National experiences varied, but there were several common influences. Exports created demand for goods produced in labour-intensive manufacturing industries, which in turn created demand for labour and increased real wages. Production for export markets also generated the foreign exchange needed to import the inputs and technologies necessary to sustain economic growth. China started to create incentives for exports in the 1980s, in order to finance imports of fertiliser and machinery, which were seen as vital to the success of domestic reforms. Imports also helped to increase the efficiency of production, enabling local firms to enter global markets on a competitive basis. Finally, because export growth was linked to major investments in education, it was possible to sustain improvements in productivity and other welfare indicators.

However, export growth has generated its own problems. Inequalities are growing across the region – in some cases, as in China, dramatically so. This poses a threat to future efforts to reduce poverty. While living standards have increased, labour conditions remain highly exploitative, especially for the growing number of female workers who have been drawn into export sectors. Serious environmental problems have emerged, posing a threat to public health. Yet these outcomes are a consequence of domestic policy failures, not an inevitable consequence of trade. The case of East Asia demonstrates that it is possible to reap enormous benefits from progressive integration into the world economy, provided that the process of integration is well managed. By the same token, there are other developing regions – notably sub-Saharan Africa – which demonstrate the simple truth that it is perfectly possible to combine weak performance on exports with social, economic, and environmental disaster.

Broad-based export growth

Exports can improve the income and welfare of poor communities by contributing to overall economic growth. However, the pattern of growth also matters. Exports are most effective in reducing poverty when they create demand in markets in which poor people have an important stake, such as labour-intensive manufacturing and agriculture. The degree to which poor people benefit will depend partly on factors such as access to infrastructure, education, and health care, as well as on the structural forces, including gender relations, that shape the distribution of opportunity and reward in the market place.

Smallholder agriculture
Agricultural exports produced by smallholder farmers in countries with relatively low concentrations of land ownership can generate important benefits for rural poverty reduction (Datt and Ravaillon 1998). Given that rural poverty accounts for more than

Figure 2.5
Per capita export values: selected regions 1999 ($)

Source: World Bank 2001c

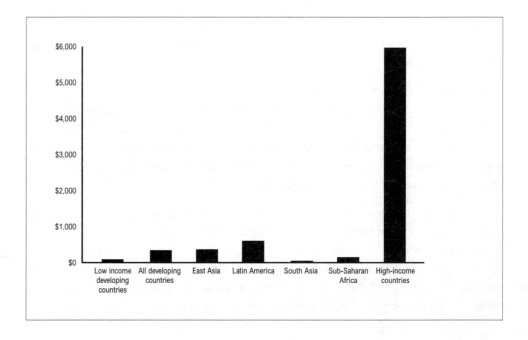

two-thirds of poverty world-wide, and that women play a major role in agriculture, this has important implications.

Vietnam demonstrates what is possible when exports support broadly pro-poor domestic reforms. Following the introduction of the economic renovation programme – or *Doi Moi* – in 1986, farmers were allowed to increase sales to the market, and agricultural taxes were cut. Productivity grew rapidly as farmers took advantage of new market opportunities and increased their use of fertilisers. During the 1990s agricultural output was growing at almost five per cent per year, far outstripping demand in local markets (Government of Vietnam 2001). Export markets provided an important source of demand for sustaining growth. During the past 15 years, Vietnam has made the transition from being a small importer of rice to being the world's second largest exporter. At the end of the 1990s, these exports generated more than $1bn in foreign-exchange earnings.

Export growth helped to underpin other reforms that contribute to advances in human development. Rice is the mainstay of the Vietnamese economy, accounting for just under half of household revenue from agriculture. Widespread participation in the rice economy meant that export growth not only increased the income of producers, but also created demand for rural labour. The proportion of households living below the national poverty line fell from nearly one-third in the 1990s to one-tenth in 2000, a decline of 300,000 people per annum. Educational and nutritional standards have improved. Once again, the advances have been unevenly distributed, and many of the poorest producers lack access to the marketing infrastructure and productive resources needed to take advantage of export opportunities. The volatility of world prices has also caused serious problems for households. Yet the link between export growth and poverty reduction is undeniable.

Few markets are more hostile to developing countries than the market for primary commodities such as coffee and cocoa, as Chapter 6 will argue. Even here, however, export opportunities have contributed to poverty reduction. This is illustrated by the testimony of Alice Lukoba, interviewed in Uganda for this report. She is a 34-year-old widow farming four acres of land near the town of Luwero, located about 40 miles to the north of the capital of Kampala. Her husband was killed during the country's civil war. At the end of that war, the entire district – once a major coffee-producing centre – resembled an economic wasteland. In 1987 nearly two-thirds of farmers were living below the poverty line. Luwero was a symbol of the devastation that can be wrought by the twin blights of civil war and gross economic mismanagement.

Today, it is a symbol of something better. In 1987, government taxation and exchange-rate over-valuation meant that farmers in Luwero received 10 cents for every $1 of coffee that they produced for export. Many, including Alice Lukoba, stopped producing and retreated into subsistence agriculture. That changed at the end of the 1980s, when the government of Uganda removed taxes on coffee exports, introduced market-based exchange rates, and liberalised imports of agricultural inputs such as fertiliser. Since then, coffee production has surged, and fertiliser use has increased by a factor of three. Despite low world prices, farm incomes have improved dramatically. Between 1992 and 1997, poverty levels in Luwero fell from 45 per cent to 27 per cent (Government of Uganda 2001).

Higher incomes have enabled farmers in Luwero to diversify production. They have used the income from coffee to buy goats, cows, pigs, and hens, and to develop new lines of production. On Alice Lukoba's farm, coffee is still inter-cropped with bananas, the main household staple. But she also produces tomatoes, onions, and carrots for markets in Kampala, as well as chillis and baby aubergines that are sold to a company for export to Europe. The collapse of international coffee prices that began at the end of the 1990s is a major threat. Even so, Alice Lukoba is in no doubt about the benefits from trade: *'Life is always hard for us farmers, especially now that our coffee prices are so bad. But no farmer here will tell you that life is harder today than it was before. We were given an opportunity to get something out of our coffee – and we took it.'*

The importance of coffee, and international trade, to the livelihoods of poor farmers in Luwero was underlined by Oxfam research in two villages during 1998 (Child Health Development Centre/Oxfam 1999). Forty-two households were interviewed. On average, coffee generated approximately $180 a year in household income, just over half the proceeds from the sales of crops. It was the single biggest source of household income for most farmers, and was used to purchase cooking oil, vegetables, and beans, and to pay for health care and education. Even with low prices, most households were certain that it made sense to grow coffee and buy groundnuts and maize in local markets to supplement household production.

What has happened in Luwero is a microcosm of developments across Uganda. There are around five million smallholder farmers growing coffee in Uganda. Like Alice Lukoba, most saw their incomes rise sharply in the 1990s, and many households were lifted out of poverty. In the first half of the 1990s, the rate of rural poverty fell from two-thirds of the population to less than half: four million people were raised above the poverty line (Government of Uganda: 2001). Education and health indicators are also improving, creating a virtuous, if incomplete, circle of human development.

It is sometimes argued that agricultural exports are inherently bad for the poor, since they divert resources from domestic food production. That outcome is possible, especially if small farmers are displaced to make way for large commercial farms. However, in countries such as Vietnam and Uganda, export growth has been accompanied by improved nutrition. In Uganda, coffee is typically part of a broader inter-cropping system, with farmers growing maize, beans, and bananas alongside coffee bushes. Increased income from coffee can generate the income needed to increase food production. Simple dichotomies between food crops and cash crops are irrelevant in this context. The idea that cash-crop production leads to the cultivation of less food or lower levels of nutrition is wrong, although such outcomes are possible (for instance, if smallholders are displaced). Poverty levels among households producing food staples in Uganda have been falling at one-tenth of the rate among coffee producers (Appleton et al. 1999a).

It does not follow from this that all agricultural export production is good for poverty reduction. Large-scale, capital-intensive farming systems, generating large volumes of output but limited employment, do not convert export growth into pro-poor development. Brazil is one of the world's largest agricultural exporters. The country's soya exports are one of the main sources of animal feed for European livestock. However, export success has not been matched by commensurate advances in rural poverty reduction. The reason: the rural poor lack access to the land and marketing infra-structure that they need in order to participate in markets. Highly concentrated systems of land ownership, limited access for poor people to marketing infrastructure, and gender inequalities at the household level all weaken the link between trade and poverty reduction. The appropriate response is to overcome these barriers through more effective policies.

Unequal trading relationships and problems on world markets can limit the potential of trade to reduce poverty. Apart from their vulnerability to unstable and declining world market prices, many primary-commodity producers receive only a tiny fraction of the final value of what they grow. International trade generates large corporate profits and leaves farmers with poverty-level wages. The Fair Trade Movement is working to change this picture by developing co-operative markets which link producers and consumers.

One example is to be found in Ghana. The Kuapa Kokoo co-operative has 30,000 members, spread across the country's cocoa belt. About one-tenth of Kuapa's output is sold to fair-trade organisations in Europe, such as Twin Trading, which pays almost double the prevailing world market prices (reflecting the high quality of the cocoa) and a 'social premium' of ten per cent of the purchase price (Ransom 2001: 64). The premium helps to fund boreholes, health centres, and schools, making real improvements to the quality of people's lives. What Twin Trading and Kuapa Kokoo are trying to do in a very direct way is make trade work for poor people in one of the most hostile international trade environments. Twin Trading can pay the premium because it has persuaded consumers to meet the costs, partly on the basis of the quality of the product, but also by giving them an opportunity to use their purchasing power to benefit the poor. The arrangement humanises trade. Extending the principles of fair trade beyond the current commodity enclaves to cover all trade would generate real benefits to poor producers.

Labour-intensive manufacturing

Exports of labour-intensive manufactured goods were one of the most powerful forces driving poverty reduction in East Asia. Industries such as textiles and clothing, footwear, and electronics not only generate high levels of demand for labour: they also provide a first step on the ladder towards increased productivity and areas of production with higher value-added features, creating the opportunity for increases in real wages.

East Asia is not the only part of the developing world that has seen export growth for manufactured goods improve human development. In the early 1960s, a Nobel prize-winning economist predicted a future of mass unemployment and poverty for the island of Mauritius. In the event, real per capita incomes there have grown by three per cent a year over the past three decades, compared with less than one per cent in mainland Africa. Improvements in human welfare have been even more impressive. Life expectancy has increased by ten years, universal school enrolment has been achieved, and income inequalities have narrowed.

Increased trade has played a critical role. Despite its geographical disadvantages, in terms of distance from major markets, exports from Mauritius have been growing faster than overall economic growth. Because the main export industry was textiles and clothing, which is highly labour-intensive, unemployment levels of 14 per cent in the early 1980s had given way to full employment by the early 1990s (Subramanian 2001). As in East Asia, this success owed little to free-market philosophy: Mauritius was a highly protected economy throughout. But it powerfully demonstrates the potential advantages of trade.

During the 1990s, export growth was an engine of employment-creation in a large group of countries. In Bangladesh, an estimated 1.7 million people have been drawn into export-processing zones producing garments (Bhattacharya and Rahman 1999). Most of the workforce consists of young women, many of whom have migrated from desperately poor rural areas. The wages earned by these women are exceptionally low by international standards, and barely above the national poverty line. Yet their daily wage rates are around twice as high as those paid for agricultural labourers, and higher than could be earned on construction sites. Employment conditions in the export zones are scandalously poor, with women denied even the most basic rights. Yet for most women working in the garments sector, their employment offers a higher quality of life than might otherwise be possible.

One of Oxfam's partners in Bangladesh, Karmojibi Nairi, is working with women to improve labour standards. This organisation supports complaints over unfair dismissals and violations of social-insurance claims, and runs courses which provide legal advice on employment rights. But Karmojibi Nairi, like other organisations representing workers in Bangladesh, categorically rejects the argument for withdrawal from export markets. Along with other Oxfam partners, it is campaigning to protect and enhance access to markets in industrialised countries, not least because this is seen as a requirement for improving wages and employment conditions. One of the women working in the industry, Rahana Chaudhury, a 23-year-old mother of three children, explained why the real challenge is to make exports work for poverty reduction:

> 'This job is hard – and we are not treated fairly. The managers do not respect us women. But life is much harder for those working outside. Back in my village, I would have less money. Outside of the factories, people selling things in the street or carrying bricks on building sites earn less than we do. There are few other options. Of course I want better conditions. But for me this job means that my children will have enough to eat, and that their lives can improve.'

As ever in debates on trade, assessments of labour-intensive export growth are influenced by polarised starting points. 'Globaphobes' see only exploitation and poverty-level wages, ignoring the real choices facing real people working in export industries. 'Globaphiles' see only employment and efficiency gains, while ignoring abuses of workers' rights that should not be tolerated in any society. For millions of women, the consequences of employment in export industries have been mixed. There have been gains in one area (income), but losses in others, in the form of increased vulnerability, unfair labour practices, and heavier workloads. The real challenge is to use policies to shift the balance of costs and benefits in favour of the latter.

Local trade in action

Most trade does not even cross national borders. It takes place within and between villages, and across different parts of the same country.

In the Indian State of Rajasthan, Oxfam works with an organisation called the Urmul Trust. Created in 1991 by a group of weavers from the low-caste Dalit community, the Trust now works with weavers in 170 villages. It buys yarns from Delhi and wool from Kashmir and Rajasthan, which are supplied to a network of weavers, all of them from low-caste backgrounds. The weavers are trained in the local 'Pattu' tradition, which involves stitching strips of cloth together. Local markets for Pattu are very restricted, but the cloth has become very popular with Delhi's middle classes. Through another non-government organisation, called Dastkar, which has developed strong marketing and design skills, the weavers involved in the Urmul Trust have been linked to urban consumer markets in Delhi. The weavers receive around one-quarter of the sale price of their products.

One of the weavers is Bhauri Devi, a 25-year-old widow in a remote rural village in the Rajasthan desert, some five hours' journey from the State capital of Jaipur. She has a small farm on which she grows millet and other small grains, and grazes four goats and two sheep. The food grown by the household lasts around four months, and in the past she used to depend for the rest of the year on work as a rural labourer. The work involved cutting grass on the farms of high-caste communities, earning 40–50 rupees per day. Since training as a weaver, Bhauri produces cushion covers and shawls for Urmul Trust, for which she earns around Rs 80 a day. She is in no doubt about the benefits:

> 'I like this work. It means that I have to spend less time working on the farms of other people – and I have more time to work on our farm. Before, I had to walk for many hours to cut grass. What I do with the money from weaving is invest it in seeds and spend it on the children's education. Before the harvest, when our food stocks are low, I can do more weaving and earn enough to buy food for us. This work has made my life better.'

The work depends on a system of exchange which links extremely poor women, living in a harsh, drought-prone environment, to consumers in Delhi and suppliers of yarn cloth and dyes in Rajasthan and elsewhere. This is trade in action. Local producers have been able to go beyond the confines of the local market and to penetrate markets with more purchasing power in Delhi. In principle, international markets offer another step up the ladder.

Some Indian firms are trying to take that step by developing new markets in industrialised countries. One of the most innovative is Fab India, a company which specialises in producing and marketing handloom products manufactured across the country. Since 1993, turnover has increased from $3m to $10m. Through various networks the company now employs around 8000 craft producers. It provides co-operatives with leather from Rajasthan, textiles from Tamil Nadu and Andhra Pradesh, and jute from Kerala. These inputs are made into goods which have the quality and appeal to sell well in intensely competitive markets. Around 80 per cent of sales take place in India, mainly in Delhi and Bombay, and the rest of the products are exported. Fab India is now seeking to expand its Northern markets by opening stores in the USA, Italy, and Rome.

International markets are often complex – and international trade may differ from local trade because of the length of the marketing chain and the concentration of marketing power. One of the problems faced by Fab India is competition from large Northern retail chains, which have obvious advantages of scale, including the ability to buy in bulk and sell at ruinously low prices. But the principle of linking poor producers to larger markets than are available locally can help to reduce poverty.

The case for trade: beyond comparative advantage

Few ideas enjoy wider currency or greater status in economic thinking than that of comparative advantage. It was first advanced in 1817 by David Ricardo (Ricardo 1971); and whether or not the protagonists are aware of it, many of today's fervent controversies about globalisation are debates with the ghost of this nineteenth-century English economist.

Comparative advantage is a deceptively complicated theory, with a deceptively simple conclusion. Briefly, it holds that trade makes it possible for people to consume more goods than they would be able to without such exchange. Using a simple numerical example, Ricardo demonstrated that it was in the interests of two countries to trade, even if one country had an absolute advantage in that it could produce all goods more cheaply than the other. He showed that by concentrating on areas where they had a comparative advantage (broadly, the area in which they were most efficient), two countries could arrive at a higher level of wealth by exchanging two goods than if they each produced both goods. The conclusion of the analysis: free trade would make it possible for households to consume more goods, regardless of whether their trading partners were more or less advanced. Writing at a time when trade was widely viewed as a zero-sum game, in which a gain for one player would mean a corresponding loss for the other, this was an idea with revolutionary implications.

Current debates about comparative advantage generate great controversy. Applied crudely, as it usually is by free-market economists, the theory is of little value. What Ricardo provided was a static model, offering insights into what it might be sensible to produce in a group of countries with any particular mix of skills and resources. But skills and resources are not fixed in time. If they were, the USA would never have moved beyond its comparative advantage in land availability, and would have remained an agricultural economy (see Box 2.1). Similarly, countries like South Korea and Taiwan would never have emerged as major industrial powers unless they had changed their comparative advantage. Thirty-five years ago, they were protecting themselves from imports of US steel in order to build up a domestic industry. Today, it is the USA that seeks protection from East Asian exporters. The reason: government policies have produced changes in comparative advantage.

Through the theory of comparative advantage, Ricardo sought to establish the case for removing all barriers to trade. His immediate target was the removal of the Corn Laws, which were used in the early part of the nineteenth century to restrict imports of grains, artificially inflating the profits of landowners and the prices of food in the process. Reformers justifiably saw the Corn Laws as symptoms of a system which placed the private interests of a politically powerful group above the public good. Many latter-day reformers in the IMF and the World Bank view all trade barriers in a similar light. It is regarded as axiomatic that any restriction on trade is an attempt to promote private interests at the expense of the public.

Such thinking is fundamentally flawed. Import protection can play a role as part of a wider development strategy in developing national capacity, as governments in East Asia have demonstrated. While trade restrictions inevitably impose short-term costs (for example, by raising the costs of imports for consumers), these costs might be outweighed by longer-term benefits. There may be sound reasons of equity and efficiency for trade restrictions (Rodrik 1999). What matters in this context is the distribution of benefits from protection. Trade barriers designed to protect a small but politically powerful group of producers, such as Brazilian landowners, or farmers in the Paris Basin, have different consequences from barriers designed to protect smallholder producers, for example. In addition, any move towards liberalisation raises questions about the pace and sequencing of reforms. Standard trade theories offer few insights in any of these areas.

Another problem with the idea of comparative advantage is that international market conditions have changed since Ricardo assumed that capital did not move between

Box 2.1

The curious history of free trade

When the Scottish economist Adam Smith wrote *The Wealth of Nations* in 1776, he attributed America's rising prosperity to specialisation in agriculture: 'The principal cause of the rapid progress of our American colonies /is/ that almost their whole capitals have hitherto been employed in agriculture. They have no manufactures.' His policy advice: don't change a good thing. He advised Americans to stay on the prairies and to open their border to British manufactured goods.

Post-independence American governments saw things differently. They understood that today's comparative advantage may be tomorrow's liability. After gaining independence in the year that The Wealth of Nations was published, the former colonists set out to develop an industrial base. The first Secretary of the Treasury, Alexander Hamilton, set out an early version of the theory of import substitution. His Report on Manufactures in 1791 rejected Smith's advice and argued that manufacturing enterprises could flourish and compete, but only with import protection and 'the incitement and patronage of government'.

At the height of British enthusiasm for free trade, Abraham Lincoln remained an unashamed protectionist. On matters of trade, he would not have been a strong candidate for a job in the IMF or World Bank. In a pithy response to the arguments of British economists who were calling for the removal of American tariffs, he commented: 'I don't know much about the tariff, but I do know if I buy a coat in America, I have a coat, and America has the money.'

Such sentiments were not restricted to the New World. The first fully developed theory of infant-industry protection was developed by a German economist in the 1880s. Friedrich List did not reject the idea of comparative advantage, or deny the short-term costs of protectionism. But he argued that these costs would be massively outweighed by the longer-term costs of failure to develop manufacturing industries. In his eyes, the free-trade arguments deployed by British economists were little more than a self-interested exercise aimed at protecting their country's commercial advantage. 'England', he wrote, 'never received at the hands of nature a perpetual right to a monopoly of manufacture … In order to allow freedom of trade to operate naturally, the less advanced nations must first be raised to that stage /to which/ the English nation has been artificially elevated.'

Even classical free-trade theorists recognised that there might be sound economic grounds for temporary protection. For example, the nineteenth-century English philosopher and economist, John Stuart Mill, accepted that comparative advantage was acquired, rather than a consequence of nature. 'The superiority of one country over another in a branch of production often arises only from having begun it sooner', he wrote. Under such conditions, 'a protecting duty, continued for a reasonable time' was in his view a reasonable strategy for gaining the skill and experience needed to establish new industries.

Even Adam Smith, for all his belief in the power of the market, was less radically inclined than some contemporary IMF and World Bank staff members in his approach to trade liberalisation. He urged extreme caution where manufacturing industries employing 'a great multitude of hands' were involved. He wrote: 'Humanity may in this case require that freedom of trade should be restored only by slow gradation, and with a good deal of reserve and circumspection.'

(Sources: Landes 1998, Irwin 1996, Mill 1909, Muller 1993)

countries, that trade would take place between competing companies, and that markets were competitive. All these assumptions can be challenged. In today's economy, capital is global; a growing share of trade takes place within firms; and concentrations of market power at national and international levels create restrictive barriers.

Market failures and the environment

More serious still are the inherent limitations of the price mechanism. Market prices may fail to reflect the effects of environment-damaging activities, thereby sending misleading signals about the appropriate use of environmental resources. Producers may not have to pay for the damage that they cause the environment, leaving society – and future generations – to suffer the consequences. Markets are also unlikely to reflect the scarcity value of natural resources. These are all conditions under which international trade can promote environmental destruction, with damaging consequences for the future.

The failure of market prices to value environmental resources is not a theoretical problem. It poses a direct risk to the livelihoods of many millions of people, and it is central to debates on international trade (Boyer 2001). When commercial farmers in Bangladesh export prawns, their poorer neighbours pay the costs associated with the salination of water and consequent crop losses (see Chapter 3). In the Philippines, Oxfam works with fishing communities on a coastal-resources management programme. Their livelihoods are directly threatened by over-fishing in coastal waters by Japanese fleets. The price paid by Japanese consumers for their catch does not reflect the hardship and losses inflicted on the livelihoods of artisanal fishing people in the Philippines. The Philippines is not an isolated case. It has been estimated that around half of the world's fishing grounds are being exploited at their biological limits (UNEP 2000). International trade has also contributed to deforestation in many countries, although other factors – such as the clearing of land for agriculture – are also important (Barraclough and Ghimire 2000). Forests in tropical regions are disappearing at a rate of about 0.7 per cent a year, according to the Food and Agriculture Organization. As in the case of fisheries, the prices that consumers in rich countries pay for their hardwood floors and mahogany toilet-seats do not reflect the real costs. These include the loss of forest products, increased risk of flooding and soil erosion, loss of biodiversity, and increases in greenhouse-gas emissions.

A rapid increase in air and sea traffic has accompanied globalisation. Environmental damage inflicted by air travel is coming under increasing scrutiny. Airplanes currently account for just under four per cent of greenhouse-gas emissions, but scientists estimate that this share could rise four-fold over the next fifty years (Sheehan 2001). Because they are deposited directly in the upper atmosphere, heat-trapping greenhouse gases emitted from airplanes contribute far more to global warming than surface emissions do. Real costs are impossible to calculate in economic terms, but they are certainly not reflected in the prices paid by companies involved in the freighting of goods across borders. The same is true of global warming in general. In the last 50 years, emissions of carbon dioxide have quadrupled, and greenhouse-gas emissions are projected to rise by 50 per cent in the next 15 years (World Resources Institute 1999). Since the cost of global warming will be borne by future generations, and mostly in the developing world, they do not figure in today's national economic accounts, or – as demonstrated during the 2001 negotiations on the Kyoto Protocol – in the priorities of industrialised-country governments.

The environmental damage associated with trade has prompted some to call for a reduction in exports by developing countries, as part of a wider strategy to reduce trade flows. That approach is wrong on several counts. First, it is rich – not poor – countries that represent the real threat to the global environment. With one-fifth of the world's population, industrialised countries produce around one-half of carbon dioxide emissions, and use nearly two-thirds of the energy that fuels transportation. Second, many of the problems attributed to trade are in fact a consequence of production in general. The challenge is to make production, whether for international or domestic markets, more sustainable. Global warming can be addressed through alternative energy policies, or by taxes on carbon and air transport (Sagasti and Bezanson 2001). Similarly, unsustainable production for export purposes can be limited by taxes and prohibitions on unsustainable resource use. The deeper problem is that global economic integration is proceeding faster than the development of international co-operation to address cross-border environmental problems.

Some benefits of trade

For all its problems, the idea of specialisation, which is fundamental to the phenomenon of comparative advantage, has some obvious appeal. In our everyday lives, almost all of us exchange goods and services, entering into complex systems of exchange that bind us to dozens of producers across the world. Few people imagine that their lives would be better if they gave up using services and goods produced by others, in favour of a life of self-reliance. In the same fashion, closing off trade would deny countries the advantages of specialisation. Taken to an extreme, it would have condemned countries that lack iron ore back to the Stone Age.

One of the paradoxes in Ricardo's legacy is that many of the governments that espouse his idea violate the principles behind it. European consumers and Third World farmers would certainly be better off if the European Union's agricultural policies were guided less by vested interests and more by the principles of comparative advantage. Similarly, US consumers and millions of people in the developing world stand to benefit from more open North American markets, and from policies which are not designed to favour textile magnates of South Carolina, farmers' lobbies, and the steel industry.

The idea of specialisation and market integration that is embodied in the theory of comparative advantage provides some insights into the potential benefits of trade (McCulloch, Winters, and Cirera 2001: Ch 2), which include the following.

- **More rapid economic growth.** International trade is an important source of wealth generation. Exports grew at more than twice the rate of world GDP in the 1990s. As a result, participation in trade has become an increasingly important determinant of economic growth. Exports also support growth in other ways. For example, they generate the foreign exchange that countries need in order to import essential technologies. Lacking sufficient foreign exchange, many countries in Africa have been suffering 'import strangulation', with manufacturing industries operating below their full capacity because they lack imported spare parts, and farmers unable to obtain fertilisers and equipment.

- **Access to larger markets.** International trade gives producers and firms in developing countries access to larger markets with more developed purchasing power. Taiwan, Korea, and Singapore could never have sustained the growth of high value-added manufacturing exports in areas such as micro-electronics solely on the basis of domestic markets. In the space of ten years, India has become the world's second largest exporter of computer software, generating more than $3bn annually. Once again, this would not have been possible within the domestic economy. The potential gains from access to global markets are potentially much larger for countries with small populations and/or low levels of average income, given the limitations of their domestic markets.

- **Access to ideas and technology.** Imports can provide a source of new technologies needed to boost productivity and competitiveness (Feenstra et al. 1997). In East Asia, trade gave companies access to the machinery that helped develop competitive industries in areas such as machine tools. In India, by contrast, high tariffs and import licences restricted the ability of local firms to get access to new technologies, raising the costs of inputs to small and medium enterprises, and ultimately to consumers.

- **Access to cheaper goods.** Import barriers act as a tax on imports. They drive a wedge between world prices and domestic prices, increasing costs to consumers and returns to producers of the protected product. In some cases, import protection is justified as part of a longer-term strategy aimed at developing national capacity. In others, it directly hurts the poor and constrains efforts to reduce poverty. For example, almost one million people die each year in sub-Saharan Africa from malaria, the vast majority of them children. Yet some of the worst-affected countries, such as Zambia and Senegal, impose tariffs of 25 per cent or more on mosquito nets (Bannister and Thugge 2001: 7). These tariffs cost lives. In Vietnam, poor people need bicycles for taking their children to school, making essential purchases, and taking their goods to markets. Ownership of a bicycle can reduce the time allocated to these tasks, releasing labour for other areas of work; yet the government of Vietnam artificially raises the costs of bicycles through import barriers aimed at protecting jobs in the national industry. The choices are difficult, but in this case the costs to the poor far outweigh the gains. (Box 2.1). Improving the access of poor people to imported goods can indirectly help to reduce poverty. In East Asia, imported technologies helped to lay the foundations for rapid export growth. Smallholder farmers in Uganda have benefited from improved access to fertilisers. Grameen Telecom – a subsidiary of the Grameen Bank – leases imported cellular phones to members of women's credit societies, giving them better access to market information. The women report an increased capacity to negotiate with traders, resulting in lower prices for inputs and higher prices for outputs (Burr 2000).

As a guide to policy formulation in developing countries, the idea of comparative advantage has suffered from gross over-simplification. It has been applied in ways which have failed either to predict problems or to recognise the limits of free markets. Building on Ricardo's initial ideas, trade economists have adapted the idea of comparative advantage to argue that free trade is inherently good for developing countries. Reduced to its essentials, the standard theory asserts that countries trade with each other on the basis of their inherent specialisation, which for developing countries (in the eyes of trade theorists) means unskilled rural and urban labour. Through free trade, according to this argument, rich countries will increase demand for the goods produced by this labour, thus generating employment, raising income, and reducing poverty in the process.[4] This narrow reading of trade theory has been converted into policy practice in many developing countries, notably through the influence of the IMF and the World Bank. As Chapter 3 will argue, the outcomes have been very different from those predicted. Under globalisation, economic integration is increasing returns to assets – such as land, capital, and education – to which poor people have restricted access. It is also reinforcing inequalities based on gender and other forms of deprivation. As in other markets, people enter global markets with unequal levels of strength – and they leave them with unequal rewards.

Box 2.2

Priced out of reach:
bicycles and motorbikes in Vietnam

'If I had money, what I would do first is to buy a bicycle for my child to go more easily to school.'
– Woman living in Xop Thang village in Ky Son province in Vietnam, a mountainous region on the border with Laos.

Decisions taken by developing-country governments about the phasing and sequencing of trade liberalisation in their domestic markets can have substantial implications for poor people. In Vietnam, the government has significantly reduced tariffs on the majority of imported goods, with a small number of exceptions. Imported bicycles and motorbikes are two of these, facing tariffs as high as 50 and 60 per cent respectively. The tariffs protect domestic producers of bicycles and motorbikes, but increase the costs of these items to consumers.

Bicycles are an essential means of transport for millions of ordinary people throughout the country. In remote rural areas, owning a bicycle is not just convenient; it can make a crucial difference to people's lives, by providing transport to take goods to market and children to school. Yet the cost of buying a bicycle is prohibitive for many poor people. Even the cheapest available bicycle costs almost twice the average monthly income of people living in rural communities. Motorbikes are becoming more popular in rural areas and are the aspiration for even some of the poorest people. However, the cheapest Chinese motorbikes assembled in Vietnam are sold for a minimum of VND 8 million,[5] which prices them out of reach of the vast majority of people.

The beneficiaries of this import regime are a number of companies, many of them State-owned enterprises, which employ around 100,000 people in the manufacture of bicycles, motorbikes, and spare parts. Seventy thousand of them work in the bicycle industry for an average monthly income of between VND 500,000 and 700,000. Workers assembling motorbikes can earn as much as VND 1 million per month. The tariffs have inadvertently encouraged the smuggling of Chinese bicycles into Vietnam (they are said to account for 5-7 per cent of the market), which has exerted some downward pressure on the prices of locally produced bikes.

If tariffs on bicycles and motorbikes were to be phased out or substantially lowered, millions of low-income Vietnamese people would benefit from more affordable access to these essential means of transport. Some jobs would inevitably be lost in domestic companies, but there is anecdotal evidence that people in Hanoi would prefer to buy Vietnamese-made bicycles, rather than cheaper imports, because of perceptions about quality and value for money. This suggests that a market for locally produced bicycles may remain, even in the face of increased competition from cheaper imports.

(Source: Thanh 2001)

CHAPTER 3
Left behind: poor countries and poor people in the international trading system

Rising tides are supposed to lift all boats. Over the past two decades, international trade has created a rising tide of wealth, but some boats have risen more rapidly than others, and some are sinking fast. In the previous chapter we examined the potential of trade to reduce poverty. This chapter documents the failure to realise that potential. It shows how unequal trade is limiting the rate of poverty reduction, reinforcing global inequalities, and marginalising poor countries and poor people.

The first part of this chapter briefly considers the global record on poverty and inequality. It shows that, contrary to the predictions made for globalisation, gaps in wealth are widening and impeding progress towards poverty reduction. Increased integration through trade could narrow these gaps, if developing countries were able to capture a bigger share of world markets. Instead, the domination of the global trading system by a small group of rich countries is reinforcing divergences in income. A world that is already unequal is becoming more polarised.

The second part examines some of the forces which marginalise developing countries in the global trading system. It shows that success in the export market has been highly concentrated, and that some impressions of successful performance are misleading. Many apparently dynamic exporters are confined to low-value-added operations, locked into simple assembly operations which offer limited opportunities for up-grading technologies and building local capacity. The process of globalisation appears to be weakening the capacity of poor countries to integrate into world markets on terms that are conducive to long-term development.

The third section shifts the focus from countries to people. Conventional trade theory predicts that the poor will benefit from more trade through employment creation in labour-intensive sectors. Unfortunately, theory and reality have parted company. Lacking the resources and assets needed to benefit from the opportunities provided by trade, many of those who have been drawn into employment are being left perilously close to the poverty line. Low wages are not the only problem. The expansion of trade

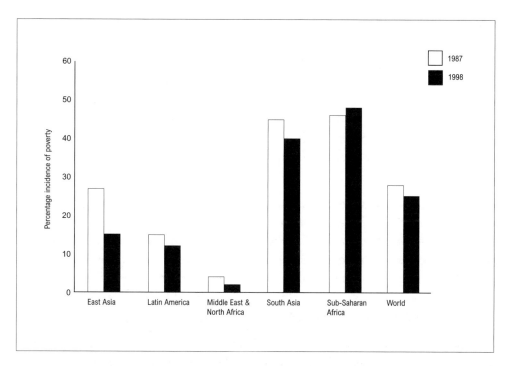

Figure 3.1
Incidence of income poverty
1987and1998

Source: World Bank

has been linked to the intensification of gender-linked inequalities and increased exposure to risk and ill-health. Export growth can also damage the natural environment, further marginalising the poor in the process.

Reinforcing poverty and inequality: international trade and the 'trickle-down' effect

Poverty and inequality in the new order

It was once believed that globalisation would lead the world into a bright new era of rapid poverty reduction and falling levels of inequality. Economists confidently predicted a process of income 'convergence', with increased flows of trade and investment enabling poor countries to catch up with average incomes in rich countries. Some believe that the early promise has been delivered. 'Global integration', declares the World Bank, 'is already a powerful force for poverty reduction' (World Bank 2001a). That assessment is difficult to reconcile with the facts.

Global poverty: money, vulnerability, and time

On the evidence of the World Bank's own figures, the impact of global integration on poverty reduction appears less powerful than often suggested. Extreme poverty declined only slowly in the 1990s. The proportion of the world's population living on $1 a day fell from 28 per cent in 1987 to 23 per cent in 1998. At the start of the twenty-first century, 1.1 billion people are struggling to survive on less than $1 a day, the same figure as in the mid-1980s (World Bank 2001d). The proportion and number of people living on less than $2 a day, a more relevant threshold for middle-income countries, show similar trends. In other words, the wealth that flows from liberalised trade is not trickling down to the poorest, contrary to the claims of the enthusiasts of globalisation.

Behind this global picture there are important regional differences (Figure 3.1). The contrasting experiences of East Asia and Latin America, two regions that have been rapidly integrating into the global economy, show that there is no simple relationship between globalisation and poverty reduction. The incidence of poverty in East Asia has fallen by 10 per cent, whereas in Latin America it remains the same as in 1987, and there are now another 15 million people living below the poverty line. The incidence of poverty in South Asia has fallen, but not fast enough to negate the effects of population increase, so that another 48 million people are below the poverty line. In Africa, the incidence of poverty increased in the first half of the 1990s before falling back by the end of the decade to the levels of the mid-1980s, leaving an additional 73 million people in extreme poverty.

Progress towards poverty reduction is clearly shown to be inadequate when measured against international development targets. In the mid-1990s, the international community adopted the goal of halving world poverty by 2015. The actual rate of decline achieved since the mid-1980s (around 0.2 per cent per year) is approximately one-tenth of that required to meet the 2015 target. Only East Asia is currently on track; sub-Saharan Africa would need to more than double its current per capita growth rate and reduce inequalities to meet the target (Hanmer 2000).

Income poverty is one of the most powerful determinants of human welfare. However, other indicators of capability, such as health and education, are just as important (Sen 1999). Progress in both of these areas has been far slower than required to meet the 2015 targets. For example, the goal of universal primary education may now be out of reach. On current trends, there will still be 75 million children out of school in 2015 (Watkins 2001a). Slow progress in education and the widening gap in health standards between rich and poor countries are both a cause and a consequence of income poverty.

Poor people tend to define their poverty in terms that differ from those used by economists. Apart from deprivation in areas such as income and health, they attach a great deal of weight to less easily measurable, though no less powerful, determinants of the quality of life, such as insecurity and vulnerability. Attempts to measure the relationship between globalisation and these broader indicators are fraught with difficulty. However, there is strong evidence that people living in poverty perceive the pressures on their lives to be intensifying. One of the largest surveys of opinion among poor people, conducted by the World Bank, concluded: 'What poor people shared with us is sobering. A majority of them feel worse off and more insecure than in the past' (Narayan 2000:1).

At one level, vulnerability is an inevitable consequence of globalisation. As countries become more inter-connected, they become more exposed to the fluctuations of world markets, as do the livelihoods of their populations. All countries are affected by mutual interdependence, but developing countries have the least capacity to protect their citizens from its associated risks.

There is another level at which vulnerability is socially determined. When women talk about the quality of their lives, they often refer to pressures on their time and to their physical exhaustion. 'Time poverty', as it has been dubbed, is on the increase, especially in countries enjoying rapid export growth. As women are drawn into labour markets, their access to paid employment has increased (Folbre 1994). So too has their working day. Long hours of paid work are added to long hours of unpaid work in the household and time spent in caring for sick relatives and nurturing children. National economies have been free-riding on unpaid female labour, in the sense that the services that women provide generate real wealth and human benefits on a cost-free basis. As the time pressures on women increase, through their participation in the creation of household income and export earnings, both the 'care economy' and their personal endurance are being stretched, often to breaking point (UNDP 1999).

Inequality

International income distribution is important for poverty reduction. Other things being equal, the larger the share of the global economy captured by developing countries, the higher their average income. Even small steps towards redistribution could have pronounced effects on poverty reduction. Unfortunately, the steps are being taken in the wrong direction.

During the 1990s, high-income countries maintained their share of global wealth, even though their share of world population fell. At the end of the decade, they accounted for 78 per cent of world GDP and 14 per cent of the world's population. At the other end of the spectrum, low-income developing countries saw their share of world population rise and their share of world income fall to less than three per cent. Measured in terms of purchasing power parity,[1] the average income gap between poor and rich countries widened in the 1990s from a ratio of 1:5.4 to 1:7.3.

Inequalities of this order in the global economy have important implications for the relationship between economic growth and poverty reduction. If the income generated by growth is distributed on the basis of prevailing income distribution, it creates at best a modest 'trickle-down' effect, while widening the average income gaps between rich and poor countries. From every $1 of wealth generated in the global economy, high-income countries receive about 80 cents, and low-income countries, with the most extreme concentrations of poverty, and with 40 per cent of the world's population, receive around three cents.

In the absence of redistributive measures, it is very difficult to close income gaps as wide as those that prevail in the world economy. The problem can be illustrated through a simple arithmetical example. If developing countries were to increase their average incomes by three per cent a year, and average incomes in high-income countries were to increase by one per cent a year, it would still take approximately 70 years before absolute incomes in both sets of countries increased by an equal amount.

Distribution is important for poverty reduction at a global level for the same reason that it matters at a national level. Economic growth determines what happens to average income, not to the incomes of the poor. The larger the share of any increment to growth captured by the poor, the faster the rate of poverty reduction (White 2000). In the global economy, the very small share of growth captured by poor countries weakens the link between world economic growth and incomes in the developing world.

In a global economy it is appropriate to ask what is happening to income distribution across all countries, treating the world as if there were no borders. Researchers at the World Bank have attempted this exercise, using surveys covering more than 90 per cent of the world's population for the period 1988-1993 (Milanovic 1998). The results provide a powerful contradiction to some of the more benign assessments of globalisation: they show that the poorest 10 per cent of the world have only 1.6 per cent of the income of the richest 10 per cent. The World Bank study also identified widening average income gaps between countries as the main factor behind widening global inequalities.

Figure 3.2a
The world is less equal than any
country: Gini co-efficient for world
economy and selected countries

Sources: Milanovic 1998, World Bank 2001c

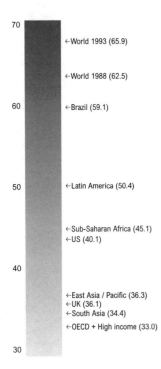

The full extent of global inequality is not widely appreciated. Measured by the Gini co-efficient,[2] the global economy ended the 1980s more unequal than any country. In the first half of the 1990s, the Gini co-efficient increased by a further three points (Milanovic 1998). This represents almost twice the rate at which inequality increased in the USA and the UK during the 1980s, a period which saw income gaps widen at levels that were unprecedented in the post-1945 era (Figures 3.2(a) and 3.2(b)).

Northern governments rightly stress the need for developing countries to give the poor a bigger stake in national wealth; but they have a different approach to global wealth. In the global economy, high-income countries make even the most avaricious national elites of highly unequal countries like Brazil look generous by comparison. It is almost unthinkable that the patterns of income inequality emerging under globalisation would be tolerated by any government. Indeed, most would regard such extreme inequalities as a recipe for social breakdown and conflict. Yet in the case of the global economy and the process of globalisation, what would be unacceptable at a national level is regarded as an immutable fact of life.

Economists are dedicating much time and effort to charting trends in inequality. They hotly debate the precise direction of trends, measurement techniques, and projections for the future, but they miss the central point, which is that levels of inequality under globalisation are both intolerable in themselves, and inconsistent with a commitment to poverty reduction.

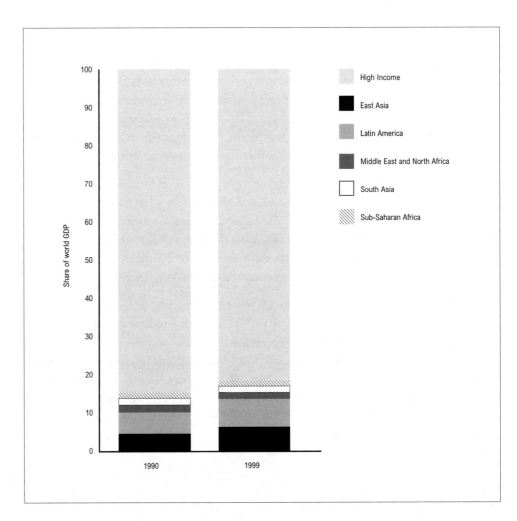

Figure 3.2b
Shares of world GDP
1990 and 1999

Source: IMF 2001a

Export performance and global inequality

International trade seldom figures prominently in debates about global income distribution. This is unfortunate. As globalisation takes deeper roots, international trade relations are having an increasingly important effect on the distribution of world income. Increased trade could narrow inequalities between rich and poor countries; instead, it is reinforcing the gaps in income.

As the share of exports in world GDP rises, it follows that the share of world export markets captured by various countries will have an increasingly important bearing on their relative and absolute income levels. As shown in Chapter 2, if poor countries increased their share of world exports, it would have the effect of raising average incomes. Unfortunately, at the end of two decades of rapid globalisation, there is still a huge discrepancy between the distribution of world population and the distribution of export activity.

Unequal shares of export markets reflect and magnify wider income inequalities. High-income countries generate three-quarters of world exports. Developing countries, with almost four-fifths of the world's population, generate less than one-quarter of total exports. Globalisation may be revolutionising international trade, but in the case of distribution the position is one of entrenched continuity in the midst of change. Figure 3.3 shows that the gap between the distribution of world population and the distribution of exports is not narrowing on any scale. Among the main findings are the following.

- East Asia accounts for the entire increase in world-market share achieved by developing countries. It expanded its world-market share by four per cent in the 1990s, to just under ten per cent.

- Sub-Saharan Africa has suffered a catastrophic loss of market share, extending over three decades. During the 1990s, the region lost another quarter of its world market. It now accounts for only 1.3 per cent of world trade.

- South Asia increased its share of world markets from 0.8 to one per cent.

- Latin America increased its world-market share from one to five per cent of the total, although this was almost entirely due to exports from Mexico.

Although export growth in developing countries was more rapid than in high-income countries in the 1990s (7 per cent versus 5.6 per cent), there were wide regional variations. Growth rates for Africa were less than one half of the high-income average, while Latin America achieved equivalence. This helps to explain why sub-Saharan Africa is falling further behind in both relative and absolute terms. Only East Asia and South Asia exceeded high-income growth levels, the latter from an exceptionally low base.

The unequal distribution of export activity reinforces wider income inequalities. Even though developing countries have been increasing their share of world exports, the resulting income gains have been smaller than for rich countries. This is for the obvious reason that a small increase in a large initial figure is worth more than a proportional increase in a smaller figure. Thus low-income developing countries as a group increased per capita income from exports by $51 during the 1990s, while high-income countries generated a gain of $1938 (Figure 3.4). Even East Asia has fallen behind in absolute terms, despite having an export growth rate that is double the high-income average. The per capita value of its exports increased by $234, compared with $1493 for the USA, even though its exports were growing at twice the rate. For sub-Saharan Africa, export

Figure 3.3
Unequal shares: regional shares of
world exports (1990 and 1999)
and population (1999)

Source: World Bank 1992, 2001c

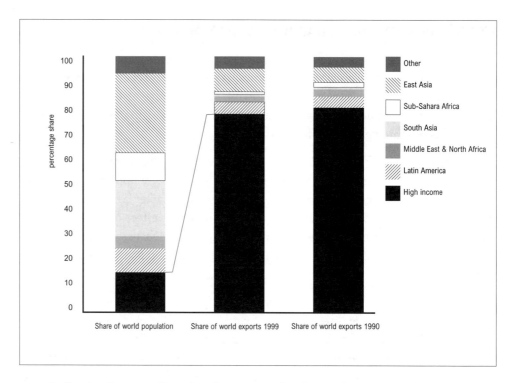

marginalisation has contributed to the region's fast-diminishing share of world income. Whereas the value of its per capita exports rose by $46, a modest industrial-country exporter like the UK enjoyed an increase of $2701.

Figure 3.4
Per capita increase in export
earnings (1999 levels over 1990
levels): selected regions and
countries

Source: Calculated from World Bank 2001d

Optimistic assessments of globalisation and its implications for poverty reduction are contradicted by a consideration of shares of the world export market. The three regions with the worst record on poverty reduction in the 1990s have seen their share of global exports either stagnate (Latin America), rise very slightly from a low base (South Asia), or decline (sub-Saharan Africa). At the end of the 1990s, South Asia and Africa – two regions that account for almost three-quarters of world poverty and one-third of world population – were generating only two per cent of world exports. Their failure to capture a larger share of the gains from global integration is intimately linked to their poor record on poverty reduction.

Developing countries in the international trading system: the emerging problems

Eduardo Galeano, the Uruguayan historian, once wrote: 'The division of labour among nations is that some specialise in winning and others in losing' (Galeano 1973). He could have been writing about the division of labour that is emerging under globalisation.

Some developing countries have seized the opportunities created by globalisation. They are not only increasing the volume of their exports, but also raising the quality of their exports in terms of local value-added, entry into dynamic sectors of world markets, technological composition, and employment creation. Many more countries are failing. This group includes not only the majority of primary-commodity exporters and countries in sub-Saharan Africa, but also countries that are participating in some of the most dynamic areas of international trade – on the basis of low-quality export activity. While export growth is creating employment in these countries, it is often based on simple low-cost assembly operations. Links with the local economy are minimal, and little effort has been made to create the foundations for successful integration into world markets (Lall 2000a). One consequence is that export-linked employment is highly vulnerable to competition from low-wage competitors.

Chapter 1 showed that globalisation is altering patterns of international trade in some important respects. Growth in international markets is concentrated in manufacturing, with a strong bias towards more sophisticated technological products. If developing countries are to increase their share of world exports, they need to penetrate these higher-growth markets on terms which generate high levels of local value-added production. Failure to achieve this will exacerbate income inequalities, by transferring value-added from developing countries to high-income countries. While aggregate data indicate improved export performance by developing countries in the 1990s, they tend to obscure four problems associated with current patterns of integration:

- **Export 'success' is highly concentrated in East Asia.** The region accounts for more than three-quarters of the exports of the developing world, and an even larger share of manufactured exports. Other regions are being left behind, with sub-Saharan Africa facing the most serious problems.

- **Continued dependence on primary commodities.** While the share of manufactured goods in developing-country exports continues to increase, a large group of countries remains reliant on primary commodities. Slow growth and adverse price trends in commodity markets are a major source of marginalisation.

- **Low-quality, labour-intensive exports.** High-volume exporters in areas such as textiles and garments are failing to raise the quality of their exports, with damaging implications in terms of current benefits and long-term prospects.

- **Several 'successful' high-technology economies are operating in low value-added ghettoes.** The growth of high-technology exports creates a misleading impression of successful integration. Like labour-intensive exporters, many high-technology exporters are entering world markets on the basis of low-wage, low-skill assembly work, rather than through innovation and technological up-grading. They are often passive recipients of foreign investment, lacking an industrial development strategy.

The limits to export success

Developing countries have been increasing their share of world markets for manufactured goods, but the picture of generalised success painted by some commentators is misleading. There are marked variations across and between regions, with large areas of the developing world playing a marginal role.

East Asia accounts for more than two-thirds of all manufactured exports and more than three-quarters of exports in high-growth technology sectors such as electronics. The region dominates both medium-technology and high-technology markets (Figure 3.5a and b). At the other end of the scale, both South Asia and sub-Saharan Africa have seen their already small share of manufactured exports shrink since the mid-1980s. Latin America has also fared badly, despite the region's image as a dynamic and successful player in the globalised economy. If Mexico is excluded from the equation, the Latin American share of developing-country manufactured exports is falling.

Regional concentration overlaps with national concentration. In each area of export activity for manufactured goods, just five developing countries – China, Korea, Taiwan,

Figure 3.5a
Shares of leading exporters of
manufactured products in the
developing world: top five and ten
exporters 1998

Source: Lall 2001a

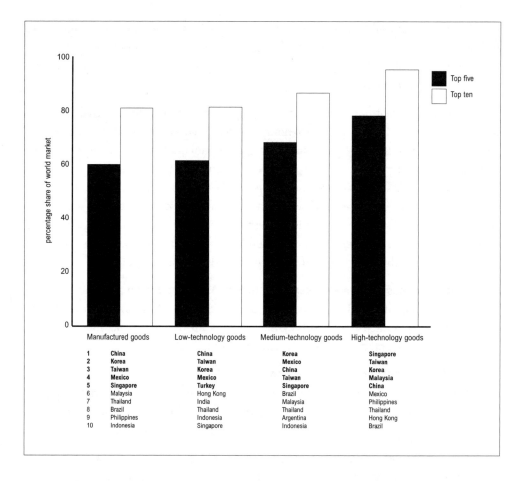

Figure 3.5b
Regional shares of developing-
country manufactured exports,
1985 and 1998

Source: Lall 2001a

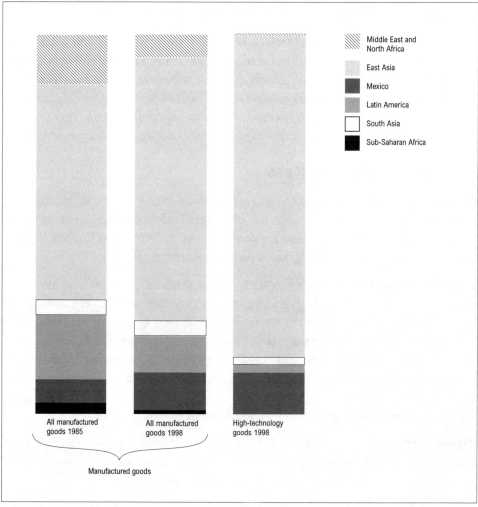

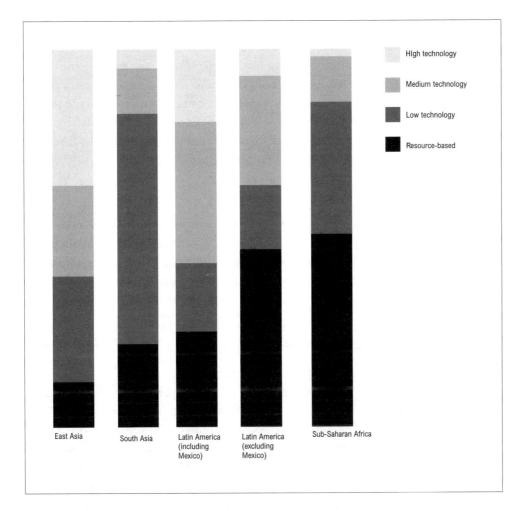

Figure 3.5c
Distribution of manufactured
exports by technological category
(1998)

Source: Lall 2001a

Mexico, and Singapore – account for almost two-thirds of all manufactured exports
from the developing world by value. National concentration is equally marked in the
medium-technology and high-technology sectors. In each case, just ten countries
account for more than 80 per cent of total exports. No African countries appear in the
top ten, or anywhere near it. In South Asia, only India figures, mainly by virtue of the
rapid growth of its computer software industry. With the exception of East Asia, export
structures are dominated by resource-based and low-technology goods (Figure 3.5c).

The picture that emerges is a sobering one for enthusiastic advocates of globalisation. It
suggests that the enormous increase in intra-product and intra-company trade that is
driving export growth under globalisation is concentrated on a very small group of
countries. The vast majority remain excluded from the growth points in world markets,
raising the imminent prospect of widening inequalities – not just between the
developed and developing worlds, but also within the developing world.

Primary commodities and agriculture

The expansion of trade under globalisation may be symbolised by the micro-electronics
industry, but many developing countries continue to participate in the global economy
on the basis of trading relationships established in the colonial period. In today's world
economy, dependence on primary commodities offers an almost automatic route to a
diminishing share of world exports and world income, with its attendant implications
for living standards.

Dependence on primary commodities is most acute in sub-Saharan Africa and among the 49 Least Developed Countries (LDCs). In sub-Saharan Africa, commodities account for about half of merchandise exports. Many depend on just a few agricultural commodities (coffee, cocoa, tea, and palm oil) and minerals. More than 50 countries in the developing world depend on three or even fewer commodities for more than half their export earnings (International Task Force on Commodity Risk Management 1999). The LDCs' share of world trade has shrunk to around 0.5 per cent, less than one-quarter of the level in the second half of the 1980s.

Even though low-income countries have the highest level of commodity dependence, a large group of middle-income countries – and millions of producers in those countries – are similarly affected (Page and Hewitt 2001). For example, contrary to the reputation that Latin America has acquired as a major exporter of manufactured goods, the share of commodities in its export earnings rose during the 1990s. In East Asia, commodities continue to play a central role in the export structures of high-growth technology exporters such as Indonesia, Malaysia, and the Philippines (UNCTAD 1999a).

While there are marked variations across commodity markets, most have in common four adverse trends which do not bode well for countries that seek a larger share of world trade.

- **Slow market growth.** Over the last three decades, growth rates for exports of primary products have lagged far behind those for manufactured goods. Since 1985, the share of primary commodities in world trade has halved, to 11 per cent. Within the commodities sector, agricultural trade has fallen dramatically as a share of world trade. In the 1990s, it grew at less than two per cent a year, or one-quarter of the rate for manufactured goods. The share of food and agriculture in total merchandise trade fell from 17 per cent to 10 per cent between 1980 and 1997 (OECD 2000).

- **Adverse price trends.** The terms of trade (the price of exports compared with the price of imports) for Africa's commodity exports were one-fifth lower at the end of the 1990s than in the early 1970s. One estimate suggests the losses to be equivalent in financial terms to one-half of aid flows into Africa. Without the deterioration in terms of trade since 1970, Africa's share of world export markets would have been twice as large as it is today (United Nations 2001a).

- **Low value-added.** Most commodities are exported in unprocessed form. Since it is processing and marketing that add value along the supply chain, only a tiny (and diminishing) share of final value stays in the exporting country (see Chapter 6).

- **Market competition.** Exporters of primary commodities and agricultural products face acute pressures from subsidised exports by industrialised countries. Markets for products such as sugar, cereals, beef, dairy, and some edible oils are dominated by rich countries, which subsidise their own farmers to the extent of $1bn a day[3](see Chapter 4). Developing countries account for only one-third of world agricultural exports, which is the same as in 1970 (OECD 2000).

As Chapter 6 will demonstrate, the prospects for sustained recovery in global commodity markets range from small to non-existent. There is certainly little chance for the poorest countries to reverse the long-term trend towards a diminishing share of world trade. Rapid diversification out of primary commodities, allied to international measures to achieve more stable and remunerative prices, is thus imperative.

Labour-intensive manufactured goods: the slippery slope

Labour-intensive manufacturing exports offer potential twin benefits for poverty reduction. In the short term, they create employment for low-income groups in general, and for women in particular. In the longer term, they can provide a base for industrial development, enabling countries to acquire the knowledge and skills needed to enter more dynamic areas of production with higher value-added. Unfortunately, labour-intensive export activity can also leave countries trapped in low-skill, low-wage sections of the global economy.

Low-technology, labour-intensive goods account for more than one-quarter of developing-country exports, with textiles and garments representing more than half of the total. Many countries in South Asia, the Caribbean, and Latin America have integrated rapidly into the global economy on the basis of these exports. During the period 1990–1999, increased exports of garments resulted in the export/GDP ratio in Cambodia increasing by a factor of six (to more than one-third); in Bangladesh the corresponding ratio doubled. As an intermediate point on the way to higher levels of technological content in exports, labour-intensive goods can provide the foundations for a successful export strategy. As an end point, they offer a declining share of world trade and extreme wage pressures.

Exporters of labour-intensive manufactured goods face many of the same pressures as primary-commodity exporters, albeit in less intensive form. Export growth for low-technology goods is far slower than for high-technology products. Growth rates averaged 10 per cent and 13 per cent respectively for the period 1985–1998 (Lall 2000e). At the same time, terms of trade for exporters of textiles and garments, which account for more than half of low-technology exports, are falling at around two per cent a year (Maizels 2000a). Like primary-commodity producers, exporters of labour-intensive goods have to run just to stand still, increasing the volume of exports in order to generate the same amount of foreign exchange. World market prices in turn exercise a downward pressure on wages, with adverse consequences for poverty reduction.

Foreign investment has played an important role in generating export growth. The magnet for that investment has been cheap labour and preferential access to (or proximity to) major markets. Important gains have been made in terms of employment generation and export earnings. However, export activity driven by foreign investment has for the most part been characterised by weak links to domestic firms. In many cases, entire factories have been transplanted into the host economy, where they operate as enclaves. Machinery, raw materials, and other inputs are almost entirely imported, with the export factory operating as little more than an assembly site. Local value-addition under these conditions is minimal.

The tensions between short-term export 'success' and long-term development prospects are much in evidence in the free-trade, or *maquiladora*, zones of Central America. From modest beginnings in the early 1990s, these zones have emerged as focal points for integration into global markets, and as economic hubs for export growth. But export growth has not been integrated into effective strategies for economic development.

The case of Honduras demonstrates the problem. On the indicator of global integration favoured by the World Bank, this is a country that looks like an export success story. Exports now account for 42 per cent of GDP, putting Honduras in the first division of the globalisation league table. The *maquiladora* industry has led export growth. It now

Box 3.1

Export success in Bangladesh?

At the end of the 1970s, Bangladesh was a typical exporter of primary commodities, with a limited rate of export growth. Today, after a decade of rapid export growth in manufactured goods, the country is promoted by the World Bank and others as a model globaliser. That assessment is at best partially justified. Exports of garments and textiles have transformed Bangladesh over the past decade. At the end of the 1970s, the sector accounted for $1m in export earnings. It now generates $4.2bn, equivalent to three-quarters of the country's total export earnings. The 2800 factories operating in the sector provide around 1.7 million jobs, mainly for women.

But behind the façade of a dynamic export-led economy there are serious problems. One major weakness is limited backward linkages between garment exporters and the local textiles industry. Of the 2.4 billion metres of fabric used each year by factories in the export-processing zones (EPZs), only four per cent are supplied by local industry. Local value-added is between one-quarter and one-third of export earnings, and product diversification is very limited.

Apart from the attraction of Bangladesh as an export base, the magnet for foreign investment has been low wages. Average wages in Bangladesh are between $1 and 1.50 per day, less than half the daily rate in India. For practical purposes, the EPZs are used as a low-cost assembly platform. There has been little investment to increase technological capacity. As a result, Bangladesh's garments sector caters mainly to the lower end of the international market, where price competition is most intense, and where value-added is lowest.

Failure to diversify and up-grade exports has left the country exposed to a serious threat. Unlike most exporters, Bangladesh stands to lose from the liberalisation of import markets in industrialised countries. This is because the Multi-Fibre Arrangement (MFA) imposes quotas on potentially more competitive suppliers, such as India and China. It is the combination of these quotas and Bangladesh's cheap labour that has made the country an attractive site for foreign investors. As Europe and the USA remove these quotas, under a WTO agreement to phase out the MFA by 2005, Bangladesh could lose markets, along with its foreign investors.

Government and donors have moved far too slowly to address this problem. It has been estimated that $1.5bn is required to put in place the spinning, weaving, and knitting units that could provide stronger backward linkages. Yet government has failed to provide serious incentives in this area, adopting instead, with the support of donors and the IMF/World Bank, a policy of 'leave it to the market'.

Sources: Bhattacharya and Rahman 2000, Mainuddin 2000

accounts for more than one-quarter of total employment and 90 per cent of manufactured exports. However, the contribution of the export sector to national development is weak. Domestic value-added accounts for only one-quarter of the total value of exports, depriving the country of an important source of foreign exchange (Agosin 2000, Gitli 1997).

This is typical of the pattern for *maquila* exports across the region and beyond. The reason: export growth is weakly integrated into the domestic economy. *Maquila* exports from Central America are basically sewn garments, assembled from components imported by TNCs from Taiwan, Hong Kong, and South Korea, and exported to the United States. Their contribution to development is mainly as a source of employment for women and foreign-exchange earnings, rather than as a platform for entry into more dynamic areas of world trade.

The Central American model is the rule rather than the exception. Much of the developing world is suffering from a surfeit of low-quality investment and low-quality export growth in labour-intensive manufacturing. In South Asia, Bangladesh is widely cited by the World Bank and the IMF as an export-led success story. Here too, the evidence is superficially compelling. Exports of garments have grown at more than double the rate of GDP over the past 15 years, generating $4.2bn at the end of the 1990s. However, as in the *maquilas,* the links with the rest of the economy are weak (see Box 3.1). Local value-addition has so far been very small, amounting to only 25–30 per cent of the value of exports (Bhattacharya and Rahman 2000a). Foreign investors obtain virtually all their inputs from overseas, thereby restricting the transmission of export growth through local employment markets.

Low-value-added production has been associated with limited product diversification. Many 'successful' clothing exporters have failed either to broaden their export base, or to move into more dynamic areas of world trade. This group includes Bangladesh, Sri Lanka, Pakistan, Cambodia, and much of the Caribbean, and countries in the Middle East and North Africa (Lall 2000a, Mortimore 1999). Future prospects for this group are poor, unless they broaden their export base. Clothing offers limited opportunities for technological up-grading and transition into more remunerative areas of international trade, unless governments develop active industrial development policies.

The hi-tech, low-value ghettoes

High-technology exports such as electronics, and medium-technology exports such as auto and engineering products, are of special interest for developing countries seeking to integrate into global markets. These are the fastest-growing areas of international trade, and among the areas with the highest-value-added elements. They also have the most beneficial long-term development potential, because of their power to generate technological learning, linkages with other manufacturing sectors, and association with foreign-direct investment. However, exporting high-technology goods will not automatically lead to long-term development. As in labour-intensive manufactured products, many countries are entering global markets primarily as assembly sites for imported goods, capturing a limited share of export values and generating weak linkages to the rest of the economy.

Simple data on the share of total exports captured by medium-technology and high-technology products provide a weak guide to export quality. On the basis of such data, countries such as Mexico are performing on a par with Korea and Taiwan; and the Philippines and Malaysia are performing at levels comparable to Singapore. (See Figure 3.6.) Such a picture is a distortion of reality.

Mexico typifies the pattern of low-quality, high-technology export growth that is emerging under globalisation. Many commentators promote Mexico as a model of what can be achieved through increased trade and investment. Exports have grown at an impressive rate, averaging more than 14 per cent a year. The share of exports in GDP has increased from one-fifth to one-third over the same period. By any conventional measure, Mexico is now near the top of the super-league for globalising economies. It is the world's second-largest exporter of medium-technology manufactured goods, after Korea and ahead of Taiwan, and the sixth-largest exporter of high-technology products.

Figure 3.6
Shares of medium-technology and
high-technology products in
manufactured exports (1998),
selected countries

Source: Lall 2001a

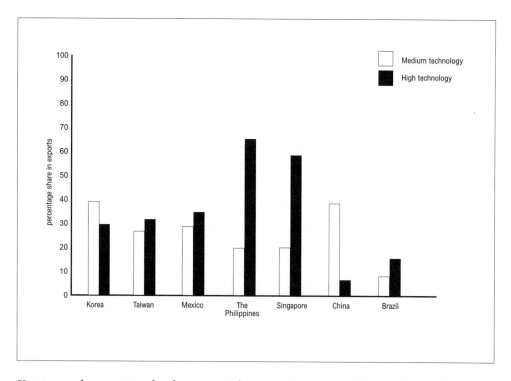

Yet on any longer-term development indicators, Mexico would be in the depths of the lower leagues. Export growth has been driven by the relocation of corporate investment and the simple assembly of imported parts, with minimal local value-added. It has provided (low) wage employment on a large scale, but failed to provide a platform for accelerated growth and poverty reduction.

The auto industry has been the site of some of the most dynamic export growth in Mexico. Exports increased five-fold, to $21bn, between 1990 and 1997 alone; Mexico is now the single largest supplier of engines and passenger vehicles to the USA. The catalyst for this export boom has been the relocation to the Mexican *maquiladora* zone of Ford, General Motors, and Chrysler. For example, Ford has invested more than $3bn to produce sophisticated engine and vehicle assembly units for the North American market (Mortimore 1998a). Intra-company trade has been driving Mexican export growth. There is nothing in principle that makes this bad for development. TNC investment can act as an important conduit for transferring skills and technology. It can also provide countries with access to large corporate markets, as it clearly has in the case of Mexico. But the quality of export growth is determined by the extent to which it is built on dynamic linkages within the local economy. On this test, Mexico fails disastrously.

Figure 3.7a
Mexican *maquiladora* exports:
breakdown of final value

Source: Buitelaar and Perez 2000

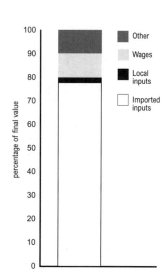

For practical purposes, the *maquila* factories are sites for the assembly of components manufactured in the USA. Linkages with the domestic economy are exceptionally weak. Value-added is very low, at less than 20 per cent of overall production. Local inputs are all but non-existent, accounting for about two per cent of total value (see Figure 3.7a). The booming export economy generates little demand for local industry, and hence little employment and investment outside of the *maquiladora* zone (Buitelaar and Perez 2000). Thus, while the zone accounts for almost half of total employment, it generates only about one-tenth of the value-added in Mexico's manufacturing sector.

Comparisons with earlier periods of economic development in East Asia are telling. Free-trade zones never figured prominently as a strategy, but even where they were used to attract investment, they produced very different results. For instance, when Korea opened the Masan export-processing zone in the early 1970s, local inputs accounted for three per cent of the value added in production. Within a decade, that share had risen to almost 50 per cent, equivalent to 25 times the value-added level in Mexican *maquilas* today (Lall 1999). Today, the differences are equally apparent. Countries such as Mexico are at the lower end of the value-added league (Figure 3.7b). More generally, Latin America's failure to improve the quality of export growth is leaving the region further behind East Asia in terms of value-added activity (Figure 3.7c).

This is not to deny the benefits of *maquiladora* exports. They provide more than one million jobs and, even after the cost of imports has been subtracted, $10bn in foreign-exchange earnings. The problem is that *maquilas* are locking Mexico into a segment of world trade characterised by low productivity and its inevitable corollary of low wages (see below). Mexico's export success has been built not on increased technological capacity, but on proximity to the US market and cheap labour, leaving the country highly vulnerable to foreign competition. China represents a huge threat, given its lower wage costs, which average less than one-fifth of those in Mexico, and its recent entry to the WTO. At the end of the 1990s, rising labour costs prompted several large American TNCs – including the Firestone Tyre company – to relocate their assembly operations to China. Failure to develop its national skills and technology base will force Mexico either to compete on the basis of lower wages, or to face the consequences in terms of higher unemployment. Both outcomes would have adverse consequences for poor people.

Comparisons between Mexico and Korea based on simple export data are highly misleading. The same is true for the Philippines, one of the world's fastest-growing micro-electronic exporters. Electronic products now account for over four-fifths of exports, having grown at more than ten per cent a year. The export/GDP ratio has doubled, to more than one-half. However, the export boom has been driven almost entirely by semi-conductor assembly (Lall 2001b). The Philippines has been integrated into the intra-company trading systems of Japanese TNCs through foreign investment. Much of that investment has involved the relocation of Japanese companies from Malaysia, which faces problems similar to those of Mexico.

Countries that seek to attract foreign investment and generate export growth predominantly on the basis of low-cost labour face a dilemma. In order to sustain increases in real wages over time, productivity has to rise. Otherwise, there is an immediate impetus towards 'investment flight'. The transferability of new technologies, competition for investment, and the mobility of capital make it increasingly possible for TNCs to respond to rising wages by seeking out alternative sites of production. The problem is that by creating limited linkages with local firms, low-quality investment can interact with other factors – such as inadequate investment in education – which make it difficult to increase productivity.

Among the major exporters of high-technology products, Korea and Taiwan have by far the highest local content in exports. Their domestic firms undertake much of the manufacturing and provide design services, engineering and other inputs, and R&D services. As in Malaysia and the Philippines, exports from Singapore are dominated by TNCs. The difference is that in Singapore the TNCs purchase a large proportion of their inputs locally. Export growth has spawned large industries in areas ranging from electronic components to precision tools, electroplating, and industrial plastics. The varied policies of the first generation of East Asian industrialisers may not be immediately transferable to other countries, but strategies for climbing the technological ladder remain an imperative for successful integration into global markets (Lall 1998).

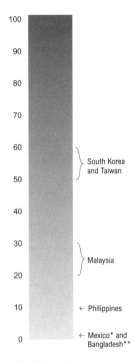

* *Maquiladora* sector
** Ready-made garments sector

Figure 3.7b
Estimated value-added*** ranges for local inputs in export production

Source: UNIDO Database

Figure 3.7c
Per capita value-added*** in manufacturing: Latin America and East Asia (1990=100)

Source: UNIDO Database

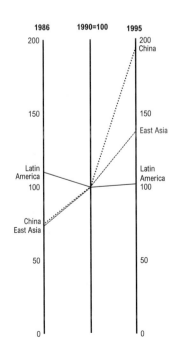

***Note: 'Value-added' refers to the difference between total revenue and the cost of bought-in materials, services and components. It thus measures the value which has been added to these bought-in materials through production processes.

Poor people and trade: who are the losers?

Standard trade theory seems to offer good news for the poor. Since developing countries generally have an abundance of unskilled labour relative to other factors of production (such as capital) and relative to industrialised countries, free trade is presumed to increase global demand for exports that embody inputs of unskilled labour, thus driving up employment, increasing incomes, and reducing poverty in the process (Wood 1994, Ben-David et al. 2000). Unfortunately, theoretical predictions have proved a weak guide to actual outcomes. Reality has been far less encouraging. Integration through trade is creating opportunities, but these opportunities are biased towards those with access to productive assets, infrastructure, and education. In the manufacturing sector, demand for products embodying skilled labour appears to be increasing far more rapidly than demand for unskilled labour.

Poverty is a powerful barrier to participation in markets. Because the rural poor lack access to the land, credit, and market information that they need, and because they often face higher transport costs, they are ill equipped to compete. Like the urban poor, the rural poor face acute disadvantages in their access to education – one of the key requirements for acquiring the skills needed to take advantage of market opportunities. Women face especially acute problems. Markets are not gender-neutral in the way that they operate (Elson 1999). Women face high levels of wage discrimination in the manufacturing sector, allied to employment practices which diminish their quality of life. In the rural sector, women producers often experience barriers to market entry and may have limited control over income. Gender-linked inequalities within the household interact with wider inequalities in the market to determine the distribution of benefits from trade.

Evidence from many countries suggests that the expansion of trade has often resulted either in the poor getting left behind, or in the intensification of exploitative and environment-damaging systems of production which challenge human-development aspirations. Failure to link integration into global markets with a strategy for the redistribution of assets upon which greater equity depends will leave the poor in an increasingly marginalised position, even in countries that achieve higher levels of economic growth.

The manufacturing sector: low wages, weak employment rights, and vulnerability

Globalisation has been associated with two important trends across much of the developing world. Exports of manufactured goods, and women's participation in the labour force, have both increased dramatically. Women now account for about one-third of manufacturing workers in developing countries, with a heavy concentration in labour-intensive sectors such as clothing, footwear, and micro-electronic assembly. In many countries, the relationship between export growth and poverty reduction continues to confound trade theory.

Wages
Wages are the most direct channel between export growth and household income. Trade theory predicts that by increasing demand for labour, export growth will increase the income of households with members working in export sectors. In some cases, this has happened. In parts of East Asia, rapid export growth has been associated with rising

real wages. But this is not a universal picture. In Latin America, export growth reached five per cent a year in the 1990s, but with little impact on the wages of poor urban workers. Numbers living below the poverty line increased in the same period.

One reason for the weak association between economic growth and poverty reduction is that growth has been weakly linked to employment creation and rising wages. Real minimum wages were lower in 1999 in 13 out of 18 countries than they had been in 1980 (ECLA 2000a). One of the apparent anomalies of economic growth in Latin America over the past decade has been a weak association both with employment and wages. In countries such as Brazil and Peru, real wages have fallen even during growth periods (Dancourt 1999, ECLA 2001). Meanwhile, urban unemployment at the end of the 1990s was twice as high as at the start of the decade, affecting another 10 million people (ECLA 2001). Unemployment increased across a large group of countries that were integrating into global markets at a rapid rate, including Brazil, Colombia, and Peru.

Wages in many high-growth export industries are low not just by the standards of international comparison, but also in relation to national poverty lines. In Bangladesh, women workers in the garment industry earn around $1.50 per day, which is marginally above the poverty line. Research in Honduras and the Dominican Republic suggests that wages for workers in export industries are often insufficient to maintain reasonable standards of nutrition. Even though wages in export manufacturing may be attractive, they do not offer an automatic escape from poverty.

Why has integration into the global trading system not led to real wage increases in many countries? At least four factors appear to have been important.

- **The skills composition of exports:** The assumption that unskilled labour will be an automatic beneficiary of export growth is flawed. In many countries, export growth has been led by sectors that generate demand for skilled labour. The Indian boom in software exports, which has generated more than 180,000 jobs, mostly for graduates of technical colleges, is an extreme example. The largely illiterate rural populations who account for about two-thirds of poverty in India are not obvious beneficiaries. In Latin America, many of the export-growth industries in the manufacturing sector have also increased demand for skilled rather than unskilled labour. The pay gap between college-educated workers and unskilled workers increased by 18–25 per cent in the 1990s, exacerbating income inequalities and reducing poor people's share in economic growth (Morley 2000, Behrman 2000, ECLA 2000b). Even the most basic assembly industries may not create employment for the lowest-income groups. The garment industry of Bangladesh has created employment for women with an average of four or five years of education, rather than those lacking basic literacy skills, which may account for the weak correlation between export growth and poverty reduction in that country.

- **The composition of labour markets:** Mass poverty, large-scale unemployment, the erosion of basic union rights, and the dismantling of wage-protection provisions generate a large supply of labour that is forced to work for wages below levels previously regarded as an acceptable minimum. The 'feminisation' of labour markets has been an important development in explaining trends in wage-levels. Labour supply has increased, with new female entrants receiving lower wages than their male peers. In a number of countries, women's participation has been accompanied by a reduction in pay gaps, though this is not a universal picture.

Moreover, even where they are narrowing, gaps remain large. In some export-processing zones, women's wages are 20–30 per cent lower than for men in the same manufacturing industry (Horton 1999, Standing 1999). On average, women earn only about three-quarters of the average male salary in manufacturing employment. Research by the World Bank suggests that less than one-fifth of this difference can be explained by levels of education, pointing to a high degree of gender-linked discrimination (World Bank 2000db). Because women, as the majority of new entrants into the workforce, are paid lower wages, this has tended to reduce the average wage. The generalised weakening of collective bargaining rights has had similar effects.

- **The composition of production:** As shown earlier in this chapter, export growth in developing countries is heavily concentrated on labour-intensive production and the simple assembly of higher-technology goods. The low-value-added activities and simple technologies involved in production result in low remuneration to workers. Productivity considerations partly explain why average wages in the Mexican *maquila* industry are one-third lower than in the rest of the manufacturing sector (Buitelaar and Perez 2000). Countries integrating into global markets through low value-added exports face intense downward pressure on wages. Not only are these highly competitive, but the transferability of production makes it possible for TNCs to respond to higher wages by relocating.

- **The composition of imports.** When countries integrate into world markets through trade liberalisation, it is not only export production that is affected. Imports can also increase, producing complicated patterns of winners and losers. If imports displace production in labour-intensive industries, while exports generate demand for skilled labour, the poor can lose out in relative and absolute terms. In South Africa, import liberalisation brought a large textiles and garments sector into competition with cheaper goods produced in East Asia. Imported textiles now account for about one-half of total consumption, up from one-quarter only five years ago. Employment in the local industry has shrunk by one-third since 1996, with 30,000 jobs lost (Simon 2001). It has become almost impossible for domestic firms to compete in high-volume, low-cost markets, dominated by countries such as China and Cambodia. Relative wages of unskilled labour are 15 times higher in South Africa than in these countries. In effect, trade is pushing down wages and transferring jobs from one developing country to another.

Vulnerability

Wages are one aspect of employment affecting human development, and security is another. Under globalisation, insecurity has increased. Labour markets have become increasingly 'flexible' – but 'flexibility' in this context has become a euphemism for the erosion of basic rights.

The deregulation of labour markets was an important element in economic liberalisation during the 1980s. Assiduously cultivated by the IMF and the World Bank, developing countries came under pressure to reduce labour costs, not just by lowering minimum wages, but also by reducing non-wage costs in areas such as social insurance. 'Flexible' labour was seen as the key to attracting foreign investment and export growth. Once again, Latin America has been in the forefront of change. In Mexico, more than one-quarter of workers do not have an employment contract, a proportion that rises to more than one-third in Brazil, Peru, Chile, and Colombia (ECLA 2000b). Fifteen years ago, formal-sector employment in Latin America provided a source of social insurance.

Today, more than one-third of wage workers in the region do not have access to social security (ECLA 2000c).

'Flexibility' is as much a consequence of the political choices made by governments as of technological change. Those choices have increased poor people's vulnerability. Risk is a standing feature of globalisation. Developments in one part of the global economy are rapidly transmitted through the mechanisms of international trade and finance to all of its participants. Integration through trade offers potential benefits, but the winners on one day may be the losers the next. Poor people are more vulnerable to risk than others, especially when they lack basic employment rights.

The levels of risk facing people employed in export industries were much in evidence during 2000. In an expanding world economy, integration can create jobs; but contraction has the opposite effect. After growth rates of six per cent a year in the 1990s, a synchronised economic downturn in the USA, Europe, and Japan reduced the growth of manufactured exports to one per cent in 2001 (World Bank 2002). This downturn was associated with a slump in US demand for micro-electronic products, thus bursting the high-technology bubble.

It used to be said that when the rich world sneezes, developing countries catch a cold. They now get a dose of potentially fatal double pneumonia. Exports of manufactured goods from developing countries fell dramatically in 2000, from more than 25 per cent to less than 1 per cent in East Asia (World Bank 2002). Exports of high-technology goods, which account for ten per cent of GDP, went into steep decline. Women who had been drawn into the industry by US demand were suddenly thrown out of work as that demand contracted. When Fujitsu announced plans to cut its global workforce by one-tenth in August 2001, it closed factories manufacturing hard-disk drives in the Philippines and Thailand and a printed-circuit-board factory in Vietnam, with total job losses of 5000 people (Landers 2001, Wall Street Journal 2001). In the same month, NEC and Hitachi announced the closures of semi-conductor plants in Malaysia. Few of the women affected had government social-insurance provision to rely on.

Women are especially vulnerable, in that they account for a large share of employment in export industries, while enjoying the least protection in terms of welfare provision (see below). When the global electronics or textiles market contracts, women account for the majority of retrenchments, and form a minority of the workforce protected through formal welfare provisions. For vulnerable people, integration in international trade can sweep away any gains almost overnight, with devastating consequences. Social-insurance provision is one of the strategies to protect gains and minimise costs.

Gender and labour markets
On a simple reading of the balance sheet, women in the manufacturing export sector would appear to be among the main beneficiaries of globalisation. Millions of jobs have been created. Reality suggests a more sober assessment of costs and benefits. Increased employment has generated important gains, in terms of both income and potential independence. At another level, it has produced outcomes that have adverse implications for human development.

Outright wage discrimination is one factor that reduces the benefits to women. Labour markets are often segmented, with women employed in occupations attracting the lowest wages (Joekes 1995). However, their employment does raise household incomes, often playing a crucial role in providing resources for meeting essential costs for food, health care, and nutrition. But these income gains have to be set against other forces that affect the quality of life for women workers, as follows.

- **Excessive work hours:** Evidence from a wide variety of countries shows that the increase in women's participation in labour markets is built on the continuation of pre-existing household labour patterns (UNDP 2001b). The result is that women typically endure far longer working days than their male counterparts. In Bangladesh, women working in the garment industry provide an average of 31 hours a week in unpaid labour in the household, more than double the average for men (Elson 1999). Women also work in export industries outside the household on average three hours a week longer than men. Such inequalities in the allocation of labour mean that increased income can exacerbate 'time poverty', with damaging implications for women's physical health and the nurturing of children.

- **Weak protection in the work place:** Women workers are often concentrated in sectors with notoriously poor levels of employment rights (see Chapter 7). One common problem is that of employers sacking young women workers who become pregnant, in order to avoid responsibility for social-insurance contributions (Joekes 1995). Compulsory overtime is common, adding to problems of time poverty. In China, 12-hour days are common practice during periods of peak demand (Tan 1999). Many countries have strong social-insurance and maternity rights enshrined in law, but enforcement is weak (see Box 3.2). Women's employment is often concentrated in occupations that carry major health hazards, including exposure to toxic chemicals and inadequate fire safety (Barrientos 1996).

- **Weak trade union rights:** Governments have severely circumscribed trade-union rights, especially in export-processing zones. In Bangladesh, the constitutional right to join a union is suspended at the entrance to the country's export zones. Elsewhere, membership is allowed in law, but restricted in practice. Only eight of the 500 companies operating in the export zones of the Dominican Republic have collective agreements with trade unions. Fewer than one in ten women working in the export-processing zones of the Philippines are members of unions (Aganon et al. 1998). Although trade unions have frequently failed to address the problems faced by women workers, their weakness makes it difficult to improve employment standards.

- **Intra-household distribution:** Paid employment provides no guarantee that women will share equitably in its proceeds. Social norms often dictate that women transfer their income to men, with important implications for the intra-household distribution of the benefits from trade. This has been reported in India, Cambodia, and Indonesia (Elson 1999). In Bangladesh, many women report intensive pressure from their families to work in the export sector, often to generate income for weddings or for a husband's family (Kibria 2001).

Box 3.2

'We have jobs but no dignity': the flower industry in Colombia

The high plains of the Savannah region surrounding Bogota, the capital of Colombia, are the heartland of one of the most extraordinary export booms of the 1990s. Colombia is now second only to the Netherlands as an exporter of flowers. The giant greenhouses dotted across the Savannah generate around $600m a year in export revenue. They provide half of all flowers sold in the USA. Only coffee, and of course coca, generate more foreign exchange.

Approximately 80,000 women work in the greenhouses of the Savannah, tending beds of carnations and roses. On an average day, one woman will pick around 400 carnations. During peak periods, such as Valentine's Day and Mother's Day, that number can double. The flowers from a day's labour will sell in US or European shops for between $600 and $800. The woman who picked them will earn a minimum wage for that day's labour of just under $2. Even with over-time payments, and working a ten-hour day, most women earn an amount that leaves them precariously close to the poverty line.

Many of the workers interviewed by Oxfam complain about inadequate income, but acknowledge that low pay is a fact of life on the Savannah. Unemployment rates are approaching 40 per cent. Many of the women have migrated to escape rural poverty. But they have serious concerns about employment conditions and security. While standards across the country are varied, the flower industry provides little security. In theory, Colombia has some of the strongest employment rights in Latin America. The right to join a union, the right to health care and unemployment insurance, and the right of all working women to 80 days of maternity leave are enshrined in law. Unfortunately, the letter and the spirit of the law are widely violated.

One of Oxfam's partners, a Bogota-based NGO called Cactus, operates a legal-advice service for dismissed flower workers in the small town of Tocanipa, on the northern Savannah. It deals with around 60 new cases each month, over half of which concern the dismissal of women during pregnancy. Compulsory pregnancy testing is common before women are granted employment contracts. In a cruel irony for an industry which generates so much profit from Mother's Day, summary dismissal has become a standard practice for avoiding employer-based contributions for maternity pay.

Workers in the flower industry face acute public-health risks from the use of agro-chemicals. Soils are sterilised with toxic methyl-bromide gas, and flowers are intensively sprayed with fungicides, insecticides, and nemoticides. One-fifth of the chemicals used in the greenhouses of the Savannah are carcinogens or toxins that have been restricted for health reasons in the USA. Women workers testify to spraying dichlorpropene, categorised by the WHO as carcinogenic, with no protective clothing and with only handkerchiefs to cover their mouths. Medical surveys carried out by Cactus show that two-thirds of Colombia's flower workers suffer from maladies associated with pesticide exposure, ranging from nausea and conjunctivitis to muscle pains and miscarriages.

Environmental problems raise further doubts about the economic benefits of the flower industry. The water table on the Savannah has been shrinking almost as rapidly as export earnings have been rising. Around the town of Madrid, the aquifer has fallen from 20 metres to 200 metres, and water now has to be imported from Bogota. In some areas, toxic residues have been found at dangerously high levels in ground-water supplies.

None of these costs is inevitable. One group of companies, called Ecoflora, has developed more sustainable strategies for reducing pesticide inputs and, by harvesting rainwater, using less ground-water. And some companies have a better record than others in protecting workers' rights and safety standards. However, the current pattern of economic growth in the flower industry would hardly appear to be compatible with a strategy for sharing the benefits of trade more equitably. Nor is it consistent with human development in its wider sense. As one woman told us: *'I knew poverty before I worked in the flower industry. But it was in the greenhouses that I learned what fear and humiliation meant. Here we have jobs but no dignity.'*

Many women feel ambivalent about employment in export industries. They recognise the benefits of waged employment to themselves and their families, while at the same time expressing anxiety about employment conditions. The garments industry in Cambodia illustrates these tensions. Seven years ago there were ten factories; today there are hundreds, producing garments for companies such as Gap and Old Navy, and generating around $750m a year in the process. Many new jobs have been created, most of them for women workers. Wages are higher than the alternatives on offer, yet many of the women interviewed in an Oxfam survey expressed ambivalence about their jobs. One summarised this in telling terms: *'In the countryside we have more freedom, but no money. In the factory we have no freedom, but we have money to support our families.'* (See Box 3.3.)

Export growth under globalisation has been associated with one form of employment reminiscent not of the computer age, but of the pre-industrial era. Labour-intensive industries such as the manufacture of garments and footwear employ large numbers of home-workers, the vast majority of whom are women. These workers are usually paid on a piece-rate basis at levels far below those in the formal employment sector. Social-insurance rights are non-existent, as is job security (Yanz et al. 1999). Although codes of practice are being developed, women home-workers continue to figure prominently among the most marginalised participants in the global trading system. In India, male domination of formal employment in the garments sector has resulted in female labour remaining concentrated in out-sourcing to households, where real income levels are falling behind (Ghosh 2000).

The rural sector: assets as a barrier to market participation

Opportunities to benefit from export production in agriculture are mediated through local markets. But structural factors, such as land distribution and distance, often prevent poor people from taking advantage of these. And, as in other markets, gender relations play a critical role in distributing opportunity and rewards.

Trade theory suggests that the rural poor will win from trade, since this is supposed to be an area of natural comparative advantage. The dramatic expansion of 'non-traditional' agricultural exports is sometimes cited as evidence of comparative advantage in operation. However, dynamic foreign-exchange gains do not always reflect strong linkages between export growth and poverty reduction. The following are among the most powerful factors explaining why the rural poor are often left behind.

- **Access to land:** Smallholder agriculture is highly effective in translating export growth into poverty reduction. It is good for growth, efficiency, and employment creation (IFAD 2001). Yet in many countries, especially in Latin America and southern Africa, land is disproportionately owned by large-scale farms that combine social injustice and economic inefficiency. More than half the rural poor in Latin America lack access to land, while the 46 largest estates in the country utilise only 17 per cent of their land (de Janvry et al. 2001). Women and other groups in society most subject to discrimination, either through law or social customs, are the least likely to have control over land. In Nigeria, only four per cent of women have title to the land that they cultivate, compared with more than 40 per cent of men. Land redistribution is a powerful weapon against poverty, and in many countries a vital requirement for achieving a wider spread of the benefits from trade. In Brazil, the Rural Landless Workers' Movement (MST) has helped to establish more than 1000 land-reform settlements, providing 145,000 families

Box 3.3

Money but no freedom:
women in Cambodia's garment factories

'In the countryside we have more freedom, but no money. In the factory we have no freedom, but we have money to support our families.' These are the words of Sovana, a 21-year-old woman working in Cambodia's rapidly growing garments industry. They express the ambivalence that many women feel about working in the industry. On the one side, most acknowledge the benefits of increased incomes. On the other, there is a widespread feeling that working in garments factories entails a loss of freedom and, in some cases, dignity.

One in five Cambodian women aged between 18 and 25 now works in a garment factory. The vast majority have migrated to Phnom Penh, the capital city, from desperately poor rural areas. Wages act as the magnet. In her rural village, Sovana earned $0.50 a day selling vegetables. In Phnom Penh she earns $55 a month, including over-time. Pay may be exceptionally low by industrialised-country standards, but for poor rural Cambodians, employment in the garments industry offers dramatic increases in income.

Most trade economists would regard Cambodia as a prime example of trade acting in the interests of the poor. Garments exports generate foreign exchange and economic growth, poor people get more income and, so the argument runs, more income means better welfare. Such simple models do not help to evaluate what is happening to women in Cambodia. Employment generates more income, but the distribution of benefits is determined partly by gender-related roles. Each month, Sovana sends between $20 and $30, half of her income, back to her family. It is used to pay for the education of her brothers and to support the household budget. After paying rent (for one room, shared with three other women), Sovana is left with less than $1 a day. So while her work is clearly increasing aggregate household income, she enjoys an unequal share of the benefits.

Sovana's case is not untypical. Health emergencies, money for education, and support for the family during times of stress place extreme demands on limited incomes. In an interview, one worker commented: *'Life is very difficult. The work is very hard. Because my salary is low, I don't save money. I pay for rental, electricity, and medicine, and have just enough to survive.'*

Non-economic dimensions of welfare also matter a great deal to garment workers. Many of the women interviewed by Oxfam complained of a sense of loneliness and isolation. *'There is no one here to care for me, even if I have more money,'* said one woman. Ironically, while rural parents often encourage their children to migrate for economic reasons, young women garment workers also complain that they are stigmatised because of social norms against women living away from the household.

Abusive labour practices are common in the industry. Women interviewed by Oxfam complained of beatings by managers, especially attacks on young new employees. Weak and ineffective trade unions mean that job insecurity is rife. Absence because of sickness is penalised by fines, and protracted illness leads to dismissal. As one woman put it: *'We know that we cannot afford to be sick for more than three days, unless we want to lose our jobs.'*

with access to unused land on large estates. Access to land has enabled these settlements to take advantage of market opportunities from which they would otherwise be excluded (Wolford 2001).

- **Marketing and infrastructure:** Poor people often face higher transport costs, as a result of weak infrastructure and distance to markets. Producers in Africa face particularly chronic problems. The density of its rural road network is 55 km per square km, compared with more than 800 in India (Collier and Gunning 1999). Rural poverty tends to be most concentrated in remote areas – such as upland Philippines, mountain regions of Vietnam, and northern Mozambique – which are more distant from markets and have least capacity to participate in trade. Inadequate provision of financial services is another factor limiting the capacity of poor producers to respond to market opportunities. In countries as diverse as Ghana, Malawi, Pakistan, and Mexico, access to credit and savings institutions is severely limited for small farmers. Just five per cent of farmers in Tanzania obtain credit from non-family sources in any given year. Poverty means that most poor people borrow credit to finance consumption rather than production (Zeller and Sharma 1998). Inadequate infrastructure makes the rural poor much more vulnerable. Operating in rain-fed areas, they have less capacity to respond to new market opportunities (which often require irrigate land). Access to irrigation is highly restricted in Africa, covering less than five per cent of its crop area. Women farmers are often severely restricted from accessing irrigation (IFAD 2001). In some areas the probability of total crop failure is about 10 per cent (Collier and Gunning 1999).

- **Weak employment rights for women in export sectors.** There has been a dramatic increase in exports of fruits and vegetables from developing countries. Commercial firms dominate exports because of their control over resources and marketing capacity. The rural poor participate in the global market primarily as agricultural labourers. Women dominate the workforce, many of them driven by poverty to seek employment as labourers. The potential benefits of employment are severely compromised by weak employment rights, which in turn generate high levels of personal vulnerability. Women account for more than half of the jobs in the deciduous-fruit industry of South Africa's Western Cape – a major source of supply to Europe. However, they represent more than three-quarters of workers who have only temporary contracts. Temporary status means wages that are about one-third lower than those for men. As a result, most women are denied access to sick pay, maternity pay, or unemployment insurance (Barrientos et al. 2001). One survey conducted among women working in the fruit-export industry in Chile found that around half of them experienced health problems linked to exposure to pesticides and toxic gases. These ranged from nausea and headaches to more serious skin and respiratory problems (Barrientos et al. 1999a). In agricultural exports, as in the manufacturing sector, women are concentrated in the most insecure and exploitative categories of employment, which reduces their capacity to benefit from exports (see Box 3.2).

- **Gender barriers in the market:** Women account for the bulk of rural production, but face a wide array of barriers restricting the potential benefits of trade. Most women in developing countries work in agriculture. They produce most of the developing world's food, and yet they have a minority stake in land ownership. In several countries in Africa, they have formal title to less than one-quarter of land holdings.

In South Asia, women face serious problems in inheriting or purchasing land (IFAD 2001). As traders, women's ability to participate in markets is hindered by poor infrastructure, bad roads, weak marketing, lack of access to credit, and poor infrastructure (Baden 1994). Gender relations at the household level mean that women may not market the crops they sell. This is one of the ways in which men can capture the benefits of market opportunities created through the commercialisation of agriculture, with potentially adverse implications for intra-household income distribution (Haddad et al. 1995).

An assessment of the conditions required in order to benefit from globalisation reveals that the rural poor in general are unlikely to figure prominently among the winners, at least in the absence of redistributive reforms. Many of them do not have access to the technologies and the market information needed to enter markets on reasonable terms. Limited access to credit and other productive resources is another constraint. High transport and input costs add to the competitive disadvantage of the poor, as do systems of public spending that bias the provision of extension services, irrigation, and health and education services towards the rich. All of these factors also leave the poor more vulnerable to competition from agricultural imports (Killick 2001).

Within the ranks of the poor, rural women are likely to be disproportionately represented among the losers. They have less command over resources such as land, credit, and capital; they face major market barriers; and there are more demands on their time. In many countries, the sexual division of labour will bias the benefits of market opportunities and cash-crop production towards men.

Deprivation in education and health care

Education and health are important dimensions of human development in their own right. They are also critical assets for successful integration into global markets. Deprivation in these areas restricts the ability of poor people and poor countries to benefit from opportunities in world trade.

For national economies, education is one of the keys to successful integration. In an increasingly knowledge-based global economy, there is no substitute for human capital. Skills are replacing other assets as the main source of a country's comparative advantage. Unfortunately, gaps in education provision, already wide, are increasing. At the end of the 1990s, boys and girls entering primary school in an industrialised country could anticipate 15–17 years in full-time education. The mean school years for developing regions are much lower, with marked gender-linked inequalities (Barro and Lee 1997).

- In sub-Saharan Africa, boys and girls spend 3.7 and 2.2 years respectively in school.

- In South Asia, girls spend 2.6 years in school and boys almost twice as long.

- In Latin America, boys and girls spend five years in school.

The overall quality of education in each of these regions is desperately low, as witnessed by high rates of illiteracy among school leavers. Improvements in education performance are a pre-condition for countries breaking out of dependence on low-wage, labour-intensive export activity, and for attracting good-quality foreign investment (Bennel 2000).

Within countries, extreme inequalities in education impede the ability of poor households to benefit from trade, and contribute to the income inequalities noted earlier. In Brazil, children from the richest ten per cent of the population receive ten years' schooling on average; children from the poorest one-third of households receive four years. In India there is a ten-year gap between the median grade completed by children from the poorest and the richest households (Pritchett 1999). Around the world, women account for two-thirds of illiteracy, and girls for a similar proportion of children not in school. These gaps, based on income, gender, and regional differences, represent a vast waste of potential, and deny the poor an opportunity to share in export growth.

Like education, good health matters to the poor, both as an end in itself, and because ill health undermines productivity. Poor countries and poor people bear the brunt of the global burden of disease and its associated costs. The economic costs of avoidable disease to poor countries are astonishingly high. Widespread prevalence of diseases such as malaria and HIV/AIDS is associated with large reductions in growth rates, and hence in capacity to participate in international trade. Malaria alone is associated with a reduction of one per cent per year in economic growth rates in several countries (WHO 2001a). The impact of HIV/AIDS has been devastating. Two-thirds of the 33 million people infected with HIV live in Africa (Sachs 1999). The disease is undermining not just health-care systems, but also the capacity of whole countries and households to participate in markets. For poor households, a single episode of sickness can lead to long-term penury. Because ill health weighs far more heavily on the poor in general, and women in particular, it reinforces wider market-based inequalities.

As in education, narrowing the health gap is a requirement for making trade work for poor countries and poor people. That is why health policy must be seen as an integral component of wider strategies for achieving more equitable forms of globalisation.

Income inequality and flexibility in industrialised countries

High-income countries dominate the group of winners emerging from current patterns of international trade, but globalisation is also producing losers in the industrialised world. As low-wage economies in the developing world become more integrated with higher-wage economies in the industrialised world, there is a downward pressure on the latter. That pressure is giving rise to acute tensions and a reaction against globalisation among those affected.

The Swingline office-stapler company illustrates why trade has become such a politically contentious issue in industrialised countries. For more than forty years, it was one of the main employers in the Queens district of New York. Today, Swingline continues to supply offices across the USA, but operates not from New York, but from a factory located on a desert hillside outside the border town of Nogales in northern Mexico. All the factory's raw materials come from the USA, and everything that is produced gets sent back across the border. The only thing that has been transferred is the employment (Macarthur 2001).

Swingline provides a microcosm of a process that is transforming the lives of communities in rich and poor countries alike. Through foreign investment, the company has been able to transfer technology that was once worked on by US employees to a country with average wages less than 12 per cent of those in the USA. When garments from India or Bangladesh enter consumer markets in industrialised countries, they embody labour rates of $0.25-$0.50 per hour. Even allowing for productivity differences and transport costs, these are very large wage gaps. In the case of Mexico, where productivity differs much less from that of the USA, average wages are one-tenth of those in the USA. These wage gaps have obvious implications for workers in industries competing against imports.

One survey by the US-based Institute for International Economics (IIE), covering the two decades to the end of the 1990s, estimated that around 6.4 million US jobs were lost in industries facing import competition (Kletzer 2001). Among the sectors most affected were garments, electrical equipment, and auto-parts. Women workers made up a disproportionate share of displaced workers, reflecting the concentration of female employment in low-wage, labour-intensive sectors. Economists point to the high level of employment creation that took place in the USA during the 1990s as a factor that mitigated the social costs of integration. However, only one-third of those who lost their jobs as a result of import competition were re-employed at equivalent or higher wage levels. When Thompson Consumer Electronics transferred its factory from Bloomington, Indiana, to Mexico in the early 1990s, 1200 jobs were lost. A subsequent survey by the US Department of Labor one year later found that only eight per cent of the workers had been re-employed at equivalent or higher wage levels (Brandon 1998).

Global integration through trade in industrialised countries has been accompanied by increased income inequalities. In the USA, the wages of unskilled workers fell by 20 per cent in real terms between the mid-1970s and 1998. Despite rapid overall economic growth, survival in the lower depths of the American economy has become increasingly difficult. Absolute deprivation has reached distressing levels. In the UK, the number of households living on below-average income tripled to 14 million over the same period, reflecting the contrasting experiences of rich and poor (DSS 2000).

Some see trade with developing countries as the main culprit for these inequalities. That assessment is wide of the mark. Imports from developing countries represent a small proportion of GDP in industrialised countries, and probably account for no more than one-fifth of widening wage inequalities (Burtless 1998). Technological change in favour of workers with higher levels of education and skills has been more important. Even so, the adjustment costs associated with trade are borne disproportionately by the poor. One survey of UK garment manufacturers found that almost half the companies covered were sub-contracting work to home-workers, in response to competitive pressures. More than three-quarters of the home-workers interviewed in the study were being paid less than the national minimum wage (National Group on Homeworking et al. 2000). As in developing countries, the vast majority of home-workers in the UK are women.

Trade and environmental sustainability

Environmental standards are at the centre of debates about trade. International issues, such as global warming and ozone depletion, tend to attract most attention. However, export production has powerful effects at a community level. Rapid increases in export production can generate large amounts of foreign exchange in the short term, while causing long-term environmental degradation, exacerbating poverty, and reducing prospects for economic growth in the future. As Chapter 7 will argue, the lethal interaction of heavy foreign investment in extractive industries with weak governance and civil conflict has had devastating consequences for sub-Saharan Africa. More generally, factoring in environmental sustainability can often change the balance sheet of winners and losers.

Nowhere is this more evident than in the fisheries sector. This is a global problem, with more than 40 per cent of stocks now being fished to their biological limits (UNEP 2000a). Having mined their own coastal waters to exhaustion, industrialised countries are now subsidising their fleets to extract fish from the coastal waters of developing countries. Fishery subsidies directed towards commercial fleets now amount to $20bn annually (Boyer 2001). These subsidies are helping to annex a resource that provides a vital source of protein and income to poor communities in developing countries.

The case of Senegal demonstrates the problem. Under a fisheries agreement with the European Union, the country's government has granted concessions to foreign boats fishing in its coastal waters. This is an important source of revenue for government, but a cause of poverty for local communities. Vast numbers of fish are caught by Spanish trawlers, many of them belonging to Europe's largest fishing fleet, owned by the Pescanova corporation. The huge drag-nets used by European fleets are reducing the number of fish that swim into near-shore areas, and breeding stocks are diminishing. The livelihoods of Senegal's 47,000 artisanal fishermen are under threat (ENDA 2001). The size of catches has been falling, and fisherfolk have been forced to go farther out to sea. The supply of fish to local markets has also been falling, reducing access to an essential source of nutrition (Dahou 2000).

Weak governance can exacerbate tensions between export success and environmental sustainability. While countries might 'win' foreign exchange through export growth, large numbers of people can lose their livelihoods. In Cambodia, Oxfam is working with local communities whose livelihoods are being destroyed through export-led deforestation. Over the past twenty years, commercial logging has contributed to the loss of nearly half of Cambodia's forests. Much of the export trade has been illegal, with Vietnamese companies exploiting weak, often corrupt, local political structures to gain access to one of the country's richest resources. In 1997, the Cambodian government received $12m from the licensing of logging activity. An estimated $185m worth of timber was illegally felled in the same year. Much of the wood was transported to Vietnam, where it was made into furniture for export to German and Danish retail outlets, often with fake 'environment-friendly' labels (Bird 2001).

The costs to local communities have been immense, as Oxfam has discovered in the course of its work with local communities who have been displaced by illegal logging, and whose livelihoods are threatened by the loss of forestry products such as nuts and berries. Wholesale deforestation is directly threatening the Tonle Sap Lake, which is one of the world's most productive inland fisheries and supplies more than 60 per cent of Cambodia's protein needs. The loss of resin trees has been especially damaging. These provide not only income, estimated at up to $500 a year for a resin tapper, but also the resin used by communities in the construction and maintenance of the boats on which their livelihoods depend.

Nothing symbolises the type of export-oriented farming activity that has blossomed under globalisation as much as the cultivation of prawns. Increasing demand in Japan, Europe, and North America has been met by increased production in countries such as Bangladesh, India, and Thailand. Aquaculture has been one of the growth industries of the decade. The foreign-exchange gains have been very large, as has the scale of the environmental damage.

Commercial shrimp farming on a large scale began in the mid-1980s, when it was supported by loans and grants from the World Bank and other donors, and by tax and export incentives from government. Today, shrimp exports generate about $320m annually, almost one-tenth of Bangladesh's total foreign-exchange earnings. Production is located across a belt between Chittagong and Khulna in the south of the country, with an estimated 145,000 hectares under cultivation on 9000 commercial farms (UNEP 1999). Few of the poorest farmers are involved in production, because of the high capital costs involved. In fact, many have lost out in a very direct sense. Land shortages have resulted in commercial farmers violently evicting small producers from their land. The immediate social costs have been compounded by long-term environmental damage. Because shrimp farming requires large amounts of saltwater to be channelled into freshwater areas, increased soil salinity has become a major problem. Local communities have also suffered as a result of the destruction of mangrove swamps, loss of freshwater fish stocks, reduced crop productivity, and a reduction in grazing land (UNEP 1999).

Even in narrowly defined economic terms, these losses have been high. According to one estimate, the economic damage is equivalent to around one-quarter of the value of exports. For Bangladesh as whole, the export earnings misrepresent the gains involved. They obscure the forces that determine how the costs and the benefits are distributed, and, by extension, who wins and who loses from export activity. Commercial farms capture almost all the profit, with government gaining some tax revenue. The most vulnerable social groups absorb the losses. For them, export 'success' has meant lower productivity and diminished access to common resources.

Badly managed export expansion is one source of environmental damage; badly managed import liberalisation is another. In 1998, Oxfam and the World Wide Fund for Nature (WWF) carried out a joint research programme in Mexico, investigating the effects of increased maize imports on the environment. Most economists argued that these imports were good for the poor, since they were reducing the costs of food. The Oxfam–WWF research found that this perspective was ignoring an important side-effect: namely, imports were also reducing prices for Mexican corn farmers (Nadal 2000).

Poor households were responding by adopting two strategies. First, they were bringing more marginal lands into cultivation, attempting to offset falling prices by expanding the volume of production in an effort to maintain household income. Second, many were seeking more off-farm employment, to compensate for the declining value of maize production, either through migration or through work on commercial farms. The overall effect was to increase the amount of ecologically fragile land in cultivation. At the same time, male migration was reducing the capacity available to carry out the labour-intensive conservation techniques needed on steep hillside farms, while also increasing the burden on women. Both outcomes had profoundly damaging implications for the livelihoods of the poor.

From local to global

At a local level, the livelihoods of the poor are directly threatened by environmental degradation. As shown above, some of those threats are a consequence of unsustainable policies linked to international trade. Other problems are inherently global in nature, though with potentially severe local consequences.

Atmospheric concentrations of greenhouse gases are increasing global temperatures at a rate that may be historically unprecedented. Projections suggest that temperatures could rise by as much as 3 degrees C by 2100 (Boyer 2001). Global warming will raise sea levels, increase the frequency of extreme climatic events, disrupt rainfall, and threaten water supplies. The resulting environmental damage will mainly affect developing countries, partly for reasons of geography, and partly because the governments of these countries lack the financial resources to respond to the problems that will emerge. The livelihoods of many millions of poor people are directly at risk.

Global warming is unambiguously a problem that originates in the consumption and energy patterns of rich countries. On a per capita basis, emissions of carbon dioxide are almost 20 times higher in the USA than in India. Industrialised countries as a group account for an estimated 60 per cent of all greenhouse-gas emissions. Yet rich countries in general, and the USA in particular, have failed to develop a strategy for reducing global warming on anything like the scale required. There are options available. Taxes on carbon and international air transport, allied to more pro-active support for alternative sources of energy, could sharply reduce emissions of greenhouse gases, without adverse consequences for economic growth and employment. The failure of the Kyoto Protocol negotiations to address the challenge provides a stark illustration of the need to support global economic integration with a commitment to manage threats to the environment through multilateral action.

CHAPTER 4
Market access and agricultural trade: the double standards of rich countries

Trade can provide a powerful engine for economic growth and poverty reduction. For that engine to function, poor countries need access to rich-country markets. Expanding market access can help countries to accelerate economic growth, while at the same time creating new opportunities for the poor. This is especially so for agricultural products and labour-intensive goods, since the livelihoods of so many people living below the poverty line are concentrated in these sectors.

Unfortunately, trade liberalisation under globalisation works against the interests of the poor. As Chapter 5 explains, developing countries have been rapidly liberalising imports, while rich countries, despite the free-market rhetoric of their governments, have remained fiercely protectionist in their approach to developing-country exports. These protectionist policies are one of the reasons why integration into world markets is not delivering its full benefits to poor countries. Tariff and non-tariff barriers penalise developing countries in precisely the areas where they have a strong comparative advantage. Poor countries seeking access to Northern markets for manufactured goods face trade barriers four times higher on average than rich-country competitors.

Reducing trade barriers in rich countries will not automatically increase the world market shares of developing countries. Many producers – especially in low-income countries – lack the infrastructure, skills, and capacity to take advantage of market opportunities. However, when market opening is combined with measures to develop supply capacity, major benefits are possible. Lacking access to land, credit, and market information, and facing high transport costs, the rural poor are the last to benefit from the opportunities created by trade. That is why developing-country governments have a responsibility to implement rural development programmes that redistribute opportunities to the poor and address the particular barriers faced by women.

The first section of this chapter documents the extent of protection imposed by high-income countries. It does so by using a Double Standards Index (DSI) – a measure of the gap between free-market principle and protectionist practice. The DSI measures a wide range of tariff and non-tariff barriers. Ranked on a simple scale, the European Union tops the DSI, although its performance is rivalled by the United States, with Canada and Japan coming close behind.

The second section considers textiles and garments, which remain the most important labour-intensive manufactured export for the developing world. Production for export has created millions of jobs, especially for women. However, restrictions on exports mean lower wages, worse employment conditions, and unemployment. As in agriculture, rich countries have pledged to phase out import restrictions in textiles and garments, but they are far behind schedule.

The third section focuses on agriculture. Trade in this area is vital for poverty reduction, since more than two-thirds of the developing world's poor live in rural areas. Also, women account for the majority of agricultural producers worldwide. International markets can provide an important source of demand for developing-country exporters, supporting livelihoods and stimulating the rural economy. Northern protectionism undermines that demand and destabilises local markets. Having pledged to cut farm subsidies, rich-country governments have increased them to record levels. As a result, developing-country producers are losing global markets and facing ruinous competition from subsidised exports in local markets. Using a new indicator to measure the gap between production costs and export prices – the Export Dumping Estimate – we highlight the extent of unfair competition between large-scale Northern agriculture and developing-country agriculture. The chapter ends by setting out an agenda for reform.

The costs of Northern protection

Trade barriers in rich countries inflict real costs on poor people in poor countries. Some of the world's most vulnerable communities are being denied an opportunity to reap the potential benefits of integration into global markets. Poor people in general and women in particular bear the brunt, since it is they who produce the goods most affected by import barriers: agricultural and labour-intensive manufactured products. Agriculture accounts for 62 per cent of women's employment in developing countries, and women make up 70 per cent of workers in export-processing zones (Chen et al. 1999).

The financial losses associated with import restrictions in rich countries outweigh the benefits of aid. Import tariffs, the least significant weapon in the protectionist arsenals of rich countries, cost developing countries around $43bn a year (Anderson et al. 2001). The total costs of all forms of trade barriers – including tariffs, non-tariff barriers, anti-dumping measures, and product standards – are more than double this amount, rising to over US$100bn, or more than double the total sum of development assistance.

Such figures understate the real impact on the poor. They do not capture the costs of protectionism in terms of reduced opportunities for employment, reduced income for essential goods such as food and health care, or the long-term economic losses associated with restricted opportunities for investment. Nor do they capture the disproportionate impact on very poor households. Because Northern governments impose the most punitive import restrictions on goods produced by the poor, they systematically diminish the potential for trade to act as a catalyst for poverty reduction.

In the agriculture sector, where two-thirds of the poor in developing countries live and work, industrialised countries' policies (including tariffs and subsidies) cause annual welfare losses of $20bn for developing countries, or 40 per cent of the value of aid flows (World Bank 2001d). Labour-intensive manufactured goods face equally intense discrimination. Losses incurred by exporters of textiles and garments alone amount to more than $30bn. This is the main source of foreign-exchange earnings for a large group of poor countries, as well as a source of employment for millions of vulnerable women workers.

Improvements to market access in these labour-intensive sectors therefore have the potential to increase equity for women. Since women tend to spend more of their income than men on the welfare of children and families, the benefits of improved market access are likely to be widely dispersed through society. Apart from causing unemployment, uncertainties caused by restrictive market-access policies can push employers to try to reduce labour costs by lowering standards and using increasingly flexible labour arrangements, which damages workers' rights.[1]

Since the Uruguay Round of world trade talks, industrialised countries have been gradually reducing their trade barriers. However, there are worrying signs of a protectionist resurgence, especially in the USA. The recent proposal by the US International Trade Commission (ITC) to raise tariffs against steel imports to 40 per cent in order to protect the ailing US steel industry is just one example of the double standards that rich countries employ to protect their own commercial interests. If implemented, the ITC proposal would affect a number of developing countries which export steel to the United States, including Mexico, Brazil, South Africa, and Argentina, many of which have already faced US anti-dumping restrictions against their steel exports.

Northern trade barriers are especially damaging because most developing-country exports are directed towards industrialised-country markets. In 2000, more than 50 per cent of Asia's exports, 75 per cent of Latin America's exports, and 70 per cent of Africa's exports of merchandise goods were destined for Western Europe, North America, or Japan (WTO 2001a). However, developing countries also apply trade barriers against each other. These restrict the development of South–South trade, undermining a potential source of economic dynamism and employment creation.

Improving market access for exports from poor countries is vital, but will not alone be sufficient to make a positive impact on employment and livelihood opportunities. Infrastructure, skills, and productive assets are also essential, if poor people are to benefit. Increased development assistance is also required, targeted to address supply constraints in poorer countries; this should be complemented by national development strategies to help poor people to take advantage of new market opportunities on beneficial terms.

Table 4.1

The Oxfam Double

Free trade rhetoric versus protectionist practice in rich countries: ten indicators of trade barriers facing poor countries in the European Union, the United States, Canada and Japan.[2]

	Percentage share of imports from developing countries (non-LDCs) subject to tariffs over 15%	Percentage share of imports from LDCs subject to tariffs over 15%	Average MFN tariff rates applied to products subject to tariff peaks over 15%	Highest tariff peak 1999 (percentage)	Producer Support Estimate (PSE) as a % of farm income, 1998 – 2000
EU	4.9	2.8	40.3	252 (meat products)	40
US	6.6	15.0	20.8	121 (groundnuts)	23
CANADA	4.8	30.2	30.5	120 (meat products)	18
JAPAN	2.8	2.6	27.8	170 (raw cane sugar)	63

Figure 4.1
Oxfam awards for double standards in trade policy

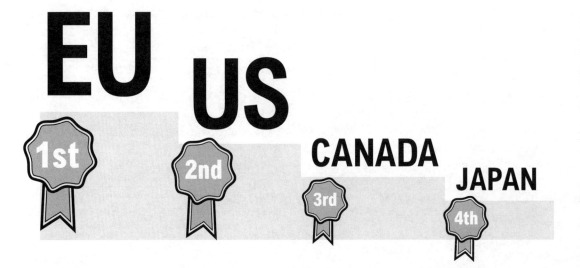

Standards Index

Extent of tariff escalation on agricultural products post-UR (average tariff on processed products as a multiple of average tariff on unprocessed products)	Average agricultural tariff – simple average post-UR bound rate	MFA phase-out: % restrained imports liberalised by 2002 compared to ATC target	Average tariff on textiles and clothing. Simple average post-UR bound rate	Number of antidumping investigations initiated against developing countries 1 July 1995 – 30 June 2000	Overall ranking based on protectionist policies[3]
2.75	20.0	24	7.9	145	1
1.25	9.0	23	8.9	89	2
3.00	8.8	not available	12.4	22	3
3.75	29.7	–	6.8	0	4

MOST PROTECTIONIST

LEAST PROTECTIONIST

The Double Standards Index

One of the problems with assessing trade barriers is that they assume so many different shapes and sizes. This makes it difficult to compare the damage inflicted on developing countries by individual industrialised countries, whose policy makers are adept at arguing that problems in one area are counterbalanced by generosity in another. In an effort to develop a comprehensive comparative indicator, Oxfam has produced a '**Double Standards Index**' (DSI). Reduced to its essentials, this compares the level of protectionist trade policies employed by the richest and most powerful trading nations against exports from developing countries. We refer to it as a Double Standards Index because it highlights the gap between free-trade principle and protectionist practice. The Index ranks the four major industrialised-country (or 'Quad') markets on ten indicators. These range from standard measurements of tariffs (including the average tariff rates applied to developing countries), the extent of tariff peaks in excess of 15 per cent, tariff escalation, agricultural subsidies, the pace at which restrictions on textile imports are being phased out, and anti-dumping actions.

Figure 4.2
Unequal treatment: average tariffs imposed by high-income countries on labour-intensive manufactured goods and agricultural goods from developing countries

Source: Finger and Schuknecht 1999

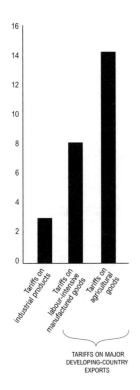

TARIFFS ON MAJOR
DEVELOPING-COUNTRY
EXPORTS

Figure 4.2 provides a simplified summary of the DSI. It shows that developing-country exports of agricultural and labour-intensive manufactured products face far higher barriers when they enter the major Northern markets than do industrial products, which are primarily exported by industrialised countries. The poorest countries face the highest barriers. Industrialised countries apply tariffs four times higher on imports of manufactured goods from developing countries than they apply to manufactured goods imported from other industrialised countries.

The more detailed results of the DSI review are summarised in Table 4.1. Among the most striking findings to emerge are the following:

- 30 per cent of Canadian imports and 15 per cent of EU imports from the least-developed countries face peak tariffs (in excess of 15 per cent).

- The average tariff on these 'tariff peak' items ranges from a low of 21 per cent for the USA to 40 per cent for the EU.

- Agricultural subsidies account for one-quarter of farm output in the USA, rising to 40 per cent in the EU and over 60 per cent in Japan.

- Average tariffs on processed agricultural products exported to Japan and Canada are more than three times higher than those facing unprocessed agricultural products.

- Average agricultural tariffs are close to 10 per cent in Canada and the USA, rising to more than 20 per cent in the EU and Japan.

- The EU and USA have eliminated only one-quarter of the textiles and clothing import-quota restrictions that they are committed to remove under the WTO Agreement on Textiles and Clothing.

- Between them, the USA and EU launched 234 anti-dumping cases against developing countries in the five years following the end of the Uruguay Round.

Taken individually, each of the trade restrictions considered in the DSI is deeply damaging to developing countries. Considered collectively, they help to explain why developing countries have been unable to increase their share of world trade, and why the links between international trade and poverty reduction are so weak. While no industrialised countries meet the criteria for providing a fair deal to poor countries, some are more unfair than others. The EU is the worst offender by a small margin, with the USA close behind.

The costs of Northern protectionism can be illustrated through economic models that predict the potential gains from import liberalisation. One such model shows that moving to full import liberalisation by the industrialised countries between 2000 and 2005 would generate gains of the following order (Anderson et al. 2001):

- more than $3bn each for India, China, and Brazil

- more than $14bn for Latin America

- more than $2bn for sub-Saharan Africa

- more than $600m for Indonesia

Large as they are, even these figures understate the potential gains from reduced trade barriers. This is because they do not take into account the dynamic effects on investment and innovation that market opportunities could generate. In the case of Brazil, one survey, covering just nine product groups, estimated potential trade gains of $831m from the removal of US trade barriers.[4]

Trade barriers in industrialised countries weigh most heavily on the poorest countries. The 48 least-developed countries (LDCs) face tariffs on average 20 per cent higher than the rest of the world on their exports to industrialised countries. This rises to 30 per cent higher for manufacturing exports (IMF and World Bank 2001a). LDCs are losing an estimated $2.5bn a year in potential export earnings as a result of the high levels of tariff protection in Canada, the EU, Japan, and the United States.

The losses in LDC export earnings resulting from industrialised-country protectionism offset the benefits of aid flows to these countries. In 1999, the Quad countries provided LDCs with almost $10bn in aid. But for every $4 of aid, the same countries took back $1 through the imposition of trade restrictions on LDC exports. This incoherence between industrialised-country trade and development policies can sometimes reach absurd proportions: trade restrictions in Canada cost LDCs approximately $1.6bn in lost export revenue, which is around five times the level of Canadian aid flows to the LDCs (Oxfam International 2001a).

Improved market-access opportunities could help to reverse the relentless marginalisation of LDCs in international trade. Providing tariff-free and quota-free access for all products exported from LDCs currently facing tariff peaks in these countries would generate an 11 per cent increase in total LDC exports (Hoekman et al. 2001). These gains would derive from increased LDC textiles and clothing exports to the USA and Canada. LDC agricultural exporters would also gain from improved access to the EU and Japan, especially for sugar and some cereals. The costs for other developing countries would be minimal, amounting to less than 0.1 per cent of their total exports. For industrialised countries, free market access would generate gains for consumers and minimal costs for producers. In contrast, the increase in total LDC exports would translate into important livelihood and employment opportunities for people living in poverty, as well as increased revenue for impoverished governments.

Despite the modest adjustment costs of improved market access and repeated pledges of action from Northern governments, little has so far been achieved. Industrialised countries have repeatedly committed themselves to provide free access for all exports from the world's poorest countries. Yet the vast majority of their initiatives to date have excluded key products of export interest to LDCs. Only New Zealand has fully opened its markets to all products exported by the LDCs.

Protectionist pressure orchestrated by politically powerful lobbies is one factor that impedes the development of market-access opportunities. The EU's 2001 'Everything But Arms' (EBA) initiative was originally intended to provide immediate free market access for all non-military exports from LDCs. However, following a concerted campaign by European producers and traditional Caribbean exporters, who feared that they would lose market share to LDC exporters, the proposal was modified so that free LDC market access for three important products (rice, sugar, and bananas) will be delayed for up to eight years.

With the introduction of EBA, some LDCs have gained export opportunities. For example, having been excluded from the EU market for sugar, Mozambique now has some (quota-limited) access to the EU over the eight-year transition period to 2009. This is expected to provide a new export market for several thousand tonnes of

Mozambique's sugar per year, which is expected to create 8000 new jobs in the sugar mills and plantations. The jobs will benefit poor people living in rural areas where there are few alternative employment opportunities, and help to stimulate the wider rural economy (Hazeleger 2001, Hanlon 2001). However, the benefits of unrestricted access would have been far greater.

All too often, the small print of ostensibly generous trade concessions limits the scope to improve export performance in developing countries. The US Africa Growth and Opportunity Act (AGOA) provides free market access for selected products exported from the 39 African LDCs. However, only 'non-sensitive' products qualify, and these face strict conditions, for example the required use of US fabrics and yarns in African textile and garment exports. Further, African countries seeking eligibility to export under the AGOA face extensive conditions, such as opening their markets to US trade and investment, and implementing market-based economic reforms.

The barriers facing developing countries

The DSI demonstrates the range of trade barriers confronting developing countries. But because it captures only broad averages, it understates both the scale of Northern protection and the implied costs for developing countries. Among the highest barriers are tariffs, tariff escalation, non-tariff barriers, product standards, and anti-dumping actions.

Tariffs

Tariffs are taxes on imports of products into a country. Because they increase the price of imported goods on the domestic market, they protect domestic producers of the same or similar goods (and their suppliers) from foreign competition. Tariffs also provide revenue for the government.

Industrialised countries reduced their average level of tariff protection from around ten per cent in the early 1980s to five per cent in 1999. However, tariffs far higher than the average rates are imposed on products of particular export interest to developing countries, in particular on staple food products, tobacco, some beverages, fruit and vegetables, food-industry products, including fruit juices and canned meat, and textiles, clothing, and footwear (World Bank 2001b). These so-called tariff peaks can exceed 100 per cent, even more. The EU applies a 250 per cent tariff on imported meat products, and the USA and Canada impose import tariffs exceeding 120 per cent on groundnuts and meat products respectively. Leather shoes exported to Japan face standard import tariffs as high as 160 per cent, with only very limited quantities of exports from developing countries allowed entry at half this tariff rate.

Tariff escalation

Escalating tariffs that rise with the level of processing undergone are especially damaging. They act as a disincentive to investment aimed at adding value locally, while at the same time discouraging diversification. This leaves many developing countries locked into volatile primary-commodity markets, characterised by low and deteriorating world prices. As we saw in Chapter 3, this is an almost guaranteed route to marginalisation in world trade. The removal of escalating tariffs would enable developing countries to capture locally a larger share of the final value of export earnings, in turn generating local employment and investment opportunities.

The processed-food sector is particularly affected by tariff escalation. Fully processed, manufactured food products are subject in the EU and Japan to tariffs twice as high as products in the first stage of processing. In Canada, tariffs on processed food are as much as 13 times higher than those on unprocessed products. Thirty per cent of all peak tariffs applied by the EU protect the food industry. These tariffs range from 12 to 100 per cent, affecting sugar-based products, cereals, and canned fruit. The situation is similar in the USA, where the food industry accounts for one-sixth of all peak tariffs, including orange juice (30 per cent) and peanut butter (132 per cent). Forty per cent of all Japanese peak tariffs protect the food industry, affecting a wide range of products from cocoa powder and chocolate to canned meat and fruit juices (UNCTAD 2000a).

Although food processing is a key export industry in many developing countries, most of their exports are concentrated in the first, relatively low-value, stage of processing. More advanced processed-food products account for a mere five per cent of LDC agricultural exports, and for only 17 per cent of those of all developing countries. In contrast, high-value processed-food products constitute 32.5 per cent of the agricultural exports of industrialised countries (ibid.).

Non-tariff barriers

Non-tariff barriers (NTBs) are frequently a more significant obstacle to developing-country exports than tariffs, which are falling. NTBs include quantitative restrictions such as import quotas, seasonal import restrictions, rules of origin (see the section headed 'Improving market access in the EU and USA'), and a wide range of product standards. NTBs can be just as effective as tariffs in restricting exports from developing countries, and are less transparent. The true level of protection afforded to European industry, for example, rises from 5.1 per cent if tariffs alone are included, to 9 per cent if both tariff and non-tariff barriers are taken into account (Messerlin 2001).

Consumer boycotts can act as effective unofficial non-tariff barriers, with devastating effects on developing-country trade. For example, the US pressure group People for the Ethical Treatment of Animals (PETA) campaigns against the use of leather produced from Indian cowhides, on grounds of animal cruelty. The resulting ban on the use of Indian leather in products imported by major European and US companies, including Gap, Marks and Spencer, and Clarks, has resulted in a seven per cent reduction in Indian leather exports, with consequent negative effects on the livelihoods of the 2.5 million people employed in the sector.

Product standards

When developing countries export to industrialised countries, they have to meet rigorous health and safety standards, especially applied to agricultural produce. Most of these standards genuinely aim to protect public health. However, the rules can be applied in a way that undermines the ability of developing countries to take advantage of export opportunities, and leaves them locked out of important markets. A recent World Bank study (Otsuki et al. 2001) showed that implementation of new EU standards to protect consumers against aflatoxin (a naturally occurring carcinogen) will cost African exporters of nuts, cereals, and dried fruits $670m a year, without generating significant health benefits.

Product standards create problems for developing countries, because they often lack the capacity to comply. The legislation that governs standards can be complex and requires detailed legal and scientific knowledge to interpret it. Product standards can cover matters ranging from packaging requirements to permitted additives, food hygiene and processing standards to pesticide residues. Monitoring and enforcing compliance with these standards requires a level of scientific and technical expertise not often available

Box 4.1

EU blocks exports of Indian bed linen

In August 2001, a WTO ruling found that EU anti-dumping duties that had been imposed on imports of bed linen from India since 1997 had been unjustified. As a result, the duties were suspended, but they have had a devastating impact on Indian companies and their workers.

Anglo-French Textiles was one of the companies affected by the EU anti-dumping action. The company is based in the southern Indian city of Pondicherry, a French outpost until 1954. Pondicherry has a population of approximately 400,000, and is ranked seventh in India in the production of cotton cloth. In 1997, Anglo-French Textiles employed 6000 people; 30,000 more were estimated to benefit indirectly, either by supplying services or other inputs to the factory, or because family members worked there.

The UK was the main market for Anglo-French Textiles, which supplied bed linen for use in the National Health Service and hotel industry. Following the imposition of EU anti-dumping duties as high as 25 per cent against its bed-linen exports, Anglo-French was unable to continue exporting to the UK. As a result, the company's turnover fell by more than 60 per cent between 1997 and 2000, from $11 million to $4 million. The company has shed more than 1000 jobs over the same period, as a result of closing a number of stitching units, introducing a voluntary redundancy scheme, and imposing a freeze on recruitment. This has meant the loss of employment opportunities for potential workers, and an overall negative economic impact on the city of Pondicherry, where Anglo-French Textiles is the biggest industry and employer.

Since the suspension of the EU's anti-dumping measures in August 2001, Anglo-French Textiles has begun to try re-building its share of the UK market. However, the company's management expects that it will take at least two years to re-gain the same level of European orders as before the anti-dumping action. There is no provision under WTO rules for companies affected in this way to seek compensation for the losses they incurred.

(Source: private communication with Anglo-French Textiles export manager)

in poorer countries. Meeting standards is not cheap: the costs of complying with legislative requirements, including testing and certification, can be as high as ten per cent of the overall product cost for some agricultural goods (DFID 2001). Even industrialised-country exporters often find it difficult to meet stringently applied standards. For example, US fresh-fruit exporters have frequently complained that the EU applies product rules in the most rigorous possible manner, effectively using them as a non-tariff barrier (BER 2001).

In some cases, product standards have an overtly protectionist outcome, whether by design or intent. Consider the case of Vietnamese catfish. In recent years, fish farmers in Vietnam have earned a decent living from increasing exports of this product to the USA. However, in November 2001, a US catfish-industry campaign persuaded Congress to change the definition of a catfish to exclude the Vietnamese species, in spite of a US Department of Agriculture ruling that there are no scientific grounds for this decision. This dubious restriction threatens the livelihoods of 15,000 Vietnamese families who had invested their life savings in buying the floating cages needed for production.

Product standards severely damage livelihoods. Fair-trade organisations seeking to promote small-scale programmes for producing honey in Africa have seen their efforts undermined by stringent EU conditions on the monitoring of pesticide residues. In some cases, precautionary action is taken to extremes. In 1997 the EU responded to a cholera outbreak in East Africa by imposing a ban on fish imports from any country in the region, without first investigating the potential dangers involved. Following intervention from the World Health Organisation, which pointed out that fish were an unlikely means of transmitting cholera, the ban was rescinded. Unfortunately, a great deal of damage had already been done. Exports of fish from Kenya to the EU fell by one-third, undermining the livelihoods of Kenya's 40,000 fishermen and their families, as well as the wider fish-processing and related industries.

Anti-dumping measures

The WTO anti-dumping agreement allows member countries to protect themselves against unfair competition from 'dumped' products. In broad terms, it aims to prevent countries and firms from gaining an unfair advantage by selling products at artificially low prices, for instance through subsidies. Unfortunately, the agreement itself is sufficiently vague to allow countries to initiate anti-dumping actions even on the most spurious grounds, and developing countries have been prime targets.

Dumping is defined as the sale overseas of a product at prices lower than those on the domestic market of the exporting country. The WTO agreement allows members to respond to dumping by imposing fines, or anti-dumping duties, which increase the price of the imports relative to domestic prices. Investigations are typically initiated following complaints by firms or industrial bodies affected. Anti-dumping duties can be imposed for up to five years. Since the new WTO agreement was signed in 1995, the EU and USA have initiated 234 anti-dumping actions against developing countries. Although some of the larger developing countries, such as Argentina and Brazil, have also started to use anti-dumping actions, many others are the targets of actions by industrialised countries. Preliminary data from 2001 suggest that rich countries are once more increasing their anti-dumping activity, with the USA and Canada initiating high numbers of cases in the first six months of the year (WTO 2001c).

The USA has developed some of the most imaginative strategies for abusing the letter and the spirit of the WTO's anti-dumping provisions. Under legislation known as the Byrd amendment, customs authorities are mandated to collect anti-dumping duties, and then transfer them to US firms alleging damage – in effect providing them with a subsidy. This practice is the subject of a WTO dispute following complaints from nine countries – including Brazil, Thailand, India, and Indonesia – that have been adversely affected.

As globalisation and technological change intensify the competitive pressures on industries, anti-dumping actions provide a quick-fix solution for those with political influence. Lacking retaliatory capacity, developing countries are often a preferred target. For example, the US steel industry has targeted rolled carbon steel from Brazil for anti-dumping actions, even though it accounts for less than one per cent of the US market.

The procedure for establishing that dumping has taken place is complex and costly, and therefore many developing countries have difficulty in challenging anti-dumping measures imposed by industrialised countries. Yet the impact of anti-dumping duties on a developing-country exporter can be devastating: the quantity of exports and production will drop, very often resulting in job losses in the company (see Box 4.1).

There can be knock-on effects in the wider economy, affecting suppliers of the company in question. And the future of the exporting company can be uncertain, affecting investment, the expansion of production, and future exports.

South–South trade and 'open regionalism'

Protectionism by high-income countries is especially damaging to developing countries for some obvious reasons: most developing-country exports are directed towards the industrialised world and, by definition, rich countries have higher levels of purchasing power. However, developing countries also face problems when they trade with each other. South–South trade has increased over the past two decades. It accounted for 40 per cent of developing-country exports in 1999, compared with 26 per cent in 1980. But the growth of trade links between developing countries has been constrained by import restrictions. The average tariff applied by developing countries to other developing countries' exports of manufactures is more than three times higher than the average tariffs imposed by rich countries. Developing-country tariffs on agricultural exports from other developing countries are also higher (World Bank, 2001b).

Regional trade arrangements provide one possible route to closer trade links, but regionalisation takes a variety of forms – not all of which are favourable for the developing world. At one level, talk of a global economy is exaggerated. An increasing share of economic activity takes place within regions and under rules stipulated in regional trade agreements (RTAs). The dominant view is that 'open regionalism', or regional agreements that extend free trade, is good for globalisation and good for poor countries. That view is wrong: open regionalism is almost a contradiction in terms, since regional trade preference implies discrimination. More importantly, regionalism is having an enormous influence on market access and the distribution of benefits from trade.

RTAs are systems of trade preferences in which members share with each other advantages that they withhold from others, except on a negotiated basis. More than two-thirds of the European Union's merchandise trade is conducted on an 'in-house' preferential basis. The USA, Canada, and Mexico – the members of the North America Free Trade Agreement (NAFTA) – also trade mainly with each other. Over half of their exports and nearly half of their imports are traded on an intra-NAFTA basis.

Developing countries have organised their own regional trade groups. In some cases, these have helped to stimulate intra-regional trade. In Latin America, the four members of Mercosur (Argentina, Brazil, Uruguay, and Paraguay) account for one-fifth of each other's exports. In South-East Asia, ASEAN member countries trade around one-quarter of their exports with other members of the regional trade bloc.[5] There have been moves towards a customs union in West Africa, and RTAs in that region and southern Africa have resulted in increased trade, even though coverage remains limited. RTAs are least developed in South Asia. The South Asian Association for Regional Co-operation, which includes Bangladesh, India, Nepal, and Pakistan, accounts for only four per cent of its members' exports, the same share as at the start of the 1990s.

During the 1990s, the spread of globalisation was accompanied by a proliferation of regional and sub-regional trade agreements. The EU has recently concluded free-trade agreements with Mexico and has launched negotiations with Mercosur. Under the new Cotonou agreement, the EU is linked to 71 poor African, Caribbean, and Pacific (ACP) States. Its vast network of preferences now covers almost every country in the world.

'Open regionalism' has also emerged as a trade-policy priority in the USA. The Bush Administration has given a renewed impetus to plans to extend NAFTA through the Americas, with the aim of concluding a Free Trade Area of the Americas by 2005.

What are the implications of all this for the distribution of benefits from international trade? According to the received wisdom, all countries will gain, since trade liberalisation is assumed to enhance growth. Leaving aside that dubious proposition, the fact remains that some stand to gain far more than others. Consider the case of NAFTA. In 1992, Mexico exported $1bn of textiles and garments to the United States. During the 1990s, this increased to $10 billion. Exports of textiles and garments from Bangladesh and India grew far more slowly, from $2 to $5 billion over the same period. NAFTA may have created trade, but the market has been biased against two of the world's poorest countries in favour of Mexico, with damaging implications for their share of world markets. Bangladesh also stands to be adversely affected by the American Trade and Development Act of 2000, which has extended preferences on textiles to competitors in the Caribbean.

RTAs can become vehicles for protectionism and trade rules that are inherently bad for poor countries, as Chapter 8 will show. As the weakest partners in the world trading system, it is developing countries that are most at risk from protectionist practices. But there are other ways in which RTAs can bias the benefits of trade in favour of rich countries. For example, the EU has negotiated preferential access to the markets of Mexico and South Africa, but neither country enjoys privileged access to the other's market, which gives European exporters an obvious advantage.

Potentially, RTAs could strengthen the position of developing countries in various ways. They can create dynamic growth centres, supporting linkages between firms and producers in developing regions. They can also spread risk, reducing dependence on a small number of Northern markets, and diminish vulnerability to a downturn in those markets. But in their current form, RTAs are helping to increase, rather than reduce, inequalities in world trade.

Textiles and clothing – how not to phase out the Multi-Fibre Arrangement

The textiles and garments sector is the single largest source of manufactured exports from developing countries by value. For many developing countries, the way in which rich countries manage these markets is a measure of their entire approach to trade and development. With considerable justification, the same countries see the Multi-Fibre Arrangement, and the failure of industrialised countries to remove it, as one of the most blatant examples of double standards in international trade.

The Multi-Fibre Arrangement

Since 1974, trade in textiles and clothing has been regulated by the Multi-Fibre Arrangement (MFA). From its inception, the MFA has been a clear departure from the principles underpinning the entire multilateral trading system. It is inherently protectionist in design, and discriminatory in application in that it is targeted against developing countries.

The MFA is essentially a system of quotas restricting the quantity of textiles and clothing products entering the Canadian, EU, Norwegian, and US markets. During the Uruguay Round of world trade talks, industrialised countries agreed to phase it out. The WTO Agreement on Textiles and Clothing (ATC) provides for its removal in four stages between 1995 and 2005. Unfortunately, importing countries have exploited every loophole in the agreement, and a few more, in order to delay liberalisation.

For developing countries, the ATC was a bad agreement which reflected their unequal negotiating strength. The elimination of quotas was 'back-loaded', with quota-free market access for about half of all imports due to enter into force at the very end of the implementation period. Under the ATC, industrialised countries were supposed to remove import quotas from at least 51 per cent of their imports of textiles and clothing products by January 2002. Although the EU and USA will have technically complied with this commitment, they will have removed quotas from only 12 per cent of textile and clothing imports that were previously restrained by import quotas under the MFA. This is because they have prioritised the 'liberalisation' of those categories of products that developing countries hardly export, such as parachutes, and the removal of those import quotas that developing countries have regularly failed to fill.[6] Norway is the only exception, since it has unilaterally removed all quotas over four years.

Contrary to the ATC requirement that WTO members would allow for continuous adjustment and increased competition in their markets, the USA declared at the start of the ATC process that it 'will ensure that integration of the most sensitive products will be deferred until the end of the ten-year period'. Similarly, the EU policy has 'considered it appropriate to retain control over quotas with a view to keeping the possibility of using them as a bargaining chip to obtain better market access in third countries'.[7]

Where Canada, the EU, and the USA have liberalised some products that were previously restrained by import quotas, these tend to be low-value yarns and garments, rather than higher-value clothing products. By January 2002, only 12 per cent of the products liberalised by the USA and Canada will be higher-value clothing products, a proportion which rises to 18 per cent for the EU.[8] Overall, it has been estimated that by 2004, the 11 principal developing-country textile and clothing exporters will still face quota restrictions on more than 80 per cent of their exports to industrialised countries (Spinanger 1999). These delaying tactics will result in a single major adjustment in January 2005, with the removal of all import quotas from around 80 per cent of previously restrained textile and clothing products, rather than the gradual adjustment that was originally envisaged. Developing-country exporters fear that this may trigger increased political resistance to liberalisation in importing industrialised countries, and the imposition of new protectionist measures such as anti-dumping actions, in addition to the already high tariffs.

Another threat from sudden changes in trading rules in textiles and clothing industries is that the costs of adjustment will be borne by women, many of whom are home-workers and therefore overlooked by government authorities. Gender bias at all levels in the labour force devalues flexible employment and women home-workers, and tends to make the livelihood and welfare impacts of such changes invisible to policy makers.[9]

Apart from the immediate injustice of industrialised countries failing to act on their commitments, developing-country exporters will continue to face problems, even after the removal of MFA quotas. Average tariffs on textile and clothing exports will be as high as 12 per cent – three times higher than the overall average tariff rate on industrial goods. A reduction in tariff protection, alongside the MFA phase-out, could lead to a growth in textile and clothing exports for many developing countries, with positive impacts on employment, investment, and poverty reduction.

Winners and losers from the MFA phase-out: the case of Bangladesh

The phase-out of the MFA will create a complicated picture of winners and losers. Developing countries as a group lose from the MFA. However, some have benefited from quotas, since these provide what amounts to a protected market. Managing the phase-out to maximise the gains and minimise the costs is a pressing priority.

No country stands to lose as much as Bangladesh, which developed its garment-export sector on the basis of guaranteed market access to industrialised countries under the MFA quota system, which sheltered its companies from competitors in India and China. Garment exports account for three-quarters of Bangladesh's total exports, having grown from $1m in 1978 to over $4bn in 2000. More than 1.5 million people, most of them women, are employed in the industry. Considerable domestic, as well as foreign, investment has been mobilised, with some companies using hi-tech techniques to produce higher-value products. Despite this, Bangladesh has found it difficult to develop backward linkages, leaving the industry highly dependent on imported inputs (see Chapter 2). This places the country at a disadvantage, compared with competitors which have developed complementary domestic industries.

There are inevitable fears that, following the MFA phase-out, Bangladesh will lose market share in industrialised countries to other exporters, such as India and China. This could leave huge numbers of Bangladeshi women without work, or forced to accept lower wages as the industry tries to reduce its production costs. Few alternative livelihood opportunities are open to them.[10] This would inevitably have an impact on poverty levels in Bangladesh, not only for the women directly affected, but also for their families, who depend on the remittances sent home from the city to pay for food, schooling, and health care.

Improving market access in the EU and the USA[11]

The Bangladeshi government and donors urgently need to turn their attention to the development of an industrial policy that strengthens local industry. At the same time, the EU and USA could do far more to reduce the costs of adjustment by improving the terms on which Bangladeshi products enter their markets. Between them, the EU and the USA account for 70 and 25 per cent respectively of knitted-garment exports, and for 46 and 49 per cent respectively of woven-garment exports.

The biggest problem facing Bangladesh in the US market is continued quota restrictions. More than half way through the implementation period of the ATC, around 70 per cent of textiles and clothing products exported by Bangladesh to the USA continue to face these barriers. Liberalisation of MFA quotas undertaken by the USA in the first two stages of implementing the ATC (in 1995 and 1998) failed to include products of export interest to Bangladesh. The third phase of implementation (due on 1 January 2002) liberalised only two items for which Bangladesh faces quota restrictions: gloves and silk trousers/shorts. This means that 80 per cent of Bangladesh's higher-value clothing exports will remain subject to quota restrictions until the end of the WTO agreement (31 December 2004). Even in the absence of quota restrictions, Bangladeshi garment exports to the USA face extremely high tariff barriers. Tariffs for many products of export interest to Bangladesh are as high as 20 per cent – five times higher than average tariffs in the USA.

The EU provides preferential market access for Bangladesh's garment exports, exempting them from its 12.5 per cent import tariff. Yet stringent rules of origin imposed by the EU inhibit the ability of Bangladesh fully to utilise this advantage. Prior to 1996, knitted garments faced a highly restrictive three-stage transformation requirement to qualify for EU preferential market access: although the original fibre did not have to originate in Bangladesh, the three processes of making fibre into yarn, yarn into knit fabric, and knit fabric into knit garments all had to take place within the country. This meant that Bangladesh's capacity to utilise its preferential access to the EU market was restricted by its limited capacity to produce yarn domestically.

Following requests by Bangladesh for greater flexibility in the rules of origin, and a dispute over its compliance with the rules, an interim arrangement prevailed between 1996 and 1998, under which the rules were relaxed but Bangladesh's garment exports were limited by quota restrictions. In 1999, the EU removed the quota restrictions and relaxed its rules of origin so that Bangladesh's knitted-garment exports made from imported yarn qualified for preferential market access. In 2000, the EU further relaxed its rules of origin by providing preferential access to the countries of the South Asian Association for Regional Cooperation (SAARC) on the basis of 'regional cumulation'. This means that Bangladesh's garment exports may qualify for EU preferential access even if the fabrics used are imported from another SAARC member country, such as India or Pakistan. However, the rules require that the value added in Bangladesh to the final exported product must be higher than the value-added of any imported inputs from any other regional country. Since the local value-added of Bangladesh's garments which use imported fabrics is generally only 25–30 per cent of the total export value, compared with 70–75 per cent of the value arising from the fabric produced in India, the majority of garment exports from Bangladesh fail to qualify for duty-free preferential access to the EU market.

The following measures would assist Bangladesh in preparing itself for increased competition in export markets after the MFA phase-out, and help to protect the jobs of more than one million women workers:

- The removal of all tariff and quota restrictions in the USA.

- The relaxation of EU rules of origin for Bangladesh's exports, to enable them to qualify for preferential (tariff-free) market access. This will require a lowering of the local value-added requirement under regional cumulation.

- The provision of technical and financial assistance to support the government of Bangladesh in developing a competitive garment-export industry, by investing in human resources and gender equity, and by creating backward linkages, for example, to increase domestic capacity to produce textiles and other inputs.

Agricultural trade – dumping on the poor

Agricultural trade and the rules that govern it have an important bearing on poverty. The majority of the world's population surviving on less than $1 a day live in rural areas, most of them working as smallholder farmers. More than two-thirds of women work as agricultural producers. Many poor and small-scale farmers produce primarily for national and regional markets. Their livelihoods depend critically on the functioning of local markets, and on effective national policies that promote rural development

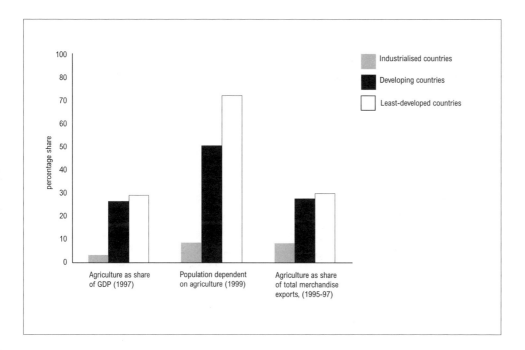

Figure 4.3
Importance of agriculture in terms
of GDP, employment, and exports
for rich and poor countries

Source: OECD, FAO

through the provision of infrastructure and the fair distribution of productive assets
such as land and credit (see Chapter 3). But a significant proportion of farmers in
developing countries produce for export markets, using the income to pay for health
care and education and to purchase essential inputs. International trade rules critically
affect these farmers' livelihoods.

Despite the growth of manufacturing exports from developing countries, agriculture
still accounts for more than one-third of export earnings in around half of all developing
countries. These exports can play an important role in poverty reduction. They generate
income and employment for vulnerable households, creating opportunities that might
not otherwise be available. But it is not only exports that have an impact on poverty. The
terms on which countries import agricultural goods are also important, not least since
this influences local prices.

Many developing countries have an obvious comparative advantage in agriculture, yet
although they have significantly increased their share of world manufacturing trade, the
same has not happened in agriculture. In the 17 years up to 1997, the developing world's
share of world agricultural markets rose by one per cent; it reached only 43 per cent in
1999. Although this share is slowly continuing to increase, industrialised countries
retain a disproportionately large market share, particularly considering their low
dependence on agriculture as a source of economic wealth, employment, and exports.

No sector of world trade is more distorted than agriculture. Global markets are
dominated by industrialised countries, for whom farming represents a negligible
amount of GDP, employment, and export earnings, largely by virtue of heavy subsidies
(Figure 4.3). So producers in developing countries suffer low prices, lost market shares,
and unfair competition in local markets. Reform of agricultural trade is a core
requirement for making international trade work for the poor. Of particular concern are:

- the scale and nature of rich countries' subsidies

- the continued practice of export dumping

- the impact of dumping on developing countries.

The scale of subsidies

Agriculture is by far the most heavily subsidised and protected sector in international trade. In 2000, rich countries subsidised their farmers to the extent of US$245bn. This represents around five times the value of annual aid flows. During the Uruguay Round of world trade talks, rich countries pledged to cut agricultural subsidies. In fact they have done the opposite. Agricultural trade is unique in that it is the only area in which 'liberalisation' has meant an increase in subsidisation, at least in rich countries.

Since 1986-88, overall budgetary outlays for agricultural support in most industrialised countries have actually increased.[12] Subsidies to agriculture take a wide variety of forms. Government intervention in agriculture in both developing and industrialised countries can be important to promote legitimate rural development and environmental objectives. The problem is that the current systems of support in the EU and USA fail to deliver the social and environmental outcomes that they claim to promote, and they have devastating effects on poor farmers in developing countries.

The OECD Producer Support Estimate (PSE) measures the scale of industrialised countries' farm subsidies. Using that indicator, the EU and the USA were spending $9–10bn more at the end of the 1990s than they were a decade earlier, with farm subsidies accounting for 40 per cent and 25 per cent respectively of the total value of production (Figure 4.4). These subsidies have a major bearing on the structure of competition in international markets, and in local food markets in developing countries. Farmers in the poorest nations are competing not just against farmers in the industrialised world, but against the financial power of the world's richest countries. US negotiators in particular like to stress their commitment to 'a level playing field' in agriculture. However, for producers in the developing world, competition is an uphill struggle: millions of smallholder farmers have to survive on less than $400 a year in total income. They are competing against American and European farmers who receive respectively an average of $21,000 and $16,000 a year in subsidies (Figure 4.5).

The sheer scale of Northern subsidisation, and the resulting unfairness of international trade, can be demonstrated by some simple comparisons:

Figure 4.4
Producer Support Estimates
($ millions): EU, US, and Japan
(1986/8 – 1998/2000)

Source: OECD

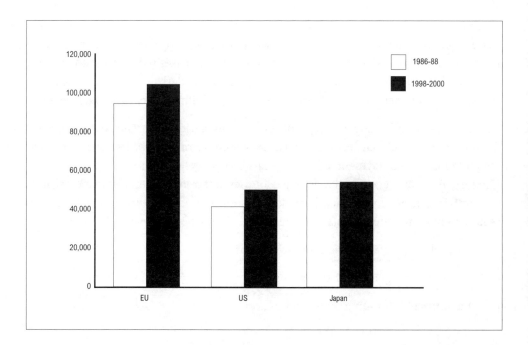

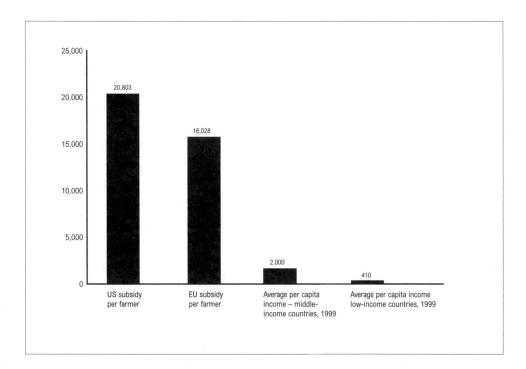

Figure 4.5
Subsidies received by US and EU
farmers (average 1998-2000)
compared with average per capita
incomes in low-income and
middle-income countries in 1999
($)

Sources: OECD and World Bank

- Total OECD agricultural subsidisation exceeds the total income of the 1.2 billion people living below the poverty line.

- The US programme of 'emergency' farm payments exceeds the UN's humanitarian aid budget.

During the Uruguay Round of world trade talks, European and US negotiators reduced the debate on agricultural trade liberalisation to a game of semantics. Having agreed in principle to reduce subsidies, they proceeded to change the definition of a subsidy to allow them to continue on a business-as-usual basis. Two particularly imaginative devices were developed under the colourful headings of 'Blue Box' and 'Green Box'. Under the 'Blue Box' arrangement, countries are allowed to provide unlimited direct income payments to farmers, provided that these are linked to 'production-limiting' programmes. One such programme is called 'set-aside', under which the EU provides income support to farmers, on condition that they remove a certain amount of land from cultivation. 'Green Box' payments include subsidies given for environmental reasons, insurance, and a range of additional measures.

When is a subsidy not a subsidy?

According to the EU, the overall level of support to agriculture matters less than the structure of subsidies. The contention is that industrialised countries have scaled down subsidies that directly encourage production, in favour of subsidies that support farm income. From a developing-country perspective, this is an unconvincing argument, for at least two reasons.

The first is that market-price support and farm payments linked to output remain the major form of producer support in rich countries, accounting for almost three-quarters of payments in 2000 (OECD 2001a).[13] Whatever their convoluted mechanisms, these programmes typically operate in the same way. Governments restrict imports and buy agricultural commodities at prices above world market levels, transferring income to their farmers. They then transfer the same commodities on to world markets, usually with the help of hefty export subsidies, pushing down world prices. Rich countries

113

spend around $7bn a year on export subsidies.

Second, far from being 'non trade-distorting', payments under the multi-coloured box arrangements can have an impact on production decisions, notably by taking the risk out of the market. In the USA, 'emergency payments' ostensibly designed to compensate farmers for losses resulting from weather damage are now provided on an institutionalised basis, regardless of losses. US apple growers receive $100m a year to compensate them for 'market losses', and the American Farm Bureau is pressing for this sum to be raised to $500m. The OECD itself has noted that these payments affect decisions about production, as they send a strong signal to farmers that they can expect to receive extra support at times of low world prices. This affects the international competitiveness of US and EU agricultural production, and the price at which these countries are able to export on world markets.

This is not to argue against the use of carefully targeted policies in the EU and USA that promote legitimate rural development and environmental objectives. But the idea that existing industrialised-country agricultural policies benefit poor and small-scale farmers and are good for the environment is a myth. On the contrary, there is overwhelming evidence that the main beneficiaries of current farm support are the largest farmers and agribusiness companies. In the EU, 17 per cent of farms receive 50 per cent of agricultural support (ABARE 2000). In the USA, the 80 per cent of farms that are small-scale receive only 16 per cent of agricultural support.[14] By concentrating subsidies in the hands of the richest farmers, agricultural policies are hastening the demise of smallholder agriculture.[15]

Apart from providing a highly regressive transfer to high-income farmers, current subsidy patterns, with their emphasis on expanding production, have encouraged the industrialisation of agriculture, with a premium on the heavy use of chemical inputs. Among the most immediate consequences are extensive environmental damage and continual threats to public health. Other environmental consequences include the pollution of lands, rivers, and water reserves as a consequence of the intensified use of fertilisers and run-off from intensive livestock production; land erosion as a result of intensive production; and a reduction in biological and landscape diversity (Fanjul 2001).

The scale of export dumping

The practice of exporting agricultural surpluses on to world markets at less than the cost of production – or 'dumping' – is one of the most pernicious aspects of industrialised-country trade policies, which the WTO has failed adequately to address. Unfair competition from dumped agricultural produce creates problems for developing countries by depriving them of foreign-exchange earnings and market share, and undermining local production, rural livelihoods, and food security.

Debates about definitions and levels of agricultural dumping are even more complex and obscure than those about tariffs. In an attempt to simplify the issue, Oxfam has developed a new indicator, drawing on the principles used in the OECD's measurement of subsidy estimates. The Export Dumping Estimate indicator looks beyond the semantic debate on how to define a subsidy, to assess a more relevant issue: the gap between export prices and costs of production.[16] For some of the major commodities traded on world markets, that gap is very large. The data are summarised in Figure 4.6. Among the main findings:

- The USA and the EU account for around half of all wheat exports. Their export prices are respectively 46 per cent and 34 per cent below costs of production.

- The USA accounts for more than one-half of all maize exports. It exports at prices one-fifth below the costs of production.

- The EU is the world's largest exporter of skimmed-milk powder. It exports at prices representing around one-half of the costs of production.

- The EU is the world's largest exporter of white sugar. Export prices are only one-quarter of production costs.

The dominance of the EU and the USA in world markets means that these dumping margins effectively set world market prices. This is because rival exporters have to follow the export price levels set by EU and the USA, or lose market share. For practical purposes, the world agricultural market is a dumping market in which prices are unrelated to costs of production.

There is no other area of international trade in which it is legitimate for exporters to sell on world markets at prices so far removed from the costs of production. The intensive use of subsidies that sustain this practice diminish the world market share of rival exporters and drive down prices, producing large foreign-exchange losses. Another effect is to create highly unequal competition in developing-country food markets. All too often, developing-country governments are willing to open their borders to cheap, subsidised imports in the interests of reducing food prices, with highly damaging implications for domestic farmers.

As the dominant exporters of a range of agricultural commodities, EU and US export prices largely determine world agricultural prices. The result is that farmers and exporters in developing countries receive prices for their crops at or below the artificially low prices set by the powerful industrialised countries' policies. Developing countries are estimated to face annual welfare losses of $20bn a year as a result of Northern agricultural policies (World Bank 2001d).

The impact on developing countries

For the agricultural sector in developing countries, the overall costs of lost market shares and lower prices are very large. Latin America is the worst-affected region, losing $4bn annually from EU farm policies alone. The impacts are particularly damaging for Argentina and Uruguay, for whom the EU Common Agricultural Policy (CAP) depresses terms of trade by seven per cent and eight per cent respectively. Estimated losses to Argentina, a country in the grip of a major financial crisis, are $2bn a year.

In domestic markets, poor farmers operating with limited resources, often in ecologically fragile areas, cannot hope to compete with products produced under heavily subsidised conditions in the EU or USA. However, trade liberalisation in developing countries is increasingly exposing domestic farmers to ruinous competition, driving down prices and undermining rural wages and employment.

In the Philippines, trade liberalisation in the corn market in 1997 reduced import prices for US corn by one-third. At the time, US corn farmers were receiving $20,000 a year on average in subsidies, while Filipino farmers in one of the main corn-producing areas on the island of Mindanao had average annual income levels of around $365. Viewed from the perspective of poor families in Mindanao, opening the market to subsidised

Figure 4.6
US and EU dumping subsidies: export prices as a percentage of production costs (selected products)

United States

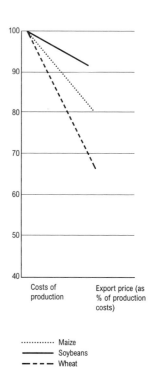

European Union

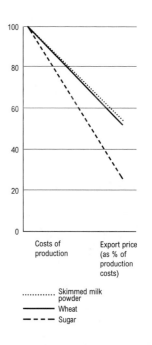

Box 4.2

A Development Box in the Agreement on Agriculture

The idea of introducing a package of enhanced special and differential treatment measures for developing countries in the WTO Agreement on Agriculture has been termed a 'Development Box'. Unlike the existing Blue and Green Boxes, whose provisions institutionalise the agricultural support policies of industrialised countries, a Development Box would provide greater flexibility for developing countries to implement policies that strengthen their domestic production, promote food security, and maintain and improve rural livelihoods.

The Development Box provisions would aim to protect poor farmers from surges of cheap or unfairly subsidised imports, enhance the efficiency of developing countries' domestic food-production capacity, particularly in key staple crops, and provide and sustain existing employment and livelihoods opportunities for the rural poor. Specific instruments would include exempting food-security crops from trade-liberalisation commitments, allowing developing countries the flexibility to raise tariffs against cheap agricultural imports that are damaging domestic production, and exempting government subsidies for low-income producers from liberalisation commitments.

(Green and Priyardarshi 2001 provides more detail on the proposed Development Box.)

US corn posed a direct threat to their livelihoods. Corn is a major cash-crop on the island, as well as being a source of food. Research conducted by Oxfam found that many of the poorest households were deriving more than three-quarters of their income from corn sales, so that any fall in household income would have devastating effects on resources available for food, health care, and education. More than half of corn farmers were already living below the poverty line, and one-third of all children below the age of five were suffering from malnutrition. In this instance, the impact of exposing poor corn farmers to competition with heavily subsidised US producers was to leave some of the poorest households worse off (Watkins 1996).

Subsidised European dairy exports have inflicted severe damage on a number of countries. In Jamaica, trade liberalisation in the early 1990s resulted in the substitution of locally produced fresh milk by subsidised European milk powder as the major input for the Jamaican dairy industry. EU milk-powder exports to Jamaica grew from less than 2000 tonnes per year in 1990-93 to more than 4000 tonnes per year in 1995-98, for which European exporters received more than four million euros per year in export subsidies. While these exports accounted for only a tiny proportion of total EU dairy trade, they dominated the small Jamaican dairy market, with devastating consequences for local producers, many of whom are women who run their own businesses. As the dominant dairy supplier on the world market, the level of EU subsidies determines – and depresses – world prices. And the level of subsidies is high: in 1999, the value of EU export subsidies on milk powder amounted to more than half the value of milk powder on the world market (Black 2001).

Many of the agricultural subsidies provided in industrialised countries enable manufacturing companies to reduce the raw-material costs on goods exported to third-country markets. This can disadvantage developing-country firms in local markets. As part of the CAP-reform process, the level of price support received by EU farmers is being reduced, and farm incomes are being supplemented by direct aid subsidies. This means that European food processors are getting raw materials at artificially depressed prices (EU cereal prices have fallen by 50 per cent since 1992 under the impact of this 'reform' process), which increases their competitiveness on world markets. On top of this advantage, EU food processors receive export subsidies on the agricultural raw-materials content of processed products equivalent to any remaining difference between EU and world market prices (this covers the sugar, dairy, egg, cereal, and rice content of manufactured goods).

In South Africa, these changes are creating subtle new forms of dumping. Although sugar prices in South Africa are lower (less than half) those in Europe, European confectionery manufacturers have been able to obtain sugar for use in exported products at prices around one-third cheaper than their South African counterparts. According to the South Africa Chocolate and Sweet Manufacturers' Association, an increase in imports of EU sugar and chocolate confectionery contributed to a 21 per cent decline in consumption of domestically produced sweets and chocolate between 1997 and 2000. This has affected production and employment in local chocolate and sweet manufacturing. The largest South African-owned sweets and chocolate manufacturer, Beacon Sweets, laid off 1000 staff between 1997 and 1999. It also cut purchases of local sugar from 40,000 tonnes in 1995 to 35,000 in 1999, with adverse consequences for rural wages and employment (Goodison 2001).

These examples illustrate the negative impacts on food security, rural livelihoods, and local industrialisation of US and EU dumping of subsidised agricultural surpluses on world markets. They highlight the need for an immediate ban on agricultural dumping, which would bring international agricultural trade rules into line with the disciplines that apply to all other sectors. More broadly, it is important that developing countries avoid making liberalisation commitments that are inconsistent with policies for rural poverty reduction and national food security. Given the distorted state of world agricultural markets, the free-market case for liberalisation is weak. WTO rules must recognise the right of developing countries to protect their domestic agricultural sectors as a means of promoting food security and rural livelihoods, the development of which will be crucial for the achievement of poverty reduction. This is one of the aims of the Development Box advocated by a number of developing countries (see Box 4.2).

Food aid

Food aid has an important role to play in responding to emergencies that arise from conflict or natural disasters. However, food-aid programmes have historically been subject to extreme abuse, with industrialised countries using them to dispose of surpluses and create food dependency. Such abuse continues today, and the US is the worst offender. The following remark by former US Secretary for Agriculture, Dan Glickman, illustrates well the US attitude to food aid: *'Humanitarian and national self interest both can be served by well-designed foreign assistance programmes. Food aid has not only met emergency food needs, but has also been a useful market development tool.'*[7] Similarly, a 1996 USAID report boasted that 'nine out of ten countries importing US agricultural products are former recipients of food assistance' (USAID 1996).

There is strong evidence of an inverse relationship between the availability of food-aid donations and the need of recipient countries: food-aid donations are typically highest during periods of low commodity prices (and high stocks), and vice versa. In 1999/2000, US food-aid donations of wheat and wheat flour increased when prices

Box 4.3

Guyana rice exports to Jamaica – undercut by US food aid

'PL480 [US food aid] was meant to boost food security,' says Dharankumar Seeraj of the Guyana Rice Producers Association. 'It was supposed to assist in the elimination of poverty, not in creating it. Yet we have seen a direct effect whereby in the very process of eliminating poverty [in one place], we have poverty being created in another region.'

Rice exports provide an important source of income for poor communities on Guyana's northern coastal plain, contributing to rural development and poverty alleviation through improved roads, schools, and health services. Following a reduction in EU trade preferences in 1996, Guyanese rice farmers switched their focus from exports to the lucrative but restricted EU market to exports to neighbouring countries in the Caribbean Community (CARICOM). In 1997, Guyana succeeded in capturing almost half the Jamaican rice market, at the expense of US sales, which had previously accounted for 99 per cent of the market.

A major set-back for Guyanese rice growers has been unfair competition from US food aid in the Jamaican market. US rice is supplied to the Jamaican government on concessional terms as food aid under US Public Law 480 (known as PL480). In response to complaints from Guyana about unfair competition from PL480 rice, a deal was struck: Jamaica would purchase 40,000 tonnes of Guyanese rice, but in exchange the rice would be milled in Jamaica. The US-owned rice mill, Grains Jamaica Limited, asked the US government to intervene, arguing that the 'explicitly stated purpose of PL480 is to build commercial customers for US agricultural goods. We recently upgraded our mill and need PL480 rice to recover this additional investment and recapture the market [from Guyanese rice].'

As a result of political pressure, combined with a surplus in the US rice harvest, Jamaica's allocation of PL480 rice was suddenly doubled for the year 2000 to 24,000 tonnes, after falling consistently throughout the 1990s. In December 1999, the US Ambassador in Jamaica and the US industry's allies convinced the Jamaican government to sign a five-year tariff-waiver to reclassify PL480 rough rice as a raw material, so that it could enter Jamaica duty-free. Simultaneously, rice was removed from the list of commodities to which CARICOM's Common External Tariff (CET) would be applied, therefore removing Guyana's preferential treatment in the Jamaican market as a CARICOM member relative to US rice imports.

However, the required consultation process to remove a product from CARICOM's list of products eligible for the CET was not undertaken and, following complaints from Guyana, rough rice has now been replaced on the list. Guyana maintains that unfair competition with rice produced in the region contravenes the mission of PL480, and it has asked the US authorities to end this abuse of food aid. No response has yet been received, but no rice was allocated to Jamaica under PL480 in 2001.

Source: Oxfam Canada, 2001

were low, the very time when recipient countries could most easily afford to obtain supplies on the world market. Conversely, when prices were high and the need for food aid may have been expected to increase, levels of US donations fell. Over half of US wheat-flour exports in this period were sent in the form of food aid, compared with less than 10 per cent for other exporting countries. Furthermore, these US wheat-flour exports were destined for a number of countries where there was no food emergency, or which have the resources to purchase food.[18]

The WTO Agreement on Agriculture binds members to ensure that the provision of food aid is not tied, directly or indirectly, to commercial exports of agricultural products to recipient countries. It also requires that international food-aid transactions be carried out in accordance with the United Nations Food and Agriculture Organisation (FAO) Principles of Surplus Disposal, which stipulate that major exporters should report all types of food-aid activity for monitoring, to ensure that food aid is directed to those in need, and that it does not interfere with normal patterns of production and international trade. Unfortunately, the FAO Principles are non-binding, and members' adherence to the notification process is sporadic. WTO disciplines need to be strengthened to guard against the abuse of food aid to dispose of domestic agricultural surpluses.

Recommendations: strategies for reform

The challenge ahead is to expand opportunities and enable the world's poorest countries and people to benefit from trade. That challenge will not be met without radical reforms to the trade policies of industrialised countries. The willingness of the rich world to undertake those reforms will predict the success – or failure – of the WTO negotiations launched in Doha in November 2001. More fundamentally, they are a test of the willingness of the industrialised world to convert its rhetoric on inclusive globalisation into practical action. Trade can realise its potential only if industrialised countries reshape the global trading system to spread opportunity more equitably.

They should start by dismantling the protectionist barriers described in this report. Industrialised countries should implement the following measures:

- Provide comprehensive duty-free and quota-free access, not just for Least Developed Countries, but for all low-income countries by 2005. Take immediate action to provide duty-free and quota-free access for all products exported by the LDCs.

- Implement an immediate across-the-board reduction of all tariff peaks in excess of 15 per cent to less than 10 per cent, with further reduction to less than 5 per cent by 2005.

- Immediately eliminate all tariff escalation on products exported from developing countries.

- By the end of 2002, implement their obligations under the Uruguay Round agreement on textiles and clothing.

- By the 2005 deadline for implementing the agreement on textiles and clothing, adopt a tariff ceiling of five per cent on all developing-country exports of these products.

- Impose a unilateral moratorium on anti-dumping actions against developing countries, and adopt a ban on anti-dumping actions against low-income countries.

- Establish a Standards Attainment Agency to assist developing countries in meeting the import standards set. The agency should be constituted with an annual budget of $2bn.

The EU and USA cannot continue with their existing agricultural policies. They are subject to a series of pressures for reform, ranging from domestic budgetary constraints (for example, arising from the planned enlargement of the EU to include a number of large agricultural economies in eastern and central Europe) to growing concern among domestic constituencies about the impact of intensive, industrialised agricultural production methods on environmental sustainability, food safety, and the situation of small and family farms and rural communities. The WTO negotiations on agriculture provide another pressure, since the Doha Declaration commits WTO members to negotiations aimed at 'substantial improvements in market access; reductions of, with a view to phasing out, all forms of export subsidies; and substantial reductions in trade-distorting domestic support'.

The key question is: how should the EU and USA address the structural problem of over-production? For it is the tendency of existing EU and US farm policies to encourage excessive production that has resulted in the use of dumping as a means of disposing of surpluses, and environmental damage arising from the intensification of production methods.

It is beyond the scope of this report to offer detailed proposals for reform of US and EU agricultural policies. However, it is possible to identify a number of principles that indicate the direction in which reform should proceed, as follows.

- **A comprehensive ban on export dumping.** The practice of export dumping, whether the result of direct export subsidies or other forms of agricultural support, must be outlawed in international trade rules. The same rules and principles that are applied to manufactured goods should be applied to agriculture, with a ban on exports at prices below costs of production. Many importing developing countries face technical and resources constraints that limit their ability to prove the existence of agricultural dumping, and therefore to be confident in imposing countervailing duties to bring the dumping prices up to the cost of production levels. One option to overcome this constraint is for the OECD to publish each year an estimate of the full cost of production, including all producer-paid costs, government-paid costs, marketing costs, and a reasonable profit, at least for all OECD member countries. Importing countries could use these figures as a reference for establishing minimum import prices. Imports at prices below these levels would be subject to countervailing duties in an amount equal to the level of dumping (Ritchie et al. 2000).

- **Recognition of the right of developing countries to protect their agricultural systems.** To protect food security, developing countries have the right to protect their domestic agricultural sectors. Given their high levels of subsidisation, the EU and USA should respect that right. Industrialised countries should support developing countries' proposals to incorporate a Development Box in the Agreement on Agriculture. This would establish a range of enhanced special and differential measures, including both domestic support and broader measures that developing countries could use to promote food security and rural livelihoods. In order to ensure that the Development Box is genuinely used to promote poverty reduction, it should require developing-country governments to target protection and support to small farmers and staple food crops.

- **Restructured subsidies to promote extensive agriculture.** Farm-income support is currently biased towards big farmers and intensive agriculture. The result is bad for equity, the environment, and developing countries. Income support should be restructured to support less intensive farming, geared towards lower output levels through carefully targeted programmes designed to achieve specific social, rural development, and environmental objectives. These are likely to include both an element of price support and the increased use of direct income payments to farmers that are de-coupled from levels of production. The payment of subsidies should be modulated to ensure a more equitable distribution of support across different groups of farmers. Transitional support should be provided to help low-income producers in industrialised countries to adjust if they are negatively affected by changes in agricultural policy.

Implementation of these reforms would provide opportunities for developing countries to increase their share of the benefits of international trade. It is the responsibility of developing-country governments to implement national policies that make trade work for the poor. As we argued in Chapters 2 and 3, of particular importance are policies that address inequalities in access to productive resources such as land, credit, and infrastructure.

CHAPTER 5
Trade liberalisation and the poor

Import liberalisation is used by the International Monetary Fund, the World Bank, and Northern governments as a standard for measuring the commitment of developing-country governments to economic reform and poverty reduction. Trade barriers are widely seen as an impediment to successful integration into global markets. The underlying presumption is that import liberalisation is good for growth and for the poor. That presumption is deeply flawed. While integration into global markets does offer opportunities for sustained and equitable growth, current approaches to import liberalisation are weakening the links between trade and poverty reduction.

In the previous chapter, we considered an aspect of international trade that has been characterised by insufficient liberalisation: the trade policies of industrialised countries. This chapter looks at the trade policies of developing countries. It argues that these policies have been characterised by an undue emphasis on rapid import liberalisation, with scant regard paid to the implications for poverty reduction and distribution. The point is not that trade liberalisation in developing countries is inherently bad for the poor. Integrated into effective national strategies for poverty reduction, well designed and properly sequenced trade reforms can create new opportunities for the poor. By the same token, trade-liberalisation programmes that create open markets without reference to the distribution of power in the market place can destroy opportunities. Many of the programmes associated with the International Monetary Fund and the World Bank fall into the latter category.

The first section of this chapter shows that developing countries, unlike industrialised countries, have been liberalising very rapidly. This has been encouraged through the system of incentives and penalties associated with IMF–World Bank loan conditions, which in turn reflect the policy priorities of Northern governments. One consequence is an unbalanced pattern of liberalisation. Developing countries are absorbing the costs associated with greater openness, while being denied access to rich-country markets.

The second part provides a critical review of the case for 'openness', as developed by the World Bank and adopted by Northern governments. That case is rooted in new adaptations of old trade theories. These theories predict a close relationship between import liberalisation on the one side, and economic growth and poverty reduction on the other. We show that the evidence in support of this case is weak. In summary, the research behind the evidence has measured the wrong things, has deduced flawed conclusions, and is generating bad policy advice. While the World Bank has moved forward in developing a more coherent agenda for poverty reduction, it has failed to integrate trade policy into that agenda.

Using a new analytical tool, the Trade Liberalisation Indicator (TLI), we highlight some of the more serious shortcomings in the World Bank's research, and most particularly its confusion over what openness means. The TLI measures trade policies (such as tariff levels and the speed and depth of liberalisation) over which governments have control, rather than the indicators of economic outcomes (such as trade/GDP ratios) upon which the World Bank concentrates. The TLI demonstrates the fact that the countries that have integrated most successfully into the global economy, such as those in East Asia, have proceeded cautiously with import liberalisation and placed more emphasis on export promotion.

The third section of this chapter sets out some contrasting cases of trade liberalisation in practice. It shows how badly designed trade-liberalisation policies can produce outcomes that are bad for poverty reduction. Protectionism is no more a panacea for poverty than rapid import liberalisation. The real challenge is to integrate trade reform into effective national strategies for poverty reduction.

Trade liberalisation, growth, and poverty reduction: the economists' new religion

Economists are sometimes criticised for their failure to agree on policy prescriptions. George Bernard Shaw once unkindly observed: 'If all economists were laid end to end, they wouldn't reach a conclusion' (Bucholz 1989). If he were writing today, he might have been forced to concede a proviso: 'unless they were talking about the benefits of open markets for developing countries'.

Openness has become the new religion of much of the economics profession. Its strongest adherents are to be found in the IMF, the World Bank, the WTO, and Northern governments. Admittedly, the latter constituency applies the principles of the faith on a selective basis: import liberalisation in the developing world is preferred to liberalisation at home. Even so, their avowed faith in openness is impressive.

No G7 communiqué is complete today without reference to the potential benefits of openness in developing countries in making globalisation work for the poor. The British government, among the strongest advocates of openness, entertains no doubts. According to its 2000 White Paper on Development: 'Empirical analysis shows that greater trade openness contributes to higher growth (...) Recent cross-country analysis shows that the poor benefit equally from the growth generated by trade openness' (DFID 2000). The IMF is equally convinced. One recent internal assessment of the Fund's approach to trade policy across a wide range of programmes concluded: 'a clear message from this review is that trade liberalisation has a positive overall effect on employment and incomes of the poor' (Bannister and Thugge 2001). The World Bank is institutionally ambivalent on import liberalisation. In some places, it acknowledges the complexity of the relationship between liberalisation and poverty reduction (for example, World Bank 2001b). In others, it gives a simple but compelling signal to policy makers: 'openness to international trade accelerates development' (Dollar and Kraay 2001a). That signal has been reinforced by the economics profession. As one of the most respected authorities on trade policy writes: 'there is widespread acceptance that in the long run open economies fare better in aggregate than do closed ones, and that relatively open policies contribute to long-run development' (Winters 2000).

The main message to emerge is that the only good trade barrier is a low one or, better still, no barrier at all. Some caveats are attached. Governments are expected to provide 'safety-nets' for the unfortunate few who might be adversely affected by short-term adjustment costs associated with trade liberalisation, such as rising unemployment. They are also expected to combine trade liberalisation with a whole set of supportive reforms, in areas ranging from property rights to health and education. But none of this detracts from the imperative to liberalise.

Trade liberalisation in developing countries

There are various ways of measuring import liberalisation. Trade barriers include tariffs on imports, non-tariff barriers (such as quotas or prohibitions on some categories of imports), and taxes on exports. Whichever indicator is used, the pace of liberalisation in developing countries over the past 20 years has been extraordinary. Since the mid-1980s there has been widespread and rapid import liberalisation, undertaken not in the context of multilateral trade negotiations but under IMF–World Bank programmes (see below) or on a unilateral basis (UNCTAD 1998). Only a relatively small group of countries in East Asia has followed a selective and gradual approach to liberalisation, gearing integration in world markets towards well-defined national policy goals and institutional capacity. Elsewhere, there has been a widening divergence between developed and developing countries in the pace of liberalisation.

At the end of the 1990s, average tariffs were around one-half of their level at the start of the 1980s in South Asia and sub-Saharan Africa, and one-third of that level in Latin America and East Asia. Non-tariff barriers were widely prevalent at the start of the 1980s, covering more than one-quarter of all imports in East Asia and sub-Saharan

Figure 5.1
Unweighted average tariffs and frequency of non-tariff barriers: selected developing regions

Source: IMF

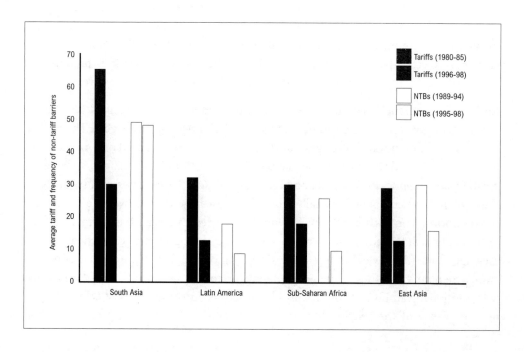

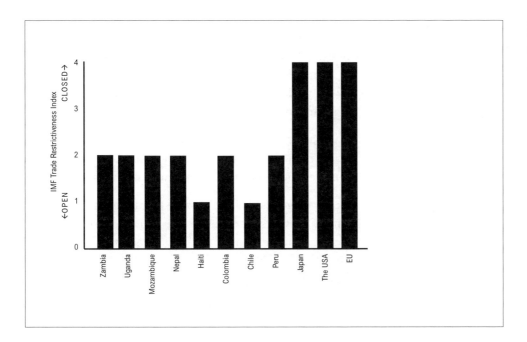

Figure 5.2
The IMF 'openness' test: selected countries (1999)

Source: IMF

Africa. With the partial exception of South Asia, these restrictions have been rolled back. Latin America, East Asia, and sub-Saharan Africa all halved the coverage of non-tariff barriers in the 1990s (see Figure 5.1).

Regional aggregates understate the scale and pace of liberalisation that has occurred in many countries. The following are not untypical examples:

- **Latin America.** Mexico halved its average tariffs between 1985 and 1987, and Colombia between 1990 and 1992. Peru's average tariff in 1991 was one-third of its level in 1989.

- **South Asia.** Between 1988 and 1996, Bangladesh cut average tariffs from 102 per cent to 27 per cent. India halved average tariffs to 47 per cent in the three years to 1993.

- **Sub-Saharan Africa.** Between 1995 and 1998, Zambia cut its average tariff rate by a factor of four, to six per cent. Ghana, Kenya, and Tanzania cut tariff rates by one-half or more during the 1990s.

- **East Asia.** China, Indonesia, the Philippines, and Thailand all halved tariff rates in the 1990s.

Composite trade indicators underline the degree of liberalisation that has taken place. The IMF's Trade Restrictiveness Index (TRI) combines the major types of trade barrier, including the average level of tariff protection, the coverage of non-tariff barriers, and export taxes. These are converted into a 10-point scale, with '1' denoting the most open and '10' the most restrictive. Countries are then assigned a ranking on this scale.

Two striking features emerge from the TRI ranking (see Figure 5.2). First, many developing countries have liberalised at an extraordinary pace. For example, Uganda, Peru, and Haiti have been among the world's most rapidly liberalising economies. Between 1997 and 2000 alone, the proportion of low-income developing countries categorised by the IMF as 'restrictive' fell from 33 per cent to 18 per cent (IMF 2001).[1] There are exceptions to the general trend. Some very strong export performers such as Vietnam, China, and Indonesia have liberalised far more slowly, while others have liberalised but remain relatively protected – an issue to which we return below.

The second strong conclusion to emerge from the TRI ranking is that many poor developing countries are now far more open to trade than rich industrialised countries. Liberalisation in developing countries has left the champions of free trade in industrialised countries trailing far behind.

- Countries such as Mozambique, Zambia, and Mali are far more open than countries in the European Union, such as the UK, France, and Germany. Sixteen sub-Saharan African countries covered by the TRI are more open than the EU.

- Peru and Bolivia are twice as open, and Haiti and Chile four times as open, as the United States and Canada. Seventeen countries in Latin America and the Caribbean are either as open, or more open, than the US economy.

The role of IMF loan conditionality

Trade-policy reform is an almost universal feature of IMF programmes, reflecting the commitment of its main shareholders – the major industrialised countries – to open markets in developing countries. When developing countries receive IMF loans, they also accept conditions requiring them to liberalise imports. These conditions, often implemented in tandem with World Bank programmes, carry considerable weight (IMF 1998). By virtue of its position at the apex of the conditionality system, the Fund is a gatekeeper to donor assistance, debt relief, and financial rescue packages. On its own evidence, IMF loan conditionality has produced some impressive results. An internal review in 1997 found that one-half of IMF programmes targeted quantifiable reductions in trade restrictiveness under their loan conditions. Whereas almost three-quarters of the countries covered in the 1997 review had restrictive trade regimes at the outset, four years later this number had fallen to one-fifth (IMF 1997, IMF 2001b).

No sector, including agriculture, is too sensitive to be prescribed the standard medicine of import liberalisation. Loans for Cambodia from the World Bank, and from the IMF's Poverty Reduction and Growth Facility (PRGF), are conditional on the country reducing average import tariffs to 15 per cent by 2001, compared with more than 40 per cent in 1998. Mali has also been required to reduce tariffs on imports of rice, as has Haiti.

The number of trade-related conditions attached to IMF loans increased during the 1990s (IMF 2001b). This was especially true for low-income countries. For this group, the average number of such conditions increased three-fold between 1988-90 and between 1997-99, helping to explain their impressive performance on trade liberalisation. These averages mask the force of loan conditionality in specific countries. The IMF's concessional loan programme, the PRGF, is heavily weighted with trade-policy loan conditions. One review of seven PRGF programmes discovered a total of 51 trade-related policy measures. These ranged from conditions for entering a programme (13 measures), to benchmarks for measuring performance (11 measures). On average, every loan advanced to PRGF countries came with seven trade conditions attached, although several countries were above average in this respect. When Tanzania accepted a PRGF loan in 2000, it also agreed to eight specific policy measures aimed at liberalising trade, including the reduction of tariff and non-tariff barriers. Yemen accepted 22 trade-policy conditions on a loan from the same account.

While loan conditionality weighs more heavily on the IMF's low-income clients, other countries are not immune. When Indonesia and Korea were forced to turn to the IMF for support in the wake of the 1997 financial crash, their loans came with 19 and 9 conditions respectively, covering a wide array of policy reforms on both the import and export sides.

IMF programmes, supported by the World Bank in many cases, have often sought to promote import liberalisation at a pace that can only be described as heroic. Both Indonesia and Bolivia were expected to go from a TRI level of 4 (already as open as the EU or the USA) to 1 in the space of three years, implying massive structural change. Under IMF-World Bank structural adjustment programmes at the start of the 1990s, Peru and Zambia went from being among the world's more closed economies to among its most open – in the space of a few years. In many ways, however, it is Haiti that stands out as the star pupil of the IMF–World Bank. The poorest country in the Western hemisphere, ranked 134 out of 162 on the UNDP's Human Development Index, Haiti became in 1986 one of the few countries to reach the elevated status of a fully open economy, with a ranking of 1 on the Fund's TRI (IMF 1999a). Guided by the IMF and the World Bank, Haiti had joined the super-league of trade liberalisers. The transition had appalling consequences for poor people, but the country is still praised by the World Bank in particular as a strong reformer (World Bank 2001b, Oxfam International 2001a).

Trade conditionality is applied irrespective of the reasons why governments seek IMF assistance. For example, Indonesia turned to the IMF following the 1997 financial crisis, which was rooted in the banking sector and exchange-rate policy. Yet financial 'rescue' came with trade-reform demands that were at best tangentially related to the underlying causes of the crisis. It is certainly not immediately apparent why IMF loan conditions required the liberalisation of imports for agricultural products and for a range of manufactured goods (Stiglitz 2001).

The scope and coverage of trade-policy conditionality implies a high level of confidence in the benefits of open markets. Before reviewing the quality of the evidence on which this confidence is based, it is worth noting some of the wider problems associated with current IMF–World Bank approaches to trade liberalisation, each of which has implications for poverty-reduction efforts.

- **Unbalanced liberalisation produces balance-of-payments pressures.** Import liberalisation has been accompanied by widening trade deficits across much of the developing world. The average deficit for developing countries as a whole in the 1990s was almost three percentage points of GDP higher than in the 1970s, even though average growth rates were lower (UNCTAD 1998). Two factors have contributed to this outcome. First, import liberalisation has led to surges of imports in many countries, with local industry being displaced. Second, trade restrictions in industrialised countries have limited export opportunities. Large trade deficits have been covered in a number of countries (notably in Latin America) by speculative flows of capital, creating instability and increasing exposure to economic risk. The Mexican financial crisis at the end of 1995, the East Asian crisis of 1997, and the Argentine crisis of 2001–02 were all, in part, a consequence of private capital flows being used to overcome balance-of-payments deficits.

- **Unequal trade negotiations.** When countries negotiate on trade reforms at the WTO, they exchange concessions. Governments agree to accept the costs implied by increased import competition, in part because they will obtain improved access to the markets of trade partners: i.e. they receive something in return for liberalising. However, under IMF–World Bank programmes, countries liberalise on a unilateral basis, receiving nothing in return. It is true that, in their policy analysis and recommendations, the IMF and World Bank give the same advice to all countries. But loan conditions are applied only to developing countries. The result is unbalanced liberalisation, under which rich-country governments do not have to reciprocate measures undertaken by developing countries.

- **World Bank–IMF loan conditionality creates a 'one system, two rules' approach to trade policy.** When rich countries liberalise, their governments are highly sensitive to the views of domestic lobbies. Democratic accountability, and the power of vested interests, inform trade-policy choices. That is why the EU and the USA have taken several decades to undertake modest liberalisation in sensitive areas such as agriculture and footwear exports. In their policy advice to developing countries, the IMF and World Bank do not have to consider issues of accountability and democracy. They are accountable primarily to their main shareholders, which are Northern governments. As the IMF and the World Bank justifiably argue, they do not discriminate in the advice they offer. Northern governments are regularly urged to liberalise. However, unlike their Southern counterparts with loan programmes, they are not obliged to follow the advice they receive. It is unthinkable that the governments of France or the USA would liberalise their agricultural systems as rapidly as is required under some IMF programmes.

- **Severing the link between trade policy and poverty-reduction strategies.** In theory, the IMF and the World Bank are committed to putting poverty-reduction at the centre of their operations. In practice, as we show below, trade-liberalisation targets are set without reference to their implications for poor people.

Growth, openness, and the poor: old arguments and new evidence

The application of IMF–World Bank loan conditions to trade liberalisation is one indicator of confidence in the benefits of openness. However, compulsion has not been the main force behind liberalisation; most developing-country governments have accepted the evidence that openness is good for economic growth, and by extension for poverty reduction. On closer inspection, that evidence is of dubious merit.

The new model consensus

Economists have been asserting for a long time that trade liberalisation is good for developing countries. Some have done so on the basis of applied theory. This school points to the gains in efficiency that are presumed to flow from resource-allocation decisions in more open markets (Bhagwati and Srinivasan 1999, Bussolo and Lecomte 1999). Others have sought correlations between openness, growth, and poverty reduction through complex econometric data analysis.[2]

Econometric research has exercised a formidable influence over policy debates, even though (or, perhaps, because) the evidence produced is seldom comprehensible to policy makers. In the mid-1980s, one study claimed that countries that were more open to trade experienced on average an unconditional increase in economic growth of 2.5

per cent a year, compared with closed economies, and that they were heading for income convergence with rich countries (Sachs and Warner 1995). Other research reached similar conclusions and produced similarly inflated claims (Edwards 1993). Such studies informed a generation of structural adjustment programmes, fuelling general euphoria about the potential of trade liberalisation in the process. IMF–World Bank staff arrived in developing countries, armed with complex studies apparently justifying their prescription of sweeping trade-liberalisation measures.

Most of the studies – and even more so the policy conclusions based on them – lacked credibility. The majority failed even the most simple test of causality: it was impossible to determine whether openness caused growth, or whether countries became more open as economic growth increased. Moreover, definitions of 'openness' were so wide-ranging as to be meaningless. Everything from exchange rates and macro-economic strategies, to import barriers and the size of government were included. One detailed review found that when import barriers were isolated as an indicator of openness, any meaningful relationship with growth evaporated (Rodriguez and Rodrik 1999). In other words, there was no relationship, positive or otherwise, between the policies advocated by the IMF–World Bank and the policy outcomes predicted. Yet import liberalisation was dogmatically pursued as an adjustment goal.

Recent years have witnessed a resurgence in econometrics as a guide to policy formulation, with the World Bank in the lead. Some of the studies have continued in the worst traditions of the past, using broad definitions of openness that confuse trade policy with other aspects of macro-economic reforms (Edwards 1998). Others have shifted the focus to more narrowly defined indicators of openness, using these to identify associations with growth. Research carried out by the World Bank's Development Research Group belongs in this latter category (Dollar and Kraay 2001a, 2001b). Almost all Northern governments, along with the IMF and the WTO, point to research carried out by the World Bank in pressing the case for import liberalisation in developing countries (for example, DFID 2000, McKay et al 2000). All of this prompts one to ask whether the new generation of research is any more robust than the last.

There are two core elements in the case presented by the World Bank.[3] The first concerns the relationship between economic growth and poverty reduction. On the basis of an econometric exercise analysing economic growth in 80 countries extending over four decades, the World Bank argues that *on average* the income of the poor rises on a one-to-one basis with overall growth. In other words, poor people capture a share of any increment to growth that reflects their existing share of income distribution. As the authors express it, in a sentence that has been reproduced many times by Northern government development agencies: 'It is almost always the case that the income of the poor rises during periods of significant growth' (Dollar and Kraay 2001a).

The second element seeks to establish a link between growth and openness. It avoids some of the pitfalls of the earlier studies by using a single indicator of openness: the ratio of trade to GDP. In an econometric study covering a sample of 72 developing countries, the World Bank examines the relationship between economic growth and the trade/GDP ratio. More specifically, it singles out the top one-third of developing countries in terms of increases in trade to GDP ratios over the 20-year period 1975-79 and 1995-97, distinguishing this group of 'globalisers' from the rest ('non-globalisers'). Some strong conclusions emerge. Among the most important, and widely cited by policy makers, are:

- Weighted for population (an important statistical device, as we show below), the per capita income of the 'globalisers' grew at five per cent a year in the 1990s, compared with 1.4 per cent for the 'non-globaliser' group.

- Growth rates for the 'globalisers' have been steadily increasing since the mid-1970s, while those for the non-globalisers fell sharply in the 1980s and recovered only marginally in the 1990s.

- Per capita income among the 'globalisers' is rising more than twice as fast as in industrialised countries, while the 'non-globalisers' are falling further behind.

At one level, it is unsurprising that such findings have attracted the attention of policy makers. The implied divergence in economic growth rates is very large. Countries that are open, on the definition used in the study, are growing at 3.6 per cent a year faster than others. On this basis, average income in a globalising economy would double every 14 years, compared with 50 years in a non-globalising economy: a growth gap that would have profound implications for poverty reduction.

On closer inspection, however, some of the numbers look less impressive. One reason for this is that averages have the effect of obscuring important differences between countries, especially when samples are weighted for population (since this means that large countries like China have a disproportionate influence). Using an unweighted average, the per capita growth rate for the globalisers in the 1990s falls to 1.5 per cent. Moreover, 10 of the 24 countries in the group have growth rates of one per cent or less. Further disaggregation reveals that one-third of the 'globalising' countries have lower average growth rates for the 1990s than the 'non-globalising' group. This would hardly appear to be a strong basis for advocating the policies associated with 'openness', even if those policies could be readily identified.

Such findings do not necessarily imply that there is no positive relationship between openness and growth. Several studies have supported the finding that openness, as measured by the share of trade in income, is related to long-term growth (Frankel and Romer 1999). The problem with these studies is one of interpretation. It is almost axiomatic that countries with growing trade/GDP ratios will have higher than average growth rates, since world trade is growing more rapidly than global GDP. However, association is not the same as causation: it could be that countries participate more in trade *because* they are growing more rapidly. The only conclusion that can be supported with any confidence is that countries tend to become more open as they become richer (Rodrik 2001a).

The selection of reference periods and thresholds for ratios can dramatically change the findings from any large cross-country sample. Dani Rodrik of Harvard University has used the same data as the World Bank study to rank the top 40 countries in terms of the increase in imports in their GDP and tariff reductions over the periods 1980-84 and 1995-97 (Rodrik 2001d). The results show a steady *decline* in growth rates from four per cent in 1975 to 2.5 per cent in 1985 and less than two per cent in 1995.

It would doubtless be possible to arrive at different results by changing these reference years and indicators. Any number of outcomes might emerge. In itself, this would suggest a case for extreme caution in interpreting results. But the strong suspicion emerges that reference years and countries have been carefully selected, and the interpretation of data presented, to produce a systematic bias in favour of a positive association between openness and growth.

What is wrong with openness?

Leaving aside statistical interpretation, the use of openness as an indicator by the World Bank produces some superficially compelling comparisons. Strongly performing 'globalisers', such as China, Vietnam, and Thailand, with a track record of rapid growth and poverty reduction, are contrasted by the World Bank with under-performing 'non-globalisers', such as Burma, Pakistan, and Honduras (Dollar and Kraay 2001b). Implied causal association is there for all to see: openness spells success, and lack of openness leads to economic failure and poverty. As one commentator puts it: 'Openness to trade has many dimensions, and all of these dimensions are positively associated with growth' (Easterly 2001).

The problem with such statements is that they are virtually meaningless in terms of their policy application. Openness as a concept in trade policy has at least two very different meanings. The World Bank uses it to describe what is essentially *an economic outcome,* captured, in this case, in the ratio of trade (defined as imports plus exports) to GDP. The Bank then undertakes a leap of imagination to a second meaning: namely, implied *policy inputs.* That leap is acknowledged, albeit cursorily, when the authors declare that 'we use decade-over-decade changes in the volume of trade as an imperfect proxy for changes in trade policy' (Dollar and Kraay 2001b). To put it mildly, it is a *very* imperfect proxy.

If the aim is to examine the relationship between *trade policy,* growth, and poverty reduction, then it is indicators of trade policy (not economic outcomes) that have to be tested. When they are tested, the World Bank view appears as an upside-down version of reality. It turns out that some of the most successful globalisers are anything but radical liberalisers, while many of the most radical liberalisers have actually achieved very little in terms of economic growth and poverty reduction.

The distinction between economic outcomes and policy inputs is an important one, especially from a policy perspective. Governments have limited control over trade/GDP ratios. They reflect a wide range of factors, including export prices and the structure of the economy (poor countries with large mineral deposits often have larger export/GDP ratios, for example). On the other hand, policies are subject to government influence. Levels of tariff and non-tariff barriers, for example, and the speed at which they are reduced, are matters of political choice.

Oxfam has developed a new analytical tool, the **Trade Liberalisation Indicator (TLI)**, which casts the debate on trade liberalisation in a new light. The TLI focuses on two important trade-policy variables: namely, the speed and depth of liberalisation.

- **Speed of reform.** The TLI attempts to capture this dimension by taking the three-year period in the 1990s during which average tariffs were subject to their most rapid reduction. Countries that cut tariffs by more than 30 per cent during this period are categorised as 'rapid liberalisers', and those that cut them by less than 30 per cent as 'slow liberalisers'. As with any indicator, this one is not unproblematic. The cut-off point is arbitrary, and tariffs are only one part of the protective apparatus deployed by governments. However, it is widely accepted that average tariff levels provide a reasonable reflection of the overall restrictiveness or openness of trade regimes (Dollar and Kraay 2001b).

- **Depth of liberalisation.** Depth matters as much as speed, not least since countries liberalise from very different starting points. A country that halves tariffs from a

Figure 5.3
The Trade Liberalisation Indicator (TLI): the speed and depth of import liberalisation in selected developing countries.

*Data from the 1980s

1 The percentage reduction in tariffs is calculated using average weighted tariffs. The formula used is as follows: [(Initial value – Final value) / Initial value] x 100. In other words, if a country cuts tariffs from 80 per cent to 40 per cent, the reduction would be 50 per cent.

2 The final level of protection has been obtained by using the IMF's Trade Restrictiveness Index (TRI) matrix, applied in this case only to import measures (the TRI also measures export taxes).

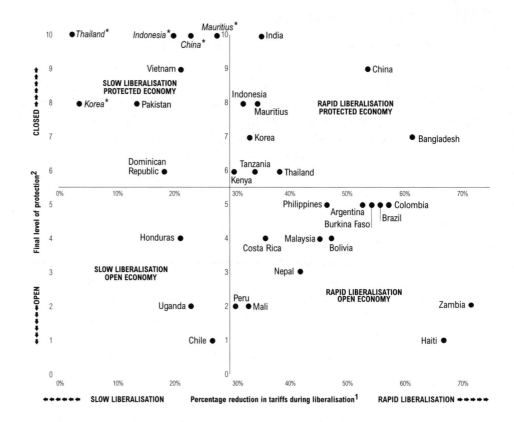

Figure 5.4
Economic growth and poverty reduction: selected groups of developing countries.

1 Growth rates have been calculated from the data in the World Bank's World Development Indicators 2000.

2 The average yearly change in poverty has been calculated as follows: [(Final headcount – Initial headcount) / number of years]

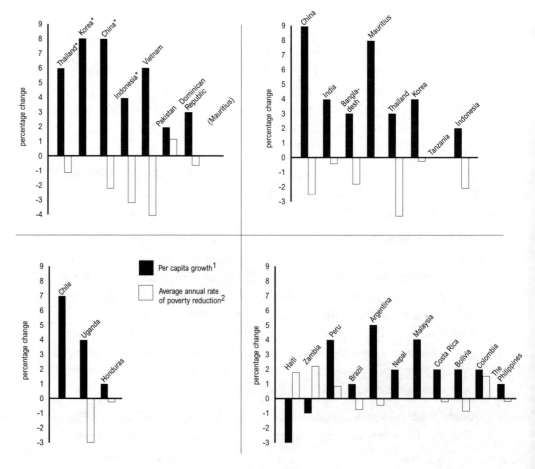

Note The data used in Figures 5.3 and 5.4 is available on www.maketradefair.com

very high level is clearly not in the same position as a country that halves already low tariffs. The TLI captures this dimension by adapting the IMF's Trade Restrictiveness Index. This ranks countries on a scale of 1–10, using the standard IMF matrix system for tariff and non-tariff barriers. However, since the focus is on understanding import policies, it does not include export taxes. Countries with a TRI of less than 5 are categorised as 'relatively open', and those ranked at more than 5 as 'relatively closed'.

Figure 5.3 shows the results of applying these indicators to a sample of 33 developing countries in the 1990s, with seven additional cases from the 1980s. What emerges is a kaleidoscopic effect. Instead of the two distinct 'camps of 'globalisers' and 'non-globalisers', there is a broad scatter of countries.

Measured by the TLI indicators of speed and depth of liberalisation, many of the developing countries that are synonymous with successful integration into global markets register as modest liberalisers. China, Indonesia, and Vietnam may be first-division 'globalisers' on the World Bank's criteria, but they are decidedly second-division liberalisers. The same would apply to Mauritius. Similarly, East Asian countries in the 1980s were able to combine high growth with high degrees of protection.

At the other end of the spectrum, many of the countries that conform most closely to the prescription in favour of rapid liberalisation are hardly models of successful integration, let alone models of good trade policies. This group, located in the bottom-right quadrangle of the scatter graph, includes Haiti, Zambia, Nepal, Mali, Peru, and Bolivia. While these countries may be world-beaters in setting import-liberalisation standards, their achievements in other areas (economic growth, poverty reduction, and human development) leave much to be desired.

This is illustrated in Figure 5.4, which provides data on economic growth and poverty reduction, measured by average annual change in the incidence of poverty. It should be emphasised that this is a relatively small sample of countries, and that there are serious problems with data on poverty levels.[4] Even so, some of the findings call into question the current tendency to celebrate and encourage openness in trade policy. Many rapid liberalisers have a weak record on both economic growth and poverty reduction. Meanwhile, many of the countries that have proceeded more cautiously on import liberalisation have sustained far higher economic growth rates and achieved a strong record on poverty reduction. Between these two extremes, a wide range of outcomes is possible.

The purpose of the TLI is not to replace the World Bank's current blueprint with another, or to imply that restrictive trade policies are inherently better for poverty reduction. Indeed, the only strong conclusion to emerge is that a diverse array of outcomes is possible. But it is this very diversity that cautions against the application of a universal set of policies in favour of rapid trade liberalisation. Far more attention needs to be paid to understanding why and how trade reforms are associated with very different outcomes in terms of poverty reduction.

Why distribution matters

As noted earlier, the argument that openness is good for growth has been closely associated with the argument that growth is good for the poor. Taken at face value, this is an uncontroversial proposition. It is certainly the case that the poor are more likely to benefit from economic growth than they are from economic decline. However, the narrow focus on growth has tended to obscure the importance of distributional factors in determining the rate at which growth is converted into poverty reduction.

The apparently simple proposition that growth is good for the poor is in fact based on another large-scale World Bank cross-country data analysis. That analysis arrived at the following conclusion: 'Income of the poor rises one-for-one with overall growth .../.../...Openness to international trade raises the incomes of the poor by raising overall incomes. The effect on distribution of income is tiny and not significantly different from zero' (Dollar and Kraay 2001a). This statement summarises much of the received wisdom on the relationship between trade reform and poverty reduction. The logic is disarmingly simple. On average, so the argument runs, the income of poor people rises in proportion to their existing share of national income. It follows that when national income rises, the income of the poor will rise with it. Other things being equal, since openness to trade raises average income, trade is good for growth and for the poor in equal measures.

The problem is that, in the case of income distribution, other things are not equal. For policy makers interested in poverty reduction, what matters is the interaction of two factors: the rate of growth, and the proportion of any increment to growth captured by the poor. In crude terms, the rate of growth decides the size of the economic cake, while distribution decides how it is sliced up.

To say that on average the incomes of the poor will rise on a one-to-one basis with overall growth is of dubious relevance to poverty reduction. If the poor account for only a small share of national income, they will capture only a small share of any increase in income. For example, with no change in income distribution, the income gain for the richest 20 per cent will be five times higher than for the poorest 20 per cent in India, 14 times higher in Mexico, and 24 times higher in Brazil. Hence, even though the income of the poor may rise on a one-to-one basis with overall growth, it will rise by less in countries with high levels of inequality (Hanmer and Naschold 1999, Stewart 2000). The fact that the income gain for the poorest quintile will be less than the income gain for the rich and for the nation as a whole implies a slower rate of poverty reduction than would be achieved if growth were combined with redistribution.

This point has profound relevance for poverty reduction. Based on existing income-distribution patterns, Brazil has to grow at three times the rate of Vietnam to achieve the same average income increase in the poorest one-fifth of the population. Similarly, Mexico would have to grow at almost twice the rate of Indonesia or Uganda to achieve a similar increase (Watkins 1998). The same rate of growth can thus produce very different effects in terms of poverty reduction across countries. As one survey of cross-country evidence has shown, countries with low inequality can expect to see from the same growth rate a 75 per cent higher rate of poverty reduction than countries with high inequality (Ravallion 2001). Even though the effects of economic growth may be the single most important determinant of poverty-reduction trends worldwide, distribution remains critical. One cross-country study, covering 143 growth episodes, has shown distribution to play a stronger role than growth in increasing the income of the poor in more than a quarter of the cases (White and Anderson 2001).

By the same token, changes in patterns of income distribution can influence poverty-reduction efforts, for better or for worse. By international standards, Bangladesh has a relatively evenl distribution of income. However, rapid export growth in the first half of the 1990s was accompanied by rising inequalities. The Gini co-efficient rose from 26 to 31 between 1992 and 1996. Without these inequalities, it is estimated that there would be 8–11 million fewer people living on less than $1 a day (based on Appleton et al. 1999b, Woodon 1999). If relatively unequal Honduras had the same Gini co-efficient as more equal Costa Rica, this would result in a seven per cent decline in the incidence of poverty (Government of Honduras 2001).

Initial inequalities interact with the pattern of economic growth to determine the rate at which rising average incomes translate into poverty reduction. Where growth is concentrated in areas where the poor are heavily represented, such as labour-intensive manufacturing and agriculture, it is likely to reduce poverty more rapidly than in other areas (such as capital-intensive farming and industry). During the first half of the 1990s, countries such as Uganda and Vietnam achieved broad-based growth based on smallholder agriculture. The ratio of the increase in per capita income to the decline in the incidence of poverty was close to 1:1 for both countries. However, for countries such as India and Peru, the ratio was around 1: 0.25, and in these cases the rural poor in particular appear to have been excluded from the benefits of growth.

There is a two-way interaction between distribution and economic growth. Research suggests that high levels of inequality not only slow the rate of poverty reduction, but also restrict the rate of economic growth. Various reasons have been identified. Where extreme inequality is a major cause of poverty, it restricts investment, undermines the development of markets, and hampers innovation (UNDP 2001a, Dagdeviren et al. 2000). This suggests that redistribution may offer a double benefit for poverty reduction, by increasing both poor people's share of the economic cake, and the size of the cake itself.

Given the vital importance of distribution, one of the first questions in the design of any trade-reform policy should be how it will affect the poor: more specifically, what policies are likely to increase not just the overall level of growth, but also the share of any increment to growth captured by populations living below the poverty line. In this context, the common presumption that liberalisation is good for growth in general is not a good starting point.

Trade liberalisation and poverty reduction

The case for rapid trade liberalisation in developing countries echoes the broader case for free trade set out in Chapter 1. It is based on the proposition that trade liberalisation is good for growth in general and for the poor in particular. The problem with this perspective is that it ignores some of the complex issues raised by trade policies. These relate to distributional outcomes, the sequencing of reforms, and the timeframe applied for measuring benefits.

The distribution of benefits from liberalisation

At its simplest, standard trade theory suggests that free trade will allow countries to

Box 5.1

Import liberalisation, poverty, and inequality in Mexico

Mexico bears all the signs of success in applying the principles of openness. Yet the country has combined rapid liberalisation with rising inequality and a poor record on poverty reduction. The design of the liberalisation programme has contributed to the problem.

Under trade reforms initiated in the mid-1980s, the country halved average tariffs to 12 per cent. Import licensing, which covered more than 90 per cent of products in the mid-1980s, covered less than one-fifth of exports by 1990. Since accession to NAFTA in 1996, Mexico has been integrating with the USA, the world's largest economy, opening up sectors such as agriculture and manufacturing to increased competition. Meanwhile, rapid export growth has increased the export/GDP ratio from less than one-fifth to almost one-third since 1990.

Rapid trade liberalisation has been associated with a weak record on poverty reduction. Despite per capita GDP growth rates of two per cent in the first half of the 1990s, the number of poor people increased. By the mid-1990s, there were 14 million more people living below the poverty line than in the mid-1980s. Rising inequality accounted for about 80 per cent of the increase, with the Gini co-efficient rising from 49 to 55. Why has rapid integration produced such modest outcomes for poverty reduction?

Distributional factors provide part of the answer. More than 80 per cent of extremely poor people in Mexico live in rural areas, with a heavy concentration in the poverty-belt States of the south. Many are involved in the production of corn. This crop accounts for about half of the total farm acreage in the country, and two-thirds in the poorest rain-fed areas. Import liberalisation has allowed heavily subsidised, cheap US corn to flood into Mexico, driving down local prices. At the time of entry to NAFTA, Mexican domestic prices were almost double subsidised US prices, threatening the livelihoods of an estimated 2.4 million farmers.

Although agricultural exports have been growing rapidly, the impact on the incomes of the very poor has been muted. In agriculture, the winners have been the large commercial farms located in areas such as the North Pacific Coast and the irrigated valley of El Bajío. Production of fruit and vegetables for export to the USA has created employment, primarily of a low-wage, temporary variety. But production is capital-intensive, and it is unlikely that new employment opportunities have outweighed the costs to the poor of import liberalisation.

In the urban sector, trade liberalisation appears to have biased income distribution away from low-waged, unskilled labour. Although foreign investment has created a large number of jobs in the *maquiladora* zone, wages are exceptionally low (see Chapter 3). Despite this, there is evidence that foreign investment is creating demand for more skilled labour.

(Sources: Lustig and Szekely 1998, World Bank 2001b, Appendini 1994)

specialise in what they do best, exporting the products in which they have a comparative advantage, and importing those that reflect comparative advantage elsewhere. Because interference with trade (whether through export taxes or import barriers) distorts prices by taxing efficient producers and subsidising inefficient ones, the presumption is that it is bad for growth, and hence bad for poverty reduction.

Trade theory assumes a pro-poor distributional bias when applied to developing countries. Because comparative advantage is presumed to lie with labour-intensive goods, increased demand for such goods through exports is expected to push up the price of labour producing them. Since poor people are most dependent on labour, trade-liberalisation models predict that they will gain in relative and absolute terms. Exports of labour-intensive manufacturing and agricultural goods are assumed to generate automatic gains for poverty reduction.

For all the certainty with which it is promoted, detailed research into the relationship between openness and the incomes of the poor provides scant encouragement for standard trade theory. One piece of cross-country research, produced by the same World Bank division that claims such strong benefits for trade liberalisation, confirmed a positive aggregate relationship between aggregate income and economic openness. However, it found that the aggregate outcome concealed important distributional changes. Openness was correlated positively with income growth among the richest 60 per cent, but negatively among the poorest 40 per cent. It concluded: 'While greater openness benefits the majority, it harms the poorest ... the costs of adjusting to greater openness are borne exclusively by the poor' (Lundberg and Squire 1999).

Like all theories, conventional trade theories are predicated on restrictive assumptions. Once those assumptions are violated, their value as a guide to policy formulation is eroded. What actually happens to poverty when countries liberalise depends on many factors. Initial distribution of income and assets, what the poor produce, gender relations within the household, and – not least – the specific types of reform undertaken all matter a great deal (Winters 2000). Where trade restrictions have benefited poor people by raising the price of the goods they produced, it can be predicted that liberalisation will hurt the poor. Under almost any conceivable set of conditions, trade liberalisation will produce winners and losers. But poor people often figure prominently among the losers. And since they frequently lack the assets, skills, and access to markets required to take advantage of new opportunities, it may be difficult for them to join the ranks of the winners. The degree to which women benefit will be determined by what they produce, and by the division of labour between men and women. There is no guarantee that any increase in growth will enable the poor to catch up, or women to share in the benefits of growth.

Labour-intensive manufacturing, employment, and wages

The rapid growth of labour-intensive manufactured exports in a number of developing countries is sometimes cited as evidence in defence of standard trade theories. These exports have unquestionably generated important benefits in terms of employment creation, especially for women. Yet the benefits have been more restricted than expected, and accompanied by considerable costs. Why have real-world outcomes confounded trade theory?

In part, the reason is that many labour-intensive sectors in developing countries were heavily protected. Far from creating employment and increasing wages among low-paid, unskilled workers, trade liberalisation has frequently undermined employment among the poor and widened wage gaps. The reason: adjustment costs have been concentrated in labour-intensive sectors, while employment creation and export opportunities have been concentrated in sectors requiring higher levels of skills and wages. This effect has been observed for a large group of countries in Latin America, including Mexico, Brazil, Chile, and Colombia (Contreras et al. 2000, Velez et al. 1999, Revenga 1997). Rapid import liberalisation in Mexico in the mid-1980s was associated with a decline of one-third in the real value of the minimum wage. Around one-quarter of this decline was directly attributable to a reduction in tariffs and other import restrictions (Harrison and Hanson 1999). While wages among skilled workers also initially declined, they rose sharply after 1998. By the mid-1990s, they were 20 per cent above their pre-liberalisation levels, while the wages of the unskilled were 10 per cent below those levels (Lustig and Szekely 1998). Rising wage inequality was one of the factors behind the slow rate of poverty reduction achieved in Mexico during the first phase of liberalisation (see Box 5.1).

The effects on employment creation associated with trade liberalisation have often been very small, with a bias towards higher levels of skill (Moreira and Najberg 2000, Marquez and Pages-Serra 1998). Although foreign investment has increased demand for labour in many countries, it reinforces that bias. This appears to be true even in Mexico's *maquiladora* zone, despite the low-skill nature of much of the assembly work undertaken there (Harrison and Revenga 1998, Cragg and Epelbaum 1996). Conversely, employment destruction is frequently concentrated in areas where the poor are disproportionately represented. This mismatch in outcomes has been an important factor behind rising inequalities.

The case of India, following its rapid trade-liberalisation programme introduced in 1991, demonstrates the point. Between 1990 and 1994, the average tariff was reduced from 125 per cent to 50 per cent (Joshi and Little 2001). The textile industry was one of the sectors most immediately affected. Between 1994 and 1996, 52 mills closed in Ahmedabad alone, with a loss of over 100,000 jobs, accelerating a process of restructuring in the textile industry that was already underway. With few alternatives in the organised sector, most retrenched workers turned to the informal sector, where their conditions in terms of wages, working hours, and welfare provision deteriorated. Retrenched workers in the informal sector reported average wages of around one-third of the level in textile factories (Howell and Kambhampati 1999).

Set against this experience, trade liberalisation has certainly created new opportunities in India. The liberalisation of investment and export incentives has fuelled a boom in high-technology products. Between 1990 and 1999, exports of information and communication technology rose from $150m to $4bn, creating some 180,000 jobs in the process (Landler 2001). In terms of net employment and economic welfare, export growth in this sector may have outweighed the losses associated with import liberalisation in textiles. However, the winners have been mainly educated workers from middle-income households, while the losers have been less skilled workers from poorer households.

There are important differences between, as well as within, countries in terms of the outcomes associated with trade liberalisation. While effects on employment have been muted in much of Latin America, labour-intensive growth has generated high levels of employment creation in parts of South Asia and East Asia. The garment and textile industries in Bangladesh, Indonesia, and Cambodia, and the micro-electronic assembly industries of the Philippines and Thailand are cases in point. Even so, there is a broad sense in which trade liberalisation under globalisation is producing unexpected outcomes. Among the main factors:

- **Changing skill composition.** Technological change and foreign investment are generating patterns of export from developing countries with a bias towards more skilled workers. The premium on literacy and education is rising, while demand (and wages) for workers lacking basic literacy skills are falling (Cornia 2000).

- **Intensified South–South competition.** East Asia is often promoted as a model of labour-intensive, export-led growth over the two decades from the mid-1960s.

Since then, globalisation has changed the world in fundamental ways. Export-orientation and increased foreign investment have intensified competition, with a large population in low-income countries entering global markets (Wood 1997). When Latin America started to liberalise in the 1980s, its workforce came into competition not just with workers in industrialised countries (where wages were higher), but with workers in developing countries (where wages were, in many cases, much lower). The average income of a Bangladeshi garment producer is $1.50 a day, compared with a Mexican minimum wage of $4 a day. The entry of China in particular into global markets has had the effect of dampening demand for labour in competitor countries.

- **Rapid transition to open markets.** One factor behind the high rate of job losses in many developing countries is the presence of enterprises that have grown up behind trade barriers. Unable to cope with a rapid surge of foreign competition on domestic markets, and lacking access to the technologies needed to compete on world markets, large numbers of firms have closed. Sub-Saharan Africa appears to have suffered heavily from this effect (Wangwe 1995).

- **Weakening of labour rights and gender discrimination.** As shown in Chapter 3, the relationship between employment creation and real wage increases has been weakened by two important factors. First, wage discrimination in the context of labour-market feminisation is reducing average wages. Second, the erosion of collective bargaining rights is limiting the ability of employees to claim a bigger share of the value of production.

Costs and benefits of liberalisation in agriculture

In agriculture, as in industry, trade liberalisation changes the returns on various assets. On the import side, it will increase competition for domestic farmers as the price of competitive products falls. For exporters, the removal of export taxes and other incentives can create new market opportunities. Capacity to adjust to increased competition and take advantage of new opportunities is determined by a wide range of factors, including access to land, marketing infrastructure, and what poor people are producing. Given that women account for around two-thirds of food production and a disproportionately large share of the rural poor, gender-determined roles in production and marketing play a crucial role.

Trade restrictions have often penalised smallholder farmers. At the end of the 1980s, export taxes and exchange-rate over-valuation meant that coffee farmers in Uganda gained only ten per cent of the world-market price of exports (Oyejide, Ndulu, and Gunning 1999). When that tax was lifted with liberalisation, exports and smallholder farm incomes rose rapidly. In Vietnam, domestic marketing restrictions meant that small rice farmers were unable to produce for global markets. The removal of those restrictions expanded market opportunities (World Bank 2000a). In both countries, the dominance of smallholder farmers over production meant that export growth had powerful effects in terms of reducing poverty (see Chapter 2).

Import liberalisation can have very different distributional outcomes. Where production is dominated by large-scale agriculture (as with sugar in the Philippines, for example), relatively rich farmers will gain and poor consumers lose as a result of protectionism. On the other hand, adverse effects would be predicted if the withdrawal of import protection exposed poor farmers to intensive price competition. In many cases, poor smallholder farmers absorb a disproportionately large share of the costs associated with

Box 5. 2

Peru: the costs of rapid liberalisation

In the early 1990s the IMF–World Bank supported one of the world's most radical trade-liberalisation programmes. It was implemented under the government of Alberto Fujimori through a 'shock therapy' programme. Peru emerged, according to the IMF's classification, as one of the world's most open economies. The design of the reforms, which was heavily influenced by powerful agri-business interests, contributed to widening inequalities in the rural sector, compounding poverty in the process.

Import liberalisation and export promotion were twin cornerstones of the Fujimori agricultural strategy. Before 1990 the average import tariff was 56 per cent. In 1991 an upper tariff rate of 15 per cent was introduced for most agricultural products, with further cuts in 1996. Marketing boards, previously used to defend minimum prices for agricultural products, such as rice, were effectively removed. Meanwhile, tax incentives and public finance were directed towards the promotion of export agriculture.

The reform programme followed intensive lobbying from a consortium of food importers and processors. Led by the Alicorp corporation, an important source of finance for the presidential election campaign, the food industry argued that lower import tariffs and the withdrawal of price support would reduce prices of basic foods, helping to reduce inflation. Alicorp itself represents the major food importers and processors, such as the Nicolini and Romero groups, for whom lower trade barriers meant access to cheaper products on world markets.

As expected, food imports increased dramatically in the wake of liberalisation. In volume terms, average food imports increased from 1.6m tonnes in the first half of the 1990s to 2.7m tonnes in the second half. Exports increased less rapidly than imports, leaving the country with an annual agricultural trade deficit of $346m for 1996-9.

Food imports now account for around 40 per cent of total national food consumption in Peru. Import growth has been especially rapid in some of the key cereals markets. Wheat imports doubled during the 1990s to 2.5 million tonnes. In 2000, imports of hard maize overtook domestic production, exceeding one million tonnes. Milk imports rose by a factor of three in the first half of the 1990s alone, before falling back slightly in the second half of the decade. Increasing imports have played an important role in forcing down the prices received by Peruvian farmers.

How has increased import competition affected rural poverty? There are variations across sectors:

Dairy farming. Twenty years ago, dairy farming was dominated by small producers in central highland areas such as Arequipa and Cajamarca. During the 1990s, as competition with imports intensified, there was an accelerating trend towards larger-scale farming around Lima and nearby coastal valleys. Traditional farmers were unable to compete with price competition from imported milk supplied by New Zealand, Australia, and, on heavily subsidised terms, the European Union.

Rice. Most of Peru's rice is produced by small-scale farmers in the southern and northern coastal valleys, and in the jungle department of San Martin. These farmers have had to absorb sharp price falls in the face of imports from Thailand and other low-cost producers.

Maize. Commercial farms in the coastal valleys around Lima and Libertad have been able to cope with increased competition. Average yields are relatively high, and transport costs to urban markets are low. By contrast, farmers in jungle areas such as San Martin have productivity levels less than half of those in coastal valleys, and face higher marketing costs. Price pressures are producing growing disparities between these two groups of producers.

Food staples. Cheap wheat and rice imports are increasing the price competition facing smallholder farmers who produce traditional Andean products such as quinua, beans, and potatoes. The availability of cheap, imported grains has accelerated changes in consumption patterns in favour of wheat-based food and rice. Per capita consumption of potatoes has fallen from 100kg per person in 1990 to 38kg in 2000.

In each of these sectors, trade liberalisation has reinforced old structural inequalities based on access to assets and markets. Smallholder peasant agriculture has fallen further behind, especially in the sierra. For the 1.5 million households in the sierra surviving on small-holdings of less than five hectares, liberalisation has been associated with accelerated marginalisation.

Developments in agriculture have been part of a broader trend. Weak and variable as it has been, economic recovery in Peru during the 1990s was accompanied by rising inequality and a deteriorating record on poverty reduction. Between the start of the reforms in 1991 and 1997, the Gini co-efficient in Peru rose by 4 points (to 50.6) – one of the most rapid increases in inequality recorded in Latin America. Over the same period, the income share of the richest one-tenth increased from 35 per cent to 39 per cent, while that of the poorest tenth fell from 15 per cent to 12 per cent.

According to the Economic Commission for Latin America, the proportion of the rural population living in poverty increased by 20 per cent in the decade to 1995, to almost two-thirds of the total.

Import liberalisation is not the primary cause of these adverse trends. Chronic under-funding of rural infrastructure, limited access to credit, and failure to develop a coherent rural development strategy have all contributed. At the same time, rapid and badly designed import liberalisation has reinforced wider pressures on poor farmers. Larger commercial farms have also faced adjustment costs, but have vastly superior access to infrastructure, credit, and markets, with the result that inequalities within the rural sector are widening.

Source: Crabtree 2001

liberalisation, while richer farmers capture a disproportionately large share of the benefits accompanying export growth. Because of the dominant role of women in the production of food crops, they are often adversely affected by import liberalisation.

This problem is illustrated by Haiti's programme of rapid trade liberalisation, implemented under IMF–World Bank auspices from the mid-1980s onwards. In 1995, import tariffs on rice were cut from 50 per cent to 3 per cent, opening the door to heavily subsidised imports from the United States. In real terms, prices for rice fell by 25 per cent in the second half of the 1990s. Unable to compete with cheap imports, domestic producers were pushed out of local markets. From a position of near self-sufficiency in 1990, by the end of the decade national production of paddy had fallen by almost half, to 105,000 tons (IMF 1999a and 2000). Subsidised exports from the USA accounted for more than half of the domestic market.

Urban populations in Haiti have benefited from cheaper rice, while smallholder rice producers have seen their livelihoods devastated. In a country where more than half of all children are malnourished, and more than 80 per cent of the rural population live below the poverty line, rice-growing areas have some of the highest concentrations of malnutrition and poverty (Oxfam International 2001a). Farmers in the Artibonite Valley, one of the main rice-growing areas, interviewed by Oxfam in mid-2001, were still suffering the consequences of increased competition. One of them commented: *'While rice is so cheap, we can never find a way out of our poverty. These imports make our lives impossible. I can no longer afford fertilisers, so I am producing less. My farm no longer grows enough even to feed this family. There is not enough money for health care and education.'*

Rice farmers have responded to the impact of lower prices on their livelihoods by cutting costs in other areas (such as health and education), and increasing off-farm employment, with women taking on more work as rural labourers. Notwithstanding the income gains for rice consumers, the country has been left dangerously dependent on food imports, which it cannot secure on a sustainable basis, for lack of foreign exchange. Moreover, increased rural poverty has been spread from the farmers most directly affected to extend across the rural economy, with adverse effects for agricultural wages and small-scale enterprises.

Import liberalisation is often designed in a manner that shields politically powerful lobbies, while subjecting marginal groups to more intense competition. In India, high tariffs have been maintained for rice farmers, but in 1996 import taxes on edible oils were dramatically cut, ostensibly to provide oil processors and consumers with access to cheaper products. Over the next two years, imports of vegetable oils increased five-fold, to five million tonnes. Malaysian palm, Indonesian coconut, and Brazilian and Argentinian soya flooded local markets, driving down domestic prices by 20--40 per cent (Sharma 2000). The consequences for rural poverty have been severe. Oilseeds are the second largest group of agricultural products in India, with about 14 million households directly engaged in production. Since the crop is extensively produced in dryland areas, where rural poverty is concentrated, the price falls would have directly affected the poor. Severe hardship was reported among oilseed producers in Andhra Pradesh and among coconut farmers in Kerala (Sharma 2000).

At the same time, trade liberalisation in India has unquestionably created new opportunities for commercial farmers. In Maharashtra and Gujarat, State governments are supporting the development of large-scale agro-export schemes for the production of grapes, vegetables, and other crops. In Andhra Pradesh, the State government is promoting through its *Vision 2020* plan the introduction of genetically modified cotton and irrigated fruit production (IIED 2001). However, participation in export markets such as these requires access to irrigated land, capital, and technologies that are beyond the means of the poor. It is difficult to see how such a model of growth is likely to improve significantly India's disastrous record on rural poverty, which accounts for over two-thirds of the national total. At the end of 1997, the incidence of poverty in rural areas was 34 per cent, the same level as in 1989 (Jha 2000). Over the same period, the rural Gini co-efficient increased by three points. Imposing a pro-rich pattern of trade liberalisation on these foundations is hardly a good basis for human development.

In countries with high concentrations of rural poverty, the combination of rapid import liberalisation in food staples and the promotion of capital-intensive export production can have profoundly anti-poor outcomes. Mexican agriculture has seen growing divergences in wealth between commercial farms linked to the US economy in the north, and smallholder agriculture in the 'poverty-belt' States of the south. By enabling subsidised corn to enter local markets at prices cheaper than many domestic farmers are able to compete with, import liberalisation has threatened the mainstay of the rural economy of the poor (see Box 5.1). In Peru, rapid liberalisation across a wide range of agricultural commodities in the early 1990s, again under IMF–World Bank auspices, has intensified inequalities between small and large producers, between farmers located close to and more distant from major markets, and between regions. Indigenous communities in highland areas, where the concentration of poverty is among the highest in the country, have seen markets for basic food staples captured by importers (Box 5.2).

Patterns of liberalisation such as these help to explain one of the anomalies revealed by the TLI: namely, the poor performance of rapid liberalisers in terms of poverty reduction. Rising inequalities reflect the development of market structures that are tending to reinforce already extreme concentrations of advantage and disadvantage.

Import liberalisation is typically accompanied by wider reforms in domestic marketing systems, which again can have benefits for the poor. In the Indian State of Gujarat, licensing requirements for the collection of gum exclude women forest dwellers from participation in the market (SEWA 1997); removing them would generate potential benefits. However, even when State marketing systems create inefficiency, the reform of these systems can damage poor people's interests. In Zambia, a government marketing board provided maize producers in poor areas with a guaranteed market and price. When it was privatised, market outlets collapsed, because there were no private traders to replace it. Competitive private markets are a requirement for protecting the poor from collusion between powerful traders, but such markets often do not exist.

No trade reform is gender-neutral. It follows that no trade policy should be designed without consideration of the potential outcomes on the distribution of income within households. The removal of barriers to women's participation in rural markets, and the elimination of wage discrimination, would appear to be universal requirements for poverty reduction.

Bias against women means that trade-policy reforms can have unintended outcomes that are bad for poverty reduction. Although export production does not necessarily result in pressure on the food-crop economy, it can have this effect. Fieldwork undertaken in southern Zambia found that nutritional standards were suffering because of pressure on women to transfer their labour from food crops to cash crops (Oxfam/IDS 1999). More generally, commercialisation can result in women losing control over the marketing of cash crops, as has been reported in Uganda (Haddad 1995). As the majority food producers, women also face the most intensive pressure as a result of import liberalisation. Research in Ghana suggests that price pressures associated with increased food imports, the loss of extension services, and limited access to alternative markets have had adverse consequences on women farmers (Lumor 1999). In the case of Mexico, the increase in male migration associated with the demise of the maize sector has increased the workload of women and children (Watkins 1997). Replacing male labour on the home farm, while at the same time being forced by income pressures to spend more hours in off-farm employment, has placed acute stresses on women.

Designing pro-poor trade-reform policies: the role of Poverty Reduction Strategy Papers

As the evidence presented in this chapter and elsewhere in the report suggests, trade liberalisation is a policy which is neither inherently pro-poor nor anti-poor. Similar sets of policies could contribute to poverty reduction in one country, yet increase poverty in another (Morrisey 2001). By the same token, trade-policy reform can widen or reduce inequalities, depending on its design, pace, and sequencing.

There are no blueprints for pro-poor trade reform, but there are some broad lessons. Ability to compete with imports and take advantage of export opportunities is partly a function of the distribution of productive assets. In countries with highly distorted patterns of asset and income distribution, failure to integrate redistributive strategies in

Box 5.3

How not to do a PRSP: the case of Cambodia

Poverty Reduction Strategy Papers (PRSPs) are supposed to place poverty at the centre of national reform programmes, breaking down the artificial division between social policies and macro-economic policies. While the concept behind PRSPs marks a step in the right direction, in terms of trade policy, application of the poverty-reduction principle has been haphazard.

Cambodia is one of the world's poorest countries. Average incomes were estimated at only $268 at the end of the 1990s, with more than one-third of the population living below the poverty line. Poverty is most marked in rural areas. Poor rural people suffer from chronic under-investment in marketing infrastructure, irrigation, and basic services. Although economic growth has been strong, averaging over four per cent in the 1990s, rural poverty has fallen very slowly, at only 0.3 per cent a year. One reason for the weak link between growth and poverty reduction is that inequalities have been widening. Between 1993 and 1997, average income increased by 12 per cent. However, the income of the poorest one-fifth rose by less than 2 per cent, while that of the richest one-fifth rose by 18 per cent.

Under a succession of IMF programmes, Cambodia has embarked on a rapid trade-liberalisation exercise. Average tariff rates have been halved since 1996, to 15 per cent. Under the terms of two memoranda signed between the IMF and Cambodia in 2001, further reforms were introduced, including a sharp reduction in maximum tariff levels. One of the aims has been to prepare Cambodia for entry to the WTO.

Rice is one of the commodities that will be subjected to rapid liberalisation. This is the mainstay of the rural economy, accounting for more than 40 per cent of value-added. Most rice is produced under rain-fed conditions, which exposes farmers to risks from droughts and floods. Although Cambodia is self-sufficient in rice, with small export surpluses at the end of the 1990s, productivity levels and marketing costs are far higher than in either Thailand or Vietnam, the world's largest and second largest exporters. How will import liberalisation affect small rice farmers in Cambodia, one of the biggest groups living below the poverty line?

The PRSP document prepared by the Cambodian government, under the auspices of the IMF and World Bank, does not even address this question. Instead, it simply asserts that increased openness will be good for growth, echoing the received wisdom on 19th Street in Washington. The omission is a serious one. Increased competition from lower-cost producers in Thailand and Vietnam would be expected to push down prices and restrict the market for Cambodian producers. While more commercial irrigated areas are in a position to withstand competition, only 12 per cent of rice farmers fall into this category. The combination of lower prices and reduced demand would have potentially grave consequences for poorer households, forcing them to seek alternative sources of income.

It could be argued that there is a free-market case for allowing cheap rice to enter the Cambodian market, given that neither Thailand nor Vietnam is a subsidising exporter. In terms of poverty-reduction strategies, current policy prescriptions raise serious problems of sequencing. With increased investment, support for infrastructural development, and increased provision of irrigation, it might be possible for most Cambodian farmers to compete with their counterparts elsewhere, or to diversify into other areas. Seeking to adjust through rapid trade liberalisation will have the effect of increasing both the social and economic costs experienced by rural Cambodians.

The PRSP for Cambodia has clearly failed to integrate trade policies into national poverty-reduction strategies. It has been guided instead by a blind faith in the virtues of open markets. An immediate requirement for reform is dialogue with farmers and research into the potential effects of market liberalisation on livelihoods.

Sources: Royal Government of Cambodia 2000, 2001; IMF 2000d; Murshid 1998

trade reform will almost inevitably increase inequalities. Even if it is possible to combine rising inequality with poverty reduction, as in China and Chile, for example, widening income disparities act as a brake on the rate of poverty reduction.

The rapid development of inequalities associated with education has only one effective solution: extended access to education and improvements in education quality. For a country like India, the 50 million children denied access to school, and the 20 per cent enrolment gap in favour of boys, represent formidable barriers to poverty reduction. In Latin America, as shown in Chapter 3, education gaps are now the single biggest force that determines income-distribution patterns.

Import liberalisation can affect the ability of governments to finance and provide services that are vital to pro-poor growth. This is because revenues from import and export taxes represent an important source of State income in a large group of countries. One IMF survey of 36 developing countries found that trade taxes accounted for nearly one-third of tax revenue (Winters 2000). In Pakistan, revenue from customs duties fell by the equivalent of two per cent of GDP in the 1990s (Anwar 2000). Inevitably, losses on this scale make it more difficult to finance spending in areas that might enhance the ability of poor people to benefit from trade. As the main providers of care, women can be expected to suffer disproportionately from any cuts in public spending associated with revenue losses.

In terms of specific trade instruments, evidence suggests that there is a strong case for reducing taxes and regulations that impede poor people's access to markets. With regard to import restrictions, more complex issues emerge. From a poverty-reduction perspective, what matters is the distribution of costs and benefits associated with the removal of such restrictions. This raises questions about sequencing and policy design. Restricting the importation of agricultural goods produced by the poor may be justified on social and economic grounds, especially if imports are subsidised. More broadly, in any labour-intensive sector it may make sense to delay import liberalisation until a wider range of complementary measures is in place, including improved infrastructure. Drastic and sudden trade liberalisation will not necessarily produce optimal outcomes, in terms of either sustainable growth or poverty reduction.

The starting point for the design of any trade-reform programme must be its integration into a broader national strategy for poverty reduction. In itself, trade liberalisation is not a poverty-reduction strategy, even if it can contribute to such a strategy. For all their recent commitment to ensure that macro-economic reform programmes are integrated into a wider set of policies for poverty reduction, neither the IMF nor the World Bank has applied this principle to trade policy. This is despite the development of Poverty Reduction Strategy Papers (PRSPs), documents that are supposed to set out in detail how IMF–World Bank programmes fit into national poverty strategies.

In a detailed review of 12 PRSPs, Oxfam found that only four even mentioned the possible impact of trade-reform measures on poverty. Of these, only two incorporated a policy response to mitigate the negative impacts of trade liberalisation. None offered even the most rudimentary assessment of the range of distributional outcomes that might result from import liberalisation, or reviewed alternative prescriptions for the pace, design, and sequencing of reform. This was despite the far-reaching liberalisation reflected in IMF–World Bank loan conditions. For example, in Cambodia the reform programme envisages large reductions in import protection for farmers in the rice sector. In a country with such high levels of rural poverty, located next to one of the world's lowest-cost rice exporters, this could have major implications for rural poverty (see Box 5.3).

The approach to PRSPs reflects a broader problem in IMF–World Bank thinking about trade reform. It is rooted in the received wisdom that trade is inherently good for growth and good for the poor. Until that is challenged, the new poverty rhetoric of the Bretton Woods agencies will remain at variance with the reality of their policies.

Trade liberalisation and growth: the limits to open markets

One of the ironies of the new consensus on trade liberalisation is that it identifies East Asia as an example of the virtues of openness. Yet the policies identified with openness were conspicuous by their absence from much of the region. The sustained growth associated with successful integration into global markets was the product of national policies that are far removed from those advocated today by the IMF and the World Bank. As the Trade Liberalisation Indicator illustrated, most countries in East Asia remain highly protected by international standards. Although there have been wide policy variations within and across countries, two common elements emerge, both of which have an important bearing on current debates.

The first concerns timing. Most countries in East Asia began to liberalise exports and provide export incentives before they started to liberalise imports. In broad terms, export liberalisation was pursued with far greater ambition than import liberalisation. Moreover, import liberalisation followed *after* countries had made the transition to higher economic growth, and after they had built up a strong base in education and economic infrastructure. Export growth provided an outlet for the productive potential unleashed through domestic reforms. In China, the reform programme started with the introduction of the household-responsibility system in 1979, under which farmers were able to market a larger share of their output. Export promotion followed, as government sought to generate the foreign exchange needed to provide the inputs for sustaining the reform programme, such as seeds, machinery, and fertiliser. In similar fashion, the foundations for Vietnam's rapid integration into the global market were laid with the introduction in 1986 of *Doi Moi,* or the Economic Renovation programme. Farmers were allowed to increase sales to the market, and agricultural taxes were reduced, boosting agricultural productivity and income.

The second element uniting a large group of East Asian countries was a set of policies that, by today's standards, would rank as highly unorthodox. They combined high levels of tariffs and non-tariff barriers with restrictions on foreign investment, and the imposition of domestic-content requirements on foreign firms. Assessed on their 'openness', Korea and Taiwan were, and remain, poor performers. World Bank analysis of price distortions associated with protectionism in the 1970s and 1980s found that both were more overtly interventionist than countries such as India, Brazil, and Mexico (Lall 1999). Countries such as Korea and Taiwan entered global markets *after* domestic firms had developed their capacity, with State support in an economic environment that was anything but open. Many of the policies used would be ruled out by IMF–World Bank loan conditions, or by WTO provisions (see Chapter 8).

East Asia used import protection as part of a strategy to raise technological capacity and productivity over the long term. There is no doubt that there were short-term costs: import barriers pushed up prices for consumers and producers. But the case of East Asia demonstrates that well-designed trade policies can create a dynamic comparative advantage. In the 1950s, Korea's fledgling steel industry would have been destroyed in open competition with its US counterpart; Taiwan's electronic sector would have suffered the same fate in the 1960s. Today, it is the US steel industry and European electronics that seek protection from East Asia, rather than vice versa. Comparative advantage has been reversed.

Import protection is not a guaranteed route to more dynamic comparative advantage. The strategy of import-substituting industrialisation (ISI) pursued by most developing countries until the 1980s involved driving a wedge between domestic prices and world-market prices to shield local industries. As in East Asia, the idea was that domestic investment and technological capacity could be spurred by protection against imports. Some spectacular failures were recorded. In sub-Saharan Africa, whole industries proved to require more subsidies from the State than they produced in income. In India, highly capital-intensive, large-scale enterprises received unnecessary protection from foreign competition, driving up the costs of inputs to small and medium enterprises, and undermining efficiency and employment (Corbridge and Harriss 2000). For all this, ISI produced growth rates for some regions, including Latin America, which compare favourably with those recorded in the 1990s (Rodrik 2001c). In general terms, high levels of import protection, applied over a long period, are likely to produce inefficient industries. However, that does not undermine the case for using temporary and selective protection to nurture infant industries that could play a vital role in supporting higher growth and successful integration into global markets. Among the many rich ironies in current debates about trade is the fact that, for much of history, industrialised countries have been in the forefront of efforts to promote such industries through restrictive trade policies.

Recommendations

Through their influence over the design and implementation of IMF–World Bank policies, industrialised countries have been able to maintain a highly unbalanced process of trade liberalisation. Developing countries have been liberalising rapidly, incurring large adjustment costs, which have been compounded by the unwillingness of rich countries to open their markets. At the same time, the IMF and the World Bank have frequently undermined the ability of poor countries and poor people to integrate successfully into the global economy. Loan conditions that place a premium on rapid liberalisation, without proper consideration of the consequences for short-term poverty and long-term development, are among the factors that prevent trade from working for the poor.

Among the measures needed to address these problems are the following.

- **The removal of trade liberalisation from IMF–World Bank loan conditions.** The proper contexts in which to discuss reciprocal trade liberalisation are the WTO and regional trade agreements, which enable governments to exchange concessions. Apart from being badly designed and poorly sequenced, IMF–World Bank loan conditionality has severely disadvantaged developing countries.

- **Retrospective credit for past liberalisation undertaken by developing countries under IMF–World Bank auspices.** IMF–World Bank staff should undertake a full review of all unilateral trade-liberalisation measures undertaken under programmes supported by the two institutions over the past decade. These measures should be converted into tariff equivalents. They should then be reciprocated by the industrialised countries through negotiations at the WTO.

- **Poverty assessments under PRSPs.** All Poverty Reduction Strategy Papers should include a comprehensive assessment of the implications of trade liberalisation for poverty reduction and income distribution. These should be published as part of a national consultation process. The same principles should be applied by developing-country governments in their trade policies.

CHAPTER 6
Primary commodities – trading into decline

Proper economic prices should be fixed not at the lowest possible level, but at the level sufficient to provide producers with proper nutritional and other standards in the conditions in which they live ... and it is in the interests of all producers alike that the price of a commodity should not be depressed below this level, and consumers are not entitled to expect that it should.
– John Maynard Keynes, 1946 (Keynes 1980)

When the institutional foundations for managing the post-war global economy were established more than half a century ago, commodities figured prominently on the international agenda. The instability, and ultimate collapse, of commodity prices in the 1920s was seen as one of the major factors that had caused the Great Depression, contributing to political turmoil and the growth of international tensions in the process. When the Bretton Woods Conference convened in 1944, the English economist John Maynard Keynes called for an institutional response to the problems posed by commodity markets (Skidelsky 2001). He warned that failure to act would threaten the potential for achieving shared prosperity. His warning voice was ignored.

History has proved Keynes right, although he under-estimated the scale of the problem. While globalisation may be transforming international trade, many countries – and many millions of producers – remain heavily dependent on the export of commodities. Trading patterns established after the discovery of the New World, and developed through slavery and colonialism, remain intact. So too do the problems that dogged commodity traders in the 1920s. Market instability and ruinously low prices are consigning whole swathes of the developing world to mass poverty and a marginal role in world trade. Cut off from the rising tide of global prosperity, there is a growing danger that countries dependent on primary commodities will become increasingly desperate enclaves of despair.

Viewed from the industrialised world, the crisis in commodity markets is invisible. Over the past four years, the prices received by coffee farmers in Africa, Asia, and Latin America have fallen by more than half. In three years, developing countries saw the value of their coffee exports fall from around $13 billion to $7 billion, even though they exported more coffee. Few of the consumers who buy their products contemplate what it would mean for their own lives and their families if their own wages were halved. But in the developing world, low prices result in worsening nutrition, children being taken out of school, and increased vulnerability. Whole economies are being deeply damaged – as are international development efforts. Losses sustained in primary-commodity markets undermine the value of what many countries in Africa and elsewhere receive in aid and debt relief.

As in other areas of trade, changes in market prices produce winners and losers. The winners in this case stand between the rich-country consumer and the producer. Low world prices give the handful of transnational companies (TNCs) that dominate world markets for products such as coffee, cocoa, tea, bananas, and other crops access to cheap resources which produce enormous profit margins. Increased corporate profit and increased Third World poverty have gone hand-in-hand.

This chapter assesses the scale of the crisis in international commodity markets, analyses its underlying causes, and considers the human costs. The first section sets out the extent of commodity dependence and examines the financial costs of adverse price trends. The second part considers some of the main factors that influence these trends, which are rooted in structural over-supply. The third part reviews attempts to manage markets in a more benign fashion, focusing on the achievements and limitations of fair trade, and on the history of commodity agreements. The final section presents an agenda for change, including Oxfam's proposal for a new institution on primary commodities, and a new approach to international commodity-market management.

The costs of commodity dependence

Over the past 30 years, the share of non-fuel commodities in world trade has been declining almost without interruption. National economies have suffered in terms of reduced prospects for economic growth and pressure on their balance of payments. For households, global market pressures have damaged people's livelihoods and reduced their sense of security.

Trading into decline

In the 1990s, world trade in primary commodities was growing at less than one-third of the rate for trade in manufactured goods, and the gap is widening (UNCTAD 1999b). As a result, countries dependent on primary commodities have been left trailing behind more dynamic exporters. More than 50 developing countries depend on three or fewer commodities for more than half of their export earnings (International Task Force 1999). Dependency is most pronounced in sub-Saharan Africa; there are 17 countries for which non-oil exports account for three-quarters or more of export earnings. In many cases, a large share of export earnings is earned by a small group of products. Coffee alone accounts for 60–80 per cent of export earnings for Ethiopia and Burundi. Cotton accounts for around half of Burkina Faso's export earnings, and cocoa for nearly one-quarter of those for Ghana (UNCTAD 2001a, World Bank data 1999–2000).

One symptom of dependence on primary commodities is a high level of vulnerability to debt. Inability to sustain imports, coupled with excessive borrowing on the strength of brief commodity booms, has had devastating consequences. Thirty-seven of the countries categorised by the IMF and World Bank as Heavily Indebted Poor Countries

(HIPCs) rely on primary commodities for more than half of their merchandise export earnings. For 15 countries in this group, export earnings from commodities generated more than 90 per cent of export revenue (International Task Force 1999). The heavily indebted countries produce more than half of the world's cocoa, and more than a quarter of its coffee. As these figures indicate, for a large group of poor countries, primary commodities must generate the foreign exchange needed to import essential goods such as oil, technology, and agricultural inputs. It follows that export prices for these commodities have an important bearing on the capacity of countries to reap the benefits of integration into global markets.

While there have been periodic rises, graphs of world market prices for most primary commodities show an unmistakably downward trend. In 2000, prices for 18 major export commodities were 25 per cent lower in real terms than in 1980. For eight of these commodities, the decline exceeded 50 per cent (Table 6.1). The 1990s saw particularly

Decrease by 0-25%		Decrease by 25-50%		Decrease by over 50%	
Banana*	-4.4	Aluminium	-27.2	Cocoa	-71.2
Fertiliser	-23.1	Coconut oil	-44.3	Coffee	-64.5
Iron ore*	-19.5	Copper	-30.9	Lead	-58.3
Phosphate rock	-21.6	Cotton	-47.6	Palm oil	-55.8
Tea	-7.5	Fishmeal	-31.9	Rice	-60.9
		Groundnut oil	-30.9	Rubber	-59.6
		Maize	-41.6	Sugar	-76.6
		Soybean	-39.0	Tin	-73.0
		Wheat	-45.2		
*note: 1980-1999					

Table 6.1
Price-decreasing commodities, real terms, 1980-2000

Source: IMF, International Financial Statistics Yearbook, various issues

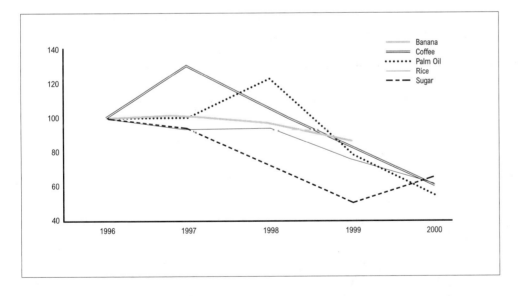

Figure 6.1
Decline in real prices 1996-2000 (index 1996=100) for developing countries' top 5 commodities (excluding tobacco)

deep price cuts for the five biggest non-oil commodity exports, as shown in Figure 6.1. The breadth and depth of the slump in non-fuel commodities during the last two years of the 1990s was particularly acute, with UNCTAD's composite index registering a decline of one-third (UNCTAD 2000b). Beverages have been the worst-affected sector. The World Bank's monthly index of beverage prices (which averages prices for coffee, cocoa, and tea) declined by 71 per cent between 1997 and 2001. Although metal prices have been less dramatically affected, there are some notable exceptions. For example, prices for copper halved between 1996 and 2001 (World Bank 2002).

Losses associated with adverse price trends can be very large. In 2000/01, developing-country coffee exporters sold nearly 20 per cent more coffee on to world markets than in 1997/98, for which they received 45 per cent less foreign exchange. Had exporters received the same price in 2000/01 as they did during 1997/98, they would have been around $8 billion better off. For individual countries the losses have been very large indeed, undermining the financial savings from debt relief. Uganda provides a stark illustration. In 1994/95, when coffee prices were high, the country's export revenues from this crop amounted to some $433m. In 2000/01, Uganda exported roughly the same volume, but it earned the country just $110m.[1] To put this figure in context, the revenue gap was equivalent to more than three times the amount that Uganda received in HIPC debt relief in 2001. The country in which coffee originated has also suffered. In just one year, from 1999/00 to 2000/01, Ethiopia's export revenues from coffee exports slumped from $257m to $176m, owing to a combination of lower production and falling price. In 2002, Ethiopia's projected savings on debt servicing (from HIPC and other debt relief) will be $58m.

Stark as they are, absolute price levels understate the problems facing commodity-dependent economies. What matters for an exporting country is less the absolute price that it receives, and more the purchasing power generated. This is especially true for countries that depend very heavily on primary commodities for foreign exchange. One way of capturing purchasing power is to look at the terms of trade, or the export prices received for commodities relative to the price of imports. As shown in Figure 6.2, primary-commodity exporters have suffered a devastating deterioration in terms of trade in relation to industrialised countries. In the 1990s alone, this amounted to a relative price decline of 10 per cent. This was a continuation of a long-term trend in prices stretching back to the 1930s (Maizels 2000b), which helps to explain the inability of a large group of developing countries to increase their share of world markets. It has also been a major source of balance-of-payments pressures.

The region that has suffered most from unfavourable terms of trade is sub-Saharan Africa. The UN estimates that for every $1 in aid received by sub-Saharan Africa since the early 1970s, $0.50 has been lost as a result of deteriorating terms of trade (UNCTAD 2001b). In broader economic terms, one UN source estimates that Africa's share of

Figure 6.2
Terms of trade for industrialised and developing countries

Source: International Financial Statistics Yearbook, 2000

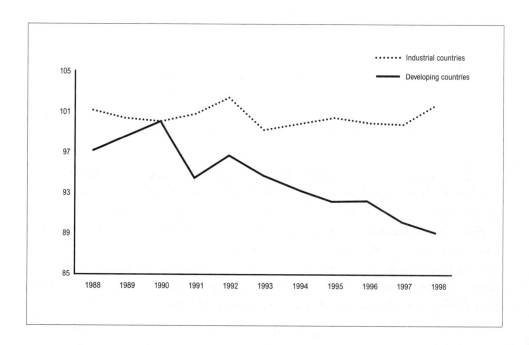

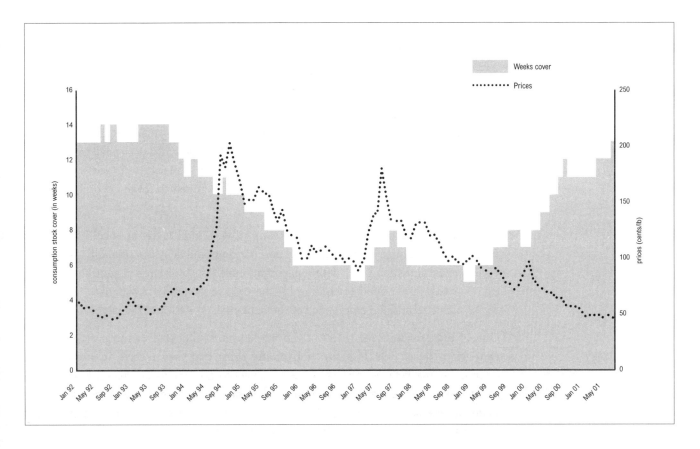

Figure 6.3
Coffee: stocks and international prices, 1992-2001

world trade would be double its current level if the region had not suffered a terms-of-trade loss. Current levels of per capita income would be 50 per cent higher. This translates into a loss of $155 per capita (UNCTAD 2001b). To put this figure in context, current aid transfers to sub-Saharan Africa amount to $20 per capita. In other words, deteriorating terms of trade have cost more than seven times as much as Africa receives in aid. It is impossible to calculate what this has meant in terms of poverty, ill-health, and vulnerability. However, it is clear that there are very real human costs associated with world market trends.

Oil-importing countries have faced serious balance-of-payments pressures associated with losses in terms of trade. Even though the price of oil has fallen recently, it has not fallen as fast as the prices of many of the commodities on which low-income countries depend. In the case of Uganda, the terms-of-trade loss associated with exchanges of coffee for oil exceeded the equivalent of two per cent of GDP for 1999/2000 (IMF/IDA 2001).

Declining prices and deteriorating terms of trade have been compounded by the problem of price volatility. This matters for the governments of commodity-exporting countries and for households, since instability makes planning difficult. It is hard for farmers to undertake investment, or governments to make future spending commitments, when they have little idea what next year's income flow will look like. Commodity markets deliver instability in extreme form. Taking average prices for the 1980s and 1990s, it is not uncommon for the prices of primary commodities to fluctuate from below 50 per cent to above 150 per cent of the average on a year-to-year basis. More worrying, research has shown that, for most commodities, price slumps last longer than price booms, and the magnitude of the price falls in a slump is slightly larger than that of price rises in subsequent booms (Cashin and McDermott 1999). Figure 6.3 illustrates the variability of coffee prices. It shows that prices rose by a factor of four in 1994–95, fell by more than half over the next two years, and doubled over the next year, before heading on a steady downward trend after 1997.

Cocoa prices have been subject to similar wild variations. Between 1998 and 2000, international prices fell by nearly half. The implied foreign-exchange loss for Ghana, the world's second largest cocoa exporter, amounted to 15 per cent of export earnings. This is not an isolated example. In just two years, from 1990 to 1992, Benin, Chad, and Mali lost around one-quarter of their total export earnings, following a sharp fall in the world price of cotton (OECD 1997). Such losses inevitably translate into acute economic pressures, as governments and households seek to adjust to lower income levels by reducing consumption.

Dependence on primary commodities, coupled with high levels of volatility in world prices, results in huge fluctuations in export earnings and debt sustainability. If foreign-exchange earnings fall while debt-repayment obligations remain constant, the share of export earnings allocated to creditors – the debt-service ratio – will rise. This was a major factor behind the emergence of the debt crisis in Africa in the 1970s.

One of the problems for many of the world's most indebted countries is that their capacity to repay debt is a function of the price that they receive in international commodity markets. When that price is subject to extreme variations on a downward trend, it becomes very difficult to define the point at which debt repayments impinge on national development capacity. Current approaches to measuring and evaluating debt sustainability under the HIPC Initiative do not help.

When the IMF and the World Bank measure sustainability under the HIPC Initiative, they do so primarily on the basis of debt-to-foreign-exchange ratios, concentrating on the share of export earnings absorbed in debt repayments. Unfortunately, their forecasts of commodity prices reinforce a bias towards over-optimism in their projections for export growth, and hence for debt-repayment capacity. Forecasts in the official IMF–World Bank papers that analyse debt sustainability often fail to reflect historic averages. For example, a recent study (Martin and Alami 2001) found that 21 of the 28 countries analysed have projected export-growth rates above recent trends. This suggests that the IMF and the World Bank may be systematically over-stating debt-repayment capacity, and under-stating the financial requirements for debt relief.

Household poverty and vulnerability

International data on prices give some insight into the pressures faced by commodity-exporting countries. They help to explain why they have been unable to integrate into world markets on more dynamic terms. Ultimately, however, the price pressures stop at the level of individual households. For the people producing these commodities, ruinous international prices mean reduced purchasing power and increased exposure to risk. The UN estimates that more than one billion people depend on commodity production for their livelihoods. Many are smallholder farmers, with women occupying a central role. For traders in international markets, changes in prices register as blips on computer screens and as opportunities to generate profit. But for the people who produce the commodities in which the traders deal, changes in international markets determine their quality of life.

In many developing countries there is an intimate relationship between world-market prices and poverty levels. There are around 20 million households across Africa, Latin America, and Asia growing coffee, mostly on small farms. In Uganda, almost one-quarter of the entire population earns a living from coffee. Two and a half million smallholders grow cocoa, mainly in West Africa. In Ghana almost half of all cultivated land is dedicated to cocoa farming, on which an estimated eight million people depend, either directly or indirectly for their livelihoods. In the south of India and the Philippines, millions of livelihoods depend on the trade in coconuts. In addition to small farmers, many millions of agricultural labourers, one of the social groups most prone to poverty, work for others, growing and picking commodities destined for world markets. On the tea estates of India and Sri Lanka, largely female workforces pick leaves destined for rich-country markets. In Peru, Chad, and Mali, rural migrant labourers plant and pick cotton. In Guatemala, coffee estates are a major source of employment for some of the country's poorest people. For all of these people, small farmers and labourers alike, changes in world-market conditions can exercise a profound influence, for better or for worse.

For people, as for countries, exposure to volatile world markets brings high risks. Falling commodity prices can sweep away the benefits of painstaking development work. In the Nilgiri Hills of India, Oxfam partners have been working with tribal communities who are mobilising to regain access to common lands expropriated by commercial farmers. Some success has been achieved. Tea cultivation was successfully introduced, with production for exports supporting income growth. However, the picture changed dramatically in 1997, not because of local conditions, but as a result of the East Asian financial crash. When the Indonesian rupiah collapsed in 1997, it made Indonesian tea far cheaper than tea grown in Nilgiris, and thus forced down export prices. Production had fallen by 40 per cent by 2000, with damaging consequences for local livelihoods (Thekaekara 2001).

Adverse world-market trends can produce highly damaging outcomes in commodity-dependent countries affected by conflict. Between 1997 and 2000, declining world prices and a fall in coffee production caused by armed conflict reduced the value of Burundi's coffee exports by $100m – equivalent to 12 per cent of GDP. Inevitably, the resulting economic pressures and limits on government financing interact with political tensions, introducing another destabilising element into an already fraught situation (IMF 2001c).

Coffee farmers have been among those worst affected by the protracted crisis in international markets. At the end of the 1990s, international prices slumped to levels that were comparable in real terms to those prevailing in the years of the Great Depression. Between 1988 and 2001, prices fell by two-thirds (World Bank 2002). Inevitably, the livelihoods of millions of small farmers have suffered. The crisis in the international coffee economy has been converted through the mechanisms of international trade into a deep social and economic crisis which has driven millions into poverty.

The village of Kishimundu in the lush foothills of Mount Kilimanjaro is a microcosm of the crisis in the international commodity economy. Coffee is the mainstay of the local economy, providing the income that families use to pay school fees, meet health-care costs, and buy essential materials like cooking oil. Small farms, or *shambas*, precariously located on steep hillsides, intercrop coffee with bananas, beans, and vegetables, the deep roots of the coffee bush helping to bind the soil and prevent erosion. It is a sustainable system that has been passed down across generations – and it is now under threat from collapsing international prices. Towards the end of 2000, Oxfam staff worked with local researchers and interviewed dozens of coffee farmers in Kishimundu and other villages as part of an international research programme. One of the poorest was a 37-year-old widow, Tatu Museyni, with two children, Angera and Mary, aged 15 and 13 respectively, and both still in primary school. The household *shamba* had 30 coffee bushes. In 1998, she was being paid $1 per pound for her coffee. At the time of the interview, Tatu Museyni had sold her crop for $0.30 per pound, leaving her with an income of $35. These are her words:

> 'The price of coffee is destroying me. It is destroying this whole community. I cannot even afford to feed and clothe my children. How can I send them to school? Education is very important. It will give them a better life. But now I cannot pay for the school fees and books. Sometimes they are chased out of school because they cannot pay. Because I have so little from selling coffee, I will have to find work cutting grass or weeding on commercial farms.'

Tatu Museyni's experience demonstrates how adverse trends in world commodity prices can devastate local communities. Lower prices force women farmers to spend more time and effort generating income from other sources, often adding long hours to already excessive working days and reducing the time available for child-care. Reductions in household income have other gender-related impacts, given the responsibilities placed on women to meet health-care and education needs.

The combination of high levels of absolute poverty and acute dependence on commodities makes sub-Saharan Africa especially vulnerable. To the extent that international opinion registers that there is a problem in developing countries, it is assumed that the problem is an African one. That assumption is wrong. When commodity prices fall, the effects are felt across a far wider group of countries, including many of those that have achieved a significant degree of diversification.

The case of Mexico demonstrates the problem. Over the past decade, the country has emerged as one of the world's fastest-growing exporters of high-technology products. But there are still more than 250,000 small-scale coffee farmers. Most of them are indigenous indians, and most live in the southern 'poverty belt' States of Chiapas, Ooxaca, Puebla, and Guerrero. The coffee harvest also generates an additional half a million seasonal jobs each year for rural labourers. Over one-third of the rural population in the southern states lives below the poverty line. The incidence of poverty is far higher in the major coffee-producing areas, which suffer from poor infrastructure and inadequate provision of basic services. Male migration to urban centres has left a growing number of female-headed households in rural areas, with women operating coffee farms and generating income through work in rural labour markets.

During 2001, Oxfam's partners carried out extensive interviews in the region of Chiapas, one of Mexico's main production centres. Coffee production in the area is dominated by small-scale farming. More than 80 per cent of plots are less than five hectares in size, mostly on steep hillsides. Indian farmers have developed coffee production as part of a highly sophisticated agricultural system. Coffee bushes are uniquely well suited to hillside production, since their deep roots help to bind the soil. They are inter-cropped with food crops such as beans, which fix nitrogen in the soil and act as a fertiliser, and with yellow, white, and red maize. Along with the guanabana fruit, macadamia nuts, and lemons, coffee provides a source of cash income for food, tools, and other household expenses.

At the time when the Oxfam interviews were carried out, just after the 2000 harvest, the coffee economy in Chiapas was in deep crisis. Traders were paying farmers less than one-third of the level paid two years earlier. Many farmers reported that coffee was no longer a viable economic proposition. As one put it:

> *'Right now the trader pays us 40 cents per pound. This is not enough. For coffee farmers ... it is a joke. The coffee plot is not worthwhile. It cannot support a household. That is why people are selling off their plots. It is sad to see, because so much work has been invested. If people don't sell, men are abandoning their fields and going to the north. There's no work here for poor people.'*

Across Chiapas and other coffee-producing areas, the slump in world prices was changing the lives of whole communities. Families reported that they would be unable to meet the costs of health care and education, or undertake basic repairs on their homes. Men were being forced to migrate, placing additional pressure on women and children to generate income. Household incomes were falling, with potentially grave consequences in an area marked by such high levels of poverty and social deprivation. In as much as coffee continues to be produced, the trade is based on the low value attached to women's labour and time.

In the case of Mexico, declining world prices for coffee have had important implications for poverty and inequality. They have reduced household income in States with the highest incidence of poverty, while at the same time widening income gaps: between the high-growth states of the north and the poverty-belt States of the south, between indian and non-indian people, and between rural and urban populations.

Agricultural labourers

Agricultural labourers suffer some of the deepest poverty, and experience some of the most severe exploitation, in the developing world. Their problems have been compounded by trends in world-market prices, especially in countries that have failed to protect basic labour rights.

There is a high concentration of poverty among those employed in markets linked to the commodity trade. Because many of these markets are seasonal (with demand for labour rising during harvesting and then falling), there is a high degree of temporary and seasonal labour. The price paid for that labour, and the welfare conditions provided, are intimately linked to world prices. Even though there is no guarantee that higher prices will produce better conditions, there is a high level of probability that lower prices will force down already low levels of income and cause a deterioration in employment standards. For example, in Peru falling world prices for cotton have forced down wages and reduced employment for temporary rural labourers, many of whom are desperately poor migrant workers from highland areas.

Low wages are a standard feature of life in employment that is linked to commodity markets. The tea industry is a prime example. In India, Bangladesh, and Sri Lanka alone, an estimated 1.5 million people work in the tea industry. The International Labour Organisation (ILO) estimates that 5–10 per cent of these are children. At the best of times, wages on tea plantations are abysmally low. Average earnings in India are estimated at $0.60 a day. In Sri Lanka in 1999, Oxfam interviews with women tea workers found cases where the net wage amounted to $12.90 per month. One woman interviewed on an estate owned by Tata Tea, one of the largest producers, was supporting six dependants on this sum (Oxfam 2001a).

The vulnerability caused by low wages is compounded by weak employment rights. Young girls are often at the centre of exploitative practices. The cotton-seed industry in the Indian State of Andhra Pradesh is estimated to employ approximately 250,000 girls, working as pickers in cotton fields. Apart from being deprived of an education, these girls face risks from the inhalation of dangerous pesticides. In the Indian tea estates, large numbers of pickers are employed on a casual basis. The work is seasonal, with employment ranging from 30 days a month in peak periods to fewer than 20 days a month later in the season. Workers have no job security, no social insurance or maternity benefits, and no entitlements to other benefits, such as education and housing, that are provided for permanent workers. Women workers make up the great majority of seasonal workers. When prices in the international tea market fell in 2000, it was inevitably the casual workforce who bore the brunt of the costs, in terms of reduced employment, lower incomes, and increased vulnerability.

In some cases, such as Guatemala's coffee plantations, workers have formal rights that are not respected by their employers, and not enforced by their governments. Coffee accounts for more than one-quarter of Guatemala's export earnings. Much of it is produced on large plantations. Permanent workers live in barracks, but plantations also hire migrant workers during harvest periods, usually indigenous Mayan indians from the poorer north. Under national law, plantation owners are supposed to provide education, access to health care, and a minimum wage. They often fail to discharge their responsibilities. In 2000, an independent assessment of labour conditions found that half of the workers were paid less than the statutory minimum wage of $2.48 per day (Neuffer 2001).

Similar problems are reported in India. In theory, the Plantation Labour Act of 1951 exists to protect the rights of estate workers, but it is very poorly enforced. Not one tea garden in Assam or West Bengal has fully implemented all the provisions of the Act. In other cases, the law provides inadequate protection for the rights of seasonal employees. In the Sri Lankan tea industry, some 300,000 Hill-country Tamils are without citizenship, placing considerable constraints on their freedom of movement as well as their ability to participate in political life (Oxfam 2001a).

Exploitative employment practices are partly a consequence of weak legislation and the non-enforcement of basic rights by governments, and partly the product of trends in world-market price. Even with the right motivation, it can be difficult to pay living wages when the world market offers poverty-level prices. The combination of bad conditions and low prices prevents the benefits of participation in world trade from trickling down to millions of smallholder farmers and labourers in poor countries.

World markets: what is going wrong?

Commodity producers face two sets of interlocking problems when they enter world markets. The first is one of structural over-supply. Production in a number of markets is growing more rapidly than demand, leading to large stocks and low prices. The second is that producers capture only a small share of the final value of their production, as primary commodities, on their way from farm-gate to supermarket shelves, pass through export, processing, and retailing systems. This is where most of the value is added, and where powerful corporate interests dominate.

Structural over-supply: the root cause of low prices

As in all markets, prices in primary-commodity markets reflect underlying conditions of supply and demand. However, supply-and-demand conditions in commodity markets differ from other markets in a number of respects. One difference is product-related. When a Ghanaian farmer plants a cocoa tree, there will be a three-year wait before it starts producing, and five years before it becomes fully productive. Similarly, when a Peruvian farmer plants a coffee tree, the first harvest will take place in two years' time, but it will take another three years before optimal yields occur. Although farmers can influence production levels, for example by applying more or less fertiliser, output is weakly related to world prices. Plants will grow fruit – whatever world prices do. For households dependent on coffee or cocoa for their cash income, it may make good sense to harvest that fruit, even during periods of very low prices. There may be no other source of cash income available. And even if there is, the returns to labour may be higher for coffee or cocoa than, say, for farm labour or selling food crops.

Like supply, demand for primary commodities is less responsive to price than demand for goods in other markets. When the price of cars goes down, more cars are sold; there is a strong link between price and demand. In most primary-commodity markets, that link is far weaker. Falling world prices have a limited impact on demand, partly because of the natural limits to consumption, and partly because the price of a commodity typically represents a tiny share of the value of the products bought by consumers. Even dramatic falls in prices for tea, coffee, and cocoa will have a negligible effect on consumer prices and demand. For example, prices for coffee at the end of the 1990s were one-quarter of the level in 1995. This price change had no effect on world demand, which continued to rise at a trend level of around 1.5 per cent per annum.

Productivity gains compound the problem. In markets where demand is unresponsive to price changes, increases in productivity will tend to push down prices. And there have been considerable advances in productivity in most commodity markets. Average yields for the major agricultural export commodities have increased by about one-third since the early 1980s. Over time, any excess of supply over demand will translate into increased stocks, which will in turn force down prices. Since falling prices do not rapidly translate into output decline on any scale, the imbalance between supply and demand can persist for years. In 2001, prices for cotton were less than half of those prevailing in 1990, but production was 10 per cent higher. In the case of coffee, production levels were one-quarter higher at the end of 2000 than in 1990, despite the protracted decline in prices.

Divergence between supply and demand has an inevitable outcome: namely, a large accumulation of stocks. At the end of the 1990s, the ratio of global stocks to annual consumption had reached exceptionally high levels for a number of commodities (UNCTAD (2001a).² Stock levels have a major bearing on prices. Excessive stock levels provide an effective guarantee against future price rises, unless future supplies are disrupted as a result of natural forces (such as climate or pest problems) or government policies to restrict output.

 In a market where prices are falling, the only way to maintain income is to increase the volume of output. This is precisely what many commodity exporters have been doing. The problem is that this closes the vicious circle: producers export more, which pushes down prices, and then seek to increase exports again, which produces a similar outcome. In other words, primary-commodity exporters have to run, simply to stand still in terms of generating foreign exchange. In many cases they are unable to run fast enough. For example, Ghana increased cocoa production from 320,000 to 450,000 tonnes between 1996 and 2000, an increase of almost one-third. But a 40 per cent decline in price over the same period meant that the export value of production was worth one-third less in terms of foreign exchange.

The factors that drive over-supply vary from product to product. Among the most important influences are the following.

- **New entrants to the market.** Low-cost producers have entered a number of commodity markets. From insignificant levels in the mid-1970s, Indonesia has been expanding cocoa production at more than 20 per cent a year. It is now the world's third largest exporter of cocoa. Smallholder productivity levels are far higher than in West Africa, reflecting the low age of tree stock. The devaluation of the Indonesian rupiah in the wake of the 1997 financial crash has given a further boost to exports, which have risen by 15 per cent since then. In the 1990s, Vietnam emerged as the second largest exporter of coffee, despite chronically depressed price levels. Output almost doubled between 1997 and 2002, with Vietnam's share of the world market rising from 7 to 11 per cent of the total (World Bank 2002).

- **Substitute products and bio-technology.** Product standards in rich countries can directly affect export prospects in poor countries. For example, in May 2000 the European Union passed a directive modifying the definition of chocolate to allow a range of vegetable fats to be used as partial replacements for cocoa butter. Implementation could cost exporting countries more than $500m at 2000 price levels.[3] The application of bio-technology poses further threats. Major confectionery companies have taken out patents on genetic codes for flavour-producing proteins occurring in cocoa plants. For example, Mars has patented proteins occurring in Amelonado cocoa (one of the highest-quality West African varieties). These could be artificially manufactured to enhance the flavour of products containing less cocoa butter.

- **Agricultural subsidisation in industrialised countries.** The $1bn a day spent by Northern governments on subsidising agricultural production is contributing to over-supply, excessive stocks, and low prices in commodities such as sugar, cereals, dairy, and meat (see Chapter 4).

- **Poor information.** Extreme price volatility means that producers have no viable means of estimating future prices, and therefore lack the information needed to inform decisions about the economic viability of future production levels.

- **Changing patterns of economic growth in industrialised countries.** Primary-commodity exporters, especially in the minerals sector, have been affected by two important changes in developed countries. First, new technologies have made it possible to develop substitutes for metals: fibre-optics have replaced copper wire in telephone systems, and industrial plastics are replacing aluminium, for example. Second, the main growth centres in industrialised countries are now knowledge-based industries such as telecommunications, information processing, computers, and analytical instruments. Growth in these industries generates lower levels of demand for minerals than growth in traditional manufacturing industries, which in turn use minerals less intensively than formerly (Page and Hewitt 2001).

In some cases, these changes are irreversible. In others, as is the case with agricultural policy and research on bio-technology, governments have more influence over the future. The choice over whether or not to use that influence in the interests of primary-commodity producers is, of course, a political one.

The marketing chain: coffee and cocoa

'Next time you enjoy a cup of Nescafe, stop and think about how more than 100 million people involved in the coffee growing industry have worked together to help you "open your day".' *(Nestlé 1998)*

At one level, the Nestlé public relations team is absolutely right. Every year, the company buys more than ten per cent of the world's coffee crop (Nestlé 1998). Every second of every day, about 3300 people pick up a cup of Nescafe. There is no question that Nestlé is the single most powerful presence in the international coffee market. As in other markets, Northern-based TNCs dominate a marketing chain that connects millions of small farmers and labourers in developing countries to rich-country consumers. Power relations along this chain operate to transfer the wealth generated in developing countries to rich countries and TNCs.

Most commodities are exported from developing countries in unprocessed form, which means that the value added by processing remains in industrialised countries. Developing countries account for more than 90 per cent of cocoa-bean production, less than half of cocoa-butter production, one-third of cocoa powder, and four per cent of chocolate (UNCTAD 2000c). This sliding scale has important implications for the share of final value captured by the exporting country, since each stage of processing adds value. Developing countries may dominate cocoa production, but two-thirds of the cocoa butter used for manufacturing is produced in the consuming countries of the industrialised world (Landell Mills 2000). Germany grinds more cocoa than the world's largest producer, Côte d'Ivoire, and Britain grinds far more than Ghana. Export sales from cocoa-producing countries amount to around $2bn a year, while chocolate sales by confectionery manufacturers produce in excess of $60bn. It is a similar story in coffee. Most international trade in coffee is in 'green coffee', or beans that have been subjected to drying, washing, and hulling (Ponte 2001). The EU is a major exporter of roasted coffee, accounting for 15 per cent of world trade – and the most profitable end of that trade. As in the case of cocoa, this means that most of the value-added in the coffee trade occurs in rich countries.

Trade barriers help to reinforce this pattern. Through the practice of tariff escalation, or import duties that rise with the degree of processing undergone by a commodity, Northern governments systematically hamper the efforts of developing countries to capture a larger share of the value of their products. Most processed edible oils face sharply rising import duties. Tariff escalation is deeply damaging to developing countries. It undermines investment in labour-intensive industries and blocks one route out of dependence on volatile, low-value-added commodity markets. By the same token, tariff escalation has the effect of transferring value generated in world trade from poor countries to rich countries, and from poor farmers to powerful food companies. They reinforce the global inequalities and poverty described in Chapter 3.

Most major global commodity markets are dominated by small groups of transnational companies. Consumers in the rich world are linked to producers in developing countries through complex systems of processing, logistics, and marketing which extend from the smallholder farm to the supermarket shelf or 'designer coffee' retail outlet. Consolidation of market power does not mean that there is no competition. But it does mean that in global markets fragmented suppliers are competing with small groups of powerful corporate buyers.

In the case of coffee, there are two sets of key players operating in world markets: international traders and roasters. Just three international traders – Neumann, Volcafe, and Cargill – control around one-third of world-market share, and the top six companies control one-half of it (Ponte 2001). The level of concentration among coffee roasters is even more marked. Just two companies – Nestlé and Philip Morris – account for half of the world-market share for roasted and instant coffee. The top five companies (the previous two plus Sara Lee, Procter and Gamble, and Tchibo) control more than two-thirds of the market.

The world cocoa market has been transformed over the past decade through a wave of mergers and acquisitions. In 1980, there were more than 30 major trading houses in London alone that bought cocoa on a large scale. Today, the four largest cocoa-processing companies – Archer Daniel Midland (ADM), Barry Callebaut, Cargill, and Hosta – account for about 40 per cent of global cocoa-processing capacity (ICO 1998). When the major chocolate companies such as Nestlé, Cadbury Schweppes, and Mars are added to this group, there are around nine companies accounting for over 70 per cent of total capacity.

The millions of suppliers – small farmers desperate to sell their crop for precious cash, or local traders and exporters – are negotiating at an enormous disadvantage in the face of competition from the multinationals. Furthermore, they often have limited access to market information which would help them to negotiate better and interpret the signals that the market gives about future prices. The imbalance in power between the millions of smallholder farmers producing for world markets and giant food and beverage companies is extreme.

Market power is reflected in the distribution of benefits from world trade. Producers do not figure prominently. During 2000, Oxfam interviewed smallholder coffee farmers in the Kilimanjaro region of Tanzania. They reported that the farm-gate price for coffee beans was around $0.28 per pound, representing only around nine per cent of the average retail price of roast and ground coffee in the USA and around four per cent of the retail price of gourmet 'Kilimanjaro' coffee (Oxfam 2001b). Of the average cup of coffee sold in a coffee bar, it is likely that the farmer would receive less than one per cent of the retail price.[4]

While low world prices are devastating poor communities, there is little evidence of their being transmitted to consumers. In the midst of one of the biggest slumps in a number of commodity markets for 50 years, consumer prices have continued to rise. This disparity matters. Although, as previously noted, consumer demand is fairly insensitive to falls in the price of basic commodities, not all consumers ignore prices entirely.

It is of course the case that raw-material inputs account for a small share of the costs of marketing and retailing. Companies invest heavily in branding their products through advertising and packaging, activities that are critical to corporate strategies for expanding market share. Smallholder farmers producing commodities such as coffee and cocoa for world markets are located at the starting point in what has been called 'buyer-driven supply chains'. These chains are characterised by three conditions:

- **Large numbers of producers, and limited entry into the market.** Large numbers of smallholder farmers are driven into commodity markets by the need for cash and the absence of alternative livelihood options. The result is that large numbers of producers, most of them lacking market information, confront a small number of buyers. Small farmers are operating in 'buyer-driven' supply chains (Gibbon 2000).

- **'Market-driven' pricing.** In the past, government marketing boards often set minimum prices in an effort to protect farm incomes, reflecting the strategy used in US and EU farm policies. The dismantling of State marketing boards has removed this floor from the market, enabling traders to purchase at unregulated price levels.

- **High barriers to entry for new buyers and marketers.** The economies of scale associated with size and vertical integration, the costs of branding, and the costs of market intelligence are major barriers to entry into international trade markets and Northern retail markets.

The interaction of these three conditions leaves farmers in a very weak position in the global supply chain. Research suggests that coffee farmers are receiving a diminishing share of the total income from their coffee. In the 1970s, an average of one-fifth of total income was retained by producers. During the first half of the 1990s, that share fell to 13 per cent, while the share gained by consuming countries had increased to almost 80 per cent (Talbot 1997). This represents a very large transfer of resources from those who can least afford it.

Declining world prices may spell disaster for millions of smallholder farmers, but for the companies in the right place in the value chain, it can mean greater commercial power and profits. In coffee, the winners are mainly the roasters, among them Nestlé. In soluble coffee, the company has a global market share of 57 per cent, three times the level of its nearest rival, and operating margins estimated at 26 per cent. In the words of one recent commercial bank review of the coffee sector: 'Nothing else in food and beverages is remotely as good' (Deutsche Bank 2000). As one Nestlé document put it at the end of 2000: 'Trading profit increased by 15 per cent and margins improved, thanks to favourable commodity prices' (Nestlé 2000, Crawshaw 2001). In other words, low coffee prices may be bad for Third World poverty, but they are good for Nestlé.

The liberalisation of marketing boards

Not all of the problems facing commodity producers are rooted in world markets. Smallholder farmers often face serious disadvantages in local markets, including poor infrastructure and limited access to inputs. In some cases, these disadvantages have been compounded under IMF–World Bank adjustment programmes which have liberalised State marketing boards.

It should be acknowledged that these marketing boards were a disaster for development across much of sub-Saharan Africa. Introduced by colonial authorities, they were used by post-independence governments to impose heavy taxes on smallholder farmers (Bates 1981). All too often, the proceeds enriched powerful vested interests. During the 1980s and 1990s, the activities of marketing boards were dramatically curtailed, often under the auspices of IMF–World Bank programmes. However, liberalisation has brought new problems in its wake, some of which have compounded problems on world markets and threatened the livelihoods of smallholders.

Under the old regime, smallholder farmers were required to sell to marketing boards at prices stipulated by governments, and which were typically set far below export prices. In the early 1980s, cocoa farmers in Ghana were getting six per cent of the export price for their produce (Frempong 1991). Similarly, coffee farmers in Uganda and Tanzania were receiving 10–15 per cent of the export price (Oyejide, Ndulu, and Gunning 1997). The marketing boards were responsible for a ruinous system of taxation which not only deprived farmers of income, but reduced incentives to invest and produce. They were at least partly responsible for the catastrophic loss of market share suffered by Africa in its key commodity exports.

Market liberalisation has produced some important benefits. The share of export price received by farmers has tended to increase, even though falling world prices have limited the benefits (Akiyama et al. 2001). Coffee farmers in Tanzania and Uganda now receive 60 per cent and 80 per cent respectively of export prices; cocoa farmers in Ghana and Cameroon receive 40 per cent and 70 per cent (Gilbert 1997). The problem with liberalisation lay in a failure to develop strategies that addressed the very real economic problems associated with marketing boards (namely, high taxation and corruption), without negating some of their more positive aspects. In many countries, the marketing boards were the main source of credit, fertilisers, and other inputs; when Tanzania's coffee board was dismantled, input provisions collapsed, leaving poorer farmers unable to take advantage of new market opportunities. At the same time, government decentralisation transferred revenue-raising authority to local councils, resulting in heavy and uneven taxes. By the end of the 1990s, effective taxes on export crops approximated those imposed before the liberalisation of marketing (World Bank 2000b).

The wider problems that have been documented since liberalisation include the following:

- a reduction in yields, due to the collapse of extension systems, loss of access to credit, and sharply increased fertiliser prices;

- pressure on small farmers to operate through a monopolistic private trading system;

- extreme vulnerability to price volatility, made worse in the absence of functioning insurance or credit markets;

- loss of market access, or a steep reduction in producer prices, for the poorest and most isolated farmers, due to the end of pan-territorial pricing and marketing systems;

- a reduction in export quality, due to the dismantling of quality-control systems, resulting in lower prices and a tarnished reputation on world markets.

Nobody would argue that the policies of marketing boards were designed with the best interests of smallholder farmers at heart. Yet in the absence of public intervention, smallholder farmers have been left as very unequal and unprotected actors in global markets. Instead of regulating markets to protect smallholder producers from the risks associated with extreme price volatility, and the inequalities associated with the concentration of economic power, governments have left them unprotected.

Box 6.1

Problems of cocoa-market deregulation in West Africa

Even if the share of the export price captured by farmers has risen, the sudden deregulation of the cocoa sector has caused significant harm to smallholders, at least in the short term. In the long term, the problems of access to credit and inputs as well as public goods, such as crop research or quality controls, remain unresolved. This is particularly detrimental to the smaller and more vulnerable producers, and as such is probably adverse to poverty reduction in cocoa-growing areas. Because men dominate the cultivation of cocoa, the growth in exports has adversely affected women, whose production is pushed to marginal lands, and who suffer reduced extension services, credit, and marketing support for their food crops (Stichele 1998).

In Côte d'Ivoire, the absence of any kind of preparations prior to liberalisation led to chaos on the market. Previously, the Ivorian marketing board had a financing system in place to phase sales throughout the year. When the old system of forward-selling up to two-thirds of the crop was abandoned, all the producers sold their harvest at the same time and flooded the market, causing international prices to collapse. The subsequent collapse in price (40 per cent within a year, during 1999–2000) caused considerable social unrest in the country, as cocoa growers protested at the way in which the government had liberalised their industry.

Liberalisation has also led to declining quality and yields, which reduces the premiums available on international markets for high-quality cocoa from Nigeria, Ecuador, and Cameroon (to choose three examples). In Nigeria, the premium paid for cocoa ranged between £50 and £100 per ton in the 1980s, but fell to zero in the 1990s. This was because the quality-control function of the marketing board was discontinued after the market was deregulated, and the sale of small beans could no longer be prevented.

Source: Oxfam, 'The Cocoa Market: A Background Study', pp.21-3, 2001

The rise of fair trade and the demise of commodity agreements

The fair-trade movement has been one of the most powerful responses to the problems facing commodity producers. It has given consumers an opportunity to use their purchasing power to tilt the balance, however slightly, in favour of the poor. At one level, the fair-trade movement is a product of an earlier attempt to manage world markets through international commodity agreements aimed at stabilising prices at reasonable levels. The effective collapse of those agreements in the 1980s saw the withdrawal of the international community from developing a collective response to the problems facing commodity producers. In the absence of a renewed effort to secure responsible market management, there is a limit to what fair trade can achieve.

Fair trade – achievements and limits

In the Ashante capital of Kumasi, in the heart of Ghana's cocoa belt, stands one of the most high-profile challenges to the current commodity-trading system. The Kuapa Kokoo (Cocoa Co-operative) has more than 30,000 members, operating in 160 local organisations (Ransom 2001). Formed in 1993, it combines the roles of a cocoa-purchasing agency, a trust fund operating on behalf of its members, and a marketing organisation. It provides a link between Ghana's cocoa farmers and consumers in rich countries, mediated partly through the UK-based Twin Trading organisation, which is part of a growing fair-trade movement (Twin 2000). That movement is seeking to give consumers a choice in how they use their purchasing power. More specifically, it is attempting to create an awareness of the problems outlined in this chapter, and to give consumers a practical means of doing something to address them.

When Kuapa Kokoo sells its cocoa into the fair-trade market, it receives a guaranteed minimum price. The lower world prices fall, the higher the premium provided through the fair-trade price. For example, in 1999 the fair-trade price was approximately 75 per cent above the world-market price (Oxford Policy Management 2000). When world prices rise above the minimum, Kuapa Kokoo's fair-trade partners pay a 'social premium' in the form of cash transfers. The premium is invested in community-level development programmes, ranging from school construction to health-care provision, and water supply and sanitation. The fair-trade link has also helped to open new, higher-value-added markets. Kuapa Kokoo provides cocoa butter to the retail chain, The Body Shop, and has entered, with Twin Trading, into a joint venture with the Day Chocolate Company (Oxford Policy Management 2000). Through fair-trade links, consumers in industrialised countries can now contribute to a market which seeks to address the three core problems facing cocoa producers: low prices, price instability, and low value-added activity.

Fair-trade organisations span a wide range of commodities and activities. They include agencies (such as Oxfam, Traidcraft, and Twin Trading) with close links to producer groups and their own retail outlets; labelling organisations (such as Max Havelaar in the Netherlands and the UK Fairtrade Foundation); co-operatives such as Equal Exchange in the USA; ethical business (ranging from mainstream companies such as the Body Shop to Green and Black's chocolate company, and NGO-sponsored products such as Café Direct); and a range of umbrella organisations. The scale of fair-trade operations is a proof of the level of consumer concern (Twin 2000). The retail value of fair-trade products sold in Europe, through supermarkets and the fair-trade movement's own channels, is believed to exceed Euro260m.

Smallholder farmers have derived real benefits from fair trade. In southern Belize, a co-operative of Mayan farmers in Toledo district is now a source of supply for Green and Black's chocolate, 'Maya Gold'. The company, which markets the chocolate under the Fairtrade Mark ('a consumer label which guarantees a better deal for Third World producers', according to the Fairtrade Foundation, which awards it), provides them with a five-year rolling contract and a guarantee that they will buy all cocoa that meets their quality standards (Fairtrade Foundation 2000). Such arrangements make a real difference to the lives of producers. As one producer, Christina Peck, explains: *'From the money we get from cacao, we have made a concrete floor in our house to replace the dirt floor, and our children are now able to go to secondary school ...only fair trade has given us a good price'* (Fairtrade Foundation 2000).

The fair-trade movement has enabled some coffee farmers to survive the protracted price slump in world markets. In Tanzania, co-operatives such as the Kilimanjaro Native Co-operative Union (KNCU) have benefited not just from the price premium, but also from technical support and advice on measures for raising quality standards. In the United States, a product-certifying organisation called TransFair USA has developed links with roasters of gourmet beans and with large supermarket chains. Thanks to its lobbying, farmers in Latin America at the end of 1999 were receiving double the prevailing market prices. If it succeeds in its efforts to capture five per cent of the $18bn US market by 2005, the benefits for smallholder farmers could be very large (Carlton 1999, Alden 2000).

For all its achievements, there are limits to what the fair-trade movement can do. Despite their rapid growth, fair-trade markets remain small enclaves. Even Kuapa Kokoo sells less than five per cent of its members' output through fair-trade channels. While the share is higher for some co-operatives, fair trade has not fundamentally changed world markets, even in its core beverage sectors. Less than one per cent of total tea, coffee, and cocoa sales are carried out on a fair-trade basis (Oxford Policy Management 2000). Moreover, in many commodities, such as palm oil and coconut oil, the fair-trade market presence is almost non-existent.

The fair-trade movement occupies a marginal position in a world market that is consigning millions of people to poverty. Expanding world-market share by persuading consumers to pay a small price-premium would help, but the barriers to market entry are formidable – and in Europe, at least, the rate of growth in fair-trade goods is slowing down. Unless the principles of fair trade are applied beyond the existing market enclaves to the global market, the structural tendency towards over-supply will leave poor countries and poor producers facing increasingly intense market pressures.

The fact that some major traders now attempt to paint themselves as fair traders is a testament to the success of the fair-trade movement. In the coffee sector, Nestlé now presents itself to the public as the world's largest 'fair trade' organisation. As one company document proclaims: 'We believe in paying fair prices and have followed a policy of working in partnership with developing world producers ...Within the limitations of a complex, often imperfect world trading system, we seek to make fair trade a reality' (Nestlé 1995). According to Nestlé, its 'fair trade' status derives from the fact that it buys an increasing amount of its coffee, currently around one-tenth of the total, directly from farmers' co-operatives, rather than international traders. But Fair Trade is about the price that producers receive. Currently the market price – or even a premium to the market price – cannot cover most farmers' costs, let alone provide them with a decent income.

Managing over-supply: the collapse of commodity agreements

In the mid-1970s the world's governments embraced the idea of a new international economic order – one that would share the benefits of international trade more equally between North and South. Primary commodities were high on the agenda. It was recognised that, for many of the poorest countries, long-term development prospects were being undermined by price trends in commodity markets. What emerged was a half-hearted experiment in international commodity-market management. That experiment collapsed under the weight of political indifference, under-funding, and weak policy design. The episode provides an instructive lesson for any effort to tackle the crisis outlined in this chapter.

In 1964 a new phase of policy began, with the first United Nations Conference on Trade and Development (UNCTAD). At that conference, industrialised countries acknowledged for the first time that the development needs of Third World countries had to be addressed through a coherent programme of action on primary commodities. The Integrated Programme for Commodities (IPC), launched under UNCTAD auspices in 1976, sought to provide it. Its objective was to create market structures which achieved remunerative and stable prices, while taking into account the interests of consuming countries. In order to achieve these objectives, a Common Fund was established to maintain buffer stocks that would be increased (through purchasing operations) when prices were low, and reduced (through sales) when prices were high (Singer and Amjari 1992).

The resulting international commodity agreements (ICAs) had a brief lifespan. At the end of the 1970s, they covered a wide range of commodities, including tin, sugar, rubber, coffee, cocoa, and jute. By the end of the 1980s, all of them except for rubber (since discontinued) had either collapsed or abandoned their price-stabilising functions (Gilbert 1996). Today, the agreements on coffee and cocoa are little more than forums for sharing information and managing administrative matters.

The reasons for the collapse of ICAs have been exhaustively analysed. While they varied from case to case, there were some common elements. The hostility of Northern governments to market interventions that they saw as inherently inflationary helped to undermine the effectiveness of the ICAs. Another problem was the attempt to defend reference prices that were far removed from underlying market realities. Buffer-stock operations were simply too small to absorb the huge increase in supplies of commodities such as coffee, cocoa, and sugar on world markets, which in turn drove down prices (Gilbert 1995). Failures of South–South co-operation also played a large part. New low-cost suppliers of coffee and cocoa in East Asia were well placed to benefit from the higher prices generated by African and Latin American governments who were restricting supplies, and had little interest in restricting their own output.

Whatever the disappointing past record of ICAs, some of their underlying principles were clearly sound. In particular, they recognised that supply management was a key requirement for achieving more remunerative prices. Their mistake was to confuse other functions. Using buffer stocks to raise prices, as distinct from moderating price cycles, was a deeply flawed approach, especially given the chronic under-funding of buffer-stock arrangements. As European and North American agriculture-policy makers have discovered to their cost, using public funds to buy up commodities produced at controlled prices that bear no relation to world prices is a prescription for disaster.

As world prices continue their relentless decline, some producing countries have resurrected the principles of supply management. In 2000 the Cocoa Producers Alliance, whose members account for 85 per cent of world output, drew up plans to hold back sub-standard beans, intending to push up prices. The aim was to generate an upturn in prices by cutting supply by around 10 per cent (Stainer 1999, 2000). In an effort to signal their intent to world markets, the governments of Ghana, Nigeria, and Côte d'Ivoire announced plans to burn up to eight per cent of the 2000/2001 crop. Chronic over-supply has prompted similar action among coffee producers. In May 2000, the Association of Coffee Producing Countries (ACPC) adopted a 'retention' plan drawn up by Brazil and other Latin American producers. The aim was to hold back 20 per cent of stock from the market until prices rose from their existing levels of $0.50/lb to $0.95/lb (Oxfam 2001d).

Neither of these plans has been translated into meaningful action. The problems have been all too familiar. Exporting countries have desperate needs for foreign exchange, however low export prices fall. Most lack the storage capacity to withhold stocks from the market, or the financing capacity to buy produce from farmers without exporting it in the same year. Moreover, there are deep-rooted South–South tensions. Exporters in East Asia see Brazil's attempts to support higher coffee prices as part of a wider strategy to enlarge Latin America's world-market share at their expense. For their part, governments in Africa and Latin America accuse East Asia of seeking to 'free ride', taking advantage of the higher prices generated by the withholding of stocks by others.

The record of ICAs over the past 25 years, and of commodity-market interventions more broadly, suggests little cause for optimism. Rich-country governments argue that the failure of such interventions proves the case for free trade. But this assessment is flawed and disingenuous for two reasons. First, whatever the failures of the ICA period, the current status quo is unacceptable. As this chapter has shown, international commodity markets are producing poverty and instability on a huge scale. The free market is failing the poor.

Second, Northern governments have a habit of ignoring their own contribution to the downfall of ICAs. Their willingness to favour the interests of powerful food companies in getting cheap raw materials rather than the interests of developing countries in getting remunerative prices has been a major factor in shaping commodity markets. Moreover, the argument that market-management agreements are inherently doomed is only partly supported by history. Before its collapse, the tin agreement had stabilised prices for almost a quarter of a century, and, for all its problems, OPEC succeeded in controlling oil prices for the decade after 1974. Moreover, governments of developed countries do intervene in other types of market where they consider their own interests to be at stake, for instance in the currency markets.

Returning to the ICA model of the 1970s is not a realistic option, but neither is continuing with business as usual. There is an urgent need for imaginative new solutions to the very old problems posed by commodity markets, and for concerted international co-operation to make those solutions happen.

Ways forward and recommendations

In 1980, in the midst of another commodity crisis, the first Brandt Report recalled the vision of some of the founders of the Bretton Woods institutions. Like John Maynard Keynes, Willy Brandt's commission called for international action to tackle a problem that lies at the heart of global poverty and instability. The central demand of the report was for measures aimed at 'the stabilisation of commodity prices at remunerative levels' (Brandt 1980). Unfortunately, the Brandt Report coincided with the start of a systematic assault on international commodity agreements, which were seen as inherently bad for inflation in rich countries.

Times have changed. Yet, despite the scale of the crisis now gripping much of the developing world, commodities remain absent from the international development agenda. Failure to tackle this issue will result in millions of producers in the developing world remaining excluded from the rising prosperity associated with globalisation. Existing institutions and trade rules are failing to respond to the challenge.

An agenda for change

The time for piecemeal solutions to the commodity crisis has passed, as has the time for the standard Northern-government response of ignoring the problem. Occasional phases of co-operation between exporting producers will prove insufficient in the future, as they have in the past. World trade faces a systemic crisis, to which it needs a systemic solution. That solution includes new institutional responses, along with new approaches to market regulation – and new practices on the part of TNCs.

Oxfam's proposals for reforms, presented in more detail below, include the following elements.

- **The creation of a commodities institution.** This institution should deliver reform in four key areas:

  – Market intervention and long-term supply management.

  – Diversification and value-added in exporting countries.

  – Use of insurance for farmers to manage the risk of price collapse.

  – Funding to deliver these measures.

- **The reform of corporate strategies.** Companies should pay prices that keep farmers and their families out of poverty. Companies should pay fair prices in long-term contracts and support the creation of more stable and remunerative markets.

- **The creation of a WTO working group on trade and commodities.** Trade in commodities could play a vital role in generating wealth for developing countries, and promoting their economic growth. The WTO must address itself to this challenge.

An institution for commodities

Public campaigning is a vital first step towards getting commodities on to the agenda of the WTO, but it needs to be supplemented by international action. That is why Oxfam is advocating the establishment of a new institution. In the short term, Oxfam calls on the UN Secretary General to establish a high-level task-force on commodities to analyse the underlying causes of the crisis in commodity markets, and produce recommendations within a year to the UN and the G8. The recommendations would include estimates of short-term and long-term financing requirements and potential sources of such funding. They would also devise a strategy for reducing the debts of commodity-dependent exporters to sustainable levels through a reformed HIPC Initiative.

Whatever the detailed recommendations in each area, any international solution must start from a recognition of three basic facts. First, the crisis in commodity markets is a systemic one. It is rooted in the nature of commodity markets and extends across a wide range of products. Second, in most product groups the problem is one of structural over-supply and price instability. It follows that effective action requires supply management and action to reduce price volatility. Third, international markets are marked by extreme inequalities of power, and an extreme concentration of corporate power. Governments must ensure that these inequalities do not artificially bias the benefits of trade away from poor countries and poor people.

International commodity agreements (ICAs) have a critical role to play in addressing the problems outlined in this chapter. The current debate on ICAs is a sterile affair, contrasting the failures of the past with the presumed virtues of the 'free market' present. There is no doubt that the previous generation of ICAs failed. But only the most insular of commodity economists and a few corporate executives would regard a perpetuation of the status quo as a viable option. The world cannot afford to allow commodity markets to continue creating the mass poverty and inequality that will ultimately threaten our common interest in shared prosperity.

A new institutional framework

Who is to deliver action on commodities? The body that does so must have the trust of both producing and consuming nations. It must be funded in a way that is commensurate with the scale of the problem. It must have influence with governments and other international institutions.

Established institutions are not delivering the sort of bold thinking and action that developing countries deserve. The issue of commodities is rarely considered as central to the development goals of the poorest countries, and initiatives on commodities, when they are launched, are too small in scope and impact. That is why there is a need for a new institution that would tackle the problems of commodity trade and its impact on development targets. This institution, which would include existing commodity-related agencies, would oversee policies designed to achieve remunerative and stable prices for commodity producers, as well as longer-term plans to help countries to escape from the commodities trap.

These policies will require international financing. The same is true for the additional debt relief that will be needed in order to ensure that commodity-dependent countries achieve debt sustainability. Funding could come from a number of sources. As ever, political willingness to think audaciously will determine whether these sources are ever tapped. Existing funds, within the EU, donor governments, and international financial institutions, could be earmarked. But broader sources of funding will also be needed. One option is taxes on imports and exports of particular commodities in crisis. An import tax on a crop when prices slumped could be offset by an export tax when prices soared. The ring-fenced proceeds could be recycled to the countries in need. Clearly, such a regime would have to be agreed internationally, to avoid the risk of large black-markets developing. Taxes would be established for a limited time and triggered in the case of severe imbalances in the market.

Market intervention and supply management

In the context of long-term declining prices, some commodities face a more acute crisis than others. Coffee is one example. Prices have plunged far below the costs of producing the crop, creating widespread misery among small farmers. Here market intervention is the only rational course of action. A large proportion of excess supply should be removed from the coffee market – a move that should help to improve prices as well as overall quality levels, as the worst-quality coffee would be diverted.

In the longer term, there needs to be a renewed effort by producing and consuming nations alike to bring supply into line with demand, on a more systematic basis, across a range of commodities. Crucial to this effort is the need to separate the objective of raising prices from that of stabilising prices. One of the reasons why the first generation of ICAs failed was that they sought to combine these two very different functions. New commodity agreements can be made to work in ways that benefit both consumers and suppliers. In coffee, curbing over-supply by means of quality criteria would be an innovative advance.

However, commodity agreements must also incorporate strategies for those countries or communities that may be excluded from these shifts in the market and can no longer compete in a particular commodity. Poor farmers must have alternatives and safety nets, just as farmers in the developed world do.

Lastly, companies that dominate the trading and retailing of particular commodities must support efforts to create a more sustainable and stable market. Profit margins may benefit if the price of a raw material such as coffee collapses, but no industry can thrive if suppliers go to the wall. Self-interest dictates that companies can no longer stand back and watch as the market claims millions of victims.

Price volatility and insurance

Price volatility has been identified as potentially the biggest problem for producers (Varangis and Larson 1996). Farmers cannot plan ahead, find it difficult to obtain credit, and can be pressured into selling their crops at bad prices. In coffee, multinationals and traders use financial instruments to hedge their exposure to fluctuations in price. The smallest producers, who are paid the least in this market, bear the most risk. Poor farmers need a comprehensive plan to help them to insure against the risks of sudden collapse of prices. Pilot projects are underway to explore this option, and the idea needs to be championed and funded on an ambitious scale. Governments could use the provision of subsidised insurance to help to promote development objectives and to give farmers incentives to produce in a sustainable manner. At a local level, insurance or options to sell a crop at a pre-determined price could make use of existing financial intermediaries. Such schemes could also be useful in stimulating the formation of producer associations and co-operatives to share the cost of the premiums.

The impact of such measures on poverty reduction could be considerable. Farmers who know what price their crop will earn are more likely to be able to get credit for the other essentials in their lives. They will be under less pressure to sell to unscrupulous buyers. They will also know whether a price recovery is expected. This would give them information on which to base important decisions: such as how much time they and their family should spend on cultivating the cash crop and how much they should devote to subsistence farming, and how much to spend on inputs, such as fertilisers.

Diversification and added value

Developing countries that depend heavily on the export of one or two non-fuel commodities, and whose ability to add value to those commodities remains limited, risk remaining trapped in poverty and instability. The benefits of adding value to a commodity can be very considerable. The difference in price between, say, loose unwashed carrots sold in a UK supermarket and washed carrots chopped up into little batons is enormous: the latter can sell for 15 times the price of the former, according to a study for UNCTAD (Humphrey and Oetero 2000). The extra profit, however, is rarely, if ever, earned by the producer country.

Clearly, diversification into other crops or other economic activities will be dictated by the geographic, social, and economic conditions particular to each country. It is a long and painful process. Action on one commodity needs to take into account the markets for other commodities. Likewise, adding value to a product requires access to capital, investment in infrastructure and fixed assets, and development of new skills in logistics and marketing. All too often, multinational companies hold all the cards.

International action to promote diversification and value-added must address the entrenched interests of rich countries.

- Multinationals should be exposed to the scrutiny of competition law, to ensure that they are not using their power to exploit suppliers in developing countries.

Companies should promote attempts by producing nations to establish home-grown processing and value-adding businesses.

- Northern governments should remove tariff and non-tariff barriers, especially the particularly pernicious ones that penalise value-added goods exported from developing countries.

- Any country that develops a credible diversification plan to tackle poverty should be supported by international donors.

Reforming corporate practices

Multinational companies should not be allowed to stand by and watch thousands of their suppliers lose their livelihoods. Prices in certain commodities, such as coffee, are scandalously low, and companies cannot expect to continue doing business in a way that is consigning millions to terrible poverty. Multinationals must not be allowed to benefit from a market that is failing the poor.

There are three main areas where positive corporate action is required. First, companies should pay prices that allow farmers and their families to live. They should make more use of long-term contracts with co-operatives, thus reducing risk for poor farmers.

Second, it is in the interests of companies that commodity markets are stable and fair, for both consumers and producers. Companies should press the international institutions and governments to make this happen.

Third, companies should adopt responsible purchasing policies. They should establish supply chains that can be independently and comprehensively monitored. Consumers have a right to know the conditions in which crops are grown, and companies who buy these crops should make this information available. Companies must take their share of responsibility in tackling chronic problems of over-supply. They should not undermine producers' attempts to improve quality.

A WTO Working Group?

The WTO must take the issue of commodities seriously. This is an area of trade that is vital to the interests of most developing countries, and its neglect in the world's trading body is causing untold misery. The mandate of such a group would include the following:

- to reaffirm the legality of international commodity agreements under the GATT/WTO rules;

- to press for the dismantlement of trade barriers that discourage agricultural diversification in developing countries: barriers that include subsidies, non-tariff barriers, and impediments to technology transfer.

The case for change

The various objections to the approach outlined above are not difficult to anticipate. Rich-country governments will question the need for institutional reform as an unwarranted extension of multilateralism. Such arguments are not convincing. Northern governments extend the remit of other Bretton Woods institutions when it suits them: for instance, the mandate of the WTO on matters of investment, financial services, and intellectual property. Moreover, the General Agreement on Tariffs and Trade (GATT), the predecessor of the WTO, explicitly accepted the case for commodity-market intervention.

The same governments will join powerful food companies in arguing that supply management is anti-market and bad for business. In which case, they might stop to ask themselves why they are spending so much public money to support supply management in their domestic agriculture. They might also wish to ask the 'free market' US government why it is responding to a crisis of over-production in its steel industry by seeking an international supply-management agreement.

As for the accusation that supply management is bad for business, that depends on how business is conducted. There is a growing awareness in several food industries that low prices constitute a threat to the consistency and quality of supply. Given the small share of commodities in the final value of most products, it is unlikely in the extreme that remunerative prices for producers would make business unsustainable, let alone generate serious inflationary pressure. The real choice that faces industry is between short-term (and short-sighted) profit imperatives, and a long-term stake in an industry that combines profitability with sustainability.

In the last analysis, it is not difficult to use text-book economic theory to show that market interventions have real costs. But so does the refusal to intervene in markets that are failing. The ultimate choice is not between a free-market idyll and an interventionist nightmare. It is between locking producers and consumers into market relations that reinforce poverty, and making global markets work in the interests of shared prosperity.

CHAPTER 7
Transnational companies: investment, employment, and marketing

Transnational companies (TNCs) are the driving force behind globalisation. Through their production, trade, and investment activities, they are integrating countries into a global market. Through their control over resources, access to markets, and development of new technologies, TNCs have the potential to generate enormous benefits for poverty reduction. However, that potential is being lost. The weakness of international rules, bad policies and weak governance in developing countries, and corporate practices which prioritise short-term profit over long-term human development are undermining the capacity of poor countries – and poor people – to benefit from international trade.

TNCs themselves are redefining their role. The notion of 'corporate citizenship' has taken deep root (Mcintosh 1998). Like citizens, corporate entities now insist that they have rights and responsibilities. The rights that they claim are commercial. International trade agreements and intense competition for foreign investment between developing countries has led to a dramatic extension of these rights. In contrast to commercial rights, the economic and social 'responsibilities' assumed by TNCs are largely voluntary in character. That is, they are the subject of self-regulation, rather than government enforcement. As part of the bargain to attract investors, many governments have weakened employment protection. As we argue below, the new balance of rights and responsibilities implied by corporate citizenship has not been good for development.

This chapter examines the role of TNCs in development in three areas. The first section considers Foreign Direct Investment (FDI), which is now the main source of financial transfers from rich to poor countries. FDI activity is heavily concentrated in a small group of countries, and the net transfers associated with it are far lower than headline figures suggest. However, good-quality investment can facilitate dynamic economic gains. It can support the transfer of technologies, create linkages between foreign and domestic firms, and enable local firms to gain access to new skills and markets. Unfortunately, much FDI fails the quality test. It is locking many developing countries into the low-value-added ghettoes of world trade described in Chapter 3. Foreign investment in extractive industries has a particularly poor development record, especially in countries affected by conflict.

The second section considers the role of TNCs in employment. As direct employers, TNCs account for a small, though rising, share of workforce participation in developing countries. Indirectly, through their global sourcing and wider investment activities, TNCs generate a very large number of jobs. They also strongly influence employment conditions. The clear message of this report is that TNCs' voluntary self-regulation is failing the poor. It is producing poverty-level wages and severe forms of exploitation, with female workers suffering the worst excesses.

The third part examines the failures of corporate codes of conduct. The final part briefly examines the role of TNCs in marketing. It identifies some of the problems associated with the ability of large companies to influence consumers' tastes, sometimes – as in the case of infant-formula milk and tobacco – to the detriment of public health. The chapter concludes by presenting an agenda for reform.

The role of foreign investment

Most governments and international financial institutions see foreign investment by TNCs as one of the keys to successful integration into the global economy. Efforts to attract TNCs through liberalisation, tax concessions, and reinforced rights for investors have been a dominant theme in development policy over the past decade. Many developing countries have adopted the simple strategy of attracting as much FDI as possible, without concern for the quality of that investment.

Governments seek to attract TNCs for the assets that they provide, such as capital, technology, and skills. But FDI has a mixed record: in some cases it has helped to generate dynamic economic growth, with attendant social benefits, but in other cases it has been of more doubtful benefit. Enthusiasts for FDI have tended to exaggerate the financial gains and understate the costs of poor-quality investment.

The potential benefits of TNC investment

By definition, TNCs have advantages that are associated with access to capital, technologies, and markets that firms in developing countries might lack. There are four principal advantages.

- **Access to finance.** TNCs can provide an important source of capital. For countries experiencing foreign-exchange constraints, FDI can act as an important source of financing for imported technologies. Because FDI tends to be more stable than other private-capital market transfers, such as portfolio lending, it is less prone to disruption. The catalyst for the East Asian financial crisis in 1996 was a huge outflow of funds, as commercial banks and institutional investors called in loans. The resulting losses were equivalent to more than 10 per cent of GDP for some countries (based on data in IMF 1999b). By contrast, FDI remained constant throughout this period.

- **Skills and technology.** Relative to local firms, TNCs are well placed to provide the tangible and intangible assets needed to raise skills, technologies, and technical capacity to higher levels. Through their investment in research and development (R&D) and control over patents, TNCs control the new technologies on which competitiveness in global markets depends. Many technologies are now available only through internalised company transfers, and their share in the overall total is rising. This is especially true of valuable new technologies based on expensive R&D. FDI has the potential to provide the local affiliates of TNCs with access not merely to new technologies and markets, but also to the management and organisational methods, quality-control standards, and marketing strategies that are important to commercial success.

- **Access to markets.** Participation in TNC networks provides firms in developing countries with access to the large internal markets associated with intra-company trade (see Chapter 1), and to consumer markets through retail chains. Small and medium-sized firms in developing countries often lack the marketing capacity and knowledge to enter markets in industrialised countries.

- **Research and development.** Through their capital resources, TNCs are able to dominate global R&D. To the extent that developing countries are able to capture some of these resources for the development of local technological capacity, it can help to narrow the gap between them and the industrialised world. In an increasingly knowledge-based global economy, that gap is a major source of inequality in world trade. Expenditure on research ranges from $674 per capita in the USA, to $12–15 in countries such as Mexico and Brazil, to less than $1 in many low-income countries (Lall 2000b). FDI has been associated with investment in research, but only in selected countries. Companies such as Cisco systems, Texas Instruments, and Hewlett Packard have set up software R&D facilities in India. Similarly, the Sony corporation has established nine R&D units in Asia, including a number of design units.

It should be emphasised that these are *potential* benefits, rather than automatic outcomes associated with FDI. Whether or not the potential is realised depends upon policy choices made by governments, and on corporate strategies.

Foreign direct investment: quantity and distribution

At the start of the 1990s, FDI flows to developing countries were equivalent to aid flows. Today, transfers of aid are dwarfed by investment flows. Total development-assistance transfers amount to less than one-quarter of the $208bn provided in FDI, and the gap is widening. While other private capital transfers, such as bond and equity flows, also grew rapidly in the 1990s, FDI still accounts for around two-thirds of total capital flows.

The decline in aid flows has hurt many developing countries. Although it coincided with a surge in FDI, very little private capital goes to the poorest countries. The 15 recipients of the largest amounts, such as China, Thailand, Indonesia, Malaysia, Brazil, and Mexico, account for more than four-fifths of the total. China alone receives one-quarter of FDI inflows – more than South Asia, sub-Saharan Africa, and Latin America combined. Almost entirely neglected is sub-Saharan Africa, which receives just over one per cent of FDI. Thus the countries that are most desperately in need of increased financial resources to integrate more successfully into the world trading system are being left behind.

To the extent that FDI enhances the ability of developing countries to benefit from trade, it is widening South–South differences. Claims that it is reducing broader North-South

Figure 7.1
Ratio of profit repatriation to FDI:
selected regions (1991-1997)

Source: UNCTAD 1999c

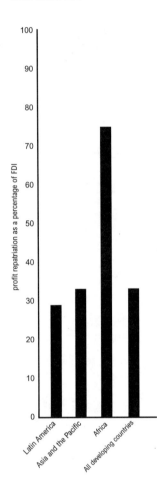

inequalities should be treated with extreme caution. While FDI flows to developing countries have been increasing more rapidly than flows to industrialised countries, rich countries continue to dominate. More than three-quarters of FDI is still directed towards industrialised countries, and the share of developing countries has been shrinking over time, from around one-third in the mid-1990s to one-quarter today. Measured in simple financial terms, the stock of FDI in developing countries amounts to $282 per capita, compared with $3626 per capita in high-income countries (based on data in UNCTAD 1999c). Even Latin America, with less than $1000 per person, has only one-third of the per capita FDI stock of the industrialised world. Even so, foreign capital plays an increasing role in developing countries. It now accounts for more than 11 per cent of fixed capital investment (ten times the share in 1980), and almost one-third of that in manufacturing.

Net transfers of FDI

Measured as a transfer of financial resources from rich to poor countries, the benefits of FDI have been wildly exaggerated. Simple accountancy helps to explain why. Figures on FDI inflows are often assumed to represent a net transfer of resources, which they do not. Repatriated profits constitute a financial outflow which must be set against any inflow associated with FDI. These are very large. For every $1 transferred to developing countries in the form of FDI, around $0.30 leaves in the form of repatriated earnings (see Figure 7.1). For sub-Saharan Africa, profit repatriation represents three-quarters of FDI inflows. In other words, for every $4 that enter through FDI, $3 leave in the form of profit transfers (World Bank 1999).

High levels of profit repatriation reflect the high rates of profit associated with FDI. In national accounting terms, the profit rate of return can be thought of as equivalent to an interest charge. For developing countries, that interest charge averaged around 15 per cent in the second half of the 1990s (and twice that level for Africa), which was twice as high as the rate of interest on sovereign loans (UNCTAD 2000e). It follows that FDI is a very expensive source of financing, unless it comes with wider benefits that generate higher levels of growth in the long term.

Profit remittances are the most obvious foreign-exchange cost associated with FDI. However, imports of goods and services associated with foreign investment also impose costs, which are reflected in the balance of payments. These costs can be very large. In Mexico, imports by foreign investors in the period leading up to the financial crash at the end of 1995 are estimated to have increased the current-account deficit in the balance of payments by an amount equivalent to more than 2 per cent of GDP (Woodward 2001). Similarly, the rapid increase in Thailand's import-to-GDP from 25 per cent to 49 per cent between 1990 and 1997 was largely due to a rise in import dependency associated with FDI (UNCTAD 1997). Foreign-investment projects were importing more than 90 per cent of their machinery, and more than half of their raw materials. According to UNCTAD, the high import costs and profit remittances associated with FDI had a *negative* overall effect on the balance of payments. In both Mexico and Thailand, the balance of payments pressures generated by import-intensive FDI added to the financial pressures that culminated in financial collapse.

Not all FDI takes the form of an external transfer. Some of it is financed through domestic savings in developing countries, rather than new foreign capital. For example, more than one-quarter of investment by US TNCs operating in Brazil and Mexico is financed by retained earnings. By international standards, this is exceptionally high, amounting to three to four times the level in France and Germany (US Department of

Commerce 1998). Taking into account profit repatriation and investment through retained earnings, the foreign-currency transfers provided through FDI in Latin America are less than half of those implied by headline FDI figures (see Figure 7.2).

The costs of attracting and keeping FDI must also be placed on the balance sheet. Many governments go to extraordinary lengths to attract foreign investors, often by providing financial inducements. Large TNCs in particular are in a position to encourage bidding wars. For example, in the second half of the 1990s, the governments of Rio Grande do Sul and Bahia in Brazil gave General Motors and Ford respectively financial packages worth $3bn in total to locate factories in their States (Hanson 2001). Other losses sustained by governments include those revenue losses associated with tax incentives and tax holidays (see below). Such costs are hidden from FDI accounts, in the sense that they are incurred in national budgets, rather than through the balance of payments. However, they represent a real financial loss.

Some of the costs associated with FDI are inherently difficult to quantify. The large internal markets of TNCs mean that a substantial part of their international transactions can bypass national scrutiny. Profit levels, and hence tax liability, can be understated by over-charging affiliates for services, licensing fees, and imports of technologies, thereby depriving the host government of revenue. This is a major problem in the USA, where federal tax authorities have responded by adjusting tax claims to take into account assessments of global profits (UNCTAD 2000e). However, few developing countries have the administrative capacity to prevent revenue losses through sophisticated tax-avoidance schemes. One estimate, endorsed by the OECD, suggests that developing countries may be losing up to $50bn annually through corporate tax avoidance (Oxfam 2000a).

The quality of investment

The conviction that foreign investment is good for development and a guaranteed route to success in world trade has diverted attention from important policy issues. Instead of focusing on strategies for generating good-quality investment that develops productive capacity, governments of rich and poor countries, along with international financial institutions, have prioritised quantity over quality. The result is a preponderance of bad-quality investment, marked by weak linkages to domestic firms, and linked in turn to low-productivity, low-wage employment.

When TNCs invest in industrially advanced countries, they typically interact on an intensive basis with local firms, contributing new skills and technologies and building capacity. This is a feature of good-quality investment. Such investment implies the transfer of skills, technologies, and productive capacity needed to create employment at higher levels of productivity, thereby creating the conditions for rising wages. It also implies strong linkages with domestic firms through the creation of new markets (Lall 2001c). Much of the activity associated with the explosion of FDI in the 1990s would not meet these criteria.

One of the most widely cited indicators for 'success' in FDI is the impact of TNCs on export performance: evidence from a large group of countries points to a very strong impact. In countries such as China, Mexico, Indonesia, Bangladesh, and Malaysia, TNCs account for more than one-quarter of exports (UNCTAD 2000e). Export growth reflects the growing ascendancy of TNCs in the domestic economies of many developing countries. In Latin America, TNCs expanded their share in the sales of the region's largest 500 firms from around one-quarter at the start of the 1990s to almost

Figure 7.2
Foreign investment in Latin America (1998)

Source: UNCTAD 1999c

100%

$31bn — Real transfers from parent companies 44%

$19bn — Retained earnings* 27%

$21bn — Profit repatriation 29%

0%

*The figure is the average for Mexico (30%) and Brazil (24%)

one-half at the end of the decade (ECLA 2000d). However, as we saw in Chapter 3, export 'success' is not the same as development success.

The Mexican maquiladora model

One country that has come to symbolise the 'quantity not quality' approach to FDI is Mexico. Since the late 1980s, foreign investment has been a central part of a national development strategy aimed at integration with the North American economy through NAFTA. Successive governments have eased the rules on regulation, allowing FDI into virtually every economic sector. At one level, the results have been spectacular. Flows of FDI averaged more than $10bn a year in the second half of the 1990s. More than half of these inflows have gone into manufacturing, predominantly into high-technology sectors such as automobiles, electronics, and computers. Exports have boomed, with their share in GDP rising to almost one-third by the end of the 1990s. The *maquiladora* zone accounts for more than half of these exports, reflecting the direction of FDI flows. Foreign companies now account for two-thirds of Mexico's exports (ECLA 1999).

FDI-led export growth in Mexico reflects the restructuring of corporate production to take advantage of the opportunities provided by NAFTA. Foreign TNCs have used Mexico as a site for assembling products for re-export to the North American market, importing most of the components and technologies used in production. Ford's state-of-the-art engine-assembly plant in Chihuahua exports more than 90 per cent of its production, and uses almost no local inputs other than labour. Although Volkswagen decided to produce its new Beetle model exclusively in Mexico, its Puebla plant remains essentially a site for assembling imported components.

The surge in exports of cars and automobile components from Mexico reflects the heavy investment by TNC car firms in restructuring their operations. The international trade data may record rapid growth in Mexico's auto exports, but much of the real growth has been in exports from Ford Chihuahua to Ford in Detroit, and other forms of intra-company trade. The local supplier industry has found it difficult to raise technological levels to the standards demanded by foreign TNCs, partly because of the absence of a credible national strategy to support up-grading, or to promote linkages between these TNCs and local firms (Mortimore 1998a).

The same picture emerges in other high-technology sectors, such as computers. Proximity to the US market (which reduces delivery times), preferential market access, cheap labour, and an investor-friendly regulatory system have acted as magnets for FDI. Large TNCs such as IBM, Hewlett Packard, and NEC have made big investments in Mexico. The Sanyo corporation moved its entire portable-computer manufacturing operation from Japan to Mexico at the end of 1997. Meanwhile, the Acer corporation, which is the main assembler of portable computers for IBM, Hitachi, and Fujitsu, is now one of the largest assembly operations in the country. Enthusiastic comparisons have been drawn with other sites in the global high-tech market place. The State of Jalisco in the northern border region has been dubbed Mexico's 'Silicon Valley', with exports of computer products having grown from $1.5m in 1994 to $6.5bn in 1998. One of the most important investors in Jalisco – and one of the largest exporters in Mexico – is IBM. The company assembles more than one million laptop computers for export in the State and invested more than $2.5bn in 1998, making this one of its most important overseas investment sites (ECLA 1999). Yet, despite the volume of FDI and the pace of export growth, linkages between exporters and local firms are negligible.

Contrasts between Mexico and East Asia are pertinent. The dominant Korean and Taiwanese firms have very strong national linkages, a highly diversified export base, and high levels of technological capacity, and are highly competitive in global markets. By contrast, export 'success' in Mexico is characterised by very low levels of value-added (less than two per cent in the *maquiladora* zone), high levels of dependence on just one market (the USA), weak national linkages, dependence on foreign capital and imported technologies, and a reliance on cheap labour.

Export-processing zones

Developments in Mexico are part of a broader pattern of FDI emerging under globalisation. As governments have shifted the focus towards export-led growth strategies, many have established export-processing zones (EPZs), aimed at attracting foreign investors. These EPZs provide investors with extensive infrastructural support, along with subsidised access to production sites, and long tax holidays. With one or two notable exceptions, they are failing to provide a basis for export success.

EPZs have been at the centre of export growth in labour-intensive products. However, much of the investment now flooding into EPZs belongs in the 'low quality' category. Attracted by cheap labour for the assembly of imported goods, investors have little interest in raising the skills of their work forces, or in establishing linkages with local firms.

Export-led success under the EPZ model is often short-lived. In the 1980s, the Dominican Republic was able to diversify out of its dependence on agricultural-commodity exports by expanding its production of garments for the US market. However, the country's increasing share of the North American market owed less to domestic competitiveness than to the arrival of US subsidiaries and their subcontractors in the country's EPZ. When wages increased, foreign investors relocated to lower-wage economies in Central America. Because the export industry never established domestic linkages or generated a national supply base, export growth did little to raise long-term capacity (Vicens et al. 1998).

Weak domestic linkages and dependence on low-wage, low-skill assembly operations are not the only problems associated with EPZs. By offering extensive tax inducements, national governments weaken their revenue-raising capacity. Export-processing zones typically offer tax-free holidays of between five and ten years, although in some cases, as in Honduras, they are granted on a permanent basis (Agosin et al. 2000). For Bangladesh, the implied revenue losses associated with tax concessions in the EPZ amount to around $84m per annum.[1] To put this figure in context, it amounts to about one-seventh of the national budget for primary education.

Extensive tax concessions to attract FDI are part of a vicious circle. If poor countries are to increase the quality of export growth and foreign investment, they need to invest in economic infrastructure, and in human capital. The problem is that when the most dynamic growth sector of the economy is a tax-free zone, it is difficult to generate the revenues needed for public investment.

Research and development

One of the most important potential benefits of foreign direct investment is the upgrading of domestic technological capacity. Local investment in research and development has a critical role to play. Unfortunately, FDI is often associated with a down-grading of R&D capacity. Several experiences from Latin America illustrate this. In 1996/97, a number of foreign TNCs bought up large Brazilian auto-parts producers, such as Metal Leve, Freios Varga, and Cofap. The R&D facilities of the local firms were subsequently down-graded or closed. In the high-technology sector, the French company Alcatel purchased Elebra Multitel, one of Latin America's most advanced producers of switching systems. Two other companies producing switching systems, Zetax and Batik, were also taken over.

In each case, the research and development programmes of the Brazilian company were scaled down, and the focus moved from the development of new products to the adaptation of imported products and processes generated by the parent TNC (Cassiolato and Lastres 1999). Reflecting the down-grading of local capacity, import penetration has increased dramatically. In the early 1990s, only ten per cent of the auto parts used in Brazil were imported. That share has now increased to exceed one-quarter. The share of imports in high-technology goods has doubled to almost three-quarters over the same period. Similar developments have taken place in Argentina. Research into privatised utilities taken over by foreign TNCs found that only one telephone company retained a research and development unit. This had no link with parent-company R&D operations (Chudnovsky 1999). In the automobile sector, previously a focal point for investment in research, the main technological activity undertaken by firms acquired by foreign TNCs is the adaptation of products developed by, and transferred from, the parent company.

Mergers and acquisitions

There is an important distinction to be drawn between different types of FDI. Potentially the most beneficial form for developing countries is 'greenfield investment', involving the creation of new productive capacity. However, since the mid-1990s, mergers and acquisitions have been the driving force behind FDI, with privatisation programmes figuring prominently. While there is a variety of experiences, the long-term development gains associated with this form of FDI have been over-stated.

Worldwide, there was a fourfold increase in merger and acquisition activity between 1990 and 1995. At the end of the 1990s, such activity accounted for around one-half of all FDI flows to Latin America. The manufacturing sector was virtually bypassed by these flows, which were directed mainly towards banking, telecommunications, and utilities. Among the showpiece models have been the $20bn 'Operation Veronica', under which Telefonica Espana purchased companies in Argentina, Brazil, and Peru, the takeover by major Spanish banks of financial-sector companies, and the purchase of energy companies (ECLA 2000d). Such activity has often facilitated a transfer of ownership from State companies to private monopolies. In countries where regulatory systems and institutions are weak, and where resources are scarce, the efficiency gains are at best unproven.

In East Asia, the surge in FDI after the financial collapse of 1997 was less a product of good-quality investment than a symptom of distress sales by local firms, with foreign buyers taking advantage of currency devaluation to purchase at bargain prices. Mergers and acquisitions accounted for $25bn in 1999, more than one-quarter of all FDI flows (Zhan 2001).

Attracting high-quality investment

The problems associated with many current FDI practices do not detract from its considerable potential for supporting national development strategies for achieving broad-based economic growth and poverty reduction. There is no blueprint for tapping that potential. However, there are two broad lessons to emerge from more successful countries. First, good-quality foreign investment is unlikely to emerge in countries lacking a commitment to improving human-capital levels. Second, governments must abandon passive strategies towards FDI and adopt more active approaches to attracting and managing new investment flows.

Box 7.1

Successful strategies for FDI: the case of Costa Rica

In the mid-1990s, Costa Rica abandoned its passive policy on foreign investment and set a new course. The aim was to integrate FDI into a national strategy for entering new high-technology markets, while at the same time increasing local technological capacity and creating new skills, to develop a competitive advantage based on human capital, rather than cheap labour. Selective and targeted approaches to FDI replaced the 'open-door' approach of the past.

The new policy direction reflected a growing awareness that Costa Rica could not compete against Mexico and other Central American countries by relying on unskilled labour and low wages. Electronics and related activities were seen as an alternative to traditional EPZ activity, such as garment assembly. Government invested heavily in expanding the Technology Institute of Costa Rica to generate the skills needed to improve performance. At the same time, government and the private-sector Coalition for Development Incentives (CINDE) worked together to identify strategic TNC partners in electronics and other knowledge-intensive industries.

Intel was identified as a potential catalyst for changing the nature of FDI. The company was seeking sites to locate a plant in Latin America, with Brazil and Mexico thought to be the favoured candidates. Both countries offered extensive inducements for the investment. Costa Rica offered incentives of a different variety. It invested heavily in new courses in micro-electronics at the Technology Institute. Following consultation with Intel, plans were developed for improving transport infrastructure, increasing electricity supply, and providing the company with exclusive telecommunications facilities.

In 1996, Intel decided to build a $300m semi-conductor assembly and testing site in Costa Rica, having rejected alternative sites in Brazil and Mexico. The company has now moved beyond simple assembly and testing to invest in a new centre for software development and the design of semi-conductors. It has also invested heavily in staff training, and in developing teaching and research facilities in universities and the Technology Institute.

It would an exaggeration to say that financial incentives have not figured in Intel's calculations. The Costa Rican government has provided the company with subsidised electricity, and like all foreign investors it received a six-year tax holiday. Yet the incentives that a small country like Costa Rica can provide are dwarfed by countries such as Brazil and Mexico, while the tax holiday is short by Central American standards. Instead of seeking to integrate into the global economy on the basis of cheap labour, Costa Rica has attempted to develop more dynamic forms of comparative advantage.

The results have been impressive. Today, Costa Rica exports more software per capita than any other country in Latin America. Unlike Mexico, export growth – exceeding 10 per cent a year – has increased demand for skilled labour, and increased real wages.

Sources: Spar 1998, ECLA 1999, Reinhardt 2000

In some circumstances, even EPZs have been made to work effectively. For example, Mauritius sustained rapid export growth through its export zones for more than two decades. Unlike many of today's cases, such as Mexico and Honduras, government policies established strong links between the EPZs and national firms. The rising levels of productivity associated with export production in Mauritius were reflected in rising real wages; the same minimum-wage provisions were applied in the EPZ as in the rest of the economy (Subramanian 2001). The experience of Costa Rica is also instructive.

In the mid-1990s, the country abandoned its efforts to attract FDI on the basis of cheap labour and actively sought partnerships with TNCs willing to undertake long-term investments in new technologies and skills training (see Box 7.1).

To this more recent example may be added some lessons from experience in East Asia. Thirty years ago, the TNC investment community in Singapore was dominated by companies producing low-value, labour-intensive products, such as textiles and simple electronics. Those companies have now gone, with the blessing of the Singapore government. As labour costs rose, they relocated elsewhere in the region, to be replaced by TNCs engaged in the production of precision instruments, aeronautic equipment, and micro-electronics. The Singapore government managed the transition through heavy investment in technical education, under the auspices of the Vocational and Industrial Training Board, creating the skill base needed to penetrate markets with higher value-added (Lall 2001c).

Other governments in the region have adopted similar approaches, often from different starting points. For example, Taiwan placed far more emphasis than Singapore on the development of local firms, often restricting TNC activity and enforcing backward linkages through rules requiring 'local content'. These rules specify that foreign investors must purchase a certain share of their inputs locally. However, the Taiwanese government has also actively facilitated links with TNCs. Through the Computing and Communication Laboratory, it has promoted the transfer, diffusion, and development of new micro-processor technologies, enabling local manufacturers to develop their own versions of new chip-based technologies. It has also negotiated on behalf of local companies with IBM and Motorola to develop licensing arrangements (UNCTAD 1999c).

The high costs of extraction

Many of the world's poorest countries are integrating into the global economy as exporters of mineral resources. With the liberalisation of trade and investment, the involvement of TNCs in finding, mining, and exporting these resources is increasing. Foreign investment is generating billions of dollars in foreign-exchange earnings. However, resource extraction attracts more than its fair share of bad-quality investment, and often fuels conflict and environmental destruction.

Foreign investment in minerals exploration and export has an obvious attraction for governments: it promises windfall revenues and foreign-exchange gains. But the longer-term economic logic is less compelling. Minerals appear to offer a pure form of static comparative advantage: countries either have them in commercially exploitable quantities and locations, or they do not. The problem is that exploitation of short-term comparative advantage can generate long-term costs. This is especially true in weak and conflict-affected States which lack the institutional capacity to manage mineral booms effectively.

The economics of commodity dependence

Investment in minerals production and export can have adverse consequences for long-term development, locking countries into patterns of export activity that are prone to boom-and-bust cycles which generate weak gains for human development.

One of the problems with resource extraction is that it tends to be a capital-intensive rather than a labour-intensive operation. While activities such as mining can create large numbers of jobs, the capital costs of job creation are far higher than in manufacturing or agriculture. Most large-scale mining operations employ large amounts of capital and small amounts of labour.

Whatever the short-term advantages for government revenue, dependence on primary-commodity exports can inflict damage on the rest of the economy. Over-reliance on minerals leaves countries operating in a segment of world trade that is characterised by slow growth and adverse terms of trade, with damaging implications for long-term growth prospects. Price instability is another problem: most minerals are subject to periodic cycles of extreme fluctuations in prices. Slumps in price can severely deplete government revenues, undermining capacity to maintain basic services. Peaks in price have the adverse side-effect of enabling governments to borrow excessively on international markets. Ecuador used the oil boom in the 1970s to borrow heavily. Today, its national debt exceeds $16bn, and over one-third of government revenue is allocated to servicing the debt. The benefits of oil revenues are being transferred to foreign creditors through debt servicing. Meanwhile, despite the rapid growth of oil exports, there are more people living below the poverty line today than in the mid-1970s.

One effect of rapid increases in minerals exports is to drive up the exchange rate, making imports cheaper and exports more expensive. As a result, local manufacturing industry and agricultural producers are faced with more intense competition, and exporters face disadvantages in international markets. One classic example is Nigeria, where the exchange-rate movements that accompanied the oil export boom in the 1970s led to a catastrophic loss of market share for smallholder producers of cocoa and edible oils, and a massive increase in food imports. The Nigerian economy won windfall foreign-exchange gains, but millions of smallholder farmers suffered (Andrae and Beckman 1985).

There is often a close association between the exploitation of mineral resources and the exploitation of the public purse. The wealth generated by mineral exploitation, and the resources available to extractive TNCs, are often vast, relative to national wealth. The ease with which revenues from minerals can be manipulated by unscrupulous officials makes corruption particularly likely. In Indonesia, revenues from mining concessions were ruthlessly plundered by the regime of President Suharto. In countries with weak regulatory structures and systems of financial accountability, large revenue flows can compound problems of governance. In 1998 the government of Angola was awarded $870m in the form of 'signature bonus payments' for oil concessions in blocks dominated by BP-Amoco, Exxon-Mobil, and Elf. While signature bonus payments are not technically illegal, these one-off payments frequently bypass the Ministry of Finance and the Central Bank, and often remain unrecorded. According to Angola's Foreign Minister, these funds were earmarked for the 'war effort' (Human Rights Watch 2000).

International efforts to improve the use of mineral revenues often fail. In the case of Angola, pressure from the IMF and NGOs for an audit of the country's oil accounts in preparation for a concessional loan became irrelevant when a private bank in the USA made a loan of $455m. This case illustrated the way in which private interests can subvert public interests (Seymour 2001).

Conflict, environmental threats, and the rights of indigenous communities

In much of the developing world, resource extraction is intimately linked to conflict, environmental damage, and the violation of the rights of local populations. Large amounts of FDI are directed towards mineral exploitation in countries affected by ethnic strife or regional tensions. Bitter struggles for control over revenues have been at the heart of some of the most protracted conflicts, from Angola and Liberia to Colombia. At the same time, mineral extraction often takes place on the lands of indigenous people. Lacking enforceable claims to their land rights, these communities are frequently and violently displaced.

Revenues from minerals often directly finance civil wars. In Angola the government finances military spending with revenues from oil, while the opposing force of UNITA pays for its weapons through diamonds. Oil accounts for 90 per cent of government revenue, but the enormous wealth generated by minerals extraction is being used to destroy, rather than develop, the country. At the end of the 1990s, defence spending accounted for more than 40 per cent of revenue, and health and education services combined accounted for only seven per cent (Oxfam 2001e). In the Sudan, oil revenues amounting to $365m per annum are being used to prosecute a vicious civil war. The government stands accused of displacing local populations by force to make way for companies holding oil concessions, such as Talisman (Canada) and Petronas (Malaysia) (Christian Aid 2001). Meanwhile, the infrastructure created by oil companies can be used by government for military purposes.

Even with the best of intentions, it is often difficult for companies to insulate their operations from civil conflict. When BP-Amoco invested heavily in oil exploration in the Casanare region of Colombia, it was operating in a zone characterised by political violence and extensive abuses of human rights. The company's security arrangements, designed to protect its own facilities and staff, led to an increased presence of security forces, private as well as State (Inter-Agency Group 1999). The discovery and exploitation of oil in the Department was accompanied by an increase in violence and human-rights abuses, as both guerrilla forces and paramilitary organisations increased their operations.

Mineral deposits are often located in ecologically fragile areas and on the lands of marginalised groups. These groups are frequently the last to benefit from the foreign-exchange gains generated through minerals trade – and the first to suffer the consequences of environment-damaging production methods. Where large mineral deposits are located on the lands of indigenous communities and other groups who lack political power, commercial imperatives can result in severe damage to the environment and abuse of human rights.

In Indonesia, Oxfam has been working in areas of East Kalimantan where prawn farmers have seen their livelihoods destroyed by oily waste from Unocal's off-shore gas and oil fields. Elsewhere in the same country, copper mining has wrought environmental havoc, with large TNCs benefiting from local political structures that operate against the interests of vulnerable communities. People living downstream from mines have seen their livelihoods destroyed by reckless waste-disposal policies that have caused siltation and flooding (see Box 7.2). Some forms of minerals exploitation are associated with extreme threats to public health. In Ghana, Oxfam's partners have recorded dangerously high levels of mercury and other toxic substances in water in gold mining areas. The weakness of national regulatory authorities and a concern to maximise foreign-exchange revenues can take precedence over the need to protect public health.

Governments have often been willing to remove local communities in the interests of making way for minerals extraction, and increased revenue for the budget. This remains a major threat. For example, in Ecuador, Peru, and Bolivia, there are significant overlaps

---

Box 7.2

Copper mining and destruction in Indonesia

'Our environment has been ruined, and our forests and rivers polluted by waste. The sago forests which served as our primary food source have become dry, making it hard for us to find food.'

These are the words of Tom Beanal, a spokesperson for communities in Papua New Guinea affected by the Freeport copper mine in the mountains of West Papua, Indonesia. The mine, operated by a US-based TNC, stands on one of the largest deposits of ore ever discovered. Since production started in 1991, it has been progressively expanded and now produces more than 200,000 tons per day.

The vast amounts of waste generated by the mine – exceeding 100,000 tons per day – are dumped in the river. Downstream, the social and environmental effects have been disastrous. Massive silt deposits have raised water levels, causing the river to breach its banks and flood the lowland forests occupied by the Kamoro people. Whole swathes of forest and vegetation have been destroyed. Malaria, previously reported only in minor outbreaks, has reached epidemic proportions.

In a desperate attempt to defend their livelihoods, local communities have protested against the activities of the copper mine, demanding that it should compensate them for their losses and develop less destructive waste-disposal methods. Their actions have met with a brutal response. In 1995 the National Human Rights Commission reported that 37 people had been killed, and dozens tortured by security forces.

The Freeport mining company has condemned the behaviour of security forces.

Source: Atkinson 2001a

---

between unexploited mineral deposits and the traditional territories of indigenous peoples. In Ecuador, the World Bank is providing loans to open up additional swathes of the Amazon forest to exploitation by foreign companies, and the construction of a new oil pipeline which is expected to double the volume of production. While TNCs are often careful to distance themselves from outright abuses of human rights, they often tacitly support and encourage such violations.

Sub-Saharan Africa

Of all developing regions, it is sub-Saharan Africa that has paid the highest penalty for its abundance of mineral resources. It has been estimated that the continent of Africa contains around one-third of the world's total mineral reserves. It is a major producer of oil gas, diamonds, and uranium. More than three-quarters of the FDI entering the region is aimed at resource extraction.

Across much of the region, mineral extraction is intimately connected with the financing of civil wars, corruption, and economic mismanagement. Apart from a few countries such as Botswana and South Africa, the vast wealth generated by export activity has produced minimal benefits for human development. In some cases it has been associated with intense suffering, as in Angola and Sudan. In Angola, UNITA produced diamonds valued at $3.7 billion between 1992 and 1998. Those revenues funded UNITA offensives which brought to an end two peace processes, in 1992 and 1998 (Seymour 2001). But it is not solely resource extraction through FDI that can exacerbate underlying sources of conflict. Imports of timber by French companies from

Liberia have furnished Charles Taylor, the country's President, with an off-budget fund of around $100m a year (Global Witness 2001). Investigations by a UN team in 2000 found that these funds were being used to finance rebel groups in Sierra Leone.

UN expert panels have produced detailed reports on war economies, naming and shaming some of the companies involved. In the case of diamonds, a certification scheme has been developed by governments and industry in order to identify and isolate goods marketed by rebel groups or governments involved in conflicts. That system has achieved some success in breaking the link between diamond trading and revenues to fuel armed conflict. However, in the case of most minerals the complexity of supply networks, allied to the large revenues available, and to a lack of political will on the part of importing companies and countries, makes effective monitoring difficult (Seymour 2001).

Nowhere are the destructive forces unleashed by the combination of weak States and abundant mineral wealth more apparent than in the Democratic Republic of Congo (DRC). Since the days when King Leopold of Belgium treated the country as his personal treasure-chest, plundering its ivory, rubber, and metals, the Congo has been a victim of unscrupulous trading practices and weak governance. Today, an on-going war has cost the lives of 2.5 million people. That war is being driven in part by a struggle to control and exploit natural resources. Instead of generating revenues to rebuild the country's social and economic infrastructure, extractive industries are being looted by individuals and neighbouring countries (Oxfam 2002).

The political geography of conflict in the DRC reflects the geography of mineral deposits. Troops from Rwanda are concentrated in areas such as Kisangani, which is rich in diamonds, and Katanga, the centre of the country's coltan and copper reserves. Since its intervention in DRC, Rwanda has increased its exports of coltan, demand for which has soared with the growth of the global micro-electronics industry, from 83 tonnes to 1440. It is implausible that an expansion of this magnitude could have been achieved on the basis of domestic production. Forces of the Ugandan army have been deployed far beyond border areas into regions such as North Kivu and Ruwenzori, with large mineral and timber deposits. Exports of gold from Uganda have risen at an astonishing rate since its armed forces began operating in DRC, in line with a transfer of gold from Ituri and other gold-rich areas now controlled by Ugandan troops. Uganda has also emerged as an exporter of diamonds. Joint ventures between the DRC government and other parties to the conflict have added to the plunder. One Zimbabwean company, whose board includes senior officials of the ruling ZANU-PF party, has been granted what is probably the world's largest logging concession – an area of 33 million hectares, which is ten times the size of Switzerland. The concession involves a partnership with a DRC company called Combiex, whose majority shareholder was former President Laurent Kabila.

The UN Panel of Experts, created by the Secretary General to investigate the underlying causes of the conflict, has observed direct links to external interests. It has accused the governments of Rwanda and Uganda of giving their tacit, and in some cases explicit, consent to the transfer of mineral wealth. After interventions justified on the grounds that the conflict in DRC posed security threats, troop deployments in mineral areas that have no bearing on security are actively intensifying conflict and reinforcing poverty (Oxfam 2002). Beyond the neighbouring States, the international trading system is generating the impetus for plunder. High levels of foreign demand for minerals create opportunities for profits and foreign-exchange earnings, illustrating how global markets can compound the effects of conflict and weak governance (see Box 7.3).

Box 7.3

Coltan wars – the price of a mobile phone

Coltan has been called the 'magic dust' of the micro-electronics industry. It makes mobile telephones work. Highly resistant to heat, it is used as a coat for electronic components in mobile phones, play stations, and military aircraft. The ore is nearly as heavy as gold – and not much cheaper. At its peak, in December 2000, coltan was worth $380 per pound on world markets.

For countries such as Australia and Canada, coltan generates large amounts of wealth and prosperity. In theory, it could do the same for the Democratic Republic of Congo (DRC), which is estimated to hold up to 5 per cent of the world's reserves. But in eastern DRC, coltan is at the centre of a brutal conflict that has claimed thousands of lives and led to hunger, disease, and mass displacement. The Rwandan army controls much of the mining of coltan, transporting the ore to Kigali. Analysts calculate that some $250m has been generated through this route (more than Rwanda's recorded exports). Uganda has also engaged in the looting of coltan, and there are documented cases of civilian massacres linked to its military efforts to secure mining areas.

Revenues from coltan are at the core of the appalling suffering in a civil war that has left thousands of people dead and a quarter of a million displaced. In the words of a damning UN Panel of Experts on the coltan trade: 'the only loser in this business venture is the Congolese people'. It is not clear what route coltan takes after it has been plundered in eastern DRC. However, it appears likely that some of it ends up in mobile phones, computers, and other electronic items. One report suggests that as much as 8 per cent of the coltan used in the USA may originate in the Democratic Republic of Congo.

Sources: Essick 2001, McGreal 2001, Oxfam 2002

TNCs and employment rights

Wages and employment standards have a critical relevance to the distribution of benefits from international trade. As we saw in Chapter 3, low wages and poor employment standards explain why the expansion of trade has failed to generate the expected human-development benefits in many countries.[2] TNCs are implicated in both problems.

TNCs and the supply chain

Leaders of the movement for corporate social responsibility place much emphasis on the need for good employment practices. In the words of the Chairman of BP (British Petroleum):

> 'A company which abuses its workforce…is flying in the face of civilised thinking all over the world. Such a company is acting irresponsibly in an area over which it has direct influence. And in a world of increasing transparency and global communications, such a company is also foolish.' (Sutherland 1997)

This statement raises two complex questions about corporate responsibility. First, what constitutes a TNC workforce? And second, what counts as an abuse?

One obvious answer to the first question might be 'the workforce of the TNC concerned'. It would be partly correct. With the growth of international production and investment flows, direct employment by TNCs is increasing in developing countries, although it still accounts for only a tiny minority of total employment.

Estimating precise numbers is notoriously difficult, but a widely used calculation puts the figure at between 17 and 26 million people (UNCTAD 1999c). There are large variations. For example, TNCs account for well under one per cent of employment in India, but for 10–15 per cent in Vietnam, Mexico, and Brazil, and over 40 per cent in Malaysia and Singapore.

The reason why the above answer is only partly correct is that the majority of employment generated by TNCs is within global production networks, often operating through long and complex supply chains. The sports company Nike formally employs about 20,000 people worldwide, but estimates that there are approximately 500,000 people employed in making its products. Micro-electronic firms such as IBM and Motorola operate plants in many countries, but those plants are connected through sub-contracting arrangements to other companies. Garments retailers such as Gap are at the end of complicated supply chains, often extending beyond the factories of sub-contractors into the houses of women home-workers who do embroidery and stitching.

Not all companies in the supply chain are Northern-based TNCs. Companies from Taiwan produce garments for European retailers in Bangladesh and Honduras, and computer chip-boards in Mexico. Hong-Kong-based companies employ an estimated three million workers in China. These workers are supplying everything from plastic dolls for Walt Disney to computer circuit-boards for Hewlett Packard. In the food sector, individual supermarkets in Europe and North America are linked to thousands of producers. Sainsbury's, a UK supermarket chain, is not untypical. The company has about 2000 suppliers providing its 'own brand' goods, but these suppliers are linked in turn through their own supply networks to millions of farms across the globe (ETI 2001). Should Sainsbury's accept responsibility down to the farm-gate level, or for the workers who mine the tin used in factories that supply it?

There is no easy answer to this question, but it is clear that the sheer size of TNCs and their domination of global markets give them an enormous capacity to influence employment conditions. With that influence comes a responsibility that goes beyond the gates of its own factories, although ultimate responsibility for employment conditions resides not in corporate boardrooms but with governments.

The second question –what constitutes an abuse? – is no easier to answer than the first. Corporate executives are swift to point out that their companies tend to provide better wages and conditions than their domestic rivals, which is generally true. They also point to exemplary codes of conduct enshrining the principles set out in the conventions of the International Labour Organisation. However, TNCs are one of the driving forces in creating an increasingly competitive global economy. As developing countries compete against each other to attract foreign investment, many have relaxed their minimum-wage protection. Associated with low wages are often poor conditions of employment, weak trade-union rights, and lack of social-insurance provision, which helps to keep down labour costs and creates vulnerability. Women in particular have been drawn into this type of employment.

While TNCs may not be responsible in a legal sense for creating these conditions, they none the less act as a link between Northern consumers and highly vulnerable workforces. Moreover, they are directly responsible for generating some of the pressures that reduce wages and weaken employment rights. Suppliers, agents, and licensees are frequently engaged in fierce competition to win their contracts, and are offering tender-prices that reflect a less than scrupulous approach to employment conditions, respect for minimum wages, and the provision of basic employment rights. Many factory owners complain that they are being put in an impossible position. In the words of the owner of a large Bangladeshi factory producing garments for big High-Street names:

> 'Every week I have somebody here telling me that I need more windows, more crèche facilities, better sick-pay arrangements, more breaks and so on. Then they tell me "Don't forget, you are competing against China – you need to keep your prices low". I am operating in a cut-throat market. It is not this factory that sets prices and wages, but the companies that buy our products. How am I supposed to pay for better conditions, when I'm operating on non-existent profit margins?'

Debate over the role of TNCs has crystallised around two issues examined below: wages and employment conditions.

The great wage debate

Much of the debate about TNCs and wage levels in developing countries has an air of unreality. Critics point to wage rates that are extremely low by rich-country standards and accuse companies of exploitative practices (Featherstone and Henwood 2001). Corporate executives and their advocates respond by asserting that low wages are a product of low productivity, inadequate education, and weak infrastructure, and by insisting that TNCs pay more than local firms (*Economist* 2001a). Critics call for a living wage, rather than a poverty wage. Corporate executives and renowned international economists return fire with stern lectures on what they describe as 'market realities' (Srinivasan 2001, Bhagwati 2000). None of this addresses the real issues at stake.

Low wages are a major cause of poverty in developing countries. The failure of export growth to push up the wages of the unskilled – notably women – is another factor that contributes to poverty. It is not simply that wages in export sectors dominated by FDI are low in comparison with those received by workers in rich countries: they are also low in absolute terms.

Women workers in the Bangladeshi garment industry earn $1.50–$2.00 per day in the country's export-processing zones. The lower end of this range is slightly below the national poverty line, the upper end slightly above it. This helps to explain one of the anomalies of Bangladesh's experience over the past decade: the coincidence of high growth and persistent poverty. Driven by export growth, average incomes have been rising at around two per cent a year in the 1990s, but poverty levels have declined only marginally.

In many cases, the wages paid to workers in export industries are close to poverty-line levels. Women working a 12-hour day in El Salvador earn less than $5 a day, or $0.60 an hour – less than one-third of the estimated subsistence costs for a family of four (see Box 7.4). In Honduras, the minimum wage is less than $0.50 an hour. This figure is not only very low by international standards. In 1998, a review carried out by the US Department of Commerce concluded, in a masterly understatement, that: 'the minimum wage in Honduras is considered insufficient to provide a decent living' (Pitts 2001).

Box 7.4

Wages in El Salvador: Hermosa's story

Hermosa is a single mother with three children who works in a garment factory in El Salvador, making sports shirts and shorts for Adidas, Puma, and Nike. In early 2000 she was interviewed about her income and daily expenses. These worked out as follows (converted to US dollars per day):

Round trip by bus to work	$1.14
Breakfast and lunch	2.28
Supper for herself and children	1.95
Rent in a crowded shared house	1.68
Gas and electricity for the house	0.63
Total	$ 7.68

In addition, she pays school fees for the three children of $5.57 per week – and there are additional occasional expenses, such as shoes for the children (between $11 and $17 a pair) and medical expenses (a visit to the public clinic costs $3.43).

To survive, Hermosa has to work as much over-time as she can, which usually means a 12-hour shift each day. Her base rate of pay at the factory is the official minimum of 42 *colones* for an eight-hour day (equivalent to $4.80 per day, or 60 cents an hour). This gives her an income of $7.20 for her 12-hour day, given that there are no extra rates for over-time – barely enough to cover the essentials, much less the extras.

Her day begins at around 4.30am, when she collects water and prepares the children for school. Often she does not arrive home until 8.15pm in the evening, after working the 12-hour shift. When asked if the family had any savings, she replied *'No, but we do have debts. Sometimes we cannot pay the rent.'*

The National Foundation for Development (FUNDE) in El Salvador estimates that a reasonable subsistance wage for a worker supporting a family of four would be about 5000 *colones* ($570) a month, or 165 *colones* ($18.81) per day. This includes the costs of food, housing, health care, clothing, education, and transport, but does not include any savings or discretionary spending on things such as entertainment.

(Source: Ministry of Labor: 'Monitoring Report on the Maquila and Bonded Areas' USAID/SETEFE/Ministry of Labor, July 2000, www.nlcnet.org/elsalvador)

Researchers in Mexico have reached similar conclusions. Wage levels for the 1.2 million workers employed in EPZ factories are desperately low. The national minimum wage of $4 a day, which many of these workers receive, is considered insufficient to cover basic household needs for a family. This is the conclusion of a report prepared by an Oxfam partner agency, the Coalition for Justice in the *Maquiladoras:*

> In community after community, maquiladora workers can afford only to live in make-shift houses without water and electricity. Even to talk about nutritious diets is a luxury. People work long, productive hours for the world's biggest corporations and still cannot provide the most basic needs for their families ... The foreign-based corporations that benefit from free trade have a moral obligation to pay their workers a sustainable wage.

It is of course the case that productivity differences have a bearing on relative wages, although the wage gap between Mexico and the USA is much wider than the productivity gap. It is also true that wages in the *maquiladora* zones of Mexico or Honduras, or the export-processing zones of Bangladesh, compare favourably with wage rates for agricultural labour. Rural poverty helps to create a steady supply of labour, even at poverty-wage rates. But the important question is whether or not TNCs could be doing more to support higher levels of wages. Many answer in the negative. The standard argument is that low wages are part of a country's comparative advantage, and that wage increases will result in investment flight and job losses. The broad approach was well expressed by Nike's Chief Spokesperson during 2001. When asked if the company could afford to pay higher wages in Asia, he responded: *'If you exponentially increase labour costs, that impacts on costs of production, which then means the retail cost may increase, which then reduces the amount of items sold'* (cited in Atkinson 2001). This is from a company which pays $2 in wage costs for a pair of trainers retailing at $67. Doubling wages would have the effect of adding three per cent to consumer prices.

Contrasts between corporate wealth and the near-poverty-level wages often paid to workers in developing countries are striking. In Bangladesh and Cambodia, women workers earn less than $40 a month sewing clothes for Gap and other companies. In Cambodia they are requesting modest wage increases, from $1 to $2 a day, to meet their families' basic needs. Corporate executives are quick to argue that the resulting cost inflation would mean loss of jobs. But for a company such as Gap, whose Chief Executive Officer Millard Drexler made more than $39 million in 2000, those arguments stretch plausibility. If his salary were to be distributed to Bangladesh's women garment workers, it would translate into an increase for each of them of about $4 a day, a three-fold rise in the daily wage rate (Global Exchange 2001b).

Other factors are as important as productivity in explaining wage levels in developing countries. Discrimination against women, restrictions on union rights, and a general erosion of employment-based insurance provision have all lowered labour costs. Many governments have created EPZs that offer more 'flexible' labour regimes than in the rest of the economy, including restrictions on collective bargaining rights. In some cases, working hours and minimum-wage provision do not apply, or can be safely ignored. When women garments workers enter the export-processing zones of Bangladesh, they leave their labour rights at the gate. Union membership is banned, there is no minimum wage provision, and no institutional mechanisms for claiming their social-welfare rights (see Box 7.5). TNCs may not create these conditions, yet they often encourage governments to create them – and they benefit from the lower-cost labour that they provide. Moreover, when TNCs operate or source from EPZs, they signal a willingness to depart from establish wage and employment norms, and inevitably exercise a downward pressure on wages.

What of the argument that TNCs pay more than local companies? Evidence on this score is mixed. Some widely cited research has claimed that wages paid by US TNC affiliates to workers in developing countries average double the local manufacturing wage (Graham 2001). Similarly, researchers in Indonesia found that foreign plants were paying wages 60 per cent higher than private domestically owned plants (Lipsey and Sjoholm 2001). Leaving aside the obvious point that TNCs are better placed to pay higher wages, other factors are important in explaining these differences. In general, foreign affiliates in developing countries are concentrated in higher-technology areas

Box 7.5

'Only investors have rights': women workers in Bangladesh

Bangladesh is one of the world's poorest countries. In the eyes of many economists, it is also one of the outstanding success stories of globalisation. The country has one of the world's fastest-growing garment industries. Inflows of foreign investment have helped to generate an export boom, creating economic growth and employment in the process. The benefits in terms of wealth creation are undeniable; the implications for women workers are more ambiguous.

There are more than one million women working in garment factories in EPZs, producing goods for companies such as Wal-Mart, Marks and Spencer, Adidas, and Gap. Machinists earn $1–$1.50 for a 14-hour day – a very low wage, but more than they can earn in alternative activities, such as labouring on construction sites. Most of these women have migrated to Dhaka, the hub of the garments industry, from poor rural areas in the regions of Comilla, Faridpur, and Barisal, where there are limited opportunities for off-farm employment. Most have had poor educational opportunities: on average, women working in garment factories have had four years of schooling, and one-quarter have none at all.

When women workers enter a factory in an export-processing zone, they leave their employment rights at the gate. Bangladesh enshrines basic labour rights such as the right to join a union, minimum wages, and social-insurance provision, both in its constitution and in national laws. But the law establishing EPZs cancelled these rights. Union membership is outlawed. In the event of a grievance, workers must appeal to an Industrial Relations Manager appointed by the EPZ management board. Employers' compliance with minimum-wage law is voluntary, and widely ignored. The Bangladeshi government has waived other legal obligations on factory owners in the EPZ. For example, the Chief Inspector of Factories is not authorised to carry out health and environment checks, or safety inspections.

Beyond the EPZs, there is a wide range of standards in the textiles and garments industry. Some factories, especially those linked to large retail chains in industrialised countries, meet high standards. Others, including some of their suppliers, do not. In theory, national legislation complies with some of the best international standards. In practice, compliance is variable, since there are only 54 factory inspectors for the whole of Bangladesh. Inadequate provision for the health and safety of workers has had fatal consequences. In November 2000, 47 workers died and hundreds more were injured when a fire swept through the Chowdhury Knitwear and Garments factory. Workers were unable to escape, because fire escapes were inadequate and doors were locked during working hours. Most of those who died were women under the age of 25, and eight of the dead were children.

Social-welfare rights are widely violated in the garments sector. Women interviewed by Oxfam complained of enforced over-time, abusive behaviour by managers, and unfair dismissals. Many had lost jobs after becoming pregnant, as their employers sought to avoid taking on responsibility for maternity payments. One woman, Aziza, a 23-year-old mother of two children, related her story as follows:

'I lost my first job when the manager found out that I was pregnant. They had no right to sack me. I came to Dhaka with my sister, and we found work in a South Korean company. The work is very hard, but the money is good – much better than I could earn as a domestic or as a labourer. Conditions are not so good. The supervisor shouts at us women and even pushes us sometimes. And we have no security. Two years ago I was in hospital for ten days, and off work for three months. The company promised me health benefit, but they never paid it. I am in debt now because of health costs. They gave me my job back, but I was sacked after one month when the manager found out that I was pregnant. I didn't receive any unemployment insurance. Now I have a new job. But I cannot feel secure.'

One of Oxfam's partners in Bangladesh, Karmojibi Nairi, is working with women garment workers and providing training courses in employment law, and health and safety provisions. It is attempting to provide women with the skills and confidence needed to improve their work situations. As the Director of Karmojibi Nairi puts it: *'What you have to understand is that many of the women working in this industry are very vulnerable. They have little education, they are often alone, and there are strong cultural barriers against women speaking up for themselves. It is easy for the EPZ management boards and their companies to exploit them, especially when their legal rights are so weak.'*

and employ better-educated workforces. There is little evidence that they pay higher wages in comparable areas of production, especially in labour-intensive sectors. In the case of Indonesia, foreign investment is concentrated in sectors (such as basic metals) with higher levels of output and productivity than domestic investment (which is concentrated in areas like food, textiles, and leather).

Employment conditions

Poor conditions of employment, lack of consideration for the health and safety of workers, and inadequate social-welfare provision create vulnerability for workers working for the export trade. As we saw in Chapter 3, women workers are especially concentrated in sectors such as garment manufacture, micro-electronics, and agro-exporting activity, where market conditions create intense pressure on employment standards. By virtue of their dominant position in their supply chains, TNCs play an important role in creating these conditions.

In countries that lack effective protection of employment rights, pressure on sub-contractors to meet stringent delivery deadlines can translate into forced overtime. In March 2000, Oxfam researchers interviewed workers from factories in Indonesia producing sports shoes for Nike. Women reported being pressed by management to work 70 hours a week. Refusal to work over-time could result in their dismissal (Atkinson 2001a). Research in China has revealed similar conditions. While Chinese labour law stipulates a maximum working week of 44 hours over six days, working days of 10–12 hours are normal when orders are high (HKCIC 2001, Labour Rights in China 1999). Forced over-time can have profoundly damaging consequences, creating intolerable individual stress and problems of finding reliable child-care facilities.

Effective trade unions give employees a voice. Many countries have sought to silence that voice in the interests of reducing labour costs. Various ideological pretexts have been found to justify such action. In 1982 the Chinese government removed the right to strike from the constitution, on the grounds that the State had 'eradicated problems between the proletariat and enterprise owners'. Malaysia has restricted trade-union rights, claiming that this will facilitate 'national economic development'. Elsewhere, labour rights are recognised in law, but not in practice. For example, legislation in the Dominican Republic allows for membership of trades unions, but only eight of the 500 companies operating in the EPZ have collective agreements. Much of the anti-union pressure applied by TNCs is informal. In El Salvador, a Ministry of Labour report concluded in July 2000: 'there exists an anti-union policy in the *maquilas*. Any attempt at organisation is repressed ... it is very common for supervisors and chiefs of personnel to threaten workers with firing if they belong to a union or attempt to form one (Pitts 2001).' While TNCs justifiably claim that they do not write anti-union legislation, few seek to challenge it – and many take advantage of it.

Minimum-wage laws can help to ensure that workers receive a reasonable share of the benefits from trade and establish a bottom line. As in industrialised countries, the precise level of bottom line is a matter of debate. But there is strong evidence that minimum-wage provisions can provide protection for the poor without damaging employment, subject to effective enforcement. Unfortunately, many governments continue to see minimum-wage protection as a barrier to foreign investment – a view encouraged by many TNCs. Some developing countries, such as Malaysia, refuse to implement such laws. Others apply them on a partial basis. Firms sub-contracted by TNCs often violate minimum-wage provisions. According to one survey, only one in five workers in the Bangladeshi textiles industry earns the legal minimum wage or above. That wage is equivalent to around $0.50 a day (ICFTU 2001). In China, labour law guarantees a minimum wage. However, when the Hong Kong Christian Industrial Committee conducted interviews with workers from twelve factories in Guangdong province in 2000, it found that women were being paid the minimum wage for a 40-hour week, even though they were often working for more than 50 hours (HKCIC 2001).

Weak employment rights and non-existent trade unions are often associated with dangerous work practices. Fires and industrial accidents are a constant feature of the special economic zones in China. Less well publicised are the health risks involved in working in the micro-electronics industry. Malaysian women working in the plating section of electronics factories report health problems ranging from miscarriages to respiratory difficulties. The injuries, risks, and long-term damage suffered by unprotected workers represent a labour cost that is not reflected in export prices.

Few TNCs contract home-workers directly, but they figure prominently in sub-contracting work in some sectors. Low pay is a common feature of home-based work. The predominantly female workforce is usually paid by piece rate, with levels set far below the equivalent for a minimum wage (ICFTU 1999). Research on the garments industry has found piece-rate payments equivalent to less than half of the minimum wage. In some cases, no margin is allowed for rejects, which depresses income further. Often women are forced to work long hours, to extremely tight deadlines (Yanz et al. 1999). Household poverty and low earnings often force home-workers to put their children to work. It is common for young girls to be kept out of school to help their mothers. One survey of home-workers in the Indian State of Gujarat found women and children contracted by textile factories working for more than nine hours a day (Jhabvala 1992).

Codes of conduct and beyond

As international trade strengthens the ties between producers in poor countries and consumers in rich ones, concern to prevent unacceptable abuse of labour rights has intensified. Consumers are demanding something more than low prices. High-profile campaigns have signalled that they care also about social responsibility – and many institutional investors have registered that concern. TNCs have responded by adopting voluntary codes of conduct. These are supposed to set and enforce standards which reflect wider international values. Evidence suggests that voluntary codes are no substitute for government enforcement of basic rights.

The dominant approach in TNCs has been the adoption of voluntary guidelines. Since

Levi Strauss started the trend in 1991, codes of conduct have become widespread. Most codes stipulate standards to be met on matters such as worker safety, social-insurance provision, and compliance with national laws in areas such as over-time. Many TNCs now have whole departments dealing with social responsibility and the implementation of these codes. Social auditing has become a standard feature of company reporting. Some codes have been adopted on an industry-wide basis. For example, the European Textile Union and the employers' association, Eurotex, have adopted a code of conduct applicable to all members.

At their strongest, codes of conduct have generated some real benefits. Individual companies have worked to improve conditions along their supply chains, demanding compliance with minimum standards. In the Dominican Republic, Grupo M, the largest employer in the free-trade zone, initiated major improvements in employment standards in the mid-1990s to meet Levi Strauss's code requirements. Today, the company provides subsidised transport for its workers, day-care centres, medical and dental care, literacy training, and generous social-insurance benefits. The company and its workforce have profited. Staff turnover and absenteeism rates are low, and its improved reputation as a good employer has enabled it to win contracts from companies, such as Liz Clairborne, Nike, and Banana Republic, that have modelled their codes on the Levi model.

Strong codes – weak auditing

Experience with the design and implementation of codes of conduct has been mixed. Some are more comprehensive than others in the standards they set, but most suffer from weak enforcement.

There is no consensus over precisely what rights should be protected by company codes. Most have standards on health and safety, child labour, and broad contractual provisions. However, some fail to include even the core labour standards set out by the International Labour Organisation (ILO) – a body that includes representatives of business interests. Neither Wal-Mart nor Liz Clairborne refers in its codes to the right of workers to join a union or engage in collective bargaining. Others expressly discourage trade-union activity. Sara Lee Knit Products (SLKP), an American-based TNC, stipulates: 'SLKP believes in a union-free environment, except where laws and cultures require us to do otherwise' (SLKP 2000).

Even the strongest codes of conduct are only as effective as their monitoring and enforcement arrangements. Here, too, serious problems have emerged. Weak auditing standards are widely prevalent. One of the first rules of effective social auditing is that inspectors should not announce their visits in advance. Another is that they should interview workers and their representatives under conditions of confidentiality. Detailed knowledge of problems faced in specific industries is another requirement. All too often these basic rules are broken, with breaches of codes left undetected as a result. In a study conducted in 2000 of monitoring by PricewaterhouseCoopers of factories in China, Korea, and Indonesia, the investigator found that the auditors had failed to detect a number of violations. These ranged from the use of hazardous chemicals to restrictions on union activity, violation of over-time legislation, and non-compliance with minimum-wage laws (O'Rourke 2000).

The commitment of suppliers to corporate codes is essential for translating principles into employment practices. That commitment is often lacking. If suppliers have no guarantee that compliance with codes of conduct will lead to future contracts, they may have little incentive to invest in effective enforcement. 'Code fatigue' is another problem. Factories supplying a large number of retailers are required to face an equally large number of auditing exercises and reporting requirements. In Central America, many factories appear to see compliance with corporate codes as a matter of supreme irrelevance. In 1998 a US Department of Commerce investigation into the effectiveness of codes of conduct in Honduras and the Dominican Republic concluded: 'Some manufacturers did not even seem to be aware of the (relevant) code, and had no copies available'.

Like factory owners, many workers are unaware of the existence of codes of conduct, or their potential use in raising labour standards. In some cases this is because companies fail to ensure that their codes are made available to workforces in an appropriate local language, or in a comprehensible form. In others, it is because workers lack the employment security and union rights that are vital if codes are to be used as negotiating devices to raise standards. Whatever the positive achievements of the Grupo M case outlined above, the company remains deeply intolerant of trade-union rights. One of the central problems across a wide range of codes is that they are not formulated, implemented, or monitored by the very people whom they are supposed to protect.

Retailers of children's toys have some of the most highly developed codes of conduct, partly because of their high profile in shopping centres in the North, and their need to protect their reputations. The Global Manufacturing Principles developed by Mattel set out in copious detail a broad range of rights, extending from minimum wages to health and safety and the right to association. The GMP is administered by professional auditors and an independent monitoring council. Other major US importers of toys – such as Walt Disney and McDonald – have also developed elaborate codes. However, the effectiveness in implementing them is open to question.

China is the world's largest exporter of toys, with sales estimated in excess of $6bn annually. These exports are produced by around 6000 factories, most of which are located in the 'toy capital' of the world, Guangdong province in south-east China (Kwan and Frost 2001). Walt Disney's 'Buzz Lightyear', McDonald's plastic replicas of Walt Disney characters, and a wide range of Mattel products all start life in Guangdong. While these and other US toy retailers have invested heavily in auditing employment practices, there are serious questions to be answered about the implementation of their codes of conduct. Research by the Hong Kong Christian Industrial Committee (HKCIC) in 2000 found that factory managers had been given extensive advance warning of auditors' visits, and that workers had been coached in what to say. Interviews by HKCIC with workers in factories that had been approved by auditors discovered numerous violations not just of codes, but of Chinese law (HKCIC 2001). Non-observance of statutory holidays, forced (and unpaid) over-time, and non-compliance with minimum-age provisions were among the problems recorded. Such problems are not unique to the toy industry (see Box 7.6).

The case of China highlights broader problems associated with voluntary codes of conduct. Even the strongest code of conduct is unlikely to achieve results in countries where governments fail to enforce basic employment rights. That is why national laws offer the only effective strategy for change. This does not mean that TNCs have no responsibilities. As noted earlier, there are deep contradictions between the goals to which corporate codes of conduct aspire and the market conditions that TNCs create. Price pressure on sub-contractors and stringent delivery deadlines often make living wages and reasonable conditions impossible to achieve. The tensions were succinctly

Box 7.6

Export-led exploitation of Chinese labour

Nowhere are the limitations of voluntary codes of conduct more apparent than in China's special economic zones. Northern TNCs make extensive use of suppliers in these zones, many of which violate basic labour rights on a systematic basis. Two surveys published by the organisation China Labour Watch of firms operating in the Dongguan special economic zone demonstrate the problem.

The Elegant Top Shoe factory is a contractor for Reebok, Clarks, and Fila shoe companies. It employs around 6000 workers, 90 per cent of them women. Most come from the provinces of Sichuan, Hunan, and Jiangxi, and few have been educated beyond primary school. In a report published after a year of investigation into labour conditions, including hundreds of interviews with workers, China Labour Watch reported the following:

*   Workers spent on average 71 hours per week in the factory, 60 of them working. Chinese labour law establishes a normal working week at 40 hours, with four hours' over-time allowed. In other words, women were working for 16 hours a week more than permitted under the law.

*   The minimum monthly wage under law is $55 per month, but the minimum wage provided by Elegant shoes was $49.

*   Elegant Top Shoe did not provide a pension plan, employment insurance, or medical insurance, despite legal obligations in each of these areas. Most workers were employed on short-term contracts.

*   Workers were subject to extensive systems of fines for minor mistakes in their work.

*   Female workers complain of sexual harassment and abuse by male supervisors.

*   Glues, including the highly toxic substance Tolulene, were being used in finishing rooms.

*   Although Reebok had established an official complaints procedure, workers expressed fear of retaliation if they complained. Reebok inspections were announced in advance, giving management an opportunity to prepare workers with appropriate answers to questions on working conditions.

The second site of investigation was the Merton factory located in the Sang Yuan industrial area, the factory supplies McDonald, Disney, Mattel, and Warner Brothers, among others, with toy products. Similar problems were reported. Women working in the colouring section worked an average of 14 hours per day. In July 1999, teams spraying 'Buzz Lightyear' products were earning an average of $0.13 per hour. During interviews, women workers complained of burns on their hands, caused by chemical thinning agents, and chronic dizziness.

Reports such as these create pressures which have led to some improvements. For instance, Reebok has insisted that workers have the right to join a union in their Elegant Top Shoe factory. This has reportedly led to some improvements.

Whatever the merits of the voluntary codes adopted by the TNCs in question, their spirit and letter were clearly being violated by their suppliers in China. This raises important questions about the limits of TNC responsibility.

(Sources: China Labour Watch 2001a and b)

captured by an evaluation by Global Exchange of Nike's code of conduct. The report welcomed the investment that Nike had made in workers' education, but continued: 'while the education programme had expanded, wages paid in Nike factories were so low that the great majority of workers could not afford to give up overtime income in order to take one of the courses' (Global Exchange 2001a).

Beyond corporate codes: the role of trade sanctions and incentives

There has been a vigorous debate over whether or not labour rights should be enshrined in a WTO social clause, and enforced through the threat of trade sanctions. In fact, trade incentives and disincentives are already widely used, for the most part with a conspicuous lack of success. Several industrialised countries have used their Generalised System of Preferences to reward what they see as good labour practice. In 2001, the European Union added Pakistan to the list of countries deemed eligible for tariff reductions, ostensibly to reward its efforts to protect core ILO standards. The USA has used a similar approach. At the end of 1999, it rewarded Cambodia's progress on labour conditions by a five per cent increase (Elliott 2001b). Labour rights are also enshrined in NAFTA, which provides financial penalties for governments that fail to enforce agreed standards.

These approaches lack credibility. The use of GSP preferences owes more to strategic and foreign-policy considerations than to a concern to protect labour rights. In the case of Pakistan, the EU was really providing a reward for its support of the US-led coalition's war in Afghanistan. The NAFTA model has one great advantage: it is codified in legal form. The problem is that it lacks teeth. Fines for violating employment rights are miniscule, amounting to no more than 0.007 per cent of any trade affected, so that the disincentives against labour abuse are limited. Moreover, enforcement is weak and the rules are partial. The right to bargain collectively is not even subject to evaluation, and, with the exception of child labour, governments are not required to bring national laws into compliance with ILO standards (Elliott 2001a).

One strong current of thought in industrialised countries favours the use of trade sanctions to enforce standards. In the early 1990s, Senator Tom Harkin introduced legislation in the US Congress that would have banned imports of products made with child labour. In Bangladesh, the threat posed by this bill prompted a significant number of factories to expel children, many of whom ended up in even more exploitative forms of employment, such as making bricks. TNCs, UN agencies, and governments have sometimes worked together to avert such outcomes. When it was discovered that home-workers used by sub-contractors producing footballs for Adidas, Nike, and other companies included large numbers of children, the companies demanded that production be shifted to 'child-free' factories. They also supported UNICEF's efforts to provide educational opportunities for the children affected, although there is little doubt that many poor households lost income (Crawford 2000).

Trade sanctions may be justified in the case of gross violations of human rights. However, in the last analysis sanctions are a blunt instrument for addressing problems that are deeply rooted in national social, economic, and political structures. Children are driven into employment by poverty. In many cases, their earnings can mean the difference between starvation and survival. In these circumstances, trade sanctions can worsen the very problems that they are intended to address.

The power of marketing

Companies are in business to make money. They purchase inputs, process them in some way, and sell on at a profit. Making profit is a vital function in any society, since it generates the wealth on which prosperity depends. In the globalised economy, marketing is more important than ever before to profit generation, but some marketing activities pose a direct threat to long-term development prospects.

Branding images

Investment in branding is a critical ingredient for success in global markets. It creates demand and generates consumer loyalty. As markets have become global, companies have sought to create global brands with recognisable appeal on a global basis. Advertising is a critical investment for successful branding. The US company Procter and Gamble spends $5bn on worldwide advertising, and Nestlé $2bn (White 1999). Branding protects and projects a company's reputation. In the words of Raoul Pinnell, Vice-president of Shell's Global Brands and Communications Division: 'it adds value to everything'. Companies trade on their reputation. Their brand images send signals to consumers and investors. Nike ('Just do it') aims to project individual achievement, Orange ('The future is Orange') a bright future, Aventis ('Our challenge is life') a commitment to health and happiness, and so on. When companies invest in their brand names, they are creating real financial assets – and corporate takeovers are concerned as much with acquiring brands as with capturing assets.

Brands are powerful, but they are also a source of vulnerability, especially when corporate practices depart from the image presented to the public. The logo of the Nestlé corporation is a bird's nest, in which a mother bird feeds two little fledglings. It conveys a commitment to nurturing and family values. But this commitment is difficult to square with Nestlé's advertising and marketing activities. According to UN estimates, around 1.5 million children in developing countries die each year because they are inappropriately fed, in many cases having contracted infections related to bottle-feeding with infant-formula milk (WHO 2001). Most die because mothers lack access to clean water or clear instructions for usage. In 1981, governments adopted an International Code of Marketing of Breast Milk Substitutes, sponsored by WHO/UNICEF, to protect mothers and babies from the commercial marketing influences of the infant-formula milk industry. The Code includes restrictions on marketing through the health-care profession, a prohibition on marketing directed towards children aged less than one year, and requirements to give clear instructions in local languages. Nestlé has been cited by campaigners as being among the most persistent violators of the Code. Researchers have documented cases of the company providing free samples to health professionals in Côte d'Ivoire and Pakistan, large discounts on prices to young mothers in Malaysia and Mexico, and extensive advertising campaigns in China and Ghana to promote the bottle-feeding of newborn children (Association for Rational Use of Medication in Pakistan 2001a and 2001b, IBFAN 2001). Claims by the company that it was in full compliance with the International Code were rejected by the UK Advertising Standards Authority in 1999 (IBFAN 2001).

As Nestlé has discovered, to devastating effect for children born into poor households, marketing can change consumer behaviour in the most fundamental areas of life. Successful advertising and branding can shift entire consumption patterns. Take the case of the McDonald corporation, one of the great symbols of globalisation. After a decade of prolific growth, it now has 15,000 outlets in 117 countries, and is opening five new restaurants every day (Schlosser 2001). Restaurants from Beijing to Delhi and Rio de Janeiro fly the same McDonald flags and serve up the same cuisine. But the marketing goes beyond food. What McDonald serves up in poor countries are the values, tastes, and industrial practices of the American fast-food industry, which is being exported to every corner of the globe. Researchers at a primary school in Beijing found that almost all of the children recognised and could name an image of Ronald McDonald. He was seen by the children as 'funny, gentle, kind – and he understood children'. Public-health outcomes associated with McDonald-style fast-food culture are less kind. The company promotes a high-fat, high-sodium diet. This kind of diet has inflicted severe damage on the population of the USA, where children now get one-quarter of their vegetables served in the form of potato chips, and where obesity is second only to smoking as a source of preventable illness. One survey of advertising to children in the EU found that more than 90 per cent of food advertisements promoted foods high in sugar, salt, and fat (Schlosser 2001).

Marketing disaster: tobacco promotion in developing countries[3]

'Tobacco is the only product that, when used as intended, will kill one half of its consumers.'
(Gro Harlem Brundtland, Director General, WHO)

It is estimated that there are 800 million smokers, almost three-quarters of the world's total, living in developing countries, along with many hundreds of millions more passive smokers who face the risk of smoking-related disease. Of the estimated 80–100,000 young people who become long-term smokers every day, around four out of every five live in poor countries. Behind these statistics is a silent public-health emergency that is worsening by the day.

The full scale of the emergency is not widely appreciated. Tobacco is already the world's greatest preventable killer. Along with HIV-AIDS, it is the only cause of premature death whose incidence is rising – and it is rising most rapidly in the developing world. While demand for cigarettes is static in rich countries, it is growing by three per cent a year in developing countries, and by more than five per cent a year in Africa. At present, developing countries account for about half of all deaths from smoking, or two million people annually. If current trends continue, that figure will rise to seven million deaths by 2030, nearly three-quarters of the worldwide total (WHO 1999, World Bank 1999).

The scale of deaths associated with smoking dwarfs the scale of deaths from conflict and disease. In 1990, almost 800,000 Chinese people died from smoking, but the annual mortality rate is projected to rise to two million by 2020. Unless smoking can be curtailed, its share of total deaths will have doubled in three decades. Sub-Saharan Africa faces an even bleaker future. On present trends, as many Africans could die from smoking in the next twenty years as from HIV/AIDS, malaria, and maternal mortality combined.

Stark as they are, these projections understate the scale of the problem. Smoking leads to protracted bouts of illness, ranging from coronary disease to respiratory problems, lung disease, and cancer – with devastating implications for poor households, since illness translates into lost income, lower productivity, and increased vulnerability. The broader losses to society associated with lost production and health costs are beyond estimation.

Like poverty, smoking is an avoidable disease. Unlike poverty, it is a disease that is being actively promoted through the use of sophisticated marketing strategies. The global market for cigarettes is dominated by three TNCs – BAT, Philip Morris, and RJ Reynolds – each of which invests heavily in promoting its products. Philip Morris alone spent more than $3bn on advertising in 1996. A growing share of corporate advertising budgets is being directed towards developing countries. Among the core strategies:

- **Increase smoking among women.** Only seven per cent of women in developing countries smoke, compared with almost half of men. Women figure prominently in the posters advertising smoking in Asia in particular. Philip Morris has developed a brand, Virginia Slims, specifically marketed to appeal to younger women.

- **Target young people.** Tobacco companies are investing heavily in the creation of future markets, with a premium placed on capturing young smokers. In Sri Lanka and China, BAT sponsors discotheque events in which young women hand out free cigarettes to teenagers. In China, BAT has developed a young person's brand. Ironically, the logo for its brand of 555 cigarettes reads 'Be free from worldly cares'. R.J. Reynolds successfully side-stepped controls when it used a cartoon character, Joe Camel, to advertise its Camel brand. As an internal company memorandum enthused: 'Its about as young as you can get, and aims right at the young adult smoker.'

- **Selling a life-style.** As one Kenyan doctor has written: 'Many African children have two hopes. One is to go to heaven, the other to America.' Tobacco companies actively promote the association between an American life-style and smoking, most famously through Marlbro.

- **Marketing through smuggling.** Avoiding border taxes can help companies to market their brands at lower prices. Some of the biggest TNCs have been implicated in smuggling. Senior tobacco-company officials have been convicted of smuggling offences in China and Hong Kong, and RJ Reynolds and BAT have come under investigation by the US Department of Commerce and the UK Department of Trade and Industry.

- **Engineering addiction.** Since the late 1980s, farmers in southern Brazil have been growing a genetically manipulated tobacco plant that contains twice the normal amount of nicotine. The seeds are supplied by a company called Souza Cruz, a BAT subsidiary in Brazil. In 1997, the US Justice Department filed criminal charges against BAT's US subsidiary (Brown and Williamson) for exporting the seeds without a permit. One year later, BAT's Director of Leaf Blending admitted in a court deposition that the genetically altered tobacco had been added to brands destined for markets in Asia and the Middle East. Federal authorities in the USA subsequently launched an investigation into BAT's efforts to 'control and manipulate the nicotine levels in its cigarettes'. Apparently undeterred, the company was subsequently investigated by the World Health Organisation for adding sugar and honey to cigarettes. According to the WHO, the action was prompted by an attempted to develop tastes with greater appeal to young smokers.

Tobacco companies have vigorously contested efforts to curtail their marketing activities, spending millions of dollars to pay scientists and lobbyists to discredit the evidence against smoking. In an internal company document, Philip Morris pledges to 'fight the social and legislative initiatives against tobacco'. It has fought with some success, and actively claims credit for the relaxation of prohibitions on advertising in Senegal and Ecuador. Governments are often half-hearted in their protection of the public interest, allowing short-term considerations of tax revenue to outweigh long-term public health and financial considerations.

This could be about to change. In 1999 the World Health Assembly unanimously backed a resolution calling for the development of a Framework Convention on Tobacco Control. The current draft supports widespread adoption of anti-smoking programmes, higher taxes, and restrictions on the sale and use of cigarettes. However, it remains weak in other areas, especially on advertising – and powerful vested interests are seeking to dilute its content further. Negotiations are expected to be concluded in 2003. They may be the last chance to avert what is now the single greatest health threat of the twenty-first century.

An agenda for reform

Speaking at the World Economic Forum in 1999, the UN Secretary General, Kofi Annan, endorsed the idea of 'global corporate citizenship'. Calling on the business community to accept internationally agreed norms as guides to behaviour, he outlined a project to develop what he called 'a Global Compact of shared values and principles which will give a human face to the global market'.

There is no shortage of shared values. In 1998, with strong support from industrialised countries, the ILO adopted a new Declaration on Fundamental Principles and Rights at Work. This sets out core labour rights in four areas:

- the right to organise, and the right to engage in free collective bargaining (Conventions 87 and 98);

- the right to equality of treatment and equal remuneration for work of equal value (Convention 100 and 111);

- a minimum working age (Convention 138);

- the abolition of forced labour (Conventions 29 and 105).

The OECD Guidelines for Multinational Enterprises provide a further normative statement of intent. Signed by all 29 member countries (and four non-OECD countries), this document enshrines the principles contained in the core ILO conventions, along with a range of wider goals and objectives on social, economic, and environmental policy. The OECD's Guidelines are distinctive, because they are endorsed by the governments of countries in which the world's major TNCs are based. Crucially, there is also a mechanism for monitoring corporate behaviour and investigating abuses.

The problem with shared international values and norms related to labour is that they are violated with impunity by governments and TNCs. For industry and many governments, the great attraction of ILO conventions is that they are not legally binding. The UN Secretary General's global compact has the same appeal. Every year, the ILO, the competent body responsible for labour standards, produces more than 2000 reports on compliance with its conventions (Elliot). Most governments respond in the time-honoured fashion, by exercising their right to ignore them.

The starting point for change has to be a recognition that labour rights are an issue of international trade. Indeed, they are more of a trade issue than are investment rights or intellectual property. That does not mean that industrialised countries are justified in using the WTO to apply trade sanctions in an effort to raise labour standards – or that developing countries are unjustified in their concerns about the protectionist interests that influence current approaches to social clauses. But it does mean that all governments have a responsibility to enforce shared values and enshrine them in meaningful legislation, instead of simply endorsing principles which are then violated.

Achieving a more equitable distribution of benefits from international trade demands action in the following areas:

- **National governments should enact and enforce legislation consistent with ILO conventions and other standards.** All governments have an obligation to provide for the right to collective bargaining and freedom of association, along with reasonable levels of social-insurance provision. Effective national legislation is the only foundation for success in raising labour standards.

- **Employment rights in export-processing zones should be strengthened and made consistent with international norms.** Governments – and investors –should abandon the current preference for a 'two-tier' approach to employment rights, under which weaker regulation is applied to export-processing zones.

- **The WTO's Trade Policy Reviews (TPRs) should report on the impact of trade rules and practices on employment standards.** In addition to standard reporting on tariffs, non-tariff barriers, and trade agreements, the TPRs would report on trade-related employment standards. The employment report would be produced by the ILO.

- **The ILO should be strengthened.** Recognising the links between trade and labour, the ILO should be granted observer status in the WTO. At the same time, its supervisory and capacity-building role in supporting national efforts to comply with ILO conventions should be strengthened. The ILO Working Party on the Social Dimensions of Globalisation should examine as a priority the situation of women workers in export-oriented industries.

- **Governments should establish an International Protocol, under the auspices of the UN, to govern the production, trade, and consumption of natural resources from conflict areas.** It would aim to promote transparency, human-rights protection, and State responsibility and should include conflict-impact assessments as a condition for export-credit concessions. The Protocol should be legally binding.

- **Northern-based TNCs should take active steps to support social and economic progress in developing countries, as envisaged under the OECD's Guidelines for Multinational Enterprises.** OECD governments should standardise the application of these guidelines among member States to provide for more effective investigatory, monitoring, and reporting mechanisms through which companies can be held accountable. Compliance with the Guidelines should inform government decisions on contracts awarded to TNCs.

- **Companies should take active steps to implement the OECD Guidelines for Multinational Enterprises.** The responsibility set out in the Guidelines to comply with human-rights obligations should be interpreted as applying also to the impact of trade in natural resources where this causes or exacerbates conflict.

- **Companies, particularly those operating in the extractive industry, should act in concert to promote transparency in all payments to governments when operating in situations of conflict** to enable civil society to hold governments to account, and adhere to the OECD anti-bribery convention and guidelines on corruption.

CHAPTER 8
International trade rules as an obstacle to development

International trade rules matter. They can create an enabling environment for poverty reduction, or a disabling one. Good international rules do not create automatic benefits for human development, but they can facilitate policies that are good for the poor. Conversely, bad rules can outlaw such policies. Many of the rules enshrined in the WTO fall into the latter category. They threaten to marginalise developing countries and the world's poorest people within an already unequal global trading system.

The authority of the WTO has been extended into areas of public policy that have a critical bearing on poverty reduction. Its mission is nothing less than to provide the common institutional framework for the conduct of trade relations between its 144 members. However, the implications go beyond trade to other important areas of public policy. The problem is that many WTO agreements, and the manner of their implementation, reflect the negotiating strength of Northern governments, and the influence of powerful transnational companies. In some areas, the multilateral system is now little more than a smokescreen for the pursuit of private interests and the subordination of developing countries to the dictates of rich countries.

That is in nobody's interest. All countries stand to benefit from the stability that a rules-based system can provide – and developing countries stand to benefit most. Lacking the economic power and the retaliatory capacity to pursue their demands outside such a system, they need multilateralism to work. But for multilateralism to work, it has to be fair and balanced. It has to protect weak countries from the abuse of economic power, rather than concentrate advantage in the hands of rich countries. The WTO fails the test in many areas.

This chapter examines three aspects of failed multilateralism. The first section concerns the Agreement on Trade-Related Aspects of Intellectual Property Rights (TRIPs). Adam Smith once warned governments to be vigilant in protecting the public interest against the instincts of private traders. 'People of the same trade', he wrote, 'seldom meet together, even for merriment and diversion, but the conversation ends in a conspiracy against the public, or in some diversion to raise prices.' He could have been writing about the TRIPs agreement. That agreement is the product of intensive corporate lobbying, the aim of which is to create a set of trade rules designed to raise prices for technologies and products controlled by transnational companies (TNCs). The public interest will suffer, especially in the developing world. Costs of technology transfer will increase, widening the technology gap – and income inequalities – in the process.

In the area of public health, the TRIPs agreement threatens to force up the costs of basic medicines, thus posing a direct threat to public health and widening inequalities between rich and poor countries. Applied to agriculture, the TRIPs agreement will damage the food security of the poor. It threatens the right of poor farmers to save, sell, and exchange seeds, which is vital not merely to their livelihoods but to bio-diversity. In summary, the TRIPs agreement is an arrangement designed to generate large gains for a small number of winners (notably the USA and assorted corporate interest groups), and it will create a large number of losers. The latter will be concentrated in the developing world.

The second section of this chapter considers the WTO agreement on services – a category of economic activity that covers everything from banking and insurance, to health services and education. The WTO services agreement is fundamentally unbalanced. It is heavily biased towards services (such as banking and insurance) provided by powerful transnational companies (TNCs) and industrialised countries, rather than those (such as labour) in which developing countries might have an advantage. Another problem is that the agreement lends itself to interpretations that could restrict the capacity of governments to extend access to basic services to the poor.

The third section looks briefly at the way in which WTO rules are being used to restrict the ability of developing countries to develop the broader policies needed in order for them to integrate successfully into the global economy. Most of the policies applied by the high-growth economies of East Asia during their formative stages would be outlawed under current WTO rules. Applied in their current fashion, these rules are limiting the ability of developing countries to raise the quality of investment and enter new, higher-value-added areas of trade.

Trade-related aspects of intellectual property rights (TRIPs)

The Agreement on Trade-Related Aspects of Intellectual Property Rights (TRIPs) was one of the most radical innovations in the Uruguay Round. It introduced for the first time a global system of minimum standards for protection and enforcement of intellectual-property claims. The blueprint includes a minimum patent-protection period of 20 years, along with protection for industrial designs, trademarks, copyrights, and other intellectual-property rights. These standards are now being introduced in poor countries as well as rich ones. Developing countries were allowed until 2000 to introduce the new rules. Least-developed countries have been granted an extension until 2016 (Correa 2000).

The TRIPs agreement is a dream come true for lawyers who specialise in trade matters, and a nightmare for almost everybody else. The sheer complexity of the law on intellectual property, and the impenetrable nature of WTO texts, creates a very high barrier against public debate. Yet intellectual-property law has profound implications for development. This chapter focuses on patenting, which is one of the most controversial areas of intellectual-property management.

The underlying principles of intellectual-property protection are relatively simple. In general terms, the aim is to strike a balance between society's interest in creating incentives for innovation on the one hand, and promoting the widespread dispersion of inventions on the other. The case for protection derives from market failure (Maskus 2000). New inventions are often costly to develop through research and development, but cheap to reproduce. If competitors were allowed to copy an invention as soon as it entered the market, so the argument runs, there would be little incentive to invest in research – and technological progress would come to a halt. To avoid this, governments grant inventors temporary exclusive marketing rights, permitting them to charge higher prices, and thereby creating incentives for investment.

The task of achieving a balance between public and private interests has been fraught with difficulty, ever since the Venetians introduced patents to encourage the development of new inventions in water technology at the end of the fifteenth century. In the hands of absolutist monarchs in Europe, the patent system was corrupted into an arrangement designed to enrich the monarchy and its favourites at the expense of the community (Ryan 1998). In Britain, the system was so badly debased by Queen Elizabeth I and her successors that Parliament was obliged to pass legislation – the 1621 Statute of Monopolies – which restricted the duration of patent protection, and required that a patented invention should be both new and of benefit to the public (Kaufer 1989). The WTO regime is firmly in the sixteenth-century Elizabethan mould.

'Winners and losers': the financial costs of the TRIPs agreement

Even if it makes sense for each country to encourage innovation, it does not follow that all countries have an interest in adopting a single, universal blueprint. Countries at different levels of development have different needs – and different interests. The appropriate level of intellectual-property protection varies according to levels of development. The poorest countries in particular are less able to absorb the costs of more stringent protection, especially when those costs assume the form of transfers to rich countries rather than to domestic inventors.

Throughout history, countries at the top of the technological ladder have generally sought to use intellectual-property protection to prevent others from catching up (Chang 2001). As the first major industrial power, Britain attempted to restrict the export of new technologies and skilled labour, demanding that other European powers and the United States should respect British patents. It was largely unsuccessful, but the same practices have been followed by other industrial leaders – and rejected by those seeking to close the gap between them. When Thomas Jefferson, the third President of the United States, signed his country's first patent law, it explicitly rejected the application of patents to foreign inventions. As a net importer of technology, the USA had no interest in paying more for the technologies that were needed to support industrial development (Ryan 1998). Another century was to pass before the country (very partially) accepted the right of foreigners to patent products. In similar fashion, most of today's advanced industrial countries refused to grant patents throughout the formative stage of their development. The USA and Germany in the nineteenth century, like Korea, Taiwan, and Japan in the twentieth, were able to develop an industrial base by encouraging the copying and adaptation of imported technologies. In fact, several industrialised countries – among them France, Germany, Canada, and Japan – did not provide standardised patent protection until after 1960 (UNDP 2001a).

Economic theory offers an analysis of the market failures that make patents necessary, but provides no guidance on the duration and scope of such protection. Countries seeking to catch up with more technologically advanced competitors have an interest in encouraging low-cost imitation, not in pushing up the cost of imported technologies through more stringent patent protection. Those without much intellectual property to protect have little to gain and much to lose from applying the same principles as new exporters of new technologies. By the same token, owners of intellectual property have an obvious commercial interest in extracting as much revenue as possible from their inventions, regardless of the wider public good. Because the overwhelming majority of the new inventions eligible for intellectual-property protection are developed in the rich world, the TRIPs agreement has decisively shifted world trade rules in favour of industrialised countries.

Patents and uneven development

At its most basic level, the TRIPs agreement will increase the financial returns to countries and companies which control the most valuable asset in today's global economy: namely, knowledge. The exclusive marketing rights associated with more stringent intellectual-property protection will be reflected in higher prices for exporters of new technologies, and higher costs for importers.

Sophisticated economic models are not required in order to identify the principal beneficiaries of the TRIPs agreement. Industrialised countries account for about 97 per cent of all the patents in the world (UNDP 1999). Most patents provided in developing countries are for foreign companies. In the poorest countries, virtually no patent protection is provided to domestic residents. African citizens filed only 0.02 per cent of the patent applications registered in 1998 by the African Regional Industrial Property Organisation (ARIPO) (World Bank 2000c). Even in Mexico, only around one per cent of patent applications are made by domestic residents (World Bank 2002). It follows that developing countries will absorb most of the costs associated with stricter patent protection under the WTO.

The domination of patented technologies by rich countries reflects their control of global expenditure on research and development (R&D). Much of that spending takes place under the auspices of TNCs, which play an increasingly dominant role in new-technology markets. Developing countries account for 80 per cent of the world's population, but for less than four per cent of global spending on R&D, most of it concentrated in East Asia (Lall 2000b). At the other extreme (according to United Nations 1999):

- industrialised countries account for more than 90 per cent of global research and development;

- the United States is the single biggest spender on R&D, accounting for 40 per cent of total world spending;

- R&D activity is heavily concentrated within a small group of TNCs. In the USA, just 50 firms account for half of all R&D spending; in the Netherlands, four firms account for almost three-quarters of the total.

Developing countries are already paying a high price for their marginal status in the global knowledge-based economy. Payments of royalties and licence fees to patent holders in the industrialised world have been rising rapidly since the mid-1980s, reflecting the growing importance of technology for participation in world trade. In 1998, licence payments linked to technology transfers cost developing countries approximately $15bn – seven times the level in the mid-1980s (United Nations 1999). As the world's largest producer of patented technologies, the USA has captured the dominant share of revenues associated with patent protection. It is the only country to post a large net surplus on payments for technology transfer, with royalty and licence payments increasing five-fold to $33bn in the decade to 1997.

The TRIPS agreement will add to the growing financial burden of importing new technologies. One simulation exercise carried out for the World Bank suggests that the six major industrialised countries with significant surpluses on intellectual-property trade will see their revenue increase by approximately $40bn as a result of the TRIPs agreement (World Bank 2002). The USA alone will account for approximately half this amount. Given that industrialised countries are already enforcing stringent patent protection, it may be assumed that the bulk of the costs will be paid by developing countries.

The implied losses for developing countries are very large. Technology licence payments were already increasing rapidly in developing countries, even before the TRIPs agreement (Figure 8.1). They will now increase at an accelerated rate as a result of the Uruguay Round agreement (Figure 8.2). Overall transfers from developing countries in the form of licence payments to Northern TNCs will rise almost four-fold from their current levels of $15bn. Increases could range from just under $1bn for India to more than $2bn for Mexico and more than $5bn for China (World Bank 2002). These figures imply a significant strain on the balance of payments. For Mexico and India, they represent between 2 and 3 per cent of total export earnings, underlining the potential pressures on their balance of payments that importers of technology will have to absorb. For countries with persistent balance-of-payments deficits, limited reserves, and unstable export earnings, such as the vast majority of countries in sub-Saharan Africa, the TRIPs agreement will present a formidable barrier to technological development. At a time when technology is exercising an increasingly important influence over the distribution of benefits from trade, intellectual-property rules threaten to bias the market for technology even further in favour of rich countries.

Illusory benefits

Disregarding these imminent financial costs, proponents of the new WTO regimes argue that it will create long-term benefits. These are supposed to arrive in various forms. It is claimed that the TRIPs agreement will create a framework which encourages domestic innovation, while at the same time providing TNCs with incentives to invest in developing countries (Maskus 1997, Gould and Gruben 1996). Some commentators also suggest that confidence in patent protection will give foreign investors the confidence to transfer new technologies, safe in the knowledge that they will not be copied.

Such claims are inherently difficult to quantify, partly because it is impossible to assess the future implications of a regime that is new; and partly because they combine speculative psychology with speculative economics. One thing is clear: whatever the impact of patents in innovation in rich countries, their effects are likely to be far weaker in poor ones. In most developing countries, the main barriers to innovation are financial, infrastructural, and skills-based, rather than the result of weak patent protection. Moreover, by restricting the scope for copying imported technologies, stricter patents will impede innovation.

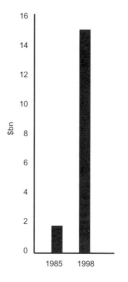

Figure 8.1
Technology licence payments by developing countries, 1985 and 1998

Source: UNIDO

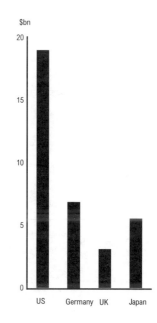

Figure 8.2
The TRIPS 'winners': estimated annual increase in income from patents as a result of the Uruguay Round Agreement

Source: World Bank

The widely held assumption that stronger intellectual-property protection will promote foreign investment is not rooted in credible evidence. Many of the countries most widely cited by the USA as gross violators of intellectual-property rights – such as China, Thailand, and Argentina – have been the main sites for foreign investment over the past decade. As to the suggestion that new technologies will follow new investment, evidence points to an opposite correlation. As Chapter 9 will show, foreign investors tend to downgrade the R&D activities of their affiliates in developing countries, even in those (such as Brazil) that already offer more stringent patent protection.

What of the broader claim that developing countries will benefit, along with everybody else, from the dynamic growth-effects associated with patenting? The problem is that these effects are largely unproven. Even in industrialised countries, there is growing concern that the patent system is being abused. Many see the rapid surge in patent claims that has taken place over the last decade as part of a corporate 'gold rush', as companies seek to turn domination of research into domination of markets. In the USA alone, patent applications are now running at 300,000 a year, twice the number in 1990. IBM is being granted ten new patents every working day. In the second half of the 1990s, the company boosted its revenues from licensing by a factor of three to $1.5bn, or one-fifth of total profits (*Economist* 2000).

Patents can be used to reward and stimulate innovation, but they can also be used to restrict competition. Minor changes to products, mundane new business methods, and even ideas that have not been brought to fruition are all being patented. Such practices are widely used for strategic purposes, annexing whole areas of research to the patent holder. This is especially damaging in areas of complex new technology, where many components may be subject to patents. Research in several sectors suggests that patents may be retarding, rather than stimulating, economic growth and innovation (Kingston 2001).

Whatever the long-term balance of costs and benefits, there is little doubt about the medium-term outcomes. The TRIPs agreement, which was the product of intensive lobbying by powerful companies and diplomatic pressure in developing countries by the USA, will generate huge rewards for its main architects. The losers will be developing countries. Rising costs of technology will translate into a widening technology gap, diminishing the potential benefits for poor countries of integrating into global markets.

The special case of medicines and public health

In its assessment of the Uruguay Round, Credit First Suisse Boston described the pharmaceutical industry as 'the greatest beneficiary' of the TRIPS agreement (Oxfam 2001f). It might have added that the greatest losers would be poor people in developing countries, for whom it will mean higher health-care costs and greater vulnerability. Developing countries ultimately accepted the TRIPs agreement, partly because of the threat of trade sanctions, and partly because of a (mistaken) belief that they would be granted concessions in other areas, such as market access. Today, a growing number of governments acknowledge the potential threat posed by TRIPs to public health.

The pharmaceuticals industry is not merely the main winner from the TRIPs agreement: it is also its main architect. Through the Intellectual Property Committee, companies such as Pfizer, Merck, and Du Pont were instrumental in persuading the Reagan Administration to force TRIPs on to the WTO agenda (Weissman 1996). As a former Chief Executive of Pfizer, Edmund Pratt, has written of the alliance between the world's most powerful government and one of the world's most powerful industry groupings: 'Our combined strength enabled us to establish a global private sector/government network which laid the ground for what became TRIPs' (cited in Drahos and Braithwaite 2002). That network continues to operate. Its activities have included recourse to threats of trade sanctions against developing countries that seek to protect public-health interests from patent claims (Oxfam 2001g).

Implications for the price of medicine

Until the early 1990s, approximately 50 developing countries either excluded medicines from eligibility for product patents, or provided shorter periods of protection, or operated conditions which restricted the claims of patent holders (Lanjouw and Cockburn 2001). Under the TRIPs agreement, no such special treatment is permitted. By 2005, all developing countries must provide patent protection for new pharmaceutical products, although the least-developed countries now have until 2016 to comply. Intellectual-property protection will apply to all products patented after these dates, although many developing countries have already implemented legislation providing exclusive marketing rights for patent holders, or are in the process of doing so.

Enforcement of the TRIPs agreement will revolutionise pharmaceutical markets in developing countries. At present, a large proportion of drug supplies in many countries comes from domestic generic-drugs industries, or from imported generic drugs. Countries with strong generic industries (such as India) are a major source of medicines for countries lacking a manufacturing base, as in much of sub-Saharan Africa. Essentially, generic companies provide copies of brand-name, or patented, drugs, usually at a fraction of the prices. The competition that they provide when their products enter the market plays a vital role in reducing the prices of drugs. By restricting their entry into the market until patents have expired, the TRIPs agreement will restrict competition and push up prices.

The overall price effects will vary from country to country. However, the large differential between the prices of generic and patented drugs suggests that they will be very large. One estimate for India projects an average price increase of at least 26 per cent, but an increase of 200–300 per cent for new patented medicines (Watal 1999, 2000).

Much of the debate on the implications of intellectual-property protection for drugs prices has concentrated on HIV/AIDS. The cases involved are instructive, because they clearly demonstrate the use of patent protection to maintain high prices, and the role of generic competition in forcing prices down. In 1999, patented anti-viral triple therapies cost between $10,000 and $15,000 per patient per year in industrialised countries. Indian generic companies were marketing triple therapies at less than $1500 (Oxfam 2001g). The price has now fallen to $295. In Thailand, drugs for the treatment of AIDS-related meningitis fell to less than 1 per cent of their previous price when the patents expired. But it is not only HIV/AIDS drugs that are affected. Indian generic companies market Ciprofloxacin, an important anti-infective drug used in the treatment of Shigella (bloody diarrhoea), at one-fifth of the price charged for the brand-name equivalent in Pakistan. Similarly, generic companies in Bangladesh produce a version of the Roche anti-infective drug Septraxon, used in the treatment of bronchitis, at one-third of the brand-name price.[1]

Of particular concern to developing countries is the fact that the patent protection will push up prices for the next generation of drugs at a time when microbial resistance to existing treatments has reached alarming proportions. Up to 70 per cent of current cases of pneumonia – the infectious disease which is the world's second-greatest killer after HIV/AIDS – are resistant to front-line antibiotics in many countries. Multi-drug resistance is also occurring in the microbes that cause diarrhoeal disease, contributing to as many as two million deaths a year (WHO 2000a). Where effective drugs for the treatment of these diseases are developed through research in industrialised countries, there is a danger that patents will price them out of reach of the poor in developing countries.

Implications for households

Any increase in prices for medicines resulting from the TRIPs agreement will have grave consequences for public health, especially among the poor. The ability of households to treat diseases will be compromised, as will the capacity of governments to provide vital medicines. Women will bear the brunt of the cost, by virtue of their higher levels of vulnerability to illness, and because they assume primary responsibility for care in the household. In a context where, according to the World Health Organisation, one-third of people in poor countries lack access to health-care provision, the TRIPs agreement poses an acute threat.

That threat derives principally from the price inflation described in the previous section. Some commentators have argued that the price of drugs is irrelevant to the poor, and that the real problem is the lack of drugs and the absence of wider health-service provision (Bale 2001). That argument is deeply flawed. While it is true that poor people lack access to health services for a complex variety of reasons, the price of medicine is a major factor. Even the most superficial survey of differences in health-financing arrangements between rich and poor countries helps to explain the reason why. When people fall sick in the industrialised world, most of the cost of their treatment is met either through public provision or through pre-paid private insurance; the financial costs incurred by households are minimal. Out-of-pocket payments in a country like the United States or the UK typically represent less than one-fifth of total expenditure on health care. However, in countries such as Tanzania and Vietnam, and across the developing world, that proportion is closer to four-fifths

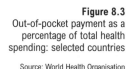

Figure 8.3
Out-of-pocket payment as a percentage of total health spending: selected countries

Source: World Health Organisation

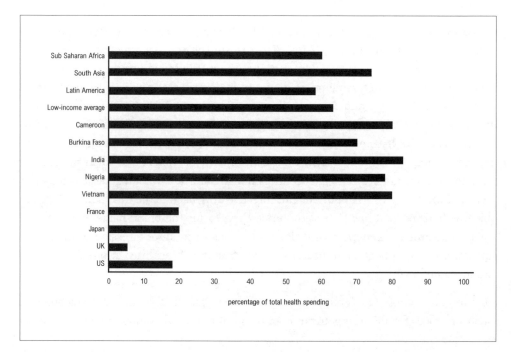

(Filmer, Hammer, and Pratchett 1997) (see Figure 8.3).

When people in poor countries fall sick, there is a very direct sense in which they, rather than the State, pay. They are less likely than better-off groups to be members of employment-based pre-payment schemes, and less likely to have access to subsidised services (WHO 2000b). Spending on drugs is by far the biggest component of household health spending, accounting for 50-90 per cent of the total (WHO 1998). The case of Burkina Faso is not untypical (see Figure 8.4). That is why the price of medicines matters.

In countries where a large proportion of the population lives below the poverty line, even small increases in prices can have catastrophic consequences. The cost of treating a single episode of sickness can absorb a large share of a household's limited resources. Research by Oxfam in two rural communities and one urban community in Uganda found poor people spending up to one-third of their monthly income during their most recent sickness episode. In the Eastern Province of Zambia, poor rural women report spending $7 to purchase antibiotics prescribed for the treatment of drug-resistant childhood pneumonia – a major cause of childhood sickness and death in the rainy season. This is a region of the country in which around three-quarters of the population struggles to survive on less than $1 a day. As one doctor said in an interview with Oxfam: 'Writing a prescription for these drugs is like signing a death certificate. We know that poor households will not be able to afford the cost – and we know the consequences.'

Research in a large number of countries consistently identifies the non-affordability of drugs as a major problem for poor households. In some cases, that problem manifests itself in the failure of poor people to seek treatment. In others, it leads to delays in seeking treatment, or the non-completion of prescribed courses. When sickness strikes a poor household, people may be forced to cover the costs of drugs by selling assets, or going into debt.[2] Women face special problems. As the primary carers, they respond to health emergencies and the high cost of medicines by intensifying their unpaid work, or cutting spending, or taking on additional income-generating activities.

It is in this context that any increase in prices for medicines can have such grave consequences for the health of the poor. Increases on the scale projected under the TRIPs agreement would inevitably exclude from treatment many of those most vulnerable to illness.

Implications for public financing

Like poor households, governments in developing countries face acute financial pressures in responding to health problems. At a global level, there is an inverse relationship between health-care financing and health-care need. Public spending in the low-income countries that account for the overwhelming majority of preventable diseases and premature deaths is often as low as $5–7 per capita per annum, compared with $1600 per capita in rich countries (WHO 1998). Spending on drugs typically accounts for a very large share of public expenditure on health, often rising to more than one-fifth of the total. However, this large share of a small budget translates into $0.50 per person in much of Africa and South Asia.

Under these conditions, the inflation in the price of drugs that is in prospect as a result of the TRIPs agreement will place further pressure on already over-stretched health-care budgets. For example, one study for Colombia projects increased costs associated with the TRIPs agreement that will be equivalent to 20 per cent of current health-care spending. This would have grave implications for the government's capacity to maintain

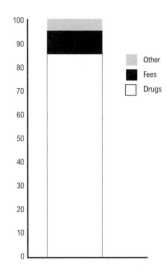

Figure 8.4
Spending on drugs as percentage of spending on health: Burkina Faso 1995

Source: World Health Organisation

access to vital drugs for the nine million people covered by the National Solidarity and Guarantee Fund – a welfare system subsidising health care for those inadequately covered through employment-based health-care schemes.

Inadequate safeguards and the 'TRIPs plus' threat

When the TRIPs agreement was negotiated, some tentative public-health safeguards were built into the system. One of the reasons for the controversy surrounding implementation is that, whatever the letter of the law, the spirit of these safeguards has been violated. Under Article 8 of the TRIPs agreement, governments 'may (...) adopt measures necessary to protect public health', provided that these are consistent with the broader principles in TRIPS. One such measure (allowed under Article 31) is compulsory licensing. Another safeguard against patent abuse is 'parallel importing'. This allows governments to import drugs from another country, in cases where the local price charged by the patent holder is higher than the sale price charged in another market. However, the provision allows governments to import only patented drugs, and not generic copies.

The gulf between safeguarding principles and practice was illustrated by the experience of South Africa. In November 1997, the South African government enacted a law enabling it to undertake parallel importing, along with other measures, in the interests of public health. The stated aim was to enhance the government's ability to provide the country's 4.5 million HIV/AIDS victims with access to affordable medicines. The law was immediately subjected to a legal challenge by 39 pharmaceutical companies, which alleged that WTO principles were being breached. They withdrew their action in the face of an international campaign co-ordinated by the South African Treatment Action Campaign, Médecins sans Frontières, and Oxfam. But in a country where HIV-AIDS has orphaned half a million children, where 50,000 children are born each year carrying the virus, and where HIV/AIDS claims more than 300 lives each day, the damage caused to human life by high prices raises fundamental questions concerning TRIPS.

The South African case was followed by another challenge to public health – and an even more spectacular reversal in policy. In March 2001, the Brazilian government announced that it would authorise local production of two vital HIV/AIDS drugs, unless the companies supplying them – Roche and Merck – agreed to reduce their prices. Spending on the two drugs was absorbing one-third of Brazil's total AIDS budget. Local firms were in a position to produce both at less than half the import price. In the event, the two companies agreed to lower their prices, but not before the USA had initiated a case against Brazil at the WTO, effectively challenging the government's right to disregard patent claims in the interests of public health (Oxfam 2001h). Once again, the case was withdrawn in the face of international protest.

The South Africa and Brazil episodes became celebrity cases in their own right. Other countries have been subjected to less publicised but equally irresponsible pressures. Using national trade legislation known as 'Special 301', the US Trade Representative (USTR) has threatened unilateral trade sanctions against a long list of countries deemed to be failing in their duty to enforce the patents of US companies. The list includes India, Egypt, Argentina, and the Dominican Republic. In each case, the USTR's office has acted after complaints from the Pharmaceuticals Research and Manufacturers of America (PhRMA), which represents giant companies such as Pfizer, Merck, and Bristol Squibb Myers (Oxfam 2001g). The target has usually been legislation that permits governments to enforce compulsory licensing and parallel importing provisions. Such practices underline the undue influence that major companies continue to exercise over the enforcement of global intellectual-property regimes.

One rule for the rich: 'TRIPs plus'

Industrialised countries themselves have applied different standards at home from those that they apply to poor countries. These double standards have called into question not just the legitimacy of the TRIPs agreement, but also the credibility of the WTO.

When the US government was responding to the use of anthrax spores in terrorist attacks against its citizens in 2001, it indicated that it would deny the claims of the Bayer corporation, producer of one of the most effective anti-anthrax drugs, unless it reduced its prices (Fushrum and Winslow 2001). Canada went a step further: the government threatened to declare a national emergency, and to authorise a local supplier to manufacture the drug under licence (*Financial Times* 2001). This was precisely what countries such as South Africa, Brazil, Kenya, and India have been demanding the right to do: namely, to assert the public-health interests of their people over the private interest of patent holders (*Economist* 2001b). Unlike Canada, most developing countries lack the capacity to produce the drugs they need. Yet TRIPS has been interpreted in a way that can restrict generic-drug exporters from supplying countries which lack the capacity to produce for themselves.

Ineffective as current safeguards in the WTO may be, they are being undermined by developments outside the WTO under the terms of regional and bilateral agreements which protect intellectual property even more stringently. Under NAFTA, there are no clauses equivalent to those in the TRIPs agreement (in Article 7 and Article 8) which specify that public-health priorities can take precedence over patent claims. Similarly, the bilateral trade agreement between the USA and Jordan weakens the ability of governments to resort to compulsory licences in order to counter monopolistic behaviour. As a result of this agreement, a Jordanian law on the provision of drugs vital to public health, stipulating that patent holders must provide 'large quantities at reasonable prices', has been removed. Potentially, the far looser wording contained in the treaty will make it more difficult for the government to introduce compulsory licensing, and easier for industry to mount legal challenges (Drahos 2001).

These efforts to develop a parallel 'TRIPs plus' system have important ramifications. Under the WTO, countries are not entitled to discriminate between trade partners. It follows that any standard that is set in a bilateral treaty must be applied to all countries. The result is that developing countries are being forced to accept obligations that far exceed WTO provisions, even before the full implications of those provisions are clear.

False promises

It has been widely argued that the TRIPs agreement will generate long-term benefits for the poor, even if there are short-term adjustment costs. These benefits are presumed to flow from the incentives provided to industry to develop new drugs. Moreover, the pharmaceuticals industry and Northern governments claim that patent protection will help to stimulate more research into diseases of the poor. That such research is vital is not in doubt. Developing countries account for more than 80 per cent of the global burden of disease, but less than 10 per cent of spending on R&D (and less than two per cent in Africa). Pneumonia, diarrhoea, and tuberculosis – three of the major killers of children, and the cause of one-fifth of the global disease-burden – account for less than one-tenth of global R&D (Gwatkin and Guillot 1999). Limited R&D has produced a limited supply of new drugs. Of the 1233 new drugs that reached the market in the two decades up to 1997, only 13 were specifically approved for tropical diseases (Pecoul et al. 1999).

The problem is that stronger patent protection will not change this state of affairs, and will do little to create incentives among generic companies to conduct their own R&D (Oxfam 2001f). The R&D costs of bringing a new drug to the market are estimated at $500m – which is beyond the resources of even the largest generic companies. In most cases, generic firms will be forced either to close down (as they lose the right to enter markets with copies of patented drugs) or to enter partnership with major global corporations. The argument that TRIPs will give these corporations an interest in developing drugs for treating poverty-related diseases is at best speculative, and at worst fanciful. Because purchasing power is so limited in poor countries, there is little incentive to increase R&D aimed at the market that they provide. Consumers in rich countries spend more than $2.2bn per annum on the drug Claritin, used to treat the symptoms of hay-fever. That is more than the total annual expenditure on drugs in the whole of sub-Saharan Africa. There is more profit to be made from treating minor allergies in rich countries than life-threatening diseases in poor ones. Like any other, the pharmaceuticals market directs investment not towards areas of greatest human need, but to areas in which consumer demand is backed by purchasing power.

Pharmaceutical companies have a vital role to play in developing and providing the drugs needed to combat disease in developing countries, but the TRIPs agreement will not facilitate that role. As the report of the Macro-Economic Commission on Health concluded, the global gap in financing will be closed only by a major international effort, backed by increased aid and facilitated through public–private partnerships (Commission on Macroeconomics and Health 2001).

Claims from industry that more stringent patent protection is vital to research, and hence to the future supply of medicines, should be treated with caution. There is no doubt that the pharmaceutical industry is more dependent on patent protection than most, and for an obvious reason: R&D costs are high, and the costs of copying are usually exceptionally low. That is why the gap between generic and patent prices is so large. There is an intimate connection in the pharmaceuticals industry between patent coverage and market judgements by the investment community. In August 2000, the American drugs firm Eli Lilly lost a legal action seeking to extend by six months the patent on Prozac, its best-selling anti-depressant drug. Within days, the company's share prices had fallen by one-third, draining $38bn from the company's capitalisation (*Economist* 2000).

The problem is that the pharmaceuticals sector has proven itself particularly skilful at exploiting the failures of the patent system. A range of practices, such as making minor changes to products at the end of their lives, are regularly used to extend monopoly rights, restrict market entry, and maintain high prices. In some cases, these practices involve deals with generic companies. In the USA, the Federal Trade Commission launched a major enquiry in 2001, investigating allegations that large pharmaceutical companies were illegally blocking low-priced generic drugs from entering the market (Spiegel 2001).

The willingness of patent offices to entertain dubious claims is another problem. In April 2000, Glaxo Smith-Kline was granted a 15-year extension on Augmentin, a powerful antibiotic first patented in 1981. Before the original patent expired on one of the active ingredients in the drug, the company had succeeded in launching a 'submarine patent' – a claim for an extension of monopoly rights, based on another ingredient that was discovered in the 1970s. In effect, the company was granted two patent lives for one piece of research (Pilling and Wolfe 2000). Such problems may appear to raise issues of distant concern to developing countries. But the ability of powerful companies to extend the duration of patents will have the effect of further inflating prices for many vital medicines, with adverse consequences for public health in developing countries.

Implications for poverty and international trade

The most immediate losers from the application of the TRIPs agreement to medicines will be households in developing countries. Each year, around 14 million people in developing countries die from infectious diseases – the equivalent of 30,000 deaths each day. The poor account for the vast majority of these deaths. Half of the victims are children (UNICEF 2000). By imposing a system of intellectual-property protection designed to benefit the interests of powerful companies rather than to meet the needs of the poor, the WTO threatens to obstruct efforts to address the health crisis that lies behind these statistics.

Repercussions will extend beyond household health into local and international markets. The poor are hurt by illness much more than the wealthy, since they depend overwhelmingly on their labour, and have limited assets on which to rely during emergencies. By increasing the costs of treating illness, the TRIPs agreement will add to pressures which restrict the capacity of poor people to take advantage of market opportunities.

The effects will be transmitted across whole economies. Disease reduces incomes and prospects for economic growth. Good health is the basis for productivity, a requirement for any livelihood, and the foundation for learning at school. For national economies, health is one of the essential foundations of development. For households, health status has an important bearing on whether people are able to participate in markets and take advantage of the opportunities provided by trade. Women in particular are affected, because of the double burden imposed on them by their vulnerability to illness, and the demands on their time that are made by their care for sick family members.

Biotechnology, patents, and food security

'Taking care of seed is essential for small farmers to survive. But now with TRIPS, the act of saving, exchanging, and selling seeds is being prohibited. Taking away the right to reproduce and share seeds is like taking away our lives. How can someone suddenly claim ownership over genetic resources?' (Leopoldo Guilaran, rice farmer, island of Negros, the Philippines)

At the beginning of the twenty-first century, biological science is poised to bring about fundamental changes in the world in which we live. The unlocking of DNA sequences has created new opportunities for advances in medical research, industry, and agriculture. If it is used wisely, the power to read and change gene sequences could bring great benefits to humanity. Yet the revolution in science also poses threats.

The biological and genetic materials that provide the main resources for the biotechnology and plant-breeding industries are also the basis for the livelihoods of the rural poor, and for food security at the household and national levels. As the farmer quoted above suggests, the application of intellectual-property rights to plants and genetic materials could jeopardise food security. With three-quarters of the world's population who live below the poverty line located in rural areas, anything that increases the costs of agricultural seed or other inputs could be damaging. So could restrictions on the right of poor farmers to retain the seeds on which next year's harvests depend.

TRIPs and beyond

The underlying principles that determine the application of the TRIPs Agreement in the area of seeds and plants are relatively straightforward, reflecting those applied to intellectual-property rights in general. In practice, however, there are serious problems in interpreting how the current TRIPs Agreement should be applied. The agreement requires countries to protect plant varieties, either through patents or through specifically designed (*sui generis*) regimes, such as plant breeder's rights. The agreement also makes the patenting of all micro-organisms and microbiological processes mandatory.[3] This requirement may effectively extend patent control over some plants and animals, if microbiological processes are used to create or modify them. The USA and EU in particular have interpreted WTO rules to allow for stronger patent protection of plants and animals.

Bio-piracy

Since patents issued in Europe and America grant effective control over the potential economic value of genetic resources derived from any country, they create an incentive for firms to acquire genetic materials from any source for the development of profitable new drugs, seeds, or other products. As developing countries account for an estimated 90 per cent of the world's biological resources, they are a natural target. This has raised concerns about 'bio-piracy'. Patents have been awarded in the USA and Europe for products and formulas that are already known to farmers in developing countries (Mayne 2002). Famous cases have included the patenting by US companies of the Mexican Yellow Enola bean, Basmati rice, and selected maize genes (GRAIN 1998). A process for extracting medicinal substances from the Indian Neem tree, known to Indian farmers for centuries, has been patented by a European company (UNDP 2001a).

As these cases demonstrate, resources may be extracted from public lands, farms, and villages and subsequently patented in another country, in effect privatising the benefits of community knowledge that has been handed down through generations. Local knowledge is not rewarded, largely because it is transmitted through oral tradition, rather than registered in Western laboratories. If communal rights were respected, or benefits shared, it would go some way towards redressing the balance of the TRIPs agreement. It is estimated that a two per cent royalty levied on genetic materials developed by local communities in the South that have been patented in industrialised countries would generate more than $5bn from medicinal plants alone (UNDP 2001a). The problem is that no framework exists for rewarding communities, partly because the TRIPs system is designed to protect private corporate investors, and partly because of the failure to implement effectively the UN Convention on Biological Diversity.

Control over seeds

For smallholder farmers, the most direct threat from patenting comes in the form of potential restrictions on the right to save, exchange, and sell seeds. Patents, by their nature, prevent third parties from engaging in such activity. The problem is that control over seeds is a fundamental requirement for food security and the protection of biodiversity. Women, who have traditionally been the keepers of indigenous genetic resources such as seeds and medicinal plants, are significantly affected by this problem.

Northern governments claim that the TRIPs agreement allows developing countries to implement *sui generis* systems that protect local interests. At best, that is a half-truth. Developing countries can opt for distinctive national legislation to protect plant varieties, subject to the general requirement that they should provide effective protection for plant breeders. In principle, this could allow countries to provide shorter periods of protection, introduce arrangements to benefit local communities, or exempt certain types of plant. However, the flexibility is more apparent than real.

Developing-country governments are coming under pressure from the USA, the EU, and corporate interest groups to adopt plant breeders' rights codified in the International Convention for the Protection of New Varieties of Plants (known by its French acronym, UPOV). This treaty has been modified over time. In 1978 it was amended, but it still allowed farmers the right to retain seeds and use protected seeds to develop their own strains. It has since been replaced by a new provision, in the form of UPOV 1991. While somewhat less restrictive than a standard patent system in law, it requires members to grant 20-year exclusive rights to plants, with the privileges of farmers at the discretion of national governments. In implementation, the USA and the EU are seeking to ensure that UPOV 1991 provides patenting applied to plants.

Against this background, there is an obvious danger that UPOV will extend corporate control over the supply of seeds to farmers. This is not a future threat: patenting is already extending corporate reach in relation to seeds. The British NGO ActionAid has calculated that there are already more than 900 patents on the five staple food crops that account for three-quarters of the world's food supply, with just four TNCs holding almost half of them (ActionAid 1999). At present, most of these patents are held in industrialised countries. The danger is that more stringent patent protection will enable companies to assert their claims in developing countries.

'TRIPs plus' applied to seeds

Developments outside the WTO are reinforcing the strength of intellectual-property regimes applied to plants. As in public health, 'TRIPs plus' provisions are becoming a standard feature of regional and bilateral treaties. The North America Free Trade Agreement (NAFTA) exemplifies this process of continuous reinforcing of protection. Under NAFTA, Mexico is required to give effect to UPOV 1991. The treaty also restricts the scope for governments to exclude plants, animals, and biological processes from patenting. When the EU negotiated its Free Trade Agreement (FTA) with Mexico, it used NAFTA as a reference point. Article 12 of the FTA commits both sides to enforce the 'highest standards' of intellectual-property protection, which includes compliance with UPOV 1991. Under the Free Trade for the Americas initiative, the USA is seeking to generalise this model across the entire region.

Bilateral agreements are adopting a similar approach. The investment treaties negotiated in 2000–01 between the USA on the one side and Vietnam, Jordan, and Nicaragua on the other side all include a requirement of compliance with UPOV 1991, in Jordan's case within one year. The US–Jordan bilateral treaty is now being used as a template for other agreements, including one between the USA and Chile (Drahos 2001). This illustrates how compliance with the WTO agreement on TRIPS has now become a bottom line, rather than a top line. Global intellectual-property protection is being gradually tightened and strengthened through a complex web of bilateral and regional treaties, each of which sets slightly more stringent conditions.

The biotechnology revolution and TRIPS

The application of more stringent intellectual-property rules to seeds and plants has become an issue of intense controversy. Industry claims that more effective patent protection will allow for a wider dispersal of benefits from biotechnological innovation. Subject to concerns about the safety of such interventions, if this were true, it would amount to a powerful case for TRIPs. Plant strains engineered to be resistant to pests and drought could generate important benefits for developing countries, especially those with the infrastructure to make them available to poor farmers. However, much of the evidence used to support the claims of industry is little more than a smokescreen for the pursuit of vested interests.

Farmers have been manipulating the genetic composition of food crops and domestic animals since Neolithic times, through the propagation and cross-fertilisation of plants with the most desirable characteristics. Crops such as wheat, barley, and corn, and animals such as goats and cows all differ from their ancestors because of selective breeding. Biotechnology is different, not just because the identification of specific gene traits enables it to produce quicker, more targeted results, but also because it allows the implantation of genes across species that are too distantly related to interbreed naturally.

In technical terms, the potential for productivity gains would appear to be very large, even if this remains unproven. Scientists can add genes and customise plant genomes for resistance to pests and pathogens in ways that were not possible before. The potential benefits include improved yields, increased pest resistance, reduced requirements for chemical pesticides and fertilisers, nutritional advances (for example, by enhancing the contents of minerals and vitamins), and disease control (National Research Council 2000).

One study in China surveyed farmers using cotton seeds modified by the implant of the Bacillus thuringiensis (Bt) toxin for controlling the cotton bollworm, which is increasingly resistant to chemical controls (Pray et al. 2000). The study claimed that the genetically modified cotton produced significant economic and environmental benefits, with a substantially reduced need for pesticide sprays, and output left unaffected. Rice has been genetically engineered to contain beta-carotene, which is a source of Vitamin A. Deficiency in this vitamin leaves approximately 230 million children at risk of blindness and respiratory infection. Taken at face value, 'golden rice', as the genetically engineered product is known, would appear to offer one potential means of improving nutritional status.

Scientific claims and counter-claims about test results of genetic modification abound. Critics rightly point out that genetic engineering is a science in its infancy, and that the genes in a living organism can mutate, multiply, and breed with other living organisms. Genetically modified organisms could have negative impacts on the genetic composition of wild plants and animals, with potentially damaging results. Leaving aside the consequences, doubts remain over whether the higher productivity recorded for Bt cotton under field-trial conditions can be replicated, especially in marginal farming areas. The response from the industry is to claim potential productivity gains and benefits for nutrition. In fact, the evidence remains open to question. Even where test sites produce impressive results, there are often questions about the extent to which the results can be replicated, especially in farming areas which lack access to irrigation and other inputs (Lappe et al. 1998). Moreover, technological innovations cannot resolve the structural problems responsible for poverty, even if they can provide part of the solution. Rural people go hungry for structural reasons, including inadequate access to land, credit, and other productive assets. If introduced into social structures marked by extreme inequalities, new technologies could further concentrate advantage in the hands of the wealthy.

Similarly, whatever the benefits of crops such as golden rice, there are more cost-effective ways of addressing problems of nutritional deficiency: enabling poor farmers to grow vegetables, for example. Even so, there is no doubt that increased productivity does have a role to play in poverty reduction. For all their initial bias in favour of big farms, the technologies that drove the Green Revolution in India did make an important contribution in terms of generating rural income and employment (Frankel 1978), albeit with environmental costs, according to some commentators. In principle, there is no reason to reject in advance the potential that biotechnology may have for enhancing the welfare of the poor.

The logic of the market prevails

The problem is that the motor driving biotechnological research, and the impetus for patenting, are disconnected from initiatives to reduce global poverty. Control over biotechnological innovation is highly concentrated. According to the Nuffield Council, six major industrial groups control the technology needed to undertake commercial research in the areas of genetically modified crops (Nuffield Council 1999). Research by the major TNCs engaged in agribusiness dwarfs public research into the application of genetic engineering to agriculture. In the mid-1990s, privately funded agricultural research exceeded $10bn. Meanwhile, the main centre for international public research in agricultural biotechnology, the Consultative Group for International Agricultural Research (CGIAR), currently spends around $25m (Cohen 2001).

One of the consequences of this pattern of spending on R&D is that commercial interests – and commercial markets – dominate innovation and the identification of future priorities. Although the share of transgenic crops grown in the developing world is rising rapidly, from 14 per cent in 1997 to almost 25 per cent in 2000, coverage is limited to a small number of relatively prosperous, export-oriented countries – and a small number of commercial crops. Herbicide-resistant soybeans remain the dominant crop, followed by maize (Juma and Watal 2000). Staple foods such as sorghum, cassava, and other root crops scarcely register. Hardly any of the newly engineered seeds on the market or in production are designed to meet the food needs of the rural poor or to enhance the productivity of smallholder farmers (Lipton 1999).

The logic of the market is reflected in the fact that commercial companies are gearing their research towards products likely to increase their profit margins and share-values. An example is the patent taken out by Monsanto on its Roundup Ready crops. These crops include soya, corn, cotton, and sugar. Their specific quality is that they have an implant of genetic materials resistant to high doses of glysophate, the main active ingredient in the company's best-selling herbicide, Roundup. The crops can withstand doses that will destroy weeds, meaning that Roundup can be applied more effectively. Patenting offers a twin benefit to companies: it increases prices for seeds and boosts sales of key inputs such as herbicides. Around half of the entire US soybean crop area is now planted to Roundup Ready seeds, as is one-fifth of the cotton crop (Lappe and Bailey 1999).

Roundup Ready is an example of the extension of corporate control over seeds and other agricultural inputs that is facilitated by patenting. The TRIPS agreement contains limited safeguards against the emergence of monopoly power, and may encourage it. The extension of patenting rights has contributed to a concentration of power in the seeds industries of a number of developing countries. In Brazil, patenting has been accompanied by a wave of mergers and acquisitions as companies seek to capture the benefits of patent control. Today, just two companies, Monsanto and Dupont, between them control three-quarters of the Brazilian market for corn (Wilkinson and Castelli 2000). The combination of stronger patent laws and reduced competition has driven up prices.

Apart from these immediate price effects, the extension of corporate control over seeds raises important concerns about bio-diversity. Rapid increases in acreage planted with genetically modified varieties of crop could push traditional varieties out of the market, with potentially serious consequences for future resistance to disease. The TRIPS agreement itself is in direct conflict with efforts to protect diversity. Under the UN Convention on Biological Diversity, governments have well-defined rights over their biological resources. The TRIPs agreement implicitly challenges these rights (Mayne 2002). It requires governments to recognise – and enforce – corporate claims over the same resources. One of the basic requirements for reform is that Article 27 of the TRIPs agreement should forbid patents on plant-based products obtained from national and international germplasm banks.

The General Agreement on Trade in Services (GATS)

'What were the services that were opened up? Financial services. Which country is the major exporter of financial services? United States. What services were not opened up? Construction services, maritime services, services of unskilled labor that are of concern to the developing world. Those remain closed.' (Joseph Stiglizt, Nobel Laureate and former World Bank Chief Economist, October 2001)

The General Agreement on Trade in Services (GATS) was the product of intensive lobbying by a coalition of some of the world's most powerful TNCs, including financial conglomerates such as American Express and Credit Suisse. The Coalition for Service Industries (CSI), which led the lobbying effort, praised the agreement as 'the constitution for liberalisation of trade in services' (Vastine 2000a). Others have been less enthusiastic. One comprehensive review concludes that GATS could 'have devastating effects on the ability of governments to meet the needs of their poorest and most powerless citizens' (World Development Movement 2001b).

The GATS agreement is one of the most complex elements in the WTO system. In a court of law, it would be of limited help in reaching a judgement. Many of its most important provisions are subject to divergent interpretations. The treaty also includes a range of exemptions, caveats, and assorted escape clauses. Despite this, the WTO services agreement poses significant threats to developing countries. Potentially, it could also offer some opportunities. The threats derive from the application of simplified free-market theories to the provision of basic services – such as water supply – that are vital to poverty reduction. The limited benefits are a consequence of the design of the GATS. Developing countries could benefit from the opening of markets for labour, but the agreement is biased towards financial services, where Northern countries and Northern-based TNCs dominate.

Services and the WTO[4]

Services have been described as 'anything that you can't drop on your foot' (World Development Movement 2000). The sector covers everything from banking and insurance to technical services, and from the provision of water, electricity, health care, and education to tourism and hairdressing.

Over the past 15 years, services have been the fastest-growing sector of the world economy. Annual trade in services has tripled to $1.2 trillion, or one-quarter of total world trade (World Bank 2002). Developing countries have shared in this expansion. Developments in information and communication technology have increased the scope for cross-border exports, ranging from the development of computer software for the TV animated cartoon show *The Simpsons* in the USA, to accounting and banking services in Barbados, to data entry for ticketing and billing services in India and Mexico. The most spectacular exporting success has been the Indian software sector, where exports grew from $225m in the early 1990s to exceed $1.75bn at the end of the decade (Mattoo 2000). But while developing-country exports have been growing, industrialised countries continue to account for more than four-fifths of world trade. As a group, developing countries are running a deficit in their services trade of about $33bn. Only five have a surplus (South Centre 2000). The USA, by contrast, operates a surplus of $80bn (Coalition for Service Industries 2001).

What the rules say

The GATS is really a system of interlocking principles, sector-specific arrangements, and liberalisation commitments. For all its daunting complexity it is, in the official view of the WTO, the single most important development in the multilateral trade system since 1945 (WTO 1999).

All sectors are covered by the agreement. The only exception is a very narrow one covering those (virtually non-existent) services that are supplied by governments solely on a non-commercial basis, or where there is no private-sector supplier.5 One of the most important aspects of the agreement is that it locks all countries into a negotiating process which aims to achieve 'a progressively higher level of liberalisation'. In committing governments to a continuous process of liberalisation, the GATS agreement goes far beyond any other agreement (Dhanarajan 2001).

Three broad principles govern the GATS. The first is non-discrimination, or the 'most favoured nation' provision, which means that any advantage provided to one supplier has to be accorded to all. The second principle is that of 'national treatment', which requires that foreign service providers are treated no less favourably than national companies. Finally, the agreement prohibits a range of policies that restrict market access. These include limits on foreign investment, restrictions on the number of service suppliers allowed and on the value of service output, and limitations concerning the type of legal entity that a service supplier should be.

There are important differences between the way in which the GATS was negotiated and the negotiation of other WTO agreements. In contrast to the negotiations on goods, those concerning services are based on a 'positive list'. Anything not on the list submitted by governments is nominally free of liberalisation obligations (Dhanarajan 2001). Theoretically, this means that countries are free to choose in which sectors to enter into liberalisation negotiations, although developing countries are already coming under pressure to undertake far-reaching action.

Trade in services is different from trade in goods, not just because service products have different qualities, but also because they imply different market arrangements. Many service transactions require the service provider and the consumer to be in the same place. Others entail the movement of service providers across borders. Four modes of supply are covered by GATS:

- **Mode 1: Cross-border supply.** This is most analogous to trade in goods, since it involves the purchase of a product, such as an insurance policy or computer programme, by a consumer in one country from a firm in another.

- **Mode 2: Consumption abroad.** This category covers activities involving people from one country visiting another to get a service, such as entertainment, education, or health treatment.

- **Mode 3: Commercial presence.** This involves a firm from one country establishing itself in another country to provide a service, such as banking or telecommunications.

- **Mode 4: Movement of individuals.** This takes place when a service provider leaves one country to provide a service in another country.

Behind the labyrinthine detail of the GATS is one revolutionary provision: it establishes the right of corporate service providers to locate themselves in another country, and to provide services to the citizens of that country (WTO 1999). This was the central demand of the USA and the EU during the Uruguay Round, and of the corporate lobby groups that shaped their negotiating positions. In this respect it represents a huge extension of investor rights and a potential curtailment of policy sovereignty for developing-country governments.

In broad terms, Northern governments are using negotiations on GATS to deepen commitments under Mode 3. For financial-service providers such as banks and insurance companies, and utility providers in water and electricity, commercial presence is a vital requirement for competing in local markets. Developing-country governments have placed far more emphasis on Mode 4. This covers the right of companies to provide services, ranging from software development to construction, involving the movement of labour.

One of the reasons for the current imbalance in the global trade in services is that global markets for labour are far more restricted than global markets for financial services, to the detriment of developing-country interests. At present, services provided through TNCs established in other countries account for about 33 per cent of the global services trade, compared with one per cent through the transfer of labour (McCulloch, Winters, and Cirera 2001). The provision of services now accounts for an estimated one-half of all direct foreign investment in developing countries, much of it directed towards privatised banks and utilities such as water and electricity.

The decision of developing countries to concentrate on Mode 4 is well judged. Labour cost is an area in which developing countries have the greatest advantage, but labour markets are subject to the greatest restrictions on trade. Immigration policies, rather than free-market principles, govern the behaviour of Northern governments in this area. There is a striking disparity between the development of global, and highly mobile, financial markets and immobile labour markets. Whereas yields on financial assets seldom vary by more than a factor of two, wages vary by a factor of ten or more.

The movement of service-supplying people is crucial to developing-country interests. For instance, despite the movement of cross-border electronic commerce, almost two-thirds of India's exports are supplied through the temporary movement of labour to clients overseas. Restrictions on movement hamper the development of markets for Indian firms. More broadly, barriers to the movement of labour, which are far higher for unskilled than skilled workers, cost developing countries billions of dollars. According to one estimate, a movement of labour from developing to developed countries equivalent to three per cent of the industrialised world's workforce would generate $200bn annually (Rodrik 2001e). Much of this would flow directly to developing countries in the form of remittances, balancing the deficit on financial and other services. Moreover, the money would be concentrated directly in the hands of workers, with obvious benefits for poor communities.

GATS 2000

WTO talks about progressive liberalisation of trade in services began in February 2000. The EU and the USA have been the prime movers, with strong inputs from various powerful business groups (see Box 8.1). Although the outcome remains uncertain, the parameters of the original agreement are being steadily pushed back in favour of rich countries and the expansion of corporate markets.

In broad terms, industrialised countries are seeking to deepen market-access commitments and extend coverage to more sectors. Once again, corporate lobby groups are seeking to use the GATS to extend commercial rights. The US-based Coalition for Service Industries has called for 'broad commitments to liberalisation in areas such as the right to establish a business presence in foreign markets, the right to own all or a majority share of that business, and the right to be treated as a local business' (Vastine 2000a). Northern governments are attempting to meet this request by proposing interpretations of GATS that may broaden out the types of services covered, while at the same time binding countries to deeper market-opening commitments.

Behind what are seemingly technical negotiations are some serious development issues. For instance, industrialised countries have proposed abandoning the request-offer approach to negotiations, and replacing it with a formula approach. This would require minimum levels of liberalisation across all sectors, denying developing countries the right to exempt services deemed vital to public welfare. Governments could be forced to extend liberalisation commitments to areas such as health care and education, allowing foreign service providers to compete with the State (World Development Movement 2002, Corner House 2001). In countries with a weak regulatory capacity, this would pose obvious dangers in terms of the fragmentation of basic services. For instance, private health-care providers might seek to concentrate resources in areas that reflected purchasing power rather than health needs.

The remit of the negotiations is being enlarged. One of the WTO committees dealing with GATS has been asked by the EU to explore the enlargement of the definition of services. The EU has expressly called for 'water for human use' (currently excluded) to be included under 'environmental services' (which are included). If this proposal is accepted, developing countries will come under intense pressure to liberalise water markets, adding to the pressures associated with water privatisation. European companies stand to gain from such an application of the GATS. Some of the world's largest water suppliers, such as Thames Water, Ondeo (formerly Suez Lyonnaise des Eaux), and Vivendi are actively seeking new privatisation opportunities (Tremolet 2001).

Box 8.1

The WTO: serving corporate interests

'Without the enormous pressure generated by the American financial services sector, particularly companies like American Express and Citicorp, there would have been no services agreement.'

As the words of WTO Services Division Director David Hartridge suggest, the GATS is a living testament to the ability of powerful corporations to insert private commercial interests into the multilateral trade agenda.

The driving force behind the development of GATS was the services industry. In 1982, American Express, Citicorp, and other financial conglomerates united to form the Coalition of Service Industries (CSI). The aim was to enlarge overseas markets for US services through a set of binding global rules, eliminating the constraints imposed by governments on commercial activity. Despite entrenched opposition from developing-country governments, the CSI was able to force the issue of service liberalisation to the top of the Uruguay Round agenda. It has influenced – and drafted – the negotiating papers of successive Administrations at the WTO. Corporate interest and US self-interest clearly overlap. The USA is the world's largest exporter of services, operating a surplus of $80bn a year (which partly balances the deficit on trade in goods).

In the European Union, the industry works through the European Services Network (ESN) – a network of high-level representatives from fifty major companies. Led by Andrew Buxton, the Chairperson of Barclays Bank, the ESN co-ordinates the activities of companies such as Goldman Sachs, SunAlliance Insurance, and HSBC Holdings. This body has extensive influence over governments and close ties with the European Commission. In the UK, a former European Trade Commissioner, Leon Brittain, chairs a group of the International Financial Services London (IFSN) network, another umbrella group dedicated to lobbying on services.

While there is nothing remarkable about big business organising to advance its interests, there is a huge asymmetry in the distribution of power and influence. Headed by a former US Assistant Treasury Secretary, the CSI is connected to the US government system through a revolving door between industry and the Administration. In Europe, the ESN and IFSN have privileged access to meetings of key committees of the European Commission dealing with services. By contrast, public-interest groups – notably those representing the interests of poor people in developing countries – have little access or influence.

(Sources: Dhanarajan 2001, Vastine 2000b)

The GATS agreement is central to national regulatory policies. Under the so-called 'test of necessity', governments are required to prove that any measure that restricts access to domestic service markets is consistent with WTO principles. In this context, that means proving that any restrictions on access to service markets are, in the words of the WTO text, 'least trade restrictive' and 'pro-competitive'. In other words, governments will have to satisfy the WTO that the regulatory framework allows maximum access to corporate service providers, consistent with an (external) assessment of government policy objectives in the sector concerned.

The imposition of an objective test clearly runs counter to the key development safeguards enshrined in the preamble to the GATS agreement. This acknowledges 'the right of Members (...) to regulate, and to introduce new regulations, on the supply of services ... in order to meet national policy objectives /and/ the particular need of developing countries to exercise this right' (WTO 1999). One of the problems in assessing whether or not this provision is being violated is the gap between the letter of WTO law and the spirit of implementation. Trade lawyers argue about the precise meaning of terms. Meanwhile, formidably powerful industrial lobbies in sectors ranging from banking and insurance to health care, education, and water supply are seeking to use the GATS as a means of levering open markets. Their motivation is commercial self-interest, rather than the public good. One of the reasons why public concern is justified is that Northern governments are using their negotiating strength to secure interpretations which reflect the interests of politically powerful constituencies.

Potential threats to development policies

Evaluating the implications of the GATS for poverty reduction is difficult. Implementation will not take place in isolation. Many developing countries are already privatising utilities and allowing foreign investors to provide services in areas such as banking, electricity, water, education, health care, and telecommunications. The GATS will interact with this process. Another problem is that the terms of implementation remain uncertain.

The GATS raises cause for concern in many respects. According to some commentators, the case for removing barriers is the same as the case for removing any trade barrier: namely, free markets are more efficient than government intervention (World Bank 2002). Such thinking is flawed. Markets for water, health care, and education are not the same as markets for television sets and cars, and they should not be governed by the same principles. Vital issues of human rights, social justice, equity, and State responsibility are at stake. These are public goods which have crucial implications not solely for the welfare of individuals, but for that of whole societies. For example, nobody is immune from the health risks generated by exclusion from clean water supplies, and all sections of society suffer from the slow growth associated with mass illiteracy.

Critics and supporters of the GATS agreement alike regard it as a vehicle for driving forward privatisation programmes. As a service-delivery strategy, privatisation is not inherently anti-poor, especially in contexts where the State has failed to provide access on affordable terms. In Argentina, privatisation in telecommunications has reduced charges and extended access for the urban poor, although not for their rural counterparts. In Peru, there were fewer than three telephones for every 100 people in the first half of the 1990s. Since privatisation, that figure has climbed to ten, and tariffs have fallen (Ugaz 2001). Developing countries can also benefit from the provision of commercial services in some areas, for instance in improving the efficiency of transport infrastructure (McCulloch et al. 2001).

The danger is that enforced liberalisation in countries with weak regulatory capacity will have deeply damaging effects in the long term, both for efficiency and for poverty reduction. Across much of Latin America, the privatisation of utilities has involved the replacement of public monopolies with private monopolies. Regulatory bodies have often been dominated by industry. Governments have systematically failed to manage privatisation in the interests of the poor, for example by requiring private providers to extend services to marginal areas. On the interpretation favoured by many Northern governments and TNCs, the GATS agreement will compound all of the problems associated with bad privatisation programmes.

The case of water privatisation in Bolivia illustrates the issue. Access to clean water is a major problem. One-third of the total population – some 2.5 million people – still lack access to clean water and sanitation (UNICEF 2000). This contributes to a situation in which infectious diseases claim the lives of one in ten children before the age of five. Like other countries, Bolivia has privatised water provision, with mixed success. Access to piped water in Bolivia's urban departmental capitals increased after privatisation by 15 per cent in the second half of the 1990s. The problem was that prices also increased, creating new pressures on the poor. In the city of Cochabamba, particularly steep increases, the product of a mismanaged privatisation arrangement, led to riots. Meanwhile, whatever the successes or failures of privatisation in urban areas, little has been done to improve access in rural areas.

The Bolivian government's efforts to extend water provision could be compromised by the GATS. One of the ways in which the government is attempting to provide water to poor consumers is to divide the water market into what amounts to two zones. Concessions are being provided to private operators in regions deemed commercially viable, subject to tariff regulations. In areas that are not commercially viable, local government has retained responsibility. Central government has the option of financing universal access in non-commercial zones, either through consumer subsidies or through transfers to local government (Ugaz 2001).

It is not clear that either option would be deemed non-discriminatory under the GATS. Similarly, the Bolivian government's tariff regulations could be deemed discriminatory if applied only to foreign water companies. Other options may also be closed down. For example, one of the ways in which some countries have extended services to poor areas is to cross-subsidise public provision through taxes on consumption in better-off areas. In cases where foreign water companies are supplying the latter, any such move could be construed as discriminatory, and therefore illegal in WTO terms.

There are legitimate fears concerning the role of the WTO in water supply. For all the inefficiencies associated with State provision, privatisation – and the commercialisation of water markets – is unlikely to meet the needs of those excluded from markets by virtue of their poverty. The danger is that powerful companies will be able to use the WTO to add to other pressures being brought to bear on developing-country governments, notably through the IMF and World Bank. A random review of IMF loan programmes in 2000 discovered that loan conditions negotiated with 12 countries stipulated water-privatisation provisions (Dhanarajan 2001).

The use of the GATS to curtail government policy choices in the interests of foreign providers could have damaging implications for one of the greatest development challenges facing the international community. An estimated 1.3 billion of the world's people do not have access to safe water at present, and that figure could double by 2035. For women and young girls in poor households, action to end the crisis in water and sanitation is an especially pressing concern. They assume responsibility for collecting water, frequently spending many hours in the task. They also carry the burden of dealing with problems associated with inadequate access to piped water, including caring for sick family members.

The WTO secretariat insists that nothing in the agreement, as currently drafted, would allow for its use as a vehicle for deregulating water markets (WTO 2000). However, there is equally nothing that excludes its application to water. The EU has explicitly called for 'water for human use' to be included in the schedules for liberalisation. It is not hard to see why. European companies dominate global markets. Two of these companies are Vivendi and Ondeo, each of which provides water to more than 100 million households. Both companies are seeking lucrative new markets in developing countries, especially those – such as Colombia, Uruguay, and Venezuela – that have yet to fully liberalise their markets.

Issues of regulation relating to GATS also loom large in the financial sector, where accelerated liberalisation could cause financial instability, as it did in East Asia. One of the dangers under the GATS is that governments will undertake liberalisation commitments on financial services that are inconsistent with their regulatory capacity. Premature liberalisation could also have fatal consequences for small and medium-sized enterprises. As in other markets, competition in service markets can produce efficiency gains for consumers. But liberalisation does not necessarily lead to more competition. Many markets for services are dominated by small groups of large firms. This high degree of concentration is often a consequence of worldwide networks, financial strength, sophisticated information technologies, and economies of scale. Developing-country service providers, most of which are small or medium-sized enterprises, are ill equipped to compete without State support and some degree of protection (South Centre 2000). Under the GATS, market interventions in these areas could be construed as discriminatory, and therefore prohibited.

It could be argued in each of these areas that there is nothing in the GATS that allows for enforced liberalisation. Defenders of the system point out that the 'positive list' approach means that developing-country governments have the right to choose what to liberalise. Leaving aside the current threats to this approach, this view ignores the fact that future governments may have only a restricted right to withdraw liberalisation commitments made by their predecessors. At the very least, GATS will close down the future space for policy choice that is available to governments. As a former Indian ambassador to the GATT has written: 'The developing countries have lost the flexibility of modifying their policy in the light of future experience' (Das 2001).

Limiting the scope for development policies

The WTO system is based upon a philosophy which sees free markets, and their corollary of trade liberalisation, as the most effective route to economic growth. Government intervention in markets is viewed as inherently inefficient and damaging to national and international interests. What the WTO offers is a guidebook for policy makers – but it is a guidebook with a difference. Non-compliance with the instructions attracts penalties in the form of trade sanctions. Developing countries are expected to comply with WTO standards, subject to some minor concessions. Unfortunately, those standards are inconsistent with policies for broad-based economic growth, and successful integration into the world economy.

Restrictions on State intervention

Forty years ago, Korea and Taiwan were poor countries with limited technological capacity. Today, they account for one-fifth of all manufactured exports from developing countries, and a similar share of high-technology exports. Of all developing countries, they have the deepest technology infrastructure. Like Japan before them, both countries were highly interventionist. They had a clear preference for promoting indigenous companies, limiting foreign investment, and developing strong linkages between the export sector and the rest of the economy (Wade 1990, Lall 1998, 1999). The following were among the most important policies:

- **Selective and time-bound import protection.** Neither country exposed its domestic market to free trade. Relatively high levels of tariff and extensive non-tariff barriers were used to give local firms the space to develop their capacity, and to provide incentives for long-term investment. The adverse effects of protectionism were offset by strong incentives to compete in export markets and face international competition.

- **Restrictions on TNC entry and investment.** Both countries restricted TNC operations. Foreign investment never represented more than 2 per cent of total investment (compared with more than 15 per cent in Mexico). Korea was the most restrictive, allowing foreign direct investment only as a means of getting access to new technologies, or promoting exports. In place of foreign investment, Korea relied heavily on 'reverse engineering', or the reproduction of imported technologies, adaptation, and domestic development. The concern in both countries was to avoid dependence on imported technologies and to create an environment in which local firms would undertake research and development.

- **Support for technological deepening.** One of the features of Korean industrial development policy was the creation of large private conglomerates, the *chaebol*. These conglomerates were given a range of subsidies in the form of credit, foreign exchange, and infrastructural support, provided that they invested capital in technology-intensive activities. The rationale for creating large-scale units was to create industrial systems capable of developing and absorbing complex technologies, without relying on foreign investment (Stiglitz 1996)

- **Flexible rules on intellectual property.** Governments in East Asia adopted intellectual-property regimes allowing local firms to copy and adapt imported technologies, thus reducing the costs of technology transfer by lowering licence fees.

- **Local content and export rules.** In cases where governments did allow foreign direct investment, they required TNCs to develop linkages with local industry (Lall 1999). The Singer Sewing Machine Company was allowed into Taiwan in 1964 because local manufacturers lacked the technology to compete in international markets. The government stipulated that Singer must procure four-fifths of all its components locally within one year. The company was required to export a considerable share of its output, while at the same time developing standardised blueprints for local firms to supply its Taiwan factory. By the end of the decade, Taiwanese firms were emerging as major exporters of sewing machines, and as the main source of supply to the local textiles industry (UN 1999).

Under WTO rules, many of these policies would be difficult to apply, or actually prohibited. Commitments to the WTO will reduce the freedom of developing-country governments in some key areas, such as intellectual-property management, the regulation of foreign investment, and tariff policy. The erosion of the principle of special and differential treatment for developing countries will further constrain their autonomy.

The TRIPS agreement is perhaps the most striking example of the WTO closing down the space for policies to develop national technological capacity. By raising the costs of technology transfer and restricting the right of importers to copy and adapt, it will rule out one set of policies successfully applied in East Asia.

The 1995 agreement on Trade Related Investment Measures (TRIMs) could have similar effects. This prohibits governments from applying any investment policies inconsistent with the general principle of non-discrimination. It is true that some measures of industrial policy are still consistent with the TRIMs agreement (Amsden 2000). For example, governments have retained the right to maintain existing local content programmes, provided that they notify the WTO. Countries such as Brazil and Indonesia have taken advantage of this in the automobile industry. In future, however, there will be less room for manoeuvre. The 'Illustrative List' of discriminatory policies attached to the agreement includes local-content requirements (UNCTAD 2000d). Countries such as Brazil and Argentina in the Southern Common Market (Mercosur) have modified the rules applying to the car industry, effectively eliminating in future the requirement on foreign investors to purchase a certain proportion of their inputs from local firms (ECLA 1998). The export and local-content performance requirements for the Chilean automobile industry have also been changed to conform to WTO rules. By freeing foreign investors of any requirements, the danger is that countries will suffer a further weakening of technological capacity and growing import dependence, as discussed in Chapter 3.

The danger is that WTO rules will preclude government policies aimed at establishing dynamic linkages between local industry and foreign investors, and at increasing the share of export value retained locally. It offers a development path on the Mexican or Bangladeshi model of export-processing zones, with a continuation of low-value-added, labour-intensive production, rather than the South Korean and Taiwan model.

In the case of import protection, the WTO does allow for some leeway. During the Uruguay Round, most developing countries bound their tariffs at levels higher than their applied rates, so that WTO negotiations have not been a major factor in trade liberalisation. However, developing countries seeking to enter the WTO – such as China, Cambodia, and Vietnam – have been required to undertake deep tariff cuts in advance, often under the auspices of IMF-World Bank programmes.

Although various safeguards are permitted for the temporary protection of domestic industries, or for higher tariffs in the event of balance-of-payments crises, these are temporary arrangements (UNCTAD 2000d). The scope and duration of exceptions are likely to be constrained. There is no provision for the use of tariffs as an element in industrial policy for the promotion of infant industry, partly because of the general presumption that tariffs will be reduced over time.

The WTO is not the only international agreement that restricts the right of governments. Regional treaties play an increasingly important role. Provisions in the NAFTA have dramatically extended the rights of companies, entitling them to challenge national environmental laws and restricting the scope for government action (see Box 8.2). The US Administration is now using the NAFTA arrangements as a model to be followed in other regional and bilateral agreements.

Special and differential treatment

One of the strengths of the WTO system is that it applies universal rules which restrict, however inadequately, the scope for bilateral power politics. Unfortunately, universality is also a weakness in one crucial respect: not all WTO members are of equal economic

Box 8.2

NAFTA: the rights of foreign investors

Over the past decade, the scope and coverage of rights enjoyed by foreign investors have been dramatically increased. There are growing concerns that corporate rights, designed to promote foreign investment, are impinging on development policies.

One focal point for public concern has been Chapter 11 of the North American Free Trade Agreement (NAFTA). This deals with the respective rights of foreign investors and the governments of Mexico, Canada, and the USA. It is important not simply in its own right, but also because it is being used as a model in the development of bilateral investment treaties, of which there are now more than 1800, and regional trade agreements. Chapter 11 provides investors with protection in areas not previously covered under investment agreements. It covers four key areas:

• **National treatment and most-favoured nation treatment.** Host governments are required to treat foreign investors no less favourably than domestic investors or other foreign investors.

• **Minimum international standards of treatment.** Although ill defined, this has been interpreted in ways which provide foreign investors with unprecedented rights in relation to governments.

• **Prohibitions on export requirements.** Governments are explicitly prohibited from requiring investors to use a given proportion of local inputs, to cover their exchange costs through exports, or to transfer technologies. Provisions in this area go much further than under the WTO.

• **Prohibitions on expropriation.** All investment agreements restrict arbitrary expropriation, but Chapter 11 has a sting in the tail. It includes restrictions on measures that amount to 'indirect' expropriation or measures 'tantamount to' expropriation. The scope is so broad as to allow virtually any of a wide range of public policies – such as taxation or environmental standards – to be treated as an act of expropriation.

Chapter 11 has given corporations a powerful tool with which to breach national regulations, threatening the sovereign rights of governments to protect consumers and the environment, and develop national industries. Companies have used NAFTA's tribunal system to launch a series of attacks on a broad range of regulatory policies by extending the notion of expropriation to include almost any action that obstructs the quest for profit. The tribunal system itself gives companies unprecedented rights, since it enables them to sue governments directly.

In 1996, the Canadian government indicated that it would ban importation of the chemical MMT (methylcyclopentadienyl manganese tricarbonyl), a petroleum additive, for reasons of environmental and public health. It acted on the basis of scientific concern over the toxicity of manganese and the threat of air pollution. It actions were promptly contested by the Ethyl Corporation, a US company which is the only manufacturer of MMT in the world. Canada lost the case and paid Ethyl $13m in compensation for lost profits.

When the government of Mexico halted construction of a hazardous waste-disposal site in the municipality of Guadalcalzar, following an environmental review, it was immediately challenged under Chapter 11. The US company Metalclad claimed that its rights to minimum international standards of protection had been violated, and that it had been subjected to a form of expropriation. The Chapter 11 tribunal upheld Metalclad's claim, forcing Mexico to pay $16m in compensation. The State of California has been sued by Methanex, the world's largest producer of methanol. The company launched the case after California's Governor issued an order banning the use of a methanol-based petroleum additive from the end of 2002, citing concerns over water pollution.

In each case, Chapter 11 gives corporate actors the scope to challenge the actions of democratically elected governments in enacting public health and environmental laws.

Citing the Free Trade Area of the Americas (FTAA), the Bush Administration, supported by powerful industrial lobbies, is seeking to have Chapter 11 extended across Latin America. Chemical and petroleum firms have been particularly powerful advocates. Current wording for the FTAA suggests that the lobbyists may well succeed, since the definition of investor interest is even broader than in the original. The danger is that this legal provision will lock Latin America into the poor-quality investment that it is currently receiving, with serious threats to public health and the environment.

strength – and they face different problems. In particular, developing countries need multilateral trade rules that enable them, within a broad-based system of accepted ground rules, to implement the policies needed to generate growth and poverty reduction.

Under the GATT, developing countries were accorded a special status. In the mid-1960s, a new 'Trade and Development' chapter was added, specifying that 'developed (countries) do not expect reciprocity for commitments made by them in trade negotiations to reduce or remove tariffs and other barriers to trade' (Fukasaku 2000). In other words, industrialised countries acknowledged that trade liberalisation had different implications in developing countries from those that applied to their own markets.

The disadvantage of this special and differential treatment was that industrialised countries did not negotiate with developing countries as trading partners. Having signed away their right to demand reciprocal liberalisation in developing countries, rich countries negotiated tariff cuts between themselves, while maintaining high barriers against developing countries. The price that developing countries paid for special and differential treatment was a weaker negotiating position. Meanwhile, other aspects of special treatment, such as improved market access, generated much rhetoric but little in the form of actual benefits.

Under the Uruguay Round agreement, things have changed dramatically. The principle of special and differential treatment is intact, but the practice has changed out of all recognition. Under most WTO agreements, the only concession granted to developing countries is a slightly longer time-frame for implementation. Given the scope of these agreements and associated administrative demands, this is a very limited provision. According to the findings of World Bank surveys, the up-front average cost of implementing the TRIPS agreement alone in a low-income country is approximately $1.5 million, with annual recurrent costs of $2 million (World Bank 2002).

There are two serious problems with the current WTO approach to special and differential treatment. First, there is a fundamental flaw in the presumption that developing countries are equipped to take on obligations similar to industrialised countries which have reached far higher levels of economic development. As we have argued earlier in this chapter, the rationale for applying Northern intellectual-property standards in poor countries is weak, both in economic terms and in broader development terms. Similarly, the idea that developing countries should liberalise on the same basis as industrialised countries, albeit at a more modest pace (at least in WTO negotiations), ignores the very real differences in adjustment capacity – and in development needs. There may be very good reasons for protecting agriculture and manufacturing – not just in the interests of protecting employment and food security, but also in the interests of developing a dynamic comparative advantage.

The second problem is that WTO rules authorise forms of intervention that are biased towards rich countries. For example, the rules allow extensive subsidies to agriculture (see Chapter 4) and manufacturing. At a conservative estimate, industrialised countries spend $51bn on direct subsidies to industry. Developing countries are ill-equipped to compete in this area, since they lack the financial resources(UNCTAD 2001c). In this context, trade policy may be the only instrument open to governments seeking to develop local capacity.

The concept of special and differential treatment is a fundamental element of the multilateral trading system. It arose from a recognition that countries at differing stages of economic, financial, and technological development have differing capacities and needs. Since the end of the Uruguay Round, there has been a dramatic erosion of the principles underpinning special and differential treatment. Developing countries are now assuming obligations that are inconsistent with policies for poverty reduction. There is an urgent need to return to some first principles on special and differential treatment, in particular to ensure that there is no WTO prohibition on policies that promote growth and poverty reduction.

Policy recommendations

Since the end of the Uruguay Round, the authority of the WTO has been extended, with crucial consequences for the poor. Having failed to address long-standing problems facing developing countries in areas such as market access, multilateral trade rules now constrain the development of national policies in a wide range of areas that are vital to poverty reduction. As shown in this chapter, these rules threaten to widen inequalities associated with trade, and to weaken the links between trade and poverty reduction.

Intellectual-property rights

Any reform must begin by abolishing the standard, universal model of intellectual-property protection. Rules should be tapered to take into account the level of development of particular countries, including their technological needs and capacities. It might make sense for middle-income countries to offer higher levels of protection than low-income countries, but it is difficult to see a rationale for all countries adopting the standards set in the industrialised world.

As part of the scheduled review of the WTO agreement, developing countries should be granted longer transition periods and greater flexibility in determining the length and scope of patent protection. In the specific case of pharmaceutical products:

- **The duration and scope of patent protection should be reduced for developing countries.** Various alternatives have been suggested. One proposal envisages a restriction of the geographical coverage of patents, with companies being required to choose whether to seek protection in an industrialised country or a developing country, but not in both (Lanjouw 2001). Another suggestion is to allow greater flexibility in the period of patent protection, with developing countries retaining the right to allow protection periods of, say, 0–10 years, depending on their levels of development and health status.

- **Public-health interests should be paramount, with people's right to health care given priority over companies' rights to patents.** The weak public-interest safeguard provided in Article 8 should be replaced by an unqualified statement that nothing in the TRIPs agreement will prevent the adoption of measures to protect public health. The political statement of intent adopted at the Doha ministerial meeting of the WTO marked a step in the right direction. It affirmed that all governments have the right to put public-health interests before patent claims. However, this commitment must be given binding legal form, including entrenched rights for the provision of compulsory licences and parallel importing.

- **All developing countries should be allowed to obtain medicines from the cheapest source, with special protection for those that lack a domestic production capacity.** Article 28 of the TRIPs agreement prevents generic companies producing and exporting copies of patented medicines. Even if governments authorise compulsory licences to over-ride patents in the interests of public health (under Article 31), production must be predominantly for the domestic market. Such licences cannot be issued for export purposes. For instance, under the TRIPs agreement, the governments of India and Brazil will not be permitted to authorise generic companies to produce copies of patented drugs for market in Africa. This arrangement can severely restrict the access of countries lacking a strong generic industry to cheap medicines. The current TRIPs agreement should be reformed, to allow countries with a generic industry to export to other developing countries that are struggling to respond to public-health problems.

As in the case of health care, the application of TRIPs in the area of genetic resources for food, agriculture, and biodiversity requires fundamentally different strategies. For adequate protection of the food security of poor people, and the genetic and biological resources upon which they depend:

- **Patent protection of plant genetic resources for food and agriculture should not be allowed under WTO rules.** This does not preclude other forms of plant-variety protection, but allows countries to protect their vital interests in respect of ensuring food security and protecting biodiversity.

- **Developing countries should retain the right to develop their own sui generis systems of intellectual-property protection for plant varieties.** Industrialised countries should not seek to enforce UPOV 1991 or other forms of TRIPs-plus arrangements, such as those envisaged under the Free Trade Agreement for the Americas.

- **The TRIPs agreement should be brought into line with the UN Convention on Biological Diversity (CBD) and the International Treaty on Plant Genetic Resources for Food and Agriculture (PGRFA).** No patents on genetic resources should be granted without the prior informed consent of, and benefit-sharing with, the communities and countries of origin.

Services

The GATS agreement should be rebalanced and more narrowly defined, with a sharper focus on the interests of developing countries – and a reduced emphasis on the interests of rich countries and transnational companies.

- **Development objectives should be prioritised during the GATS 2000 negotiations.**

Industrialised countries should undertake liberalisation commitments in areas where developing countries stand to benefit, such as temporary labour movement.

- **Public services should be excluded from liberalisation commitments.** Article 1(3) of the GATS agreement should be amended to provide for the exemption of any public service from liberalisation, regardless of the precise role played by the State in supplying that service.

- **National sovereignty provisions should be strengthened, and the negotiating mandate should be limited.** The GATS agreement should be amended to include a clear and unambiguous commitment, stipulating that governments retain the right to limit liberalisation in areas deemed essential to national development and poverty reduction. Industrialised-countries should abandon their efforts to replace the current 'positive list' approach (which allows developing countries to choose which sectors should be included in GATS negotiations) with a 'negative list' approach (which would require them to specify which sectors are not included).

Special and differential treatment

Developing countries should retain the right to develop industrial and agricultural policies that facilitate successful integration into global markets. In this context:

- **Special and differential treatment provisions should be strengthened.** Infant-industry provisions should allow developing countries to retain the right to protect key manufacturing sectors. More broadly, the time-frame for liberalisation commitments should be extended. Governments should not be required to make commitments to liberalisation that are inconsistent with national poverty-reduction strategies.

- **Governments should retain the right to regulate foreign investors.** In particular, Article 4 of the TRIMS agreement should be amended, to allow governments to impose local-content rules and other requirements aimed at establishing links between domestic firms and foreign investors.

CHAPTER 9
Making trade work for the poor

The increasing integration of developing countries into the global trading system offers the promise of more rapid progress towards poverty reduction and improved standards of living – but not if current practices continue. Trade cannot realise its potential unless rich and poor countries alike take action to make it work for the poor. That means redistributing opportunities through new rules and new forms of international co-operation at a global level, and through more effective anti-poverty strategies at a national level.

This chapter summarises some of the key policy reforms that would unlock the full human-development potential of trade. The first part focuses on measures that are necessary at the national level. Good international rules can create an enabling environment in which poor countries can successfully integrate into global markets, but it is national policies that determine the extent to which the poor share in the benefits of trade. Making national markets work for poor people is as important as making international markets work for poor countries.

The second section presents some of the ways in which the international community could co-operate to disperse the benefits of trade more widely. International trade cannot be considered in isolation from other development issues, such as aid, debt relief, and the management of capital markets. One of the problems facing the international community is that the pace of economic integration has outstripped the pace of international co-operation in these areas.

The third section shifts the focus to the governance of world trade. It argues that the World Trade Organisation is fundamentally failing poor countries and poor people. The authority of the WTO has been extended into broad new areas of public policy, thus limiting the autonomy of national governments in the process. For them there is an increasing tension between the imperative of complying with WTO rules, and the need to adopt policies which will reduce poverty. The reverse of this extension of the WTO's role into new areas is its failure to address long-standing problems in old ones, such as market access. Meanwhile, the system of trade governance is failing to respond to major new challenges posed by globalisation, including the threats arising from the enormous concentration of corporate power.

National governance and participation in world trade

Throughout this report we have argued that the policies, institutions, and rules that govern international trade at the global level contain an inherent bias against the poor. But the lives of impoverished people, and their ability to take advantage of the opportunities presented by trade, are ultimately shaped by forces which operate inside the borders of their countries: public spending, the distribution of incomes and assets, access to health and education services, to name a few. Actions at the national level are therefore a crucial complement to measures designed to reform the global trading system.

Education and health

Many of the most important requirements for successful integration in global markets extend beyond the narrow confines of trade policy. National policies on matters such as education and health services are even more basic to national prosperity than are questions of trade tariffs and non-tariff barriers to trade.

In the global economy of the early twenty-first century, education is perhaps the single most important pre-requisite for successful participation in world trade (Bennel 2000). Human capital is rapidly superseding physical capital as the principal source of wealth generation, both in national terms and at the level of individual households. High and sustainable economic growth – a critical requirement for accelerated poverty reduction – is increasingly dependent on the quality of education provision. Global income distribution in the future will reflect the distribution of educational opportunities. Similarly, within countries the links between the distribution of income and the distribution of educational opportunities are growing stronger.

As profound technological changes sweep the global economy, almost one in five adults in the developing world are unable to read or write. There are 125 million children of primary-school age not in school. As with non-literate adults, two-thirds of these children are female: a reflection of the deeply embedded gender-linked inequalities that continue to pervade education systems. The education deficit is particularly pronounced in Africa. If current trends continue, the region will account for three-quarters of all children out of school by 2015 (Oxfam 2001i). Restricted access to primary education is only a small part of the problem. Official enrolment rates disguise the full extent of the education crisis, since many children drop out of school before completing primary education. This is true even in middle-income countries. For example, in Brazil and Peru approximately one-third of children do not complete primary school. Across much of the developing world, many of those who do complete a full primary cycle emerge lacking literacy skills because of the poor quality of their education. An estimated one-third of Indian children graduate from primary school deficient in literacy skills.

The education crisis is not evenly distributed. It is overwhelmingly a crisis that afflicts the poor. In India, virtually all children from the richest one-fifth of households successfully complete their primary education, whereas fewer than half from the households of the poorest one-fifth even enrol in school. In Brazil, only 15 per cent of children from the poorest households complete primary school, compared with near universal completion for the richest (Filmer and Pritchett 1999). Gender-based gaps in education remain large: on average, South Asian girls spend three years less than boys in school, and there is a 10 per cent gap between enrolment rates for girls and boys in Africa. Interacting with these disparities, based on gender and wealth, are other inequalities; for example, rural populations suffer far more intensive levels of deprivation than do urban communities across much of the developing world.

These inequalities in education have a profound bearing on international trade. Countries with high levels of illiteracy and restricted opportunities for education, if they attempt to integrate into increasingly knowledge-intensive global markets, can expect a diminishing share of world trade and investment. Mass educational deprivation will also restrict the ability of countries and poor people to take advantage of the opportunities offered by trade. Cross-country research suggests that completion of primary education raises the output of smallholder farmers by 9 per cent, with even higher returns from girls' education (Appleton 1996). In the absence of a sustained strategy to close the education gap between rich and poor countries, and between rich and poor within countries, integration into global markets will continue to be associated with widening inequalities, with commensurate losses for poverty reduction. African governments can change their trade policies, but as long as the region has almost half of its children out of school, it can expect to suffer further marginalisation in global markets. India can maintain the rapid growth of a high-technology enclave economy; but with adult illiteracy rates in excess of 40 per cent, an average of only five years' schooling for its children (and three years for girls), and more than 30 million children of primary-school age out of school, India has little prospect of converting export growth into rapid poverty reduction.

Education should be at the heart of any national strategy for enhancing the capacity of the poor to benefit from trade. Yet in many countries it is seen almost as a distraction from the real challenges facing government. Many governments in South Asia and Africa continue to spend more on arms than on primary education services. Countries with some of the worst education indicators – such as India – spend no more than 1 per cent of their GDP on primary education. Limited public spending means that individual households must meet the costs of education through paying 'user charges'. Across much of the developing world, this tax on education denies millions of children access to school, transmitting poverty across generations and impeding economic growth.

What is true for education is also true for public health. Huge disparities in health between rich and poor countries, and rich and poor people, demonstrate clearly that ill-health is a product of poverty. Lacking access to clean water, adequate nutrition, and medical care, poor people are more susceptible to infectious disease. However, ill-health is a cause as well as a consequence of poverty. Single episodes of sickness can plunge households into deep poverty, reducing productivity and the availability of labour – the main asset of poor people – and forcing women to divert more of their time and energy to caring for sick relatives. When poor adults become sick, they are often forced to draw down their savings, sell off assets, and reduce consumption. Sickness in children impairs their capacity for learning. The effects are cumulative, and the impact on national economies often devastating. A high prevalence of diseases such as malaria, tuberculosis, and HIV/AIDS is associated with large reductions in economic growth. HIV/AIDS poses acute threats, not least because two-thirds of its 33 million victims live in sub-Saharan Africa (Sachs 1999).

Apart from being a fundamental goal of development in its own right, better health is a requirement for enabling poor people and poor countries to take advantage of the opportunities for higher living standards that international trade can provide. Yet, as in the case of education, health policy in developing countries seldom achieves the political priority – or the financial commitments – that it merits. It is estimated that one-third of the developing world's population lacks access to basic health services, and an even larger proportion are deprived of affordable medicine. Such outcomes are a reflection of inadequate resources and inequitable patterns of public spending.

Rural poverty

When countries integrate into global markets through increased trade, poor people face both opportunities and threats. There are huge potential benefits from fuller integration into rapidly expanding markets for exports, increased employment, and access to new technologies. Conversely, there are real dangers that the poor will be left behind, or that they may be subjected to exploitative labour practices, or that their livelihoods may be threatened through increased competition. Outcomes are not pre-determined. They are shaped by inherited patterns in the distribution of assets, income, and education, and by the policies that define the terms on which countries integrate.

Policies which aim to strengthen the links between trade and human development must accord priority to the rural poor – a group who account for approximately three-quarters of those living in extreme poverty worldwide. The rural poor have unequal access to the physical and financial assets needed to take advantage of trade opportunities. In many countries – such as Brazil, Bolivia, South Africa, Kenya, and parts of India – land ownership is highly concentrated. The FAO estimates that two-thirds of the rural population in Latin America are either landless, or lacking sufficient land to meet their basic needs (FAO 1998). Distorted systems of land ownership bias the opportunities provided through export agriculture away from the poor.

Weak marketing infrastructure is another barrier to participation in global markets – and infrastructure is typically weakest in areas with high concentrations of poverty. Distance to markets and poor-quality roads are a central concern for the rural poor across the developing world. High transport costs result in lower farm-gate prices, which in turn reduce household income and opportunities for employment (Delgado 1995, Minten and Kyle 1999). Highland rice farmers in Vietnam, potato farmers in Peru, and maize farmers in Kenya and Tanzania all suffer higher than average levels of poverty and lower than average access to roads. Africa faces special problems. The density of the rural road network (measured as kilometres of road per square kilometre) is only 7 per cent of that in India (Collier and Gunning 1999). In Kenya, the marketing costs for food grains are 40 per cent higher than in Indonesia, a fact which demonstrates the huge impact of infrastructure on competitiveness in local markets. The rural poor are also disadvantaged in terms of access to irrigation and to credit and extension services (IFAD 2001).

These interlocking inequalities have an important bearing on the distribution of benefits from trade. Remoteness from markets and inadequate access to roads raise the costs of marketing output, reduce farm-gate prices, and increase the costs of inputs such as fertilisers (Killick 2001). When markets are liberalised, it is often impossible for poor farmers to compete with the costs of imports in urban markets, even if the latter are not subsidised. In Peru, the loss of these markets has forced down farm-gate prices for food staples grown in highland areas. In Zambia and Kenya, farmers in remote areas are unable to compete with imports from South Africa. Without access to land, irrigation, market information, and infrastructure, the poor are equally ill-equipped to respond to export-market opportunities. For example, the rapid growth of fruit and vegetable exports in Latin America and sub-Saharan Africa has been dominated by larger commercial farms.

In countries with high levels of rural inequality, the redistribution of assets is essential if trade is to benefit the poor. Redistribution of land is a starting point. In Brazil, the Rural Landless Workers' Movement (MST) has established more than 1000 land-reform settlements, occupying land on large estates that is not being used (Wolford 2001). These settlements enable formerly landless people to grow food for their households and for local markets. Such action is not just good for rural poverty reduction: it is also in the national interest. Small farms are good for efficiency, employment, and growth. They have productivity levels which compare favourably with large farms, and they use more labour and less capital. Yet governments frequently favour large-scale commercial farms, which are less efficient in their use of resources. The World Bank recognises the importance of land redistribution, but favours market-based approaches, under which land is sold and land rights are privatised. Such approaches have achieved very limited results – for an obvious reason: namely, poor people lack purchasing power (Palmer 2001).

Beyond the need for the redistribution of land, rural poverty-reduction strategies need to place far more emphasis on investment in infrastructure used by the poor. Investment in irrigation and roads tends to be heavily concentrated in areas dedicated to commercial farming, rather than in areas characterised by high concentrations of poverty. Extension services and research priorities are often geared towards crops produced by larger farms, rather than those produced by smallholders in marginal areas. Access to rural savings and credit institutions is very undeveloped in many countries, and so access to capital is constrained.

Gender equity is of central importance to trade-related rural development strategies. In many countries, rural women are among the biggest potential losers from globalisation. As we showed in Chapter 3, they have less command than men over resources such as land, credit, and capital. In some cases, if a family begins to cultivate commercial crops, the gender-linked division of labour means that women lose control over the marketing of the produce. Rural women are more likely to be illiterate – and less likely to obtain access to the services that are needed to raise living standards. As traders, women also face in intense form the problems posed by inadequate transport infrastructures.

Urban poverty and employment

As we saw in Chapter 3, the impact on employment of integration into world markets is complex. In some cases – as in the textiles, agro-exports, and micro-electronics sectors – it is creating new opportunities for employment, especially among women. In others it is undermining employment, especially where labour-intensive industries were previously protected by high barriers against imports. But the picture of winners and losers that emerges is more complicated still. As this report has argued, employment creation is often accompanied by the emergence of 'flexible' labour practices, some of which have been associated with intensive forms of exploitation. While reducing one form of deprivation (based on income), export growth appears to be intensifying other forms.

The governments of developing countries must assume much of the responsibility not only for failing to address these new forms of deprivation, but for actively creating the conditions under which they occur. The guiding assumption, assiduously cultivated by the World Bank, the IMF, and Northern-based TNCs, has been that 'flexible' work practices are an essential response to inadequate economic growth, and a guaranteed way to increase exports and attract more foreign investment. Labour-market 'rigidities' have been blamed for a generalised lack of competitiveness. These presumed rigidities include basic trade-union rights, minimum-wage provisions, and employment rights.

As shown in Chapter 3, the imposition of flexible labour markets has been closely linked to new forms of vulnerability. From the free-trade zones of Bangladesh and Mexico to the special economic zones of China, and the agricultural export businesses of Latin America, millions of women have been drawn into very insecure jobs with very low levels of pay, often on a temporary and casual basis. Employment conditions are often very poor, with no proper health insurance, social insurance, or pension rights. In many countries, rapid export growth has failed to increase real wages.

While the reasons are complex, with significant differences between countries, the relentless assault on collective bargaining rights has inevitably contributed to the problem. It is not only workers in previously unionised sectors who have suffered. There is evidence that part of the wage premium generated by trade unions also extends to non-union workers. The same would apply to non-wage benefits associated with collective bargaining rights, including health and safety provisions, insurance, and pension schemes.

It is difficult to avoid the conclusion that labour markets have become excessively flexible. Cheap, vulnerable labour is not a guarantee of competitiveness in global markets – and even less is it a guarantee of poverty reduction (OECD 1996). While there is an obvious connection between labour costs and productivity, political intervention by governments is artificially depressing wages and employment conditions. Against this background, it is important that governments enforce the core labour standards established by the International Labour Organisation. They must also abandon the current two-tier approach to labour standards, under which women and workers in export-processing zones are accorded weaker rights.

Government regulation and the 'corruption tax'

Across much of the developing world, bad governance weakens the ability of poor people to benefit from trade. Corruption and bureaucracy often combine to act as a tax on development. That tax is highly regressive, in that it falls most heavily on the poor. It is also a barrier to good-quality investment.

The full extent of the 'corruption tax' is not widely appreciated. Each year, Transparency International publishes a Corruption Perceptions Index, which reflects the perceptions of business people, country analysts, and academics of levels of corruption in more than one hundred nations. Many of the world's poorest countries, including Kenya, Bolivia, Bangladesh, and Indonesia, record exceptionally high levels of perceived corruption in government and public administration (Transparency International 2001). In Kenya, monthly bribery payments translate into an increase of around one-third in the average cost of living for ordinary households. The daily requests by government officials for *kitu kidogo* – or 'something small' – constitute a huge burden on poor households. Small farmers, traders, and small enterprises all suffer (Turner 2002). Apart from its invidious effects on poor people, corruption raises the costs of marketing and reduces the returns from participation in trade. In Tanzania, coffee traders report paying up to ten sets of informal fees to obtain licences and to transport their produce. The costs are immediately passed back to producers in the form of lower prices.

In many countries, corruption coincides with excessive bureaucracy. One survey of foreign investors' perceptions of competitiveness in 47 countries ranked India twelfth on the basis of its supply of skilled labour; however, the same survey ranked India 45th on the basis of its efforts to tackle corruption (International Institute for Management Development 2000). Dealing with corruption and bureaucracy raises transaction costs, not just for foreign investors, but also for small and medium-sized enterprises. Managers in India report spending more than three times as long dealing with government officials as in Latin America, prompting the World Bank's Chief Economist to observe that 'bureaucratic harassment can be an art form' (Stern 2001).

Developing the institutions and capacities needed to curb systemic corruption should be seen as an integral part of any long-term trade strategy. More effective public scrutiny through parliament and civil-society bodies should be an integral element of trade policy.

Economic infrastructure

The quality of economic infrastructure has an important bearing on competitiveness in global markets. It is the channel through which domestic producers and firms enter global markets, but in many of the poorest countries it is a channel that is blocked at many points. The results are increased transaction costs, reduced competitiveness, and lower returns from trade. The problem presents itself in an extreme form in Africa. Freight and insurance payments on freight from Africa average 15 per cent of export earnings, whereas the average for all developing countries is only 6 per cent (Collier and Gunning 1999). Moreover, costs in Africa have been rising relative to other developing regions. Inefficient ports add to transport costs, which makes countries less competitive. It takes twice as long for firms operating in India to clear goods through ports as for their counterparts in Korea or Thailand, and the costs of shipment are on average 20 per cent higher (Limao and Venables 1999, Stern 2001).

Energy infrastructure has an important bearing on the domestic investment climate. Power supply is a major problem in many countries. For large domestic and foreign companies, it is a problem that can be circumvented through investment in generators. Small and medium-sized enterprises lack this option. Since these are precisely the companies that account for the bulk of employment in developing countries, weakness in power generation is an impediment to making trade work for the poor.

Technological divisions between rich and poor countries threaten to intensify the disadvantages of the poor countries and the advantages of the rich. In some industrialised countries, more than 50 per cent of the population has access to the Internet, compared with fewer than 1 per cent in India. As the high-technology revolution gathers pace, two billion people lack access to electricity. There is just one mainline telephone connection for every two hundred people in the poorest countries, compared with a ratio of 1:2 in rich countries. In the globalised economy, these inequalities translate into inequalities in access to information, opportunities, and markets — and ultimately into ever-widening inequalities in incomes.

Integrated frameworks for poverty reduction

There are some serious institutional difficulties to be confronted in developing strategies to make trade work for the poor. Most developing countries have failed to reform their trade policies as an integral element of their national strategies for reducing poverty and inequality. The compartmentalisation of policy making, coupled with a failure to develop credible poverty-reduction strategies, is at the heart of the problem of poor governance.

When Peru embarked on its rapid trade-liberalisation experiment in the early 1990s, it did so on the basis of targets which emerged following discussions between the Ministry of Finance on the one side, and the World Bank and IMF on the other. The Ministry of Agriculture was barely consulted, even though agricultural markets were targeted for rapid import liberalisation. No assessment of the implications for rural livelihoods, income distribution, or poverty was carried out in advance. The case of Peru is not untypical. In India, trade liberalisation was part of a broader reform package initiated by the Ministry of Finance. Across much of Africa, as in Peru, liberalisation strategies are frequently developed in the context of IMF–World Bank loan agreements, with financial ministries acting as the key players. Social-sector ministries are seldom consulted, except with regard to the details of implementation.

While most developing-country governments share the broad assumption that more open trade is good for the poor, few have sought to place trade reform at the centre of wider poverty-reduction strategies. Indeed, few can lay claim to institutional coherence in such strategies. In many countries, ministries of labour and social affairs have been made responsible for poverty reduction. Since these ministries carry little weight with other government departments, poverty reduction is not a priority in more powerful ministries, such as those dealing with trade and finance (UNDP 2000). Co-ordination between departments is often weak or non-existent. An important exception is Uganda, where the Ministry of Finance manages the national poverty-reduction programmes and is responsible for their cross-departmental implementation.

It had been hoped that the new framework for poverty reduction developed by the IMF-World Bank would help to integrate poverty reduction into all aspects of government policy. The aim of Poverty Reduction Strategy Papers (PRSPs) – documents drawn up by governments and agreed by the IMF–World Bank as a basis for loans and debt relief – is to devise a comprehensive approach to poverty reduction. Unfortunately, as shown in Chapter 5, experience to date has not been encouraging – especially in the case of trade. No national PRSPs to date have even provided a credible analysis of the potential impact of trade liberalisation on the poor, and none has reviewed existing commitments on trade reform in the light of such an analysis.

In view of the enormous impact of trade liberalisation – for better or for worse – on the livelihoods of the poor, it is essential that its implications are subjected to a proper assessment in advance, rather than a retrospective justification on the basis of pre-conceived theory. The timing, sequencing, and coverage of liberalisation all need to be carefully reviewed. For example, it may make sense to liberalise imports for a particular agricultural good after the implementation of an investment programme to develop the capacity of small farmers, but not before. Above all, trade liberalisation should be made part of an informed national public debate about poverty-reduction strategies.

Beyond trade: improving international co-operation

The management of world trade cannot be viewed in isolation from other aspects of international co-operation. As weaker players in the global economy, developing countries need support in other areas, and protection from some of the most destructive aspects of globalisation.

Development assistance

Ten years ago, when they met at the Earth Summit in Rio de Janeiro, rich-country governments acknowledged the critical importance of development assistance in enabling developing countries to participate in the global economy on a more equitable basis. They reaffirmed their commitment to mobilise 0.7 per cent of their gross national product annually in the form of increased aid.

In the decade since that commitment was made, levels of aid have fallen substantially. According to the OECD, official development assistance fell by $13bn between 1992 and 2000. Expenditure on aid as a share of GNP declined by one-third, from 0.33 per cent to 0.22 per cent. The United States, the world's largest economy, is its least generous major donor, dedicating only 0.10 per cent of its GNP to aid (OECD 2001b).

Reductions in aid have had a severe impact on the world's poorest countries. Per capita aid transfers to sub-Saharan African Africa fell from $34 per person in 1994 to $20 in 1999. Over the same period, aid to low-income countries as a group fell by $7bn. There is little doubt that cuts of this order have impaired the capacity of developing countries and poor people to benefit from trade. More broadly, failure to deliver on the pledge to achieve the aid target of 0.7 per cent of GNP translates into a huge loss of financial resources. If the OECD countries actually met this target, aid would increase by about $100bn a year, providing an important source of financing for human development (UN 2001c).

Not all aid is good aid, but well-targeted development assistance can make a real difference in removing some of the barriers to participation in world markets. In agriculture, aid could play an important role in providing the infrastructure needed to reduce marketing costs in marginal areas. Development assistance could enable poor producers to take advantage of export opportunities. Yet aid to agriculture has suffered worse than any other form of development assistance. At the end of the 1990s, aid flows directed towards agriculture were running at one-third of the level in the late 1980s (IFAD 2001).

It is difficult to think of anything that would help to promote more equitable trade relations than action to support the provision of good-quality primary education, free of charge, in poor countries. This is another area in which aid could make an important difference. When they met at the World Education Forum in Dakar, Senegal in 2000, developing-country governments committed themselves to the construction of national plans of action designed to achieve the goal of universal primary education by 2015. Northern governments pledged that no plan would be allowed to fail for want of financial support. The amounts required for financing universal primary education are estimated at $9–10bn per annum, or 0.02 per cent of global GDP (Oxfam 2001i). That represents a small investment, capable of generating a very large return in terms of human development. But cuts in aid, and the inertia of donors, have impeded the development of a global initiative on education.

International co-operation could play a central role in overcoming the health problems that are restricting the benefits of trade in poor countries. The Commission on Macroeconomics and Health, established by the World Health Organisation, estimates that an increase in rich-country support for health services in poor countries, equivalent to 0.1 per cent of their combined GDP, allied to additional financing by developing-country governments, could save 8 million lives a year by 2010 (Commission on Macro Economics and Health 2001). Apart from the immediate gains in terms of human welfare, the economic benefits associated with reducing the burden imposed by diseases such as tuberculosis, malaria, and – above all – HIV/AIDS would be enormous. On one estimate, they would amount to 13 times the additional inputs of development assistance. Despite this enormous potential return, aid for health services declined in the 1990s.

Debt sustainability in low-income countries

Failure to manage international debt problems can undermine the potential benefits of trade in two important ways. First, the claims of foreign creditors can divert a large share of the export earnings that are generated through export activity. This reduces debtor nations' access to essential imports and transfers the benefits of trade away from the producers. Second, debt repayments can absorb a large share of government revenues, undermining the ability of governments to finance public investment in health and education services and rural infrastructure. In both cases, unsustainable debt reduces the benefits of trade, while at the same time limiting a nation's potential to integrate successfully into the international trading system.

International co-operation to solve the problem of unpayable debt has focused on the problems of low-income countries, many of which were devastated by unsustainable debt burdens in the 1980s. The Heavily Indebted Poor Countries (HIPC) Initiative has extended debt relief to 23 countries, mostly in Africa. It has succeeded in reducing the proportion of exports directed towards debt servicing to an average of less than 10 per cent for these countries. However, creditors' demands still weigh heavily on national budgets. In 2001, the countries benefiting from the HIPC Initiative were still spending on average 12 per cent of government revenue on debt servicing (World Bank 2001e). More than half of them were spending more on debt than on primary education, and two-thirds were spending more on debt than on health services (Oxfam 2001i). Although the HIPC Initiative marked an important advance over past efforts, it is difficult to justify public-spending priorities that prioritise debt servicing above investment in education and health services, especially given the scale of deficits in these areas.

Private capital markets

The globalisation of capital markets has brought with it debt-related problems which would have been painfully familiar to central bankers and finance ministries in the 1920s. Instability in capital markets poses a major threat to the trade interests of developing countries, as the experience of a growing number of countries testifies.

In addition to foreign direct investment, the 1990s saw a huge increase in stock and bond investments in developing countries, along with a recovery in commercial bank lending. These private-capital market flows have often been speculative and highly volatile. Between 1996 and 1998, the years before and after the Asian financial crisis, portfolio investment in developing countries fell from $81bn to $37bn, and bank lending from $15bn to minus $103bn (IMF 1999c). The resulting financial collapse devastated East Asia, and was transmitted to Russia and Brazil. In 2001/2002, Argentina became the latest and most spectacular of a growing list of countries suffering from financial crisis, resulting from their inability to meet their obligations to private capital-market creditors.

The large inflows and outflows of private capital experienced by many developing countries have been extremely destabilising in terms of trade prospects. Capital inflows, often attracted by speculative opportunities in financial markets, have the effect of artificially inflating the exchange rate, making exports more costly and imports cheaper. This damages the real productive base of the national economy, generating balance of payments pressures in the process. Financial outflows expose poor countries to severe debt pressures, forcing government to raise interest rates and impose deflationary policies in order to maintain repayments. In 1998, the Indonesian economy contracted by 12 per cent and the Thai economy by 5 per cent. In Thailand, high interest rates led to the closure of up to one thousand businesses a month after the 1997 crash (Bretton Woods Project/Oxfam 2001). Unemployment rose rapidly across the region, along with poverty rates. As the contagion spread to Brazil, the government reduced public spending on social welfare services.

In the late 1920s, it was a financial crisis that acted as a catalyst for the Great Depression. As outflows of capital forced one country after another to reduce imports and squeeze the domestic economy, the international trading system went into steep decline (James 2001). During the latest phase of globalisation, systemic collapse has so far been avoided, albeit narrowly. However, the trade interests of a large group of developing countries have suffered enormous damage. Unsustainable debt owed to private creditors has restricted the capacity of governments to respond. At the end of 2000, repayments due to Argentina's creditors exceeded 90 per cent of the country's export earnings (IMF 2001d). The ultimately unsuccessful efforts to stave off financial collapse resulted in government cutting public spending by one-fifth in 2001, sending the economy into a deep recession (*Economist* 2001d). In the case of Indonesia, more than one-quarter of government revenue was being spent on debt repayments in 1999 (Oxfam 2000b).

The management of capital markets requires urgent attention, at both national and global levels. Nationally, the headlong rush towards the liberalisation of capital markets in developing countries that characterised the 1990s – a rush encouraged by the IMF and Northern governments – was clearly a mistake. One of the reasons why India was able to avoid the impact of this trend was the fact that it maintained a relatively closed capital market, even after it had embarked on rapid trade liberalisation. Capital controls enabled India to avoid an accumulation of a volatile external debt structure, which in turn helped to stabilise exchange rates (Joshi 2001). For many countries, extreme caution in opening capital markets is a precondition for successful integration into international trade.

At the international level, there are two pressing requirements that go beyond the current pre-occupation with improving information flows on lending. The first is the need for a debt-relief framework that enables governments to negotiate the rescheduling and reduction of repayment obligations. In contrast to low-income countries, middle-income countries with unsustainable debts owed to institutional investors and commercial banks have no recourse to a mechanism which limits creditor claims – with the result that creditors' demands can jeopardise long-term economic prospects, including trade prospects (Grieve Smith 2000). The second requirement is for mechanisms to restrict speculative capital flows. Governments should require lenders to maintain higher levels of reserve cover for higher-risk lending, thereby pushing up the cost of loans (Griffith Jones and Cailloux 1999).

In addition to private capital transfers, some \$1.6 trillion worth of foreign exchange is traded every day, much of it on a speculative basis. Foreign-exchange speculation on a huge scale sparked the East Asian crisis. Part of the problem in this case – as in Argentina – was the product of government efforts to defend over-valued currencies. But the threat of speculative currency attacks is a source of continued vulnerability and instability for many developing countries, almost regardless of the state of the real economy.

Support for a currency-transaction tax to deter speculation has grown in rich and poor countries since the East Asian crisis, with the French government adding its approval of the idea in 2001. Because such a tax would fall most heavily on short-term transactions, it could act as a deterrent to speculation and thus help to stabilise exchange rates (Tobin 1994). Some of the revenue generated could be used to supplement aid budgets and finance initiatives in the provision of health and education services. If the tax were levied at 0.1 per cent, and 10 per cent of the revenue were directed to aid, it would be possible to mobilise around \$40bn (estimate derived from data in UN 2001c).

Reforming the WTO governance agenda

The World Trade Organisation is an organisation that is old before its time. Created in 1995 out of the old General Agreement on Tariffs and Trade (GATT), the WTO fundamentally changed the scope and power of the multilateral system in regulating trade. In some respects, its reach and authority exceed that of the IMF and the World Bank. Yet despite its youth, the WTO is dangerously insensitive to the needs of the global trading system in the early twenty-first century. The organisation suffers from weak governance, allied to a remit which extends beyond its sphere of competence, while at the same time it is failing to address some major challenges.

Background

Like the IMF and the World Bank, the WTO owes its existence to the Great Depression of the 1930s. Its origins can be traced back to the efforts of post-1945 leaders to create new global institutions which would prevent the slide into economic decline and nationalist political tensions that led ultimately to war.

Following World War II, the architects of the post-war institutions devised a new set of rules aimed at governing how nations regulated international commerce. Their concern was to create the foundations for a trading system that would provide stability and shared prosperity. They wanted to offer a better alternative to the ruthlessly competitive approach to trade problems that characterised the inter-war period, when countries sought to transfer costs to their trade partners by raising tariffs. The International Trade Organisation (ITO), the body that they proposed, was designed to enforce rules extending beyond the regulation of trade barriers to the stabilisation of commodity markets, the development of global anti-trust arrangements, and the solution of other global financial problems (Noland 2000).

In the event, the ITO was rejected by the US Congress and never came into being. Consequently, the GATT (which had been negotiated in 1947) emerged as the only set of rules for the governance of world trade. Essentially, the GATT was a forum for negotiating reductions in trade barriers. It had no enforcement mechanisms: if a country broke the rules, nothing could be done to penalise it. Furthermore, the system left whole areas of trade – such as textiles and agriculture – outside of the rules (Hoekman and Kostecki 1995).

The transition from the GATT to the WTO was a revolutionary development. The mandate and authority of the WTO are more extensive than those of its predecessor in at least three respects. First, when countries participate in the WTO, they do so on the basis of a 'Single Undertaking': that is, they accept all of its rules unconditionally. Unlike the GATT, the WTO does not offer its members the option to choose which of its rules to enforce. Second, the rules themselves extend far beyond tariffs and non-tariff barriers. As we have seen in this report, they cover investment, services, and intellectual-property rights, and they now include agriculture and textiles. Policy issues previously considered to be the sole preserve of national governments are now subject to scrutiny by the WTO. Finally, the WTO has teeth. Through its dispute-settlement system, countries can challenge each other's policies and, in the event of non-compliance with WTO rules, demand compensation or impose trade sanctions.

Another reason why WTO rules matter is that they operate on a global scale. In November 2001, trade ministers from the WTO's 142 member countries met in Doha to launch a new round of multilateral trade talks. With the accession of China, the vast majority of world trade – and world population – is now governed by principles enshrined in, and enforced by, the WTO.

At one level, developing countries have a great deal to gain from the emergence of a strong multilateral system of trade rules. As the weakest partners in the world trading system, they lack the economic strength to pursue their interests through bilateral action or threats of sanctions. But they also lack the retaliatory capacity to defend themselves against such action or threats. Poor countries need rules more than rich ones do. However, the content of the rules also matters – as does the system of governance through which they are developed and managed. Unfortunately, the WTO fails in both of these areas.

Governance: formal democracy and informal dictatorship

In a formal sense, the WTO is a more democratic institution than either the IMF or the World Bank. Its structure is more directly representative of member states (Helleiner and Oyejide 1999). However, its formal democratic structure obscures a very large democratic deficit at the heart of the multilateral trade system. That deficit enables industrialised countries to construct the rules to their own advantage.

Whereas the IMF and World Bank are governed on the basis of 'one dollar one vote', the WTO is based on a system of 'one country one vote'. The operations of the IMF-World Bank are overseen by Executive Boards, on which voting rights are directly linked to the financial stake of governments. Thus the USA has roughly the same voting share as East Asia, South Asia, Latin America, and sub-Saharan Africa combined. Belgium has more votes than India, and Britain has more than sub-Saharan Africa (Oxfam 2000b). As a result, the countries that implement IMF-World Bank programmes have the weakest voice in management. But the WTO has a different structure. Its governing body is a ministerial conference, which meets every two years. In theory, all countries have equal voting rights. Everyday operations are conducted by a General Council which meets approximately twelve times a year and allows representation from all members on an equal basis.

Another contrast with the IMF-World Bank relates to the role of staff and management. The capacity and remit of WTO staff are very limited (restricted mainly to technical support). As a result, government representatives have more authority in relation to staff than they do in the IMF-World Bank. The total budget of the WTO is only $80m, which is less than the annual travel budget for IMF staff.

For all the appearance of a vibrant working democracy in operation, the WTO suffers from a democratic deficit in two main respects.

- **Capacity and representation.** Rich and poor countries, when defending their own interests, are in very different positions. As the WTO's remit and the scope of its activities have been enlarged, the demands on the capacity of its members' missions have increased. Five years ago there were an estimated 46 meetings of delegates each week, not counting informal discussions (Blackhurst et al. 2001) – and it may be safely assumed that there has been an increase since then. But eleven of the thirty Least Developed Countries, along with another nine developing countries, cannot afford to maintain delegations at the WTO's base in Geneva. Even a very large country such as Bangladesh has only one permanent representative at the WTO. Countries in sub-Saharan Africa suffer particularly severe under-representation, with 19 countries having one delegate each, or no delegate at all. Unequal representation in Geneva is only the most visible part of the problem. Delegates from the USA and the EU are supported by armies of commercial staff, lawyers, academic consultants, and special advisers, monitoring all aspects of WTO agreements in microscopic detail. Large teams of personnel fly in and out of Geneva for key meetings. The resulting differences in negotiating strength create inherent inequalities in the system. For example, agricultural trade is far more important to the economies of sub-Saharan Africa or South Asia than it is to Europe or North America. Yet in negotiations on agricultural trade at the WTO, sub-Saharan Africa and South Asia populations may be represented by one non-specialist representative, who will be facing large teams representing American and European interests.

- **Informal power.** Despite the WTO's principle of 'one country one vote', power relationships are extremely unequal. This fact is reflected in the new issues that have been brought under the WTO's remit. The vast majority of developing countries opposed the extension of that remit into areas such as intellectual-property rights, investment, and commercial services, yet their opposition was ignored or suppressed by recourse to the threat of trade sanctions. In its everyday operation and at its key ministerial meetings, the WTO works by consensus, not by voting. The details of any consensus are usually negotiated in informal meetings – by the so-called 'Green Room' process. These meeting are frequently dominated by the USA, the EU, Japan, and Canada, with developing countries playing a peripheral role (Woods and Narlikar 2001). For example, the Uruguay Round agreement on agriculture was negotiated by the EU and the USA, and presented to the rest of the world for signature. Tensions over the 'Green Room' approach to negotiations provoked a crisis at the 1990s ministerial conference in Seattle. The refusal of developing countries to accept the agenda dictated by industrialised countries was one factor that led to the collapse of negotiations. Since then, there have been some improvements. At the Doha ministerial meeting in November 2001, developing countries were able to secure some important changes in the negotiating agenda, notably through the efforts of countries such as Kenya and India on the issue of intellectual-property rights. More generally, exclusive 'Green Room' meetings seem now to take place less often than before. Even so, the reality of trade negotiations at the WTO is that influence is proportionately related to a country's economic strength and the size of its world market shares.

In the past, the WTO has been dominated by the interests of rich countries. The Seattle ministerial conference may have marked the end of that dominance and a move towards partial power-sharing, but most WTO members, representing the majority of the world's population, still have a limited voice. Ironically, these are precisely the members who are being asked to undertake the most radical domestic reforms in order to comply with WTO rules (Schott and Watal 2000). The consequences of the continued power imbalance in the WTO was apparent at the Doha ministerial meeting, where the governments of developing countries complained that detailed proposals for changing the agenda were rejected by industrialised countries (BRIDGES 2001)

International efforts designed to give poor countries a more effective voice in the WTO have been entirely inadequate. The main programme in this area has been the Integrated Framework (IF) – a programme established by bilateral donors to increase the effectiveness of trade-related technical assistance. Operating under the auspices of six agencies – including the IMF, the World Bank, the WTO, UNDP, and UNCTAD – the Integrated Framework suffers from an inflated, donor-driven mandate, and a very small budget, which in 2001 stood at $6.5m.

Beyond the WTO: the role of TNCs[1]

Issues of governance are not confined to what happens during trade negotiations in Geneva. International institutions like the WTO impinge more directly on the lives of people than ever before. Decisions and policies taken at an international level increasingly shape what governments can and cannot do, affecting the lives of ordinary people in important ways. In the past, people could call their governments to account for the policies that they implemented. Today, governments are able to claim that they have transferred authority to agencies – such as the WTO – that are not accountable to their citizens. This raises important questions about the forces that shape the decisions made by the WTO. How can the principles of democratic accountability be established at a national level?

Mass media interest in the WTO often focuses on street protestors and ritualised confrontations between government and non-government organisations. The press creates the impression that the demonstrators and NGOs exercise a major influence over government actions and decisions taken at the WTO. But the really important actors who determine trade policy are invisible to the general public. The design and implementation of the rules and agreements enshrined in the WTO have been heavily influenced by transnational companies (TNCs). At the 2001 ministerial meeting in Doha, representatives of civil-society groups from across the world were heavily outnumbered by corporate lobbyists. More than two hundred industry groupings were represented, many of the US-based ones as official members of the US delegation. Corporate influence over trade policy starts with commercial companies' capacity to shape the policy options that the major industrialised countries advocate at the WTO. But their influence does not stop at national borders. Unlike governments, who negotiate on the basis of national interests, TNCs have developed global networks of influence that have an important bearing on multilateral rules.

Some industry coalitions have been formidably successful in shaping WTO rules. The US Coalition for Service Industries and the Pharmaceutical Research and Manufacturers of America could, with some justification, claim copyright on large sections on the WTO agreements on services and intellectual-property rights. In the USA, the Administration has established formal channels through which TNCs can help to shape trade policies. The most important of these is the Advisory Committee on Trade Policy and Negotiations (ACTPN), whose 45 members are appointed by the President. Its six policy-advisory committees provide detailed analysis and strategies for US approaches to the WTO and regional trade agreements.

Corporate lines of communication to top policy-makers are less public in Europe, but no less important. The European Round Table of Industrialists – a group including Fiat, Daimler Chrysler, Royal Dutch Shell and British Petroleum – has exercised an enormous influence on approaches to trade policy in European governments. Within the Commission of the European Union, the most important source of guidance to national ministers on trade comes from a specialist committee – the Article 133 Committee – staffed by civil servants and officials of the Commission. Recent evidence has shown that, on various occasions, business representatives have been given access to meetings, minutes, and agendas of the Article 133 Committee – privileges denied to elected Members of the European Parliament.

Corporate lobbying is one of globalisation's growth industries. In Brussels alone, there are approximately 13,000 professional corporate lobbyists – about one for every member of the European Commission Staff. An even more potent means of exercising influence is the interchange of appointments between governments and international institutions on the one side, and big business on the other. The former EU Trade Commissioner, Leon Brittain, is now the Vice-President of Warburg Dillon Reed, and chair of a high-level finance-industry grouping – the Lotis Group – which seeks to advance the WTO agenda on service liberalisation (Wesselius 2001). Former EU Industry Commissioner, Martin Bangemann, now serves on the executive board of the Spanish telephone business, Telefonica – a huge company that is heavily involved in lobbying on investment and services. One of George Bush's chief advisers on health policy during his election campaign, Deborah Steelman, is head of a corporate lobbying firm whose clientele includes the major pharmaceutical companies (Loewenberg 2000). Many of the companies actively involved in lobying on WTO rules are also major donors to political parties. For example, PhRMA donated $17m to the Republican Party during the most recent US elections.

It would be unrealistic to argue that TNCs should cease lobbying governments. Corporations have a legitimate interest in influencing the policies of governments and the rules of the WTO, as do other groups. By definition, they also have financial skills and insights into the working of global markets. Yet it would be naïve to assume that financial power does not confer levels of influence that are denied to other interest groups. This imbalance raises important questions that are central to debates about reform of the WTO. Unlike global pharmaceutical companies, populations in developing countries who are vulnerable to ill-health had no influence over the design of the TRIPs agreement, yet they will pay higher prices for medicines as a result of it.

North American and European grain-trading companies and big farm interests dictate WTO rules on agriculture, which farmers in poor countries must abide by, regardless of their own interests. The examples could be multiplied many times over. There is a widespread – and justified – perception that private vested interests are able to prevail over the public interest in the WTO, and that Northern governments in particular have failed to set limits to corporate power. That perception is one of the reasons for the crisis of legitimacy that confronts the WTO.

Another problem is that governments of developed and developing countries alike have failed to develop credible systems for balancing commitments to the WTO, with a commitment to transparent and accountable governance at home. Voters do not elect delegates to the WTO; they elect governments, which are responsible for representing their country. The problem is that most governments can enter into agreements at the WTO without sufficient reference to public opinion or parliamentary scrutiny, even though those agreements often involve important constraints on national policy. In effect, governments have been devolving power upwards away from elected, national legislative bodies, and towards unelected, unaccountable supra-national bodies.

The mandate of the WTO

The credibility of the WTO has suffered from the efforts of rich countries to extend its authority into new areas, and from the failure of the same countries to increase its effectiveness in old areas of competence. Along with other international institutions, the WTO has also suffered from a wider failure to create a global governance system relevant to the management of a global economy.

As argued in earlier chapters of this report, the terms on which Northern governments have extended the authority of the WTO pose an imminent threat to developing countries, and to prospects for poverty reduction. Northern governments have used the WTO to promote the liberalisation of investment, even in areas where this may conflict with national economic development priorities. The TRIPs agreement will increase the cost of technology transfer to poor countries, thus making them less competitive. Rich countries have used the negotiations on the GATS agreement in an effort to open up new markets in financial sectors, extend opportunities for investors in public utilities, and restrict the right of governments to provide essential services. In each of these cases, powerful private interests have dominated, taking precedence over the interests of poor people.

In this context, there is a strong argument for enshrining in all WTO agreements the principle that, in cases where conflicts of interest arise, governments will in all cases retain the right to prioritise policies for poverty reduction. The WTO should be seen as a vehicle for promoting such policies, not restricting them.

The refusal of rich countries to address long-standing concerns of developing countries was apparent at the 2001 Doha ministerial meeting. As ever, the declaration that emerged from that meeting was full of rhetoric about the need to improve market access, but it offered little of substance in the form of concrete measures to roll back the huge protectionist barriers against the exports of poor countries. The EU, the USA, and Canada made no immediate commitment to improve market access on textiles and clothing, or to adopt wider measures aimed at removing trade restrictions on all exports from the Least Developed Countries. This did not prevent them from pronouncing the Doha meeting as the launch of a 'development round' of trade talks. The development round will not justify its name unless industrialised countries prioritise the need to make progress in areas of key interest to developing countries.

Given the past performance of the WTO, it may seem perverse to point to areas in which the trade-governance agenda needs to be extended. However, in the context of the huge transformations in the world economy that now drive globalisation, there are some very large anomalies. Nowhere are they more apparent than in WTO policy on competition. This issue has now appeared on the WTO agenda, thanks largely to the efforts of the European Union. However, the focus is on opening developing-country markets to corporate investors, notably by prohibiting rules that limit their right to compete in local markets (CUTS 2001). This is another example of an attempt to extend the WTO remit in a direction that suits the interests of rich countries. What is needed is a set of international rules on competition that will address the problems associated with the massive concentration of corporate power in the global economy. While TNCs now operate on a global scale, the legislation that governs their conduct and restricts the abuse of monopolistic power remains national. The large gap between current governance systems and the economic realities of global markets demands new multilateral rules. Those rules should extend the principles that govern the regulation of TNCs beyond national borders to the world economy.

The principles themselves are well established. Governments in industrialised countries have developed extensive legislation designed to prevent the abuse of monopoly power. In the USA, anti-trust legislation dates from the Sherman Act of 1890, when government introduced legislation to stop large companies deriving unfair advantage based on 'inequality of condition, or wealth and opportunity' (Fox and Pitofsky 1997). As corporate power has grown, governments have become increasingly vigilant in protecting the interests of the public. In 2001, anti-monopoly bodies in the USA, the EU, and Canada fined several large pharmaceutical companies – including Merck, Rhone Poulenc, and Hoffman La Roche – almost $2bn for fixing prices in vitamin markets (Oxford Analytica 2001). Authorities in Europe have blocked what would have been the world's largest merger, between Honeywell and General Electric. In the USA, anti-trust bodies have been involved in a continuing dispute with Microsoft. While the content of anti-trust legislation varies widely between countries, the broad concern is to restrict concentrations of market power which might enable companies to artificially inflate prices, limit competition, or engage in price discrimination (Fitzgerald 2001).

That concern is of direct relevance to the global trading system. In many areas of international trade, the concentration of corporate power has reached levels which would set the alarm bells ringing in any industrialised country. Global markets for food grains and most commodities are dominated by a small group of TNCs. The Cargill corporation alone accounts for more than one-quarter of all international maize sales, and Nestlé and Kraft for one-third of the world coffee market. There are also high levels of concentration in sectors such as micro-electronics.

On the world stage, TNCs are free to exploit the advantages that are conferred by monopoly power. At the same time, the rapid growth of intra-company trade has created extensive opportunities for tax evasion, enabling countries to minimise tax liabilities through the manipulation of prices. These are both areas in which international action is urgently needed, yet neither figures on the WTO agenda.

There are striking contrasts between the WTO's system of binding rulings that are ultimately enforced by trade sanctions and multilateral environmental agreements (MEAs), many of which are non-binding and voluntary. The divergence in enforceability can be a serious problem in cases where the two bodies of law contradict one another. For instance, the Montreal Protocol (on ozone depletion), the Convention on

International Trade in Endangered Species, and the Convention on Biological Diversity contain provisions that are arguably at odds with WTO rules (French 2002). Whereas the WTO is committed to removing trade barriers, each of these treaties includes provisions allowing for trade restrictions in the interests of environmental sustainability. Although no country has thus far lodged a formal WTO challenge against an environmental treaty, this remains a distinct possibility. This makes it imperative that the Doha commitment to begin negotiations on the relationship between MEAs and WTO rules should unambiguously state that the former take precedence over obligations under the latter.

An agenda for reform

Making trade work for the poor implies a broad agenda for reform, extending from national governments up to the World Trade Organisation. That agenda overlaps with wider strategies for poverty reduction. Reform of the WTO should address the democratic deficit, while at the same time promoting policies designed to meet the needs of the poorest countries and poorest people.

Specific proposals to improve the position of poor countries and poor people in the international trading system have been presented elsewhere in this report. At the multilateral level, the WTO has outgrown its increasingly unrepresentative system of decision-making. There is an urgent need for democratic renewal, and new approaches to improve transparency and accountability.

- **Increased technical assistance for poor countries through a Financing Facility for Trade-Related Capacity Building.** The main financing mechanism for capacity building in developing countries is the Integrated Framework for Trade-Related Technical Assistance, which is administered by the World Bank, the WTO, UNCTAD, and other agencies. Its budget – at $6.3m – is severely inadequate. The Financing Facility for Trade-Related Capacity Building should develop a budget of around $250m to support a co-ordinated programme of training and other activities to enhance representation among developing countries at the WTO. Funds should also be provided to build the capacity of civil-society groups to engage in debates on trade policy.

- **Greater transparency on informal influence.** National legislation should require governments to disclose all contacts and written submissions relating to trade negotiations. Instead of the current emphasis on ad hoc lobbying, governments should create formal processes for receiving and reviewing submissions on trade policy in advance of key negotiations.

- **Improved transparency and accountability in developing countries.** The WTO should develop and disseminate guidelines on best practice for national consultations between governments and civil society. Trade Policy Reviews should include an assessment of the quality of government consultations with civil society. All governments should submit to their respective legislative bodies an annual report on their activities at the WTO and the implications of those activities for poverty reduction.

- **The development of a Global Anti-Trust Mechanism.** In view of the deepening consolidation of corporate power in the global economy, a new anti-trust investigation agency should be established under WTO auspices to investigate threats to the public interest posed by monopolistic abuse.

As we have argued throughout this report, international trade can work for the poor, or against the poor. Just as in any national economy, economic integration in the global economy can be a source of shared prosperity and poverty reduction, or a source of increasing inequality and exclusion. Managed well, the international trading system can lift millions out of poverty. Managed badly, it will leave whole economies even more marginalised.

At present, trade is badly managed, both at the global level and, in many countries, at the national level. Continuing on the current path is not an option. But a retreat into isolationism would deprive the poor of the opportunities offered by trade. It would counteract a powerful force for poverty reduction. That is why we need a new world trade order, grounded in new approaches to rights and responsibilities and in a commitment to make globalisation work for the poor.

Notes

Chapter 2

1 One study of 20 countries, conducted by the World Bank, found that a 10 per cent increase in average income generated a 20 per cent reduction in income poverty, implying a ratio of growth to poverty reduction of 1:2 (Bruno et al. 1996). Other World Bank research puts the ratio even higher, at 1: 2.6 (Ravallion and Chen 1997). One of the largest cross-country data sets, covering 105 countries, compares outcomes in a range of countries, based on income-distribution patterns (Hanmer and Naschold 1999). This comparison finds a very large difference, with a ratio of growth to poverty reduction of 1:0.9 in low-inequality countries, compared with 1: 0.3 in highly unequal countries.

2 Low inequality is defined as a Gini co-efficient of less than .34, and high inequality as more than .55 (Hanmer, Healey, and Naschold 2000). The Gini co-efficient is a measure of income distribution which captures the scale of departure from a situation of perfect equality (where all people have the same income, and the Gini co-efficient is zero), to total inequality (where one person has all the income, and the Gini co-efficient is 1). The higher the number, the greater the departure from total equality.

3 The income effects of a redistribution of export activity in this context can be thought of as equivalent to a terms-of-trade gain for developing countries resulting from an improvement in relative prices.

4 The Samuelson-Stolper theory provides the standard model in applying comparative advantage to developing countries. It sets out the so-called 'factor price equalisation' theory. This holds that when countries exchange goods, the factors of production that produce those goods will converge towards a common level. In other words, when industrialised countries purchase labour-intensive goods produced in developing countries, the price paid to the factor of production in the exporting country (in this case labour) will rise. Conversely, the price paid in the importing country to workers producing the same goods will fall. (See Chapter 3 on wage inequality in industrialised countries.)

5 US$1 = 14,000 VND.

Chapter 3

1 Purchasing Power Parity (PPP) is an exchange rate between two currencies which would enable the same basket of goods and services to be bought in each country, if costs were converted at that rate. The aim is to make it possible to compare the real purchasing power of incomes. Figures derived from UNDP Human Development Reports for 1994 and 2001.

2 See Chapter 2, note 2.

3 The Producer Support Estimate (PSE) is calculated by the OECD as an indicator of the annual monetary value of transfers from consumers and taxpayers to agricultural producers. The overall PSE monetary value depends on the size and structure of a country's agricultural sector. By contrast, agricultural support expressed as a percentage of gross farm income (% PSE) shows the amount of support to farmers, irrespective of the sectoral structure of a given country. For this reason, the % PSE is the most widely used indicator for comparisons of support across countries.

Chapter 4

1 The trend towards flexible, temporary, seasonal, part-time work with no social provisions or benefits is also termed the 'feminisation of employment'. As the name suggests, women comprise the majority of workers employed on these terms, which means that they bear the brunt of the costs associated with such employment practices.

2 Tariff peaks: Hoekman, Ng, and Olarreaga 2001; PSE: OECD 2001a; tariff escalation: WTO 2001b; average agricultural tariffs: WTO 2001b; MFA phase-out: figures from the International Textiles and Clothing Bureau. Restraining countries were required to liberalise a minimum of 51 per cent of the value of their 1990 imports by stage 3 (on 1 January 2002) of the implementation of the WTO Agreement on Textiles and Clothing. While the USA, EU and Canada have all complied with this requirement technically, they have mainly removed quota restrictions from products that were not exported by developing countries, i.e. quotas that were not imposing a restriction on LDC exports. In terms of % restrained imports in 1990, the USA and EU will have liberalised only 11.7 per cent and 12.2 per cent respectively, that is 23 per cent and 24 per cent of the 51 per cent they should have liberalised by 2002. Average tariffs on textiles and clothing: WTO 2001b; anti-dumping actions: WTO 2001c, WTO 2001b, Reports of the WTO Committee on Anti-Dumping Practices 1995 - 2000 (G/L/34; G/L/123; G/L/204; G/L/268; G/L/340; G/L/404).

3 The Quad countries were ranked from 1 (least protectionist) to 4 (most protectionist) for each indicator, and their scores were added for all indicators. The resulting scores for each country were used to produce the overall ranking.

4 Communication from Rubens A. Barbosa, Brazilian Ambassador to the United States.

5 The following countries are members of the Association of South-East Asian Nations (ASEAN): Brunei, Cambodia, Indonesia, the Lao People's Democratic Republic, Malaysia, Myanmar, the Philippines, Singapore, Thailand, and Vietnam.

6 Private communication from the International Textiles and Clothing Bureau.

7 Official US and EU documents cited in Communication from Uruguay on behalf of members of the ITCB for the Second Major Review of the Implementation of the Agreement on Textiles and Clothing by the WTO Council for Trade in Goods.

8 Private communication from the International Textiles and Clothing Bureau.

9 Home-based work is an important source of employment around the world, particularly for women. Home-based workers comprise a significant share of the workforce in key export industries (Chen, Sebstad, and O'Connell 1999, cited in Baden 2001). In most countries, the proportion of home-workers who are female is high, around 70-80 per cent (Charmes 2000, cited in Baden 2001).

10 However, reducing labour costs is not necessarily an inevitable strategy for Bangladeshi employers seeking to remain competitive. A survey of large textile and clothing traders in Hong Kong showed that the essential factors of competitiveness are political stability, transportation, telecommunications, labour costs, education and training, and the 'ease of doing business', in that order. This shows that higher labour costs can be compensated for by other factors (Centre for Policy Dialogue 2000).

11 The following section on access for Bangladeshi textiles and clothing exports to the EU and US markets is drawn from Bhattacharya and Rahman 2000.

12 1986-88 is the reference period used in the WTO Agreement of Agriculture, against which reduction commitments are calculated.

13 In the EU, these payments now take the form of direct payments to farmers, reflecting production levels either now or in the recent past.

14 Environmental Working Group Farm Subsidy Database for 1996-2000, http://www.ewg.org

15 See Fanjul 2001 for a longer discussion of these issues. In Japan, almost one-third of the smallest farms have disappeared over the last decade. Between 1995 and 2000, the proportion of small rural communities in Japan declined by 3.5 per cent, with the number of towns with a population fewer than 100 households showing a decline of 24 per cent. In most European countries where rural land accounts for the majority of the territory, such as Spain, Italy, and Greece, the active rural population has been reduced to one-fifth of its numbers in the 1950s. The US Department of Labor expects that the United States will lose 13.2 per cent of all family farm jobs between 1998 and 2008, the largest projected job loss among all occupations.

16 The average costs of EU production were compiled by Andreas Schneider of Wye College, with additional information on sugar obtained from LMC International. The data sources used to compile the figures include Home Grown Cereals Authority, Eurostat, OECD Commodity Outlook, Agrarbericht,

References

UK Farm Business Survey. The US figures draw on IATP 2000.
17 102nd Landon Lecture, by Dan Glickman, 8 September 1995.
18 European Commission Démarche on US food-aid donations.

Chapter 5

1 'Trade restrictiveness' refers to measures which serve to raise the price of imports, driving a wedge between local prices and world prices. The IMF has developed a composite index of trade restrictions to rank countries on a scale of 1(very open) to 10 (very restrictive). The TRI combines the major elements of trade restrictiveness, including the average level of tariff protection and the coverage of non-tariff barriers such as quotas.
2 Econometrics involves the use of mathematical models to analyse the relationship between different variables, establishing correlations based on movement. In a simple model, econometrics can be used to analyse how movement in the price of a good is correlated to the quantity of the good demanded by consumers. In the context of the studies analysed in this chapter, econometrics has been used to analyse the relationship between economic growth and income distribution, and between economic growth and openness to trade.
3 The position summarised here refers to the work of the World Bank's Development Research Group, which reflects only one of the many views to be found among World Bank staff, albeit the one that has exercised most influence.
4 Changes in the incidence of poverty are measured by taking two comparable surveys in the 1990s. Where possible, we have used the World Bank's $1-a-day poverty line. In other cases we have used official national poverty surveys.

Chapter 6

1 Based on data from the ICO, covering the periods October 1994-September 1995, and July 2000-June 2001.
2 In 1999, the ratio of stocks to annual consumption was as follows: cocoa 40 per cent; coffee 37 per cent; sugar 49 per cent; cotton 37 per cent.
3 Derived from ICCO estimates.
4 Based on a retail price of $2 for coffee. Assumes 8 grammes of roast/ground coffee per cup.

Chapter 7

1 This figure assumes a profit rate on export production of 10 per cent and a corporate tax rate foregone of 20 per cent on exports of $4.2bn.
2 This section draws on Atkinson 2001a and 2001b.
3 This section is based on Brown 2001b.

Chapter 8

1 Based on information from Square Pharmaceuticals, Bangladesh.
2 For a review of the coping strategies associated with rising health-care costs, see Russell (1996), Watkins (2001b).
3 For an analysis of the implications for intellectual property rules on biotechnology, see Mayne 2002, on which this section draws.
4 This section draws on Dhanarajan 2001.
5 The exception is contained in Article 1(3) of the GATS. It is very narrow, in that it extends only to public monopolies providing services on a non-commercial basis. Since most public services are provided through a mixture of public and private suppliers, or include commercial aspects, they would not qualify for exclusion.

Chapter 9

1 This section draws on Dhanarajan 2002.

ABARE (2000) 'US and EU Agricultural Support: Who Does it Benefit?', Australian Bureau of Agricultural and Resource Economics, Current Issues 20.2, Canberra: ABARE

Abrams, P. and A. Harney (2001) 'Chip overload', *Financial Times,* 3 September 2001

ActionAid (1999) 'Patents and Food Security', ActionAid Briefing 5, London: ActionAid

Aganon, M. et al. (1998) 'Strategies to empower women workers in the Philippines export zones', *Philippine Journal of Labour and Industrial Relations* 18(1-2): 106-59, Quezon: University of the Philippines

Agosin, M. et al. (2000) *Globalisation, Liberalisation and Sustainable Human Development: Progress and Challenges in Central American Countries*, Geneva: UNCTAD/UNDP

Ahuja, V. et al. (1997) *Everyone's Miracle? Revisiting Poverty and Inequality in East Asia*, Washington: World Bank

Akiyama, T. et al. (2001) 'Commodity Market Reforms: Lessons of Two Decades', Washington: World Bank

Alden, A. (2000) 'Coffee with conscience', *Financial Times,* 4 October 2000

Alden, E. (2001) 'NAFTA lifts investor protection pressure', *Financial Times,* 2 August 2001

Amsden, A. (2000) 'Industrialisation under WTO Law', UNCTAD X, High Level Round Table on Trade and Development, Geneva: UNCTAD

Anderson, K., B. Dimaranan, J. Francois, T. Hertel, B. Hoekman, and W. Martin (2001) 'The Cost of Rich (and Poor) Country Protection to Developing Countries', CIES Discussion Paper No. 0136, Adelaide: Centre for International Economic Studies

Andrae, G. and B. Beckman (1985) *The Wheat Trap: Bread and Underdevelopment in Nigeria*, London: Zed Books, in association with Scandinavian Institute of African Studies

Anwar, T. (2000) 'Impact of Globalisation and Liberalisation on Growth, Employment and Poverty: A Case Study of Pakistan', Lahore: Central Bank of Pakistan

Appendini, K. (1994) 'Agriculture and farmers within NAFTA: a Mexican perspective', in V. Bulmer-Thomas et al. (eds.): *Mexico and the North American Trade Agreement*, London: Macmillan

Appleton, S. (1996) 'Education and agricultural productivity: evidence from Uganda', *Journal of International Development* 8(3)

Appleton, S. et al. (1999a) 'Changes in Poverty in Uganda 1992-97', Working Paper 99.22, Oxford: Oxford University, Centre for the Study of African Economies

Appleton, S. (1999b) 'Income and Human Development at the Household Level: Evidence From Six Countries', background paper prepared for the 2000 *World Development Report*, Washington: World Bank

Aristotle (1967) *Politics*, Oxford: Oxford University Press

Arndt, S. (1998) 'Super-specialisation and the gains from trade', *Contemporary Economic Policy* 56: 480-5, Oxford: Oxford University Press

Arnold, W. (2001) 'Japan's electronic slump takes a toll on Southeast Asia', *New York Times,* 1 September 2001

Association for Rational Use of Medication in Pakistan (2001a) 'Milking Profits: How Nestlé Puts Sales Ahead of Infant Deaths', Islamabad: The Network

Association for Rational Use of Medication in Pakistan (2001b) 'Feeding Fiasco: Pushing Commercial Infant Foods in Pakistan', Islamabad: The Network

Atkinson, J. (2001a) 'Transnational Companies, Employment and Investment', Melbourne: Oxfam Community Aid Abroad

Atkinson, J. (2001b) 'The Electronics Industry in Malaysia', Melbourne: Oxfam Community Aid Abroad

Baden, S. (1994) 'Gender Issues in Agricultural Liberalisation', Briefing on Development and Gender Report 41, Brighton: Institute for Development Studies, University of Sussex

Baden, S. (2001) 'Researching Homework and Value Chains in the Global Garments Industry: An Annotated Resource List and Binder', prepared for Women in Informal Employment Globalising and Organising, Cambridge, Mass: WIEGO

Bale, H. (2001) 'Patents and Public Health: A Good or Bad Mix?' www.pfizer-forum.com/

Bank, D. (1996) 'Cisco to support format to ease Internet traffic', *Wall Street Journal*, 9 December 1996

Bannister, G. and K. Thugge (2001) 'International Trade and Poverty Alleviation', IMF Working Paper 1/54, Washington: IMF

Barraclough, S. and K. Ghimire (2000) *Agricultural Expansion and Tropical Deforestation: Poverty, International Trade, and Land Use*, London: Earthscan

Barrientos, S. (1996) 'Social clauses and women workers in Latin America', *New Political Economy* 1(2), London: Carfax

Barrientos, S. et al. (1999a) *Women and Agribusiness: Working Miracles in the Chilean Fruit Export Sector*, Basingstoke: Macmillan

Barrientos, S. et al. (1999b) 'Gender and Codes of Conduct: A Case Study from Horticulture in South Africa', London: Christian Aid

Barrientos, S. et al. (2001) 'Ethical trade and South African deciduous fruit exports – addressing gender sensitivity', *European Journal of Development Research* 12: 140-58

Barro, R. and J. Lee (1997) 'Schooling Quality in a Cross-Section of Countries', National Bureau of Economic Research Working Paper W6198, Cambridge, MA: NBER

Bates, R. (1981) *Markets and States in Tropical Africa: the Political Basis of Agricultural Policies*, Berkeley: University of California Press

Behrman, J. et al. (2000) 'Economic Reforms and Wage Differentials in Latin America', Washington: Inter-American Development Bank

Ben-David et al. (2000) 'Trade, Income Disparity and Poverty', WTO Special Study 5, Geneva: WTO

Bennel, P. (2000) 'Human Resource Development and Globalisation: What Should Low Income Developing Countries Do?' Background Paper for UK White Paper on Globalisation and Development, Brighton: University of Sussex, Institute for Development Studies

Benson, M. (1997) 'The chips are down: California loses out on semi-conductor plants', *Wall Street Journal*, 28 May 1997

BER (Bureau Européen de Recherches) in association with the Institute of Development Studies, University of Sussex (2001) 'EU Agricultural and Fisheries Market Access for Developing and Transition Countries: EU Market Analysis', Brussels: BER

Bhagwati, J. (2000) 'Globalisation and Appropriate Governance', World Institute for Development Economics Research, Annual Lecture, Helsinki: WIDER

Bhagwati, J. and T. Srinivasan (1999) 'Outward Orientation and Development: Are Revisionists Right?', http://www.columbia.edu/~jb38/Krueger.pdg

Bhattacharya, D. and M. Rahman (1999) 'Female Employment Under Export-Propelled Industrialisation', UNRISD Occasional Paper, Geneva: UNRISD

Bhattacharya, D. and M. Rahman (2000a) 'Experience with Implementation of the WTO Agreement on Textiles and Clothing', Occasional Paper 7, Dhaka: Centre for Policy Dialogue

Bhattacharya, D. and M. Rahman (2000b) 'Seeking Fair Market Access for Bangladesh Apparels in the USA: A Strategic View', Dhaka: Centre for Policy Dialogue

Bhattacharya, D. and M. Rahman (2000c) 'Regional Cumulation Facility under EC-GSP: Strategic Response from Short and Medium Term Perspectives', Policy Briefing, Dhaka: Centre for Policy Dialogue

Bird, M. (2001) 'Campaigning on Trade Issues Works! A Report on Illegal Logging in Cambodia', Oxford: Oxfam

Bird, G. and R. Rajan (2001) 'Economic Globalisation: How Far and How Much Further?' Adelaide University: Centre for International Economic Studies, Discussion Paper 0117

Blackhurst, R., B. Lyakurwa, and A. Oyejide (2001) 'Options for improving Africa's participation in the WTO', in B. Koekman and W. Martin (eds.): *Developing Countries and the WTO: A Pro-Active Agenda*, Oxford: Blackwell

Bloom, D. and M. Murshed (2001) 'Globalisation, Global Public "Bads", Rising Criminal Activity and Growth', discussion paper 2001/50, Helsinki: WIDER

Boyer, D. (2001) 'Trade: The Connection Between Trade and Sustainable Livelihoods', Washington: Oxfam America

Brandon, K. (1998) 'NAFTA at five: promises and realities', *Chicago Tribune*, 29 November 1998

Brandt, W. (1980) *North–South: A Programme for Survival*, London: Pan

von Braun, J. et al. 'Irrigation Technology and Commercialisation of Rice in the Gambia: Effects on Women', Research Report 75, International Food Policy Research Institute, Washington: IFPRI

Bretton Woods Project/Oxfam (2001) 'Go With the Flows? Capital Account Liberalisation and Poverty', London and Oxford: Bretton Woods Project and Oxfam

BRIDGES (2001) 'New ministerial text to hand ministers and challenge in Doha', BRIDGES Weekly Trade News Digest, International Centre for Trade and Sustainable Development, 30 October 2001, Geneva: BRIDGES

Brown, G. (2001) Speech to the US Federal Reserve in New York, 16 November 2001, reproduced in 'Tackling Poverty: A Global New Deal', HM Treasury, London, February 2002

Brown, O. (2001a) 'Brand New World: the Power of Brands in the New Economy', Oxford: Oxfam

Brown, O. (2001b) 'Up in Smoke: Marketing Tobacco in the Developing World', Oxford: Oxfam

Brown, O. (2001c) 'Transnational Companies in the Global Economy', Oxford: Oxfam

Bruno, M. et al. (1996) 'Equity and Growth in Developing Countries: Old and New Perspectives on the Policy Issues', Policy Research Working Paper 1563, Washington: World Bank

Bucholz (1989) *New Ideas from Dead Economists,* Penguin (USA)

Buitelaar, R. and R. Perez (2000) '*Maquila,* economic reform and corporate strategies', *World Development* 28(9): 1627-42

Burr, C. (2000) *Grameen Village Phone: Its Current Status and Future Prospects,* Geneva: International Labour Organisation

Burtless, G. et al. (1998) *Globaphobia,* Washington: The Brookings Institution Press

Bussolo, M. and H. Lecomte (1999) 'Trade Liberalisation and Poverty', Overseas Development Institute Briefing, London: ODI

Camuffo, A. and G. Volpato (2000) 'Rolling Out a "World Car"', University of Venice Working Paper, Ca Foscari University

Carlton, J. (1999) 'A global effort for poor coffee farmers', *Wall Street Journal,* 23 November 1999

Cashin, P., J. McDermott and A. Scott (1999) *Booms and Slumps in World Commodity Prices,* Washington: IMF

Cassiolato, J. and H. Lastres (1999) 'Local, National and Regional Systems of Innovation in Mercosur', paper presented at Conference on National Innovation Systems, June, Rebild, Denmark

Castels, M. (2000) 'Information technology and global capitalism', in W. Hutton, and A. Giddens (eds.): *On the Edge,* London: Jonathan Cape

Chang, H-J. (2001) 'Intellectual Property Rights and Economic Development – Historical Lessons and Emerging Issues', Background Paper for 2001 Human Development Report, New York: UNDP

Chen, Sebstad, and O'Connell (1999), cited in Baden (2001)

Child Health Development Centre/Oxfam (1999) 'Public Health and Education in Uganda: Evidence from Four Survey Sites', Oxford: Oxfam GB

China Labour Watch (2001a) 'Merton Company Ltd', November 2001, Hong Kong: China Labour Watch

China Labour Watch (2001b) 'Dongguan Elegant Top Shoes', Hong Kong: China Labour Watch

Christian Aid (2001) 'The Scorched Earth: Oil and War in Sudan' London: Christian Aid

Chudnovsky, D. (1999) 'Multinational enterprises, globalisation and economic development: the case of Argentina in the 1990s', in N. Hood and S. Young (eds.): *The Globalisation of Multinational Enterprise Activity and Economic Development,* London: Macmillan

Coalition for Service Industries (2001) 'US Services Trade Remains in Surplus', press statement, Washington, 18 May 2001

Cohen, J. (2001) 'Harnessing biotechnology for the poor', *Journal of Human Development* 2

Collier, P. and J. Gunning (1999) 'Explaining African economic performance', *Journal of Economic Literature* 37: 64-111

Commission on Macroeconomics and Health (2001) 'Report of the Commission on Macroeconomics and Health', Geneva: World Health Organisation

Contreras, D. et al. (2000) 'Income Distribution in Chile, 1990-1998', Department of Economics, Universidad de Chile: Santiago

Corbridge, S. and J. Harriss (2000) *Reinventing India*, Cambridge: Polity Press

Cornia, A. (2000) 'Inequality and Poverty in the Era of Liberalisation and Globalisation', World Institute for Development Economics Research, Helsinki: WIDER

Correa, C. (2000) *Intellectual Property Rights, the WTO, and Developing Countries*, London: Zed

Coyle, D. (2000) 'Does the new economy change everything?' *Prospect* 49: 16-20

Crabtree, J. (2001) 'Peru: Agricultural Trade Liberalisation in Peru', Oxford: Oxfam

Cragg, M. and M. Epelbaum (1996) 'The Premium for Skills in LDCs: Evidence from Mexico', New York: Columbia University

Crawford, R. (2000) 'Adidas' Human Rights Policy and Euro 2000', INSEAD

Crawshaw, S. (2001) 'Coffee prices are slumping (not that you would know it in Starbucks)', *Independent*, 17 May 2001

CUTS (2001) 'Viewpoint on Multilateral Competition Policy', CUTS Newsletter, September, New Delhi: CUTS

Dagdeviren, H. et al. (2000) 'Redistribution Does Matter: Growth and Redistribution for Poverty Reduction', Geneva: International Labour Organisation

Dahou, K. et al. (2000) 'Socio-Economic and Environmental Impacts of Senegalese Fishery Support Mechanisms', Dakar: ENDA

Dancourt, O. (1999) 'Neoliberal reforms and macroeconomic policy in Peru', *CEPAL Review* 67, New York: UN

Das, B. (2001) 'Strengthening Developing Countries in the WTO', Third World Network, Trade and Development Series 8, Penang: Third World Network

Datt, G. and M. Ravaillon (1998) 'Farm productivity and rural poverty in India', *Journal of Development Studies* 34: 62-85

Davis, R. (1966) 'The rise of protectionism in England', *Economic History Review* 19: 306-17

Deininger, K. and L. Squire (1995) 'Measuring Income Inequality', Washington: World Bank

Delgado, C. (1995) 'Agricultural Transformation: the Key to Broad-Based Growth and Poverty Alleviation in sub-Saharan Africa', Washington: International Food Policy Research Institute (IFPRI)

Desai, M. et al. (2001) *Sharing the Spoils: Taxing International Human Capital Flows*, Washington: National Bureau of Economic Research

Deutsche Bank (2000) 'Soluble Coffee: A Pot of Gold?', London: Deutsche Bank

DFID (1999) 'Better Health for Poor People', International Development Target Strategy Paper, London: DFID

DFID (2000) *Eliminating World Poverty: Making Globalisation Work for the Poor*, London: HMSO

DFID (2001) 'Standards as Barriers to Trade: Issues for Development', DFID background briefing, London: Department for International Development

Dhanarajan, S. (2001) 'The General Agreement on Trade in Services', Oxford: Oxfam

Dollar, D. and A. Kraay (2001a) 'Growth is Good for the Poor', World Bank Policy Research Working Paper No.2587, Washington: World Bank

Dollar, D. and A. Kraay (2001b) 'Trade, Growth, and Poverty', World Bank Policy Research Working Paper No. 2199, Washington: World Bank

Dongguan Information Centre (2001) Located at http://www.3cexpo.com/english/index.asp (accessed January 02)

Drahos, P. (1995) 'Global property rights in information: the story of TRIPs at the GATT', *Prometheus* 13

Drahos, P. (2001) 'BITs and BIPs: Bilateralism in Intellectual Property', Oxford: Oxfam

Drahos, P. and J. Braithwaite (2002) *Information Feudalism*, London: Earthscan

DSS (2000) 'Households Below Average Income Survey, 1994/5-98/9', London: Department of Social Security

Easterly, B. (2001) *The Elusive Quest for Growth*, Oxford: Blackwell

ECLA (1998) 'Trade and Industrial Policies: Past Performance and Future Prospects', Santiago: Economic Commission for Latin America

ECLA (1999) 'Foreign Investment in Latin America and the Caribbean 1999', Santiago: Economic Commission for Latin America

ECLA (2000a) 'The Equity Gap: A Second Assessment', Santiago: Economic Commission for Latin America

ECLA (2000b) 'Equity, Development and Citizenship', Santiago: Economic Commission for Latin America

ECLA (2000c) 'Social Panorama of Latin America 1999-2000' Santiago: Economic Commission for Latin America

ECLA (2000d) 'Foreign Investment in Latin America and the Caribbean 2000', Santiago: Economic Commission for Latin America

ECLA (2001) 'Social Panorama of Latin America 2000-2001', Santiago: Economic Commission for Latin America

Edwards, S. (1993) 'Openness, trade liberalisation and growth in developing countries', *Journal of Economic Literature* 31: 1358-93

Edwards, S. (1998) 'Openness, productivity and growth: what do we really know?', *The Economic Journal* 108: 383-98

Elliott, K.A. (2001a) 'Finding Our Way on Trade and Labour Standards', Institute for International Economics, Policy Briefs 01-5, Washington: IIE

Elliott, K.A. (2001b) 'The ILO and Enforcement of Core Labour Standards', Institute for International Economics, Policy Briefs 00-6, Washington: IIE

Elson, D. (1999) 'Labour markets as gendered institutions: equality, efficiency, and empowerment issues', *World Development* 27(3): 611-27

ENDA (2001) 'A Case Study on the Senegalese Fisheries Sector (Report Prepared for UNEP)', Dakar: ENDA

Essick, K. (2001) 'A call to arms', *The Industry Standard*, 11 June 2001, London: Ethical Trading Initiative

Faini, R. et al. (1999) 'Trade and migration', in R. Faini et al.: *Migration*, Cambridge: Cambridge University Press

FairTrade Foundation (2000) Producers Stories http://www.fairtrade.org.uk/belize.htm (accessed February 2002)

Fanjul, G. (2001), 'Northern Agricultural Policies: The Long and Winding Road to Coherence', Madrid: Intermón

FAO (1998) 'Potential for Agriculture and Rural Development in Latin America and the Caribbean', Rome: Food and Agriculture Organisation

Featherstone, L. and D. Henwood (2001) 'Clothes encounters', *Lingua Franca* 11(2)

Feeney, P. (2001), 'Regional Trade and Investment Agreements', Oxford: Oxfam

Feenstra, R. et al. (1997) 'Testing Endogenous Growth in South Korea and Taiwan', National Bureau of Economic Research Working Paper No 6028, Washington: NBER

Filmer, D., J. Hammer and L. Pritchett (1997) 'Health Policy in Poor Countries', Washington: World Bank

Filmer, D. and L. Pritchett (1999) 'The effect of wealth on educational attainment', *Population and Development Review*, March 1999

Financial Times (2000) 'India plans to plug the brain drain', 24 April 2000

Financial Times (2001) 'Patent abuse', 22 October 2001

Finger, J. Michael and Ludger Schuknecht (1999) 'Market Access Advances and Retreats: The Uruguay Round and Beyond', World Bank Working Paper No. 2232, 1 November, Washington: World Bank

Fitzgerald, V. (2001) 'Regulating Large International Firms', Working Paper 64, Queen Elizabeth House Working Paper Series, Oxford University: QEH

Folbre, N. (1994) *Who Pays for the Kids: Gender and the Structures of Constraint*, London: Routledge

Fontana, M. et al. (1998) 'Global Trade Expansion and Liberalisation: Gender Issues and Impacts', Briefings on Gender and Development 42, London: Department for International Development

Fox, E. and R. Pitofsky (1997) 'The United States', in E. Graham and J. Richardson (eds.): *Global Competition Policy*, Washington: Institute for International Economics

Frankel, F. (1978) *India's Political Economy 1947-77: The Gradual Revolution*, Princeton: Princeton University Press

Frankel, J. and D. Romer (1999) 'Does trade cause growth?', *American Economic Review* 89: 379-99

Freeland, C. (1993) 'Blood, sweat and tears – for others', *Financial Times*, 9 Dec 1993

Frempong, J. (1991) *The Vampire States in Africa: The Political Economy of Decline in Ghana*, London: James Currey

French, H. (2002) 'Reshaping global governance', in World Watch Institute (ed.) *State of the World 2002*, London: Earthscan

Fukasaku, K. (2000) 'Special and Differential Treatment for Developing Countries: Does It Help Those Who Help Themselves?', World Institute for Development Economics Research, Working Paper 197, Helsinki: WIDER

Fushrum, V. and R. Winslow (2001) 'Cipro demand tests Bayer's capacity and public relations', *Wall Street Journal*, 21 October

Galeano, E. (1973) *Open Veins of Latin America* (translated by Cedric Belfrage), New York: Monthly Review Press

Ghosh, J. (2000) *Globalisation, Export-Oriented Employment for Women and Social Policy: A Case Study of India*, Delhi: Jawarhalal Nehru University

Gibbon, P. (2000) 'Global Commodity Chains and Economic Upgrading in Less Developed Countries', Centre for Development Research Working Papers 0.2, Copenhagen: Centre for Development Research

Gilbert, C. (1995) 'International Commodity Control: Retrospect and Prospect', Background Paper for 1994 Global Economic Prospects, Washington: World Bank

Gilbert, C. (1996) 'International commodity agreements: an obituary', *World Development* 24(1): 1-19

Gilbert, C. (1997) *Cocoa Market Liberalisation*, London: The Cocoa Association of London

Gitli, E. (1997) 'Maquiladora Industries in Central America', Geneva: International Labour Organisation

Global Exchange (2001a) 'Still Waiting for Nike To Do It', California: Global Exchange

Global Exchange (2001b) 'Global Economy Update', California: Global Exchange http://www.globalexchange.org/economy/ (accessed February 2002)

Global Witness (2001) 'Taylor-Made: The Pivotal Role of Liberia's Forests in Regional Conflict', London: Global Witness

Glewwe, P. et al. (2000) 'Who Gained from Vietnam's Boom in the 1990s? An Analysis of Poverty and Inequality Trends', Development Research Group, Washington: World Bank

Goldsmith, E. (2001) 'Development as colonialism', in E. Goldsmith and J. Mander (eds.): *The Case Against the Global Economy*, London: Earthscan

Goodison, P. (2001) 'The Future of the Common Agricultural Policy: Implications for Developing Countries', Oxford: Oxfam

Gould, D. and W. Gruben (1996) 'The role of intellectual property rights in economic growth', *Journal of Development Economics* 48: 323-50

Government of Honduras (2001) 'Poverty Reduction Strategy Paper', Washington: World Bank

Government of Uganda (2001) 'Poverty Reduction Strategy Paper', Kampala: Ministry of Finance

Government of Vietnam (2001) 'Interim Poverty Reduction Strategy Paper', Hanoi: Ministry of Finance

GRAIN (1998) 'Biopiracy', Barcelona: GRAIN

GRAIN (1999) 'Plant Variety Protection to Feed Africa? Rhetoric versus Reality', Barcelona: GRAIN

Graham, E. (2001) 'Fighting the Wrong Enemy', Washington: Institute for International Economics

Green, D. and S. Priyardarshi (2001), 'Proposal for a "Development Box" in the WTO Agreement on Agriculture', London and Geneva: CAFOD and South Centre

Grieve Smith, J. (2000) *Closing the Casino: Reform of the Global Financial System*, London: Fabian Society

Griffith Jones, S. and J. Cailloux (1999) 'Encouraging the Longer-Term: Institutional Investors and Emerging Markets', Discussion Paper Series 16, New York: UNDP

Gwatkin, D. and M. Guillot (1999) 'The Burden of Disease Among the Global Poor: Current Situation, Future Trends and Implications for Strategy', Washington: World Bank

Haddad, L. et al. (1995) 'The gender dimensions of economic adjustment policies: potential interactions and evidence to date', *World Development* 23(6)

Hanlon, J. (2001) 'Mozambique and the Potential for a Campaign in Europe on Sugar – The Position Inside Mozambique'. Pretoria: Oxfam

Hanmer, L. (2000) 'Halving Global Poverty: How Important is Income Inequality?', ODI Working Paper, London: Overseas Development Institute

Hanmer, L. and F. Naschold (1999) 'Are the International Development Targets Attainable?', London: Overseas Development Institute

Hanmer, L., J. Healey and F. Naschold (2000) 'Will Growth Halve Poverty by 2015?', ODI Poverty Briefing No. 8, London: Overseas Development Institute

Hanson, G. (2001) 'Should Countries Promote Foreign Direct Investment?', G-24 Discussion Paper Series, Geneva: UN

Harrison, A. (1998) 'Volkswagen builds its first Unix plant', *Software Magazine*, January

Harrison, A and G. Hanson (1999) 'Who Gains From Trade Reform? Some Remaining Puzzles', Working Paper 6915, National Bureau of Economic Research, Cambridge (Mass): NBER

Harrison, A. and A. Revenga (1998) 'Labour markets, foreign investment, and trade policy reform', in J. Nash and W. Takacs (eds.): *Trade Policy Reform: Lessons and Implications*, Washington: World Bank

Hazeleger, B. (2001) 'EU Sugar Policy: Assessment of Current Impact and Future Reform', The Hague: Novib

Helleiner, G. and A. Oyejide (1999) 'Global economic governance, global negotiations and the developing countries', in UNDP (ed.): 'Globalisation with a Human Face', background papers for *Human Development Report 1999*, Vol. 1, New York: UNDP

Hellin, J. and S. Higman (2001a) 'The Impact of the Power of the Multinational Companies on the Banana Sector in Ecuador', Oxford: Oxfam

Hellin, J. and S. Higman (2001b) 'Quinua and Food Security in Ecuador, Peru, and Bolivia', Oxford: Oxfam

Hemispheric Social Alliance (2001) 'NAFTA Investor Rights Plus: An Analysis of the Draft Investment Chapter of the FTAA http://www.art-us.org/Docs/Invest-eng.pdf (accessed February 2002)

Hilary, J. (2001) 'The Wrong Model: GATS, Trade Liberalisation and Children's Right to Health', Briefing Report, London: Save the Children

Hirst, P. and G. Thompson (1995) *Globalisation in Question*, Oxford: Blackwell

Hoekman, B. and M. Kostecki (1995) *The Political Economy of the World Trading System: From GATT to WTO*, Oxford: Oxford University Press

Hoekman, B, F. Ng, and M. Olarreaga (2001), 'Eliminating Excessive Tariffs on Exports of Least Developed Countries', World Bank Working Paper No. 2604, Washington: World Bank

Hong Kong Christian Industrial Committee (2001) 'Beware of Mickey: Disney's Sweatshop in China', Hong Kong: Hong Christian Industrial Committee

Horton, S. (1999) 'Marginalisation revisited: women's market work and pay, and economic development', *World Development* 27(3): 571-82

Howell, J. and U. Kambhampati (1999) 'Liberalisation and labour: the fate of retrenched workers in the cotton textile industry in India', *Oxford Development Studies* 27(1)

Human Rights Watch (2000) 'The International Monetary Fund's Staff Monitoring Program for Angola: The Human Rights Implications', 22 June 2000, updated 25 September 2000, New York: Human Rights Watch

Humphrey, J. and A. Oetero (2000) 'Strategies for Diversification and Adding Value to Food Exports: A Value-Chain Perspective', Geneva/Brighton: UNCTAD/IDS, University of Sussex

Humphreys, J. (1999) 'Globalisation and supply chain networks: the auto industry in Brazil and India', in G. Gereffi et al. (eds.): *Global Production and Local Jobs*, Geneva: International Institute for Labour Studies

IBFAN (2001) 'Breaking the Rules: Stretching the Rules', Penang: International Baby Food Action Network

ICFTU (1998) 'Fighting for Workers' Human Rights in the Global Economy', Geneva: International Confederation of Free Trade Unions

ICFTU (1999) 'World Apart: Women and the Global Economy', Brussels: International Confederation of Free Trade Unions

ICFTU (2001) 'Global Unions Report', Brussels: International Confederation of Free Trade Unions

ICO (1998) 'Cocoa and Chocolate in the 21st Century', London: International Cocoa Organisation

ICO (2001) 'Answers to Questions', London: International Cocoa Organisation

IFAD (2001) 'Rural Poverty Report', Rome: IFAD

IIED (2001) '"Citizen Juries" in Andhra Pradesh', http://www.poptel.

org.uk/iied/agri/IIEDcitizenjuryAP1.html (accessed February 2002)

IISD/WWF (2001) 'Private Rights, Public Problems: A Guide to NAFTA's Controversial Chapter on Investor Rights', Winnipeg/Washington: International Institute for Sustainable Development/WWF-US

IMF (1997) 'Trade Liberalisation in Fund-Supported Programmes', Policy Development and Review Department, Washington: IMF

IMF (1998) 'The External Review of the Enhanced Structural Adjustment Facility', Washington: IMF

IMF (1999a) 'Haiti Staff Report', Washington: IMF

IMF (1999b) 'International Financial Statistics CD-Rom', Washington: IMF

IMF (1999c) 'World Economic Outlook', Washington: IMF

IMF (2000a) 'Article 4 Consultation: Haiti', Washington: IMF

IMF (2000b) 'Cambodia: Memorandum of Economic and Financial Policies for 2001', Washington: IMF

IMF (2001a) *World Economic Outlook*, Washington: IMF

IMF (2001b) 'Trade Policy Conditionality in Fund-Supported Programmes', Policy Development and Review Department, Washington: IMF

IMF (2001c) 'Memorandum of Economic and Financial Policies of the Government of the Republic of Burundi', September 2001 Washington: IMF

IMF (2001d) 'IMF Augments Argentina Stand-by Credit to $21.5bn', External Relations Departments Press Briefing, 7 September, Washington: IMF

IMF/IDA (2001) 'Poverty Reduction Strategy Paper Progress Report', joint staff assessment, 9 March 2001, Washington: IMF/IDA

IMF and World Bank (2001a) 'Market Access for Developing Countries' Exports', Washington: International Monetary Fund/World Bank

IMF and World Bank (2001b) 'Leveraging Trade for Development: World Bank Role', paper prepared for the Joint Development Committee of the IMF and World Bank

Institute for European Environmental Policy (2001a) 'Current Operation and Impact of the CAP in the Context of EU Agriculture and its Significance for International Trade', paper commissioned by Oxfam and other members of the UK Food Group, London: IEEP

Institute for European Environmental Policy (2001b) 'The Potential Impacts of CAP Reform', paper commissioned by Oxfam and other members of the UK Food Group, London: IEEP

International Institute for Management Development (2000) 'The World Competitiveness Yearbook 2000', Lausanne: IIMD

International Task Force on Commodity Risk Management (1999) 'Dealing with Commodity Price Volatility in Developing Countries', Washington: World Bank

Inter-Agency Group (1999) 'Good Intentions are Not Enough', Recommendations of the UK Inter-Agency Group, Oxfam: Oxford

Irwin, D. (1996) *Against the Tide*, New Jersey: Princeton University Press

James, H. (2001) *The End of Globalisation: Lessons from the Great Depression*, Cambridge, Mass: Harvard University Press

de Janvry, A. et al. (2001) 'The changing role of the State in Latin American land reforms', in de Janvry: *Access to Land, Rural Poverty and Public Action*, Helsinki: WIDER

Jha, R. (2000) 'Reducing Poverty and Inequality in India: Has Liberalisation Helped?', Working Paper 204, World Institute for Development Economics Research, Helsinki: WIDER

Jhabvala, R. (1992) 'The Self Employed Women's Association: SEWA's Programme for the Organisation of Home-Based Workers', Geneva: International Labour Organisation

Joekes, S. (1995) 'Trade-Related Employment for Women in Industry', Geneva: UNRISD

Joshi, V. (2001) 'Capital controls and the national advantage: India in the 1990s and beyond', *Oxford Development Studies* 22(3)

Joshi, V. and I. Little (2001) *India's Economic Reforms 1999-2001*, Oxford: Oxford University Press

Juma, C. and J. Watal (2000) 'Global Governance and Technology', paper prepared for UNDP, New York: UNDP

Kaufer, E. (1989) *The Economics of the Patent System*, Geneva: Harwood Academic

Keynes, J. (1923) *A Tract on Monetary Reform*, London: Macmillan

Keynes, J. (1980) 'The International Control of Raw Material Prices', in *The Collected Writings of John Maynard Keynes*, Vol XXVII, London: Macmillan

Khor, M. (2001) *Rethinking Globalisation: Critical Issues and Policy Choices*, London and New York: Zed

Kibria, N. (2001) 'Becoming a garment worker: the mobilisation of women into the garment factories of Bangladesh', in R. Sobhan and N. Khundker (eds.): *Globalisation and Gender: Changing Patterns of Women's Employment in Bangladesh*, Dhaka: University Press

Killick, T. (2001) 'Globalisation and the Rural Poor', background paper for Integrated Fund for Agricultural Development: 'Rural Poverty Report 2001', Rome: IFAD

Kingston, W. (2001) 'Innovation needs patent reform', *Research Policy* 30

Klein, N. (2000) *No Logo*, London: Flamingo

Kletzer, L. (2001) *Measuring the Costs of Trade-Related Job Loss*, Washington: Institute for International Economics

Knox, A. (1997) 'Southern China: Migrant Workers and Economic Transformation', London: Catholic Institute for International Relations

Kwan, A. and S. Frost (2001) 'Rules and Regulations Versus Corporate Codes of Conduct in the Toy Sector', Hong Kong Christian Industrial Committee

Labour Rights in China (1999) 'No Illusions: Against the Global Cosmetic SA 8000', Hong Kong: Labour Rights in China

Lall, S. (1998) 'Technological capabilities in emerging Asia', in *Oxford Development Studies* 26(2)

Lall, S. (1999) 'Selective policies for export promotion: lessons from the Asian Tigers', *Research for Action* 43, World Institute for Development Economics Research, Helsinki: UN

Lall, S. (2000) 'Technological change and industrialisation in the Asian newly industrialising economies: achievements and challenges', in L. Kim and R. Nelson (eds.): *Technology, Learning and Innovation: Experience of the Newly Industrialising Economies*, Cambridge: Cambridge University Press

Lall, S. (2001a) 'The technological structure and performance of developing country manufactured exports, 1985-1998', *Oxford Development Studies* 28(3)

Lall, S. (2001b) 'Competitiveness challenges in the new Asia Tigers: Malaysia, Thailand and the Philippines', in S. Lall (ed.): *Competitiveness, Technology and Skills*, Cheltenham: Edward Elgar

Lall, S. (2001c) 'Multinational corporation, technology development and export competitiveness' in S. Lall (ed.): *Competitiveness, Technology and Skills*, Cheltenham: Edward Elgar

Landell Mills Commodities (2000) 'The World Cocoa Market and Outlook', Oxford: LMC

Landers, P. (2001) 'Fujitsu plans to cut work force', *Wall Street Journal* 21 August 2001

Landes, D. (1998) *The Wealth and Poverty of Nations*, London: Abacus

Landlor, M. (2001) 'Opportunity knocks: India's high-tech bull is ready for bear', *International Herald Tribune*, 14 March

Lanjouw, J. (2001) 'A Patent Policy Proposal for Global Diseases', Yale University, Department of Economics

Lanjouw, J. and I. Cockburn (2001) 'New pills for poor people? Empirical evidence after GATT', *World Development* 29(2): 265-89

Lappe, F. et al. (1998) *World Hunger: 12 Myths*, London: Earthscan

Lappe, M. and B. Bailey (1999) *Against the Grain: the Genetic Transformation of Global Agriculture*, London: Earthscan

Lee, J. and E. Mansfield (1996) 'Intellectual property protection and US foreign direct investment', *Review of Economics and Statistics* 78: 181-6

Legrain, P. (2000) 'Against globaphobia', *Prospect* 52: 30-5

Levine, P. (1997) 'Is Asian Growth a Threat to the West?', Working Paper 97/1, Surrey Centre for International Economic Studies, Surrey: University of Surrey

Limao, N. and A. Venables (1999) 'Geographical Disadvantage and Transport Costs', World Bank Policy Research Working Paper 2257, Washington: World Bank

Lindert, P. and J. Williamson (2001) 'Globalisation and Inequality: A Long History', paper prepared for the Annual World Bank Conference on Development Economics, Washington: World Bank

Lipsey, R. and F. Sjoholm (2001) 'Foreign Direct Investment and Wages in Indonesian Manufacturing', Working Paper 8299, National Bureau of Economic Research, Cambridge (Mass): NBER

Lipton, M. (1999) 'Reviving Global Poverty Reduction: What Role for

Genetically Modified Plants', Consultative Group on International Agricultural Research, Washington DC

Loewenberg, S. (2000) 'The Bush money machine', *The Nation,* 10 April http://www.thenation.com/ (accessed February 2002)

Lucker, W. (2000) 'Generating and sustaining backward linkages between maquiladoras and local suppliers', *World Development* 20(12)

Luhnow, D. (2001) 'How NAFTA helped Wal-Mart reshape the Mexican market', *Wall Street Journal,* 31 August 2001

Lumor, M. (1999) 'Agricultural trade and adjustment programme in Ghana', cited in J. Madeley (2000): 'Trade and Hunger: An Overview of Case Studies on the Impact of Trade Liberalisation on Food Security', Stockholm: Forum Syd

Lundberg, M. and L. Squire (1999) 'The Simultaneous Evolution of Growth and Inequality', Washington: World Bank

Lustig, N. and M. Szekely (1998) 'Economic Trends, Poverty and Inequality in Mexico', Technical Study 103, Poverty and Inequality Advisory Unit, Inter-American Development Bank, Washington: IADB

Macarthur, J. (2001) 'The Selling of Free Trade: NAFTA, Washington and the Subversion of American Democracy', Washington: NAFTA California

Maddison, A. (2001) *Monitoring the World Economy 1820-1922,* Paris: OECD

Mainuddin, K. (2000) 'Case of the Garment Industry in Dhaka, Bangladesh', Background Series 6, Urban Partnerships, Washington: World Bank

Maizels, A. (2000a) 'The Manufacturers' Terms of Trade of Developing Countries with the United States, 1981-97', Oxford: Oxford University, Queen Elizabeth House

Maizels, A. (2000b) 'Economic Dependence on Commodities', paper prepared for UNCTAD X, Geneva: UNCTAD

Mann, H. (2001) 'Private Rights and Public Problems: A Guide to NAFTA's Controversial Chapter on Investor Rights', World Wildlife Fund

Marquez, G. and C. Pages-Serra (1998) 'Trade and Employment: Evidence from Latin America and the Caribbean', Working Paper 3666, Inter-American Development Bank, Washington: IADB

Martin, M. and R. Alami (2001) 'Long-term debt sustainability for HIPCs: how to respond to shocks', *Development Finance International,* January 2001

Maskus, K. (1997) 'The role of intellectual property rights in encouraging foreign direct investment and technology transfer', *Duke Journal of International Law,* 1998

Maskus, K. (2000) 'Intellectual Property Rights in the Global Economy', Washington DC: Institute for International Economics

Mattoo, A. (2000) 'Financial services and the WTO: liberalisation commitments of the developing countries', *World Economy* 23: 351-86

Mayne, R. (2002) 'Intellectual Property and Development', Oxford: Oxfam

Maxwell, S. and L. Hanmer (1999) 'For Richer, For Fairer: Poverty Reduction and Income Distribution', Development Research Insights 31, Brighton: Institute of Development Studies, University of Sussex

McCulloch, N., A. Winters and X. Cirera (2001) 'Trade Liberalisation and Poverty: A Handbook', London: Centre for Economic Policy Research

McGreal, C. (2001) 'The cost of a call', *Guardian,* 20 August 2001

McIntosh, M. et al. (1998) *Corporate Citizenship,* London: Financial Times/Pitman

McKay, A. et al. (2000) 'A Review of Empirical Evidence on Trade, Trade Policy and Poverty', Report Prepared for Department for International Development, Nottingham University

Mehra, R. and S. Gammage (1999) 'Trends, countertrends, and gaps in women's employment', *World Development* 27(3): 533-50

Messerlin, P.A. (2001) 'Measuring the Costs of Protection in Europe: European Commercial Policy in the 2000s', Washington: Institute for International Economics

Milanovic, B. (1998) 'True World Income Distribution, 1998 and 1993', World Bank Development Research Group, Washington: World Bank

Mill, J. S. (1909) *Principles of Political Economy,* London: Longmans

Minten, B. and S. Kyle (1999) 'The effect of distance and road quality on food collection, marketing margins and traders: evidence from the former Zaire', *Journal of Development Economics* 60(2)

Mitchell, M. (2001) 'Sinking feeling', *Time,* 23 July 2001

Moreira, M. and S. Najberg (2000) 'Trade liberalisation in Brazil: creating or exporting jobs?', *Journal of Development Studies* 36(3): 78-100

Morley, S. (2000) 'The Impact of Economic Reforms on Equity in Latin America', International Food Policy Research Institute, Washington: IFPRI

Morriset, J. (1997) cited in 'The Role of Commodities in LDCs', UNCTAD/CFC, March 2001

Morrissey, O. (2001) 'Pro-Poor Conditionality and Debt Relief in East Africa', Nottingham University

Mortimore, M. (1998a) 'Getting a lift: modernising industry by way of Latin American integration', *Transnational Corporations* 7(2): 97-136

Mortimore, M. (1998b) 'Mexico's TNC-centric industrialisation process', in R. Kozul-Wright and R. Rowthorn (eds.): *Transnational Corporations and the Global Economy,* London: Macmillan

Mortimore, M. (1999) 'Apparel-based industrialisation in the Caribbean Basin: a threadbare garment?', *CEPAL Review* 767, New York: UN

Muller, J. (1993) *Adam Smith: In His Time and Ours,* New Jersey: Princeton University Press

Murshid, K. (1998) 'Food Security in an Asian Transitional Economy', Working Paper 6, Phnom Penh: United Nations Research Institute for Social Development

Nadal, A. (2000) 'The Environmental and Social Impacts of Economic Liberalisation on Corn Production in Mexico', study commissioned by Oxfam and World Wide Fund, Geneva: WWF/Oxfam

Narayan, D. et al. (2000) *Voices of the Poor: Crying Out for Change,* New York: Oxford University Press

National Group on Homeworking, Knitwear, Footwear, and Apparel Trades Union, and Women Working Worldwide (2000) 'UK Garment Workers Project: A Report on the Effects of Globalisation on UK Garment Workers', Manchester: Women Working Worldwide

National Research Council (2000) *Genetically Modified Pest-Protected Plants – Science and Regulation,* Washington: National Academy Press

Nestlé (1995) 'A Partnership for Fair Trade', Geneva: Nestlé

Nestlé (1998) 'Nestlé and Coffee: a Partnership for Fair Trade', Nestlé UK

Nestlé (2000) Nestlé Corporation Annual Management Report 2000, Geneva: Nestlé

Neuffer, E. (2001) 'Waking up to reality in global coffee trade', *Boston Globe,* 23 September 2001

New York Times (1997) 'The immigration debate', 31 August 1997

New York Times (2001) 'For coffee traders, disaster comes in pairs', 28 October 2001

Nicholson, M. and P. Taylor (1997) 'Microsoft in plan for India', *Financial Times,* 15-16 November 1997

Noland, M. (2000) 'Understanding the World Trade Organisation', Institute for International Economics, Washington: IIE

Nuffield Council (1999) 'Bioethics, Genetically Modified Crops: The Ethical and Social Issues', London: Nuffield Council

OECD (1996) 'Trade, Employment and Labour Standards: A Study of Core Workers' Rights and International Trade', Paris: OECD

OECD (1997) 'Market Access for LDCs: Where are the Obstacles?', OECD/GD (97): 174 Paris: OECD

OECD (2000) 'Agricultural Policies in Emerging and Transition Economies', Paris: OECD

OECD (2001a) 'Agricultural Policies in OECD Countries: Monitoring and Evaluation 2001', Paris: OECD

OECD (2001b) OECD Database, Paris: OECD

O'Rourke, D. (2000) 'Monitoring the Monitors: A Critique of Price Waterhouse Cooper's Labour Monitoring', Boston: Massachusetts Institute of Technology

O'Rourke, K. and J. Williamson (2000) *Globalisation and History: The Evolution of a Nineteenth Century Atlantic Economy,* Cambridge, Mass: MIT Press

Otsuki, T., J. Wilson and M. Sewadeh (2001) 'A Race to the Top? A Case Study of Food Safety Standards and African Exports', World Bank Agriculture Working Paper No. 2563, Washington: World Bank

Oxfam (2000a) 'Tax Havens: Releasing the Hidden Billions for Poverty Eradication, briefing paper, Oxford: Oxfam

Oxfam (2000b) 'The IMF: Wrong Diagnosis, Wrong Medicine', Oxford: Oxfam

Oxfam (2001a) 'The Tea Market: A Background Study', Oxford: Oxfam

Oxfam (2001b) 'The Coffee Market: A Background Study', Oxford: Oxfam

Oxfam (2001c) 'The Cocoa Market: A Background Study', Oxford: Oxfam

Oxfam (2001d) 'Bitter Coffee: How the Poor are Paying for the Slump in Coffee Prices', Oxford: Oxfam

Oxfam (2001e) 'Angola's Wealth: Stories of War and Neglect', Oxford: Oxfam

Oxfam (2001f) 'Dare to Lead: Public Health and Company Wealth', Oxford: Oxfam

Oxfam (2001g) 'Patent Injustice: How World Trade Rules Threaten the Health of Poor People', Oxford: Oxfam

Oxfam (2001h) 'Drugs Companies vs Brazil: the Threat to Public Health', Oxford: Oxfam

Oxfam (2001i) 'Debt Relief: Still Failing the Poor', Oxford: Oxfam

Oxfam (2002) 'Poverty in the Midst of Wealth: The Democratic Republic of Congo', Oxford: Oxfam

Oxfam Canada (2001) 'Guyana's Rice Farmers and the Myth of the Free Market', research performed by Michelle Beveridge, Nathalie Rowe, and Megan Bradley, and compiled and edited by Mark Fried, Ottawa: Oxfam Canada

Oxfam International (2001a) 'Rigged Trade and Not Much Aid: How Rich Countries Help to Keep the Least Developed Countries Poor', Oxford: Oxfam International

Oxfam International (2001b) 'Harnessing Trade for Development', Oxford: Oxfam International

Oxfam/IDS (1999) 'Liberalisation and Poverty', Final Report to Department for International Development, London: DFID

Oxford Analytica (2000) 'Immigrant Labour', Oxford: Oxford Analytica

Oxford Analytica (2001) 'The Vitamin Cartel', Oxford: Oxford Analytica

Oxford Policy Management (2000) 'Fair Trade Study', report prepared for DFID, Oxford: Oxford Policy Management

Oyejide, A., B. Ndulu and J. Gunning (1997) *Regional Integration and Trade Liberalisation in sub-Saharan Africa*, Vol.2, Basingstoke: Macmillan

Page, S. and A. Hewitt (2001) 'World Commodity Prices: Still a Problem for Developing Countries', London: Overseas Development Institute

Palmer, R. (2001) 'Report on International Conference on Agrarian Reform and Rural Development', January 2001 http://www.oxfam.org.uk/landrights/Agrarref.rtf (accessed February 2002)

Pecoul, B. (1999) 'Access to essential drugs in developing countries: a lost battle?', *Journal of the American Medical Association* 281: 361-7

Pérez-Grovas, V., E. Cervantes and J. Burstein (2001) 'Case Study of the Coffee Sector in Mexico', Oxford: Oxfam

Pilling, D. (2000) 'Patently Overpriced', *Financial Times*, 31 July 2000

Pilling, D. and R. Wolfe (2000) 'Drug Abuses', *Financial Times*, 20 April 2000

Pitts, J. (2001) 'Export Processing Zones in Central America', Oxford: Oxfam

Ponte, S. (2001) 'The "Latte Revolution"? Winners and Losers in the Restructuring of the Global Coffee Marketing Chain', Research Working Paper 1.3, Copenhagen: Centre for Development

Porto Alegre (2002) World Social Forum, Porto Alegre, Conference on International Trade, 1 February 2002; see www.forumsocialmundial.org.br/eng/roficial_trade_eng.asp for text of proposals

Pray, C. et al. (2000) 'Impact of Bt Cotton in China', Working Paper Series No WP-00-E18, Beijing: Centre for Chinese Agricultural Policy

Pritchett, L. (1999) 'The effect of household wealth on educational attainment: evidence from 35 countries', *Population and Development Review* 25(1)

Ransom, D. (2001) *The No-Nonsense Guide to Fair Trade*, London: Verso

Ravallion, M. (2001) 'Growth and Poverty: Making Sense of the Current Debate', World Bank Research Department, Washington: World Bank

Ravallion, M. and L. Chen (1997) 'What Can New Survey Data Tell Us About Recent Changes in Distribution and Poverty', *World Bank Economic Review* 11(2)

Reinhardt, A. (2000) 'The new Intel', *Business Week*, 13 March

Revenga, A. (1997) 'Employment and wage effects of trade liberalisation: the case of Mexican manufacturing', *Journal of Labour Economics* 15(3): 20-43

Rialp, V. (1993) 'Children and Hazardous Work in the Philippines', Geneva: International Labour Organisation

Ricardo, D. (1971) *The Principles of Political Economy and Taxation*, London: Watson and Viney

Ritchie, M., S. Wisniewski and S. Murphy (2000) 'Dumping as a Structural Feature of US Agriculture: Can WTO Rules Solve the Problem?', Minneapolis:

Institute for Agriculture and Trade Policy (IATP)

Rodriguez, F. and D. Rodrik (1999) 'Trade Policy and Economic Growth: A Skeptic's Guide to the Cross-National Evidence', National Bureau of Economic Research Working Paper 7081, Cambridge (Mass): NBER

Rodrik, D. (1997) 'Has Globalisation Gone too Far?', Institute for International Economics, Washington: IIE

Rodrik, D. (1999) 'Making openness work: investment strategies', in D. Rodrik (ed.): *The New Global Economy and Developing Countries: Making Openness Work*, Washington: Overseas Development Council

Rodrik, D. (2001a) 'Trading in illusions', *Foreign Policy Magazine* March/April 2001

Rodrik, D. (2001b), 'The Global Governance of Trade as if Development Really Mattered', paper prepared for UNDP

Rodrik, D. (2001c) 'Development strategies for the next century', in 'Annual World Bank Conference on Development Economics 2000', Washington: World Bank

Rodrik, D. (2001d) 'Comments on "Trade, Growth and Poverty"', available on Dani Ridrik home page, http://ksghome.harvard.edu/~.drodrik.academic.ksg/papers.html (accessed February 2002)

Rodrik, D. (2001e) 'Immigration Policy and the Welfare State', paper presented at the Conference on Immigration Policy, Trieste, 23 June 2001

Roosevelt, F. (1945) 'Fourth Inaugural Address', cited in *The Oxford Dictionary of Political Quotations*, Oxford: Oxford University Press

Royal Government of Cambodia (2001) 'Interim Poverty Reduction Strategy Paper', Phnom Penh

Royal Government of Cambodia (2001b) 'Social Economic Development Plan Phase II', Phnom Penh: Ministry of Finance

RSPB (2001), 'Eat This: Fresh Ideas For The WTO Agreement on Agriculture', Sandy, Buckinghamshire: Royal Society for the Protection of Birds

Russell, S. (1996) 'Ability to pay for health care: concepts and evidence', *Health Policy and Planning* 11(3): 219-37

Ryan, P. (1998) *Knowledge Diplomacy: Global Competition and the Politics of Intellectual Property*, Washington: The Brookings Institution Press

Sachs. J. (1999) 'Helping the world's poorest', *Economist*, 14 August

Sachs, J. and A. Warner (1995) 'Economic Reform and the Process of Global Integration', Brookings Papers on Economic Activity 1: 1-118

Sagasti, F. and K. Bezanson (2001) 'Financing and Providing Global Public Goods', Stockholm: Ministry of Foreign Affairs

Sara Lee Knit Products (2000) 'International Operating Principles', http://www.dol.gov/dol/ilab/public/media/reports/iclp/apparel/5c27.htm (accessed February 2002)

Sarntisart, I. (2000) 'Growth, Structural Change and Inequality: The Experience of Thailand', Working Paper 207, World Institute for Development Economics Research, Helsinki: WIDER

Schiller, D. (2000) *Digital Capitalism: Networking the Global Market*, Cambridge (Mass): MIT Press

Schlosser, E. (2001) Fast Food Nation: The Dark Side of the All-American Meal, New York: Houghton Mifflin

Schmukler, S. and Z. Lobaton (2001) 'Financial Globalisation: Opportunities and Challenges for Developing Countries', Washington: World Bank

Schott, J. and J. Watal (2000) 'Decision-Making in the World Trade Organisation', International Economics Policy Briefs No. 00-2, Washington: IIE

Sen, A. (1999) *Development as Freedom*, Oxford: Oxford University Press

SEWA (1997) 'Liberalising for the Poor', Self-Employed Women's Association, Ahmedabad

Seymour, L. (2001) 'It's about diamonds and oil', *North-South Institute Review*, Summer 2001 Ottawa: North-South Institute

Sharma, D. (2000) 'Trading in food security', *Hindu Business Line*, 1 October, New Delhi

Sheehan, M. (2001) 'Making better transportation choices', in L. Brown (ed.): *State of the World 2001*, London: Earthscan

Simon, B. (2001) 'For South African textiles, the battle cry is "export or die"', *Business Day*, Johannesburg, 23 February 2001

Singer, H. and J. Amjari (1992) *Rich and Poor Countries: Consequences of International Disorder*, London: Unwin-Hyman

Skidelsky, R. (2001) *John Maynard Keynes: Fighting for Britain, 1937-1946* Vol. 3, London: Macmillan

Smith, A. (1976) *The Wealth of Nations*, Oxford: Clarendon Press

Soros, G. (1988) *The Crisis of Global Capitalism: Open Society Endangered*, New York: Public Affairs

South Centre (2000) 'GATS 2000 Negotiations: Options for Developing Countries', Working Paper 9, Geneva: South Centre

Spar, D. (1988) 'Attracting High Technology Investment: Intel's Costa Rica Plant', Occasional Paper 11, Foreign Investment Advisory Services, Washington: World Bank

Spiegel, P. (2001) 'US to widen drug groups inquiry', *Financial Times*, 6 July 2001

Spinanger, D. (1999) 'Faking liberalisation and finagling protectionism: the ATC at its best', Kiel: Kiel Institute of World Economics (cited in IMF and World Bank 2001a)

Srinivasan, T.N. (2001) 'Living Wage in Poor Countries', Department of Economics, Yale University

Stainer, R. (1999) 'Reform roadblock?', *Coffee and Cocoa International*, May/June, Redhill, Surrey: DMG Business Media

Stainer, R. (2000) 'Exports cut to boost prices', *Coffee and Cocoa International*, June, Redhill, Surrey: DMG Business Media

Standing, A. (1999) 'Global feminisation through flexible labour: a theme revisited', *World Development* 27(3): 583-602

Stern, N. (2001) 'Building a Climate for Investment, Growth and Poverty Reduction in India', speech at EXIM Bank, Mumbai, India, 22 March, Office of Chief Economist, World Bank

Stewart, F. (2000) 'Income Distribution and Development', paper prepared for UNCTAD X High Level Round Table, February 2000, UNCTAD

Stichele, M. (1998) 'Gender, Trade and the WTO: A Ghana Case Study', Manchester: Women Working Worldwide

Stiglitz, J. (1996) 'Some lessons from the East Asian miracle', *The World Bank Research Observer* 11(2): 151-77

Stiglitz, J. (1999) 'Must financial crises be this frequent and this painful?', in P. Agenor et al.: *The Asian Financial Crisis: Causes, Contagion and Consequences*, Cambridge: Cambridge University Press

Stiglitz, J. (2001) 'Two principles for the next round: or how to bring developing countries in from the cold', in B. Hoekman and W. Martin (eds): *Developing Countries and the WTO: A Pro-Active Agenda*, Oxford: Blackwell

Subramanian, A. (2001) 'Mauritius' Trade and Development Strategy: What Lessons Does it Offer?', paper presented at seminar on Globalisation and Africa, Tunis, April 5, Washington: IMF

Sutherland, P. (1997) 'Address to Amnesty International', 26 September, London: Amnesty

Talbot, J. (1997) 'Where does your coffee dollar go to? The division of income and surplus along the coffee commodity chain', *Studies in Comparative International Development* 32(1), quoted in Ponte (2001)

Tan, S. (1999) 'The relationship between foreign enterprises, local government, and women migrant workers in the Pearl River Delta', in L. West and Y. Zhao (eds.): *Rural Labour Flows in China*, Berkeley: Institute of East Asian Studies, University of California

Thanh, H. (2001) 'Bicycles and Motorbikes for the Poor and Trade Liberalisation in Vietnam', Hanoi: Oxfam GB and Oxfam Hong Kong

The Corner House (2001) 'Trading Health Care Away? GATS, Public Services and Privatisation', Briefing 23, Dorset: The Corner House

The Economist (2000) 'Patent wars', April 8

The Economist (2001a) 'The case for globalisation', September 29-October 5

The Economist (2001b) 'Eli Lilly's drug induced depression', 12 August 2000

The Economist (2001c) 'Patent problems pending', 27 October

The Economist (2001d) 'Argentina's economy', 22 December

Thekaekara, S. (2001) 'Just Change – a Concept Paper', Nilgiris: ACCORD

Tobin, J. (1994) 'A Tax on International Currency Transactions', paper prepared for the *Human Development Report 1994*, New York: UNDP

Transparency International (2001) 'Corruption Perceptions Index', London: Transparency International

Tremolet, S. (2001) 'Not a drop to spare', *Guardian*, 26 September 2001

Turner, M. (2002) 'Bribery drives up the cost of living in Kenya', *Financial Times*, 19 January

TWIN (2000) 'Summary of the Fairtrade Movement in Europe', London: TWIN

Ugaz, C. (2001) 'Liberalisation of Utilities Markets and Children's Right to Basic Service: Some Evidence from Latin America', Brighton: Institute for Development Studies: Sussex University

UN (1999) 'World Investment Report: Foreign Direct Investment and the Challenge of Development', Geneva: United Nations

UN (2000) 'World Investment Report: Cross-Border Mergers and Acquisitions', Geneva: United Nations

UN (2001a) 'Economic Development in Africa: Performance, Prospects and Policy Issues', New York: United Nations

UN (2001b) 'Report of the Secretary-General to the Preparatory Committee for the High-Level International Inter-Governmental Event on Financing for Development', New York: United Nations

UN (2001c) 'Report of the High-Level Panel on Financing for Development', New York: United Nations

UNCTAD (1997) 'Trade and Investment Report', Geneva: UNCTAD

UNCTAD (1998 and 1999) 'Trade and Development Report', Geneva: UNCTAD

UNCTAD (1999a) 'Economic Dependence on Commodities', Geneva: UNCTAD

UNCTAD (1999b) 'The World Commodity Economy: Recent Evolution, Financial Crises, and Changing Market Structures', Geneva: UNCTAD

UNCTAD (1999c) 'World Investment Report 1999', Geneva: UNCTAD

UNCTAD (2000a) 'The Post-Uruguay Round Tariff Environment for Developed Country Exports: Tariff Peaks and Tariff Escalation', UNCTAD/WTO joint study, TD/B/COM.1/14/Rev.1, 25 January, Geneva: UNCTAD

UNCTAD (2000b) 'The Least Developed Countries 2000 Report', Geneva: UNCTAD

UNCTAD (2000c) 'Strategies for Diversification and Adding Value to Food Exports', Geneva: UNCTAD

UNCTAD (2000d) 'Industrial Policy and the WTO, Policy Issues in International Trade and Commodities', Study Series 6, Geneva: UNCTAD

UNCTAD (2000e) 'World Investment Report 2000', Geneva: UNCTAD

UNCTAD (2001a) 'The Role of Commodities in LDCs', Geneva: UNCTAD

UNCTAD (2001b) 'Economic Development in Africa: Performance, Prospects and Policy Issues', New York and Geneva: UNCTAD

UNCTAD (2001c) 'Is There Effectively a Level Playing Field for Developing Country Exports?', Policy Issues in International Trade and Commodities, Study Series 1, Geneva: UNCTAD

UNDP (1999) *Human Development Report*, New York: UNDP

UNDP (2000) 'Overcoming Human Poverty', New York: UNDP

UNDP (2001a) *Human Development Report* , New York: UNDP

UNDP (2001b) 'Choices for the Poor: Lessons From National Poverty Reduction Strategies', New York: UNDP

UNEP (1999) 'Trade Liberalisation and the Environment: A Synthesis Report', Geneva: UNEP

UNEP (2000) *Environment and Trade: A Handbook*, International Institute for Sustainable Development, Geneva: UNEP

UNICEF (2000) *The State of the World's Children*, New York: UNICEF

US Department of Commerce (1998) 'US Direct Investment Abroad: Benchmark Survey', Washington: USDC

USAID (1996) 'Annual Food Assistance Report, 1996' Washington: USAID

Varangis, P. and D. Larson (1996) 'Dealing with Commodity Price Uncertainty', World Bank International Economics Department, Policy Research Working Paper 1667, Washington: World Bank

Vastine, J. (2000a) 'Liberalising trade in services', *Cato Journal* 19(3)

Vastine, J. (2000b) 'Making Progress on Services Trade Liberalisation, Testimony Before the House of Representatives Sub-Committee on Trade', Coalition of Service Industries, 8 February, Washington

Velez, C., A. Kugler and C. Bouillon (1999) 'A Microeconomic Decomposition of the Inequality U-turn in Urban Colombia', Poverty and Inequality Advisory Unit, Inter-American Development Bank, Washington: IADB

Vicens, L. et al. (1998) 'The International Competitiveness of the Garments and Apparel Industry of the Dominican Republic', Santiago: ECLA

Volcker, P. and T. Gyohten (1992) *Changing Fortunes: The World's Money and the Threat to American Leadership*, New York: Times Books

Wade, R. (1990) *Governing the Market*, New Jersey: Princeton

Wall Street Journal (1998) 'US border town suffers from post-NAFTA syndrome', 28 August 1998

Wall Street Journal (2001) 'A slowing global economy bears down harder on Asia', 20 August 2001

Wangwe, S. (ed.) (1995) *Exporting Africa: Technology, Trade and Industrialisation in sub-Saharan Africa,* UN/INTECH, Routledge and Kegan Paul

Watal, J. (1999) 'Introducing product patents in the Indian pharmaceutical sector: implications for prices and welfare', *World Competition* 20:5-21

Watal, J. (2000) 'Pharmaceutical patents, prices and welfare losses: policy options for India under the WTO TRIPs Agreement', *The World Economy* 23

Watkins, K. (1996) 'Trade Liberalisation as a Threat to Livelihoods: the Corn Sector in the Philippines', Oxford: Oxfam

Watkins, K. (1997) 'Globalisation and Liberalisation: Implications for Poverty, Distribution and Inequality', UNDP Occasional Paper 32, New York: UNDP

Watkins, K. (1998) *Economic Growth With Equity*, Oxford: Oxfam

Watkins, K. (2001a) *The Oxfam Education Report*, Oxford: Oxfam

Watkins, K. (2001b) 'Cost recovery and equity in the health sector: the case of Zimbabwe' in G. Mwabu et al. (eds.): *Social Provision in Low-Income Countries: New Patterns and Emerging Trends*, Oxford: Oxford University Press

Weissman, R. (1996) 'A long strange TRIPs: the pharmaceutical industry drive to harmonise global intellectual property rules', *Journal of International Law,* University of Pennsylvania, Winter 1996

Wesselius, E. (2001) 'Liberalisation of Trade in Services: Corporate Power at Work' (accessed at http://www.gatswatch.org/LOTIS) (accessed February 2002)

White, H. and E. Anderson (2000) 'Growth Versus Distribution: Does the Pattern of Growth Matter?', Brighton: Institute of Development Studies, University of Sussex

White, R. (1999) 'Advertising: The Attempt to Persuade', *Understanding Global Issues* 99

WHO (1998) 'Health reform and drug financing', Health Economics and Drugs Series 6, Geneva: WHO

WHO (1999) 'World Health Report', Geneva: WHO

WHO (2000a) 'Overcoming Microbial Resistance', Message from the Director General, Geneva: WHO

WHO (2000b) 'World Health Report 2000', Geneva: WHO

WHO (2001) 'Global Strategy for Infant and Young Child Feeding', Geneva: WHO

Wilkinson, J. and P. Castelli (2000) 'The Internationalisation of Brazil's Seed Industry: Biotechnology, Patents and Biodiversity', Rio de Janeiro: ActionAid

Winters, A. (2000) 'Trade, Trade Policy and Poverty: What are the Links', London: Centre for Economic Policy Research

Wolford, W. (2001) 'Grassroots-initiated land reform in Brazil: the Rural Landless Workers' Movement', in de Janvry (2001)

Wood, A. (1994) *North-South Trade, Employment and Inequality,* Oxford: Clarendon Press

Wood, A. (1997) 'Openness and wage inequality in developing countries: the Latin American challenge to East Asian conventional wisdom', *World Bank Economic Review* 11: 33-57

Woodon, Q. (1999) 'Growth, Inequality and Poverty: A Regional Panel for Bangladesh', Policy Research Working Paper No. 2072, Washington: World Bank

Woods, N. and A. Narlikar (2001) 'Governance and the limits of accountability: the WTO, the IMF and the World Bank', *International Social Science Journal*

Woodward, L. (1962) *The Age of Reform 1815-1870,* Oxford: Clarendon Press

Woodward, D. (2001) *The Next Crisis? Direct and Equity Investment in Developing Countries*, London: Zed

World Bank (1997) 'China 2020', Washington: World Bank

World Bank (1999) 'Curbing the Epidemic – Governments and the Economics of Tobacco Control', Washington: World Bank

World Bank (2000a) 'Vietnam Development Report 2000: Attacking Poverty', Washington: World Bank

World Bank (2000b) 'Agriculture in Tanzania Since 1986', Washington: World Bank

World Bank (2000c) 'World Development Indicators', Washington: World Bank

World Bank (2000d) 'Engendering development through gender equality', *Policy and Research Bulletin* 11(3)

World Bank (2001a) 'Globalisation, Growth, and Poverty: Building an Inclusive World Economy', Washington: World Bank

World Bank (2001b) 'Global Economic Prospects and the Developing Countries 2001', Washington: World Bank

World Bank (2001c) 'World Development Indicators', Washington: World Bank

World Bank (2001d) 'World Development Report 2000/2001: Attacking Poverty', Washington: World Bank

World Bank (2001e) 'Financial Impact of the HIPC Initiative: First 23 Country Studies', Washington: World Bank

World Bank (2002) 'Global Economic Prospects and The Developing Countries', Washington: World Bank

World Development Movement (2001a) 'The Tricks of the Trade: How Trade Rules are Loaded Against the Poor', London: WDM

World Development Movement (2001b) 'In Whose Service', London: WDM

World Development Movement (2002) 'GATS: A Disservice to the Poor', London: WDM

World Resources Institute (1999) 'Environmental Change and Health', Washington: World Resources Institute

Wristin, W. (1997) 'Bits, bytes and diplomacy', *Foreign Affairs* 76(5)

WTO (1999) 'An Introduction to the GATS', Geneva: WTO

WTO (2000) 'GATS – Fact and Fiction', Geneva: WTO

WTO (2001a) 'International Trade Statistics' Geneva: WTO

WTO (2001b), 'Market Access: Unfinished Business. Post-Uruguay Round Inventory and Issues', Special Study No. 6 Geneva: WTO

WTO (2001c) 'WTO Members Report on Anti-dumping Activity', WTO press release, 27 November 2001 Geneva: WTO

WTO (2001d) 'TRIPs and Pharmaceutical Patents', Geneva: WTO

Yanz, A. et al. (1999) 'Policy Options to Improve Standards for Women Garment Workers in Canada and Internationally', Ottawa: Maquila Solidarity Network

Yusuf, S. (2000) 'Globalisation and the Challenge for Developing Countries', background paper for the 1999/2000 *World Development Report*, Washington: World Bank

Zeller, M. and M. Sharma (1998) 'Rural Finance and Poverty Alleviation', Food Policy Report, Washington: International Food Policy Research Institute (IFPRI)

Zeller, W. et al. (1997) 'Wal-Mart spoken here', *Business Week,* 23 June 1997

Zhan, J. (2001) 'Business Restructuring in Asia: Cross-Border Mergers and Acquisitions in Crisis-Affected Countries', Copenhagen: Copenhagen Business School Press

Background research papers

Aldred, A. (2001) 'Trade Issues in South Asia: A Background Note', Dhaka: Oxfam

Amador, F. (2001) 'Strategies for Rural Development in Vietnam', Córdoba: ETEA (original in Spanish)

Atkinson, J. (2001a) 'Transnational Companies, Employment and Investment', Melbourne: Oxfam Community Aid Abroad

Atkinson, J. (2001b) 'The Electronics Industry in Malaysia', Melbourne: Oxfam Community Aid Abroad

Avendaño, N. (2001) 'Liberalisation Policies in Nicaragua and their Impact on the Rural Sector', Madrid: Intermón (original in Spanish)

Bieckman, F. and C. van der Borgh (2001) 'Towards Pro-Poor Liberalisation of Trade? Trade and Poverty in PRSPs and PRGF', The Hague: Novib

Bird, M. (2001) 'Campaigning on Trade Issues Works! A Report on Illegal Logging in Cambodia', Oxford: Oxfam

Black, F. (2001) 'Update: Dumping in Jamaica, a Report on the Dairy Industry', The Hague: Novib

de Boer, J. (2001) 'Agricultural Trade and Food Security: Japan's Agricultural Policies', Madrid: Intermón

Brown, O. (2001a) 'Brand New World: the Power of Brands in the New Economy', Oxford: Oxfam

Brown, O. (2001b) 'Up in Smoke: Marketing Tobacco in the Developing World', Oxford: Oxfam

Brown, O. (2001c) 'Transnational Companies in the Global Economy', Oxford: Oxfam

Brown, O. (2001d) 'Trade and Environmental Change: a Discussion Paper for Oxfam International', Oxford: Oxfam

CEDLA (2001) 'Water Privatisation in Cochabamba (Bolivia): Impact on Consumers and Producers', Madrid: Intermón (original in Spanish)

Charveriat, C. (2001) 'Primary Commodities: Trading into Decline', Oxford: Oxfam

Chery, J. (2001) 'The Impact of Rice Trade Liberalisation on the Rice-Growing Sector in Haiti', report for Oxfam GB

Cordera, H. (2001) 'Coffee and Livelihoods in the Dominican Republic', Oxford: Oxfam

Crabtree, J. (2001) 'Peru: Agricultural Trade Liberalisation in Peru', Oxford: Oxfam

Das, A. K. (2001) 'Indian Commodities and International Trade', Delhi: Oxfam

Dhanarajan, S. (2001) 'The General Agreement on Trade in Services', Oxford: Oxfam

Drahos, P. (2001) 'BITs and BIPs: Bilateralism in Intellectual Property', Oxford: Oxfam

Eagleton, D. (2001) 'The International Rice Market: A Background Study', Oxford: Oxfam

Fanjul, G. (2001), 'Northern Agricultural Policies: The Long and Winding Road to Coherence', Madrid: Intermón

Feeney, P. (2001), 'Regional Trade and Investment Agreements', Oxford: Oxfam

Galián, C. and C. Ancona (2001), 'EU and Morocco: Winners and Losers In International Trade', Madrid: Intermón (original in Spanish)

González-Manchón, B. (2001) 'OECD Agricultural Policies: Australia, Canada, New Zealand', Madrid: Intermón

Goodison, P. (2001) 'The Future of the Common Agricultural Policy: Implications for Developing Countries', Oxford: Oxfam

Gough, E. (2001) 'Deprivation in UK Hill Farms – Case Studies for Oxfam International's Trade Report', Oxford: Oxfam

Gresser, C. 'Background Note on Garment Workers in Cambodia', produced in collaboration with Margherita Maffii and Rosanna Barbero, Phnom Penh/Hong Kong: Womyn's Agenda for Change/Oxfam Hong Kong

Habtu, Y. (2001) 'The Impact of Food Aid on Livelihood Systems: the Case of Ethiopia', The Hague: Novib

Hazeleger, B. (2001) 'EU Sugar Policy: Assessment of Current Impact and Future Reform', The Hague: Novib

Hellin, J. and S. Higman (2001) 'The Impact of the Power of the Multinational Companies on the Banana Sector in Ecuador', **Oxford: Oxfam**

Hellin, J. and S. Higman (2001) 'Quinua and Food Security in Ecuador, Peru and Bolivia', Oxford: Oxfam

INESA (2001) 'Le Café en Haïti: Situation Actuelle et Plaidoyer Pour une Amélioration de la Situation Socio-economique des Producteurs', Oxford: Oxfam

Institute for European Environmental Policy (2001a) 'Current Operation and Impact of the CAP in the Context of EU Agriculture and its Significance for International Trade', paper commissioned by Oxfam and other members of the UK Food Group

Institute for European Environmental Policy (2001b) 'The Potential Impacts of CAP Reform', paper commissioned by Oxfam and other members of the UK Food Group

Kidder, T. (2001) 'Gender and Trade Background Paper: Harnessing Trade for Gender Equity', Oxford: Oxfam

Mayne, R. (2002) 'Intellectual Property and Development', Oxford: Oxfam

Oxfam (2001a) 'The Tea Market: A Background Study', Oxford: Oxfam

Oxfam (2001b) 'The Coffee Market: A Background Study', Oxford: Oxfam

Oxfam (2001c) 'The Cocoa Market: A Background Study', Oxford: Oxfam

Oxfam (2001) 'The Impact of Rice Trade Liberalisation on Food Security in Indonesia', research by Dini Widiastuti, Widyono Sutjipto, and Bayu Wicaksono, Bangkok: Oxfam

Oxfam (2001) 'The Impact of Fish Importation and Smuggling on the Fishing Industry: a Case Study of Co-operative Fish Traders in the Philippines', research by Cesar Allan Vera and Malou Vera, Bangkok: Oxfam

Oxfam (2001), 'Rice for the Poor and Trade Liberalisation in Vietnam', Hanoi: Oxfam GB and Oxfam Hong Kong

Oxfam Canada (2001), 'Guyana's Rice Farmers and the Myth of the Free Market', research by Michelle Beveridge, Nathalie Rowe, and Megan Bradley, compiled and edited by Mark Fried, Ottawa: Oxfam Canada

Oxfam Community Aid Abroad (2001) 'Controlling the Conduct of TNCs', Melbourne: OCAA

Oxfam Community Aid Abroad (2001) 'Investment in Extractive Industries', Melbourne: OCAA

Pérez-Grovas, V., E. Cervantes and J. Burstein (2001) 'Case Study of the Coffee Sector in Mexico', Oxford: Oxfam

Pinat, J. and F. Perez (2001) 'An Overview of Regional Trade Agreements in East Asia with Reference to Growth and Poverty', Oxford: Oxfam

Pitts, J. (2001) 'Export Processing Zones in Central America', Oxford: Oxfam

Ponce, J.M. and M. Posas (2001) 'Trade Liberalisation, Rural Poverty and Alternatives for Small Producers', Madrid: Intermón (original in Spanish)

Raj, A. and S. Deva (2001) 'Indian Handlooms: An Uncertain Future', Delhi: Oxfam

Romero, J.J. et al. (2001) 'EU's Common Agricultural Policy: Critical Assessment of Internal and External Impacts', Madrid: Intermón and Córdoba: ETEA (original in Spanish)

Ruyssenaars, J. (2001) 'Unfair Fisheries Policies and Practices', The Hague: Novib

Thanh, H. (2001) 'Bicycles and Motorbikes for the Poor and Trade Liberalisation in Vietnam', Hanoi: Oxfam GB and Oxfam Hong Kong

Acronyms

ACP	African, Caribbean, Pacific Group of States
ACPC	Association of Coffee-Producing Countries
AGOA	Africa Growth and Opportunity Act
AoA	Agreement on Agriculture
APEC	Asia-Pacific Economic Co-operation
ARIPO	African Regional Industrial Property Organisation
ASEAN	Association of South-East Asian Nations
ATC	Agreement on Textiles and Clothing
CARICOM	Caribbean Community
CAP	Common Agricultural Policy
CET	Common External Tariff
CSI	Coalition of Service Industries
DSI	Double Standards Index
DSS	Dispute Settlement System
EBA	Everything but Arms
EC	European Commission
EPZ	export-processing zone
EU	European Union
FAO	Food and Agriculture Organisation
FDI	foreign direct investment
FTA	Free Trade Agreement
GATS	General Agreement on Trade in Services
GATT	General Agreement on Tariffs and Trade
GDP	gross domestic product
GSP	Generalised System of Preferences
HIPC	Heavily Indebted Poor Countries
ICA	International Commodity Agreement
IFI	international financial institution
ILO	International Labour Organisation
IMF	International Monetary Fund
LDC	Least-Developed Country
MEA	Multilateral Environmental Agreement
MFA	Multi-Fibre Arrangement
MFN	Most Favoured Nation
NAFTA	North American Free Trade Agreement
OECD	Organisation for Economic Co-operation and Development
OPEC	Organisation of the Petroleum Exporting Countries
PhRMA	Pharmaceutical Research and Manufacturers of America
PRGF	Poverty Reduction and Growth Facility
PRSP	Poverty Reduction Strategy Paper
PSE	Producer Support Estimate
R&D	Research and Development
REPA	Regional Economic Partnership Agreement
RTA	Regional Trade Agreement
SAARC	South Asian Association for Regional Co-operation
SADC	Southern African Development Community
TLI	Trade Liberalisation Indicator
TNC	transnational company
TRI	Trade Restrictiveness Index
TRIMs	Trade-Related Investment Measures
TRIPs	Trade-Related Aspects of Intellectual Property Rights
UNCTAD	United Nations Conference on Trade and Development
UNDP	United Nations Development Programme
USTR	United States Trade Representative
WHO	World Health Organisation
WTO	World Trade Organisation

Addresses

Oxfam International is a confederation of twelve development agencies that work in 120 countries throughout the developing world: Oxfam America, Oxfam in Belgium, Oxfam Canada, Oxfam Community Aid Abroad (Australia), Oxfam Great Britain, Oxfam Hong Kong, Intermón Oxfam (Spain), Oxfam Ireland, Novib Oxfam Netherlands, Oxfam New Zealand, Oxfam Quebec, and Oxfam Germany. Please call or write to any of the agencies for further information.

Oxfam America
26 West St.
Boston, MA 02111-1206
Tel: 1.617.482.1211
E-mail: info@oxfamamerica.org
www.oxfamamerica.org

Oxfam Canada
Suite 300-294 Albert St.
Ottawa, Ontario, Canada K1P 6E6
Tel: 1.613.237.5236
E-mail: enquire@oxfam.ca
www.oxfam.ca

Oxfam Quebec
2330 rue Notre-Dame Quest
Bureau 200, Montreal, Quebec
Canada H3J 2Y2
Tel: 1.514.937.1614
E-mail: info@oxfam.qc.ca
www.oxfam.qc.ca

Oxfam Ireland
Dublin Office:
9 Burgh Quay, Dublin 2, Ireland
Tel: 353.1.672.7662
E-mail: oxireland@oxfam.ie

Belfast Office:
52-54 Dublin Road, Belfast BT2 7HN
Tel: 44.28.9023.0220
E-mail: oxfam@oxfamni.org.uk
www.oxfamireland.org

Oxfam GB
274 Banbury Road, Oxford
England OX2 7DZ
Tel: 44.1865.311311
E-mail: oxfam@oxfam.org.uk
www.oxfam.org.uk

Oxfam-in-Belgium
Rue des Quatre Vents 60
1080 Bruxelles, Belgium
Tel: 32.2.501.6700
E-mail: oxfam@oxfam.be
www.oxfam.be

Novib Oxfam Netherlands
Mauritskade 9
2514 HD The Hague, The Netherlands
Postal address: P.O Box 30919, 2500 GX The Hague, The Netherlands
Tel: 31.70.342.1621
E-mail: info@novib.nl
www.novib.nl

Intermón Oxfam
Roger de Lluria 15
08010, Barcelona, Spain
Tel: 34.93.482.0700
E-mail: intermon@intermon.org
www.intermon.org

Oxfam Germany
Greifswalder Str. 33a
10405 Berlin, Germany
Tel: 49.30.428.50621
E-mail: info@oxfam.de
www.oxfam.de

Oxfam Hong Kong
17/F, China United Centre
28 Marble Road, North Point
Hong Kong
Tel: 852.2520.2525
E-Mail: info@oxfam.org.hk
www.oxfam.org.hk

Oxfam Community Aid Abroad
156 George St. (Corner Webb Street)
Fitzroy, Victoria, Australia 3065
Tel: 61.3.9289.9444
E-mail: enquire@caa.org.au
www.caa.org.au

Oxfam New Zealand
Level 1, 62 Aitken Terrace
Kingsland, Auckland
New Zealand
Postal address: P.O. Box 68 357, Auckland 1032, New Zealand
Tel: 64.9.355.6500
E-mail: oxfam@oxfam.org.nz
www.oxfam.org.nz

Oxfam International Advocacy Office
1112 16th St., NW, Ste. 600,
Washington, DC 20036
Tel: 1.202.496.1170
E-mail: advocacy@oxfaminternational.org
www.oxfam.org

Oxfam International Office in Brussels
60 rue des Quatre Vents,
Brussels
B-1080
Tel: 32.501.6761
E-mail:
david.earnshaw@oxfaminternational.org

Oxfam International Office in Geneva
15 rue des Savoises
1205 Geneva
Tel: 41.22.321.2371
E-mail:
celine.charveriat@oxfaminternational.org

Oxfam International Office in New York
Tel: 1.646.246.5448
E-mail:nicola.reindorp@oxfaminternational.org